MUSIC IN AMERICAN LIFE

Volumes in the series Music in American Life
are listed at the end of this book.

BITTER MUSIC

HARRY PARTCH

BITTER MUSIC

Collected Journals,
Essays, Introductions, and Librettos

Edited with an Introduction by
Thomas McGeary

University of Illinois Press
Urbana and Chicago

Publication of this book has been supported by a grant
from the National Endowment for the Humanities, an independent federal agency, and is also made possible through
the generous assistance of Betty Freeman and a grant from
the BMI Foundation, Inc.

Frontispiece: Harry Partch, Los Angeles, 1966.
Photograph by Mark Z. Stevens.

This book is printed on acid-free paper.

Library of Congress Cataloging-in-Publication Data

Partch, Harry, 1901–1974.
    Bitter music : collected journals, essays, introductions, and
librettos / Harry Partch ; edited with an introduction by Thomas
McGeary.
        p.   cm. — (Music in American life)
    Includes bibliographical references.
    ISBN 0-252-01660-2
    1. Partch, Harry, 1901–1974. 2. Composers—United States—
Biography. 3. Music—United States—20th century—History and
criticism. I. McGeary, Thomas, 1948–   . II. Title. III. Series.
ML410.P176A3 1991
780.92—dc20
    [B]   89-20344
                                                          CIP
                                                          MN

Grateful acknowledgment is made for permission to use the following:

Partch's unpublished writings, printed by permission of Danlee Mitchell, president, Harry Partch Foundation.

Excerpt from "Hymn to the Sun and Myself" by Ogden Nash, reprinted by permission of Curtis Brown, Ltd. Copyright 1931 by Ogden Nash.

Excerpt from *Sappho of Lesbos* by Arthur Weigall, reprinted by permission of Thorton Butterworth.

Excerpt from "Wilderness Song" by Everett Ruess, reprinted with permission of Gibbs M. Smith, Inc., Peregrine Smith Books, P.O. Box 667, 1877 E. Gentile Street, Layton, Utah 84041.

"Patterns of Music," printed with permission of the Carnegie Corporation of New York.

Excerpt from "Voyages II" from *White Buildings, Poems by Hart Crane,* reprinted by permission of Liveright Publishing Corporation. Copyright 1926 by Boni & Liveright, Inc. Copyright renewed 1954 by Liveright Publishing Corporation. Copyright © 1972 by Liveright Publishing Corporation.

"Bach and Temperament," "W. B. Yeats," "The Kithara," and "Barstow," reprinted with permission of the *Carmel Pine Cone,* 1985.

"The Ancient Magic," reprinted with permission from the *Music Journal.*

"A Somewhat Spoof," reprinted with permission of Soundings Press, Santa Fe, N.Mex.

"The University and the Creative Arts: Comment," reprinted with permission from *Arts in Society.*

"Monoliths in Music," reprinted by permission of Larry Austin, editor, *Source.*

The 1943 essay on *U.S. Highball,* reprinted with permission of the Music Division, The New York Public Library, Astor, Lenox, and Tilden Foundations.

"Revelation in the Courthouse Park," reprinted from the second edition of *Genesis of a Music* with permission of Da Capo Press.

The photograph of the Alwin Nikolais dancers in the scene from *The Bewitched,* printed with permission of the Nikolais Dance Theatre, New York.

I am first and last a composer. I have been provoked into becoming a musical theorist, an instrument builder, a musical apostate, and a musical idealist, simply because I have been a demanding composer.

I hold no wish for the obsolescence of the widely heard instruments and music. My devotion to our musical heritage is great—and critical. I feel that more ferment is necessary to a healthy musical culture. I am endeavoring to instil more ferment.

Harry Partch
1942

Contents

Acknowledgments

The inception of this anthology was in 1976 when the late Lauriston C. Marshall donated to the University of Illinois Music Library a large collection of Partch letters, documents, microfilms, and recordings that he had acquired during his many years of collaboration and friendship with Partch. Much of the material in this volume exists only because of Marshall's preservation. With this gift as its basis, now professor emeritus of music Ben Johnston and I established at the University of Illinois Music Library an archive devoted to documenting Partch's life and music. Establishment of the archive was aided by research grants to Professor Johnston from the University of Illinois Research Board, a grant from Betty Freeman, and the assistance of William McClellan, music librarian.

The most urgent use of the material collected — correspondence, documents, taped lectures, oral history interviews, scores, and recordings — was a collection of Partch's published and unpublished writings. An anthology that presented the full range of Partch's writings would forestall further misconceptions about his life and music, and would lay the foundation for a fuller and more accurate understanding and appreciation of his life, artistic ideas, musical achievements, and unique place in twentieth-century music.

For their encouragement throughout the preparation of this volume, I must thank Ben and Betty Johnston, Danlee Mitchell, president of the Harry Partch Foundation, and Judith McCulloh, my editor at the University of Illinois Press.

Publication of the present volume is made possible through the generous assistance of Betty Freeman, the BMI Foundation, and the National Endowment for the Humanities.

Champaign-Urbana, Illinois
January 1990

Introduction

Even during his lifetime, Harry Partch was recognized as the most innovative, iconoclastic, and genuinely American composer of our century. Despite the isolation of growing up in desert towns of the American Southwest, he was exposed as a child to a wide range of world music. His irrevocable break in 1930 with the tradition of European music was followed by forty intensely creative and uncompromising years devoted to creating single-handedly a complete alternative to that tradition. In this pursuit Partch became the most radical embodiment of the maverick, eclectic, individualistic American composer. Self-taught as a theorist, living on the margins of society, and ignored by most musical institutions, Partch sought musical inspiration and materials outside the European tradition. He became an instrument builder, developed a comprehensive philosophy of music, and in his last theater works realized a redemptive vision of a corporeal music.

Partch, the musical apostate, called all aspects of European music into question: its concert traditions and the specialized role of the composer and performer, its forms and abstract music, its instruments and equal temperament, and its purity of music, dance, and theater. Indeed, Partch's challenge to the tradition of Western music has its closest counterpart in the music and ideas of John Cage, with whom he is often bracketed in discussions of twentieth-century American music.

Partch would have abhorred the labels *avant-garde* or *revolutionary*—for his challenge to our Western musical tradition was not like that of Schoenberg to extend its tradition, nor like that of Ives to create a characteristically American strain of it, nor like that of Cage

to negate it. Rather, Partch's lifelong effort—begun in the 1920s—
was to create a monophonic and corporeal music that returned to
what he believed was the primal, ritualistic, corporeal state that music
had long ago abandoned: a music arising from human speech and the
natural acoustic musical intervals generated by sounding bodies; a
music no longer estranged from the physical production of sound; a
music where the audience experiences an integration of drama, dancers, and performing musicians.

His rejection of twelve-tone equal temperament and adoption of
the principles of just intonation led Partch to use a scale with forty-
three tones to the octave; and this in turn forced him to invent new
musical instruments. At first, Partch adapted to his purposes conventional instruments such as violas, guitars, and reed organs. His early
compositions from the 1930s and 1940s used these instruments in
small-scale, intimate bardic settings of Chinese poems, biblical verses,
scenes and songs from Shakespeare, and American hobo texts. As
Partch invented original percussion and string instruments—which
he increasingly designed with a sensitivity for visual and sculptural
qualities—he turned in the 1950s and 1960s to large-scale theatrical
and dramatic compositions that extended his concept of corporeality.
Oedipus (1952), *Plectra and Percussion Dances* (1952), *The Bewitched*
(1957), *Revelation in the Courthouse Park* (1961), *Water! Water!* (1962),
and *Delusion of the Fury* (1969) integrated music with dance and drama
in ritualistic theater pieces that ranged for their source material from
Greek tragedy, Japanese Noh plays, and African stories to contemporary American experience. The pivotal work marking the change
from the solo, bardic works of the 1930s and 1940s to public theater
pieces is his setting of *Oedipus,* which is at once the fulfillment of his
ideals of intoned setting of texts and the first of his dramatic works.

Partch, it must be acknowledged, is only one of many twentieth-
century composers and theorists to have experimented with just intonation and built new musical instruments. His enduring and un-
equaled achievement was to transcend mere experimentation and to
use his instruments and system of tuning to compose a large body of
works that are among the most imaginative and innovative of twentieth-century American music. Beyond the legacy of his compositions,
Partch's significance for twentieth-century music arises from his still-
provocative ideas about music and its place in human culture. In
Partch's life, music, and writings, we see sharply exposed—perhaps
more so than in any other American composer—those crucial issues
of an artist's relation and responsibility to society. And Partch's continuing importance for, and influence upon, younger musicians owes

much to his own example of personal and artistic integrity in refusing to compromise with musical institutions and social expectations.

As has often been observed, much of Partch's life and music was shaped by his parents' missionary service in China and his own childhood spent in desert towns of the Southwest.[1] His parents, Virgil Franklin Partch (1860–1919) and Jennie Childers (1863–1920), had served as Presbyterian missionaries in China in 1888–93 and 1895–1900. But after Virgil experienced a crisis of faith, both returned to the United States, their departure being hastened by the Boxer Uprising, and Harry Partch was born in Oakland, California, on June 24, 1901.

Because of his mother's poor health, by 1904 the family had moved to southeastern Arizona, where Virgil Partch worked for the U.S. Immigration Service, being stationed first at Tucson. Later that year the family moved and homesteaded a ranch one and one-half miles outside of the desert railroad town of Benson, Arizona. These were the dying days of the Old West, and this frontier town of about 300 still had boardwalks and at least a dozen saloons for the railroad workers. Partch recalled that Yaqui Indians lived in the area and that he once sympathetically watched a band of holed-up outlaws.

Partch grew up hearing music from many cultures. His mother sang Chinese lullabies and played hymns on a pump organ, and he heard local Mexican tunes, Yaqui Indian music, and music from cylinder records. In his home Partch was surrounded by Chinese books, art, furniture, and folksongs. A musical family was fostered by his mother, and the children learned to play mail order musical instruments. Partch recalled that his sister was a good violinist and that he played violin, piano, and mandolin.

The family moved to Albuquerque, New Mexico, in 1913, where Partch graduated from high school in 1919. In high school he participated in the journalism program, chorus, dramatics, oratorical contest, Spanish Club, and *The Mikado*. Partch studied piano seriously in these years and played piano or organ in silent movie theaters. By age fourteen he was composing prolifically for piano, and Partch often cited "Death on the Desert," written in 1916 (now lost), as an example of his early interest in music based on dramatic situations.

Partch's father died in 1919 in Albuquerque, and soon afterward the family moved to Los Angeles, where his mother died in a trolley accident the following year. Partch briefly enrolled in the School of Music at the University of Southern California in 1920–21 and the summer of 1922, and later stated he left because he found his teachers no older and wiser than he. In the following years spent in the San Francisco Bay Area, he frequented Mandarin theaters in San Francisco.

Having given up on both private music teachers and music schools, Partch began to read about music in public libraries and to compose music free from academic restrictions. He usually dated the beginning of his rejection of European concert music and its system of twelve-tone equal temperament to the year 1923. While working as a proof-reader for the Sacramento State Printing Office, he discovered in the Sacramento Public Library the great classic of acoustics Hermann Helmholtz's *On the Sensations of Tone,* in the translation and edition by Alexander J. Ellis—the book that began his lifelong investigations into music theory from the standpoint of acoustics and just intonation.

In 1925 he began to develop and apply his theories, making experimental paper coverings for violin and viola fingerboards and writing a string quartet (for violin, two violas, and cello) in just intonation. In May 1928 he completed the first draft of "Exposition of Monophony." Setting out his theoretical system for music in just intonation, this treatise would go through many revisions and several titles through the next twenty years. In these years of experimentation, Partch supported himself as a proofreader, taught piano, shipped out as a common seaman, or lived as a transient.

His decisive break with the European musical tradition occurred in New Orleans in 1930: in an iron potbellied stove, he burned fourteen years worth of his own music, including a symphonic poem, a string quartet, almost fifty songs, and an unfinished piano concerto. In New Orleans a violin maker had fitted a viola with a cello finger-board, on which Partch could now musically realize his theories of just intonation by using twenty-nine notes to the octave. For this viola Partch began writing what are his earliest extant characteristic compositions: settings for voice and Adapted Viola of poems by Li Po, biblical verse, and scenes from Shakespeare. In these settings, composed between 1930 and 1933, Partch sought to achieve a perfect balance between poetry and music, letting the spoken inflections, accents, and stresses of the text define melody and rhythm.

By August 1931 Partch was back in California, where he recruited two sopranos—Rudolphine Radil in San Francisco and Calista Rogers in Los Angeles—to perform his songs. In 1932 Partch and Radil performed in recitals and demonstrations in the San Francisco area, while in the following year he and Rogers performed in the Los Angeles area. The most widely reviewed of these performances was the February 9, 1932, concert in San Francisco for Henry Cowell's New Music Society of California.

With the help of a group of private sponsors organized by the Los Angeles music critic Bertha Knisely, Partch traveled to New York in the fall of 1933 in hopes of finding support and exposure for his music. Although he was unable to obtain the assistance of a soprano, he gave demonstrations alone, intoning and accompanying himself with the Adapted Viola. Among the musicians Partch met, or who supported his work, were Roy Harris, Charles Seeger, Henry Cowell, Howard Hanson, Otto Luening, Walter Piston, and Aaron Copland.

Unsuccessful applications for 1933 and 1934 Guggenheim fellowships were followed in June 1934 by a $1,500 grant from the Carnegie Corporation of New York for a research trip to England. On this trip Partch visited the poet W. B. Yeats in Dublin in mid-November to discuss his projected setting of *King Oedipus,* read in the British Museum, commissioned the construction of the Chromatic Organ (a reed organ with forty-three notes to the octave), and took a side trip to Malta and Italy.

Partch returned in April 1935 to an America in the midst of the Depression and for the next nine years experienced what he called his own personal Great Depression. The years from 1935 to 1943 constitute what is often romanticized as Partch's hobo period, the first eight months of which are chronicled in his "Bitter Music." As this journal makes clear, he resorted to life as a hobo or transient only out of necessity. Nor, contrary to the impression that has developed (and that Partch allowed to persist), did he spend these years entirely wandering: Partch frequently established residences and studios, occasionally had full-time work, and—most important—continued to compose, write, build instruments, and promote his music. In 1936–37 he worked for the Federal Writers' Project in Phoenix rewriting the Arizona tour book. The years 1937–40 were spent in the Los Angeles area, where in 1938 he built the first version of his Kithara in a high school adult education wood shop; and in 1939–40 Partch again worked for the Federal Writers' Project on the editorial staff for *California: A Guide to the Golden State.*

Late in 1940 Partch was at Big Sur, and there the Kithara was completed. In the summer of 1941, he received a letter from a friend of an acquaintance from Chicago. This letter offering a place to stay prompted the September freight train trip to that city that was recreated in *U.S. Highball.* Partch moved to Chicago, staying from the winter of 1941 through the summer of 1942, composing, constructing the first model for the Chromelodeon (an adapted reed organ), making recordings, and giving presentations in schools and studios (one of which was heard by John Cage).

Partch moved to New York in the fall of 1942, subsequently working or staying with friends in New York City, Ithaca, Chappaqua, and Boston. In these years he completed the Americana works—those compositions based on his hobo experiences in the preceding seven years. Through the efforts of Otto Luening, he gave presentations at Bennington College and the Eastman School of Music. The period of Partch's personal Great Depression was closed by the award of a Guggenheim Fellowship in March 1943 for composition of a seven-part "Monophonic Cycle," construction of musical instruments, and training an ensemble. The musical culmination of this period was the premiere of Partch's Americana compositions at the widely reviewed April 22, 1944, League of Composers concert at Carnegie Chamber Music Hall.

After an exploratory trip to Madison, Partch began a three-year association with the University of Wisconsin in October 1944. Here he was supported by a renewal of the Guggenheim Fellowship and grants from the university. At Madison he built instruments, trained an ensemble, presented lectures and concerts, saw the release of the first of a series of privately issued recordings (*U.S. Highball* and ten of the Li Po settings), and in 1947 completed the manuscript of *Genesis of a Music*, which was published by the University of Wisconsin Press in 1949.

Despite this productivity, Partch left Madison in 1947. The music school had refused to accept him on its staff (without which acceptance the university would no longer support him), and there was no longer space available for his instruments. This would be the familiar pattern of Partch's relations with academic institutions throughout his life: despite enthusiastic applause from audiences and strong support from faculty and students throughout the university, music departments generally remained hostile and unsupportive, and there was always a shortage of space for his growing ensemble of instruments.

After spending most of the next two years in southern California, in August 1949 Partch established a studio in the small coastal community of Gualala, north of San Francisco. Pianist Gunnar Johansen, who had supported Partch's work at Madison, offered the use of the smithy on his ranch, which Partch converted to a studio. Here Partch composed, built instruments, and made recordings. His work was principally supported by a Guggenheim Fellowship shared with Lauriston C. Marshall, a physicist at the University of California, Berkeley. Marshall obtained materials for instruments, solved technical problems, and privately issued a recording of the *Intrusions*. For six months in 1950, a young composer, Ben Johnston, worked with Partch at Gualala and performed in the recordings. Johnston would later be instrumental in obtaining sponsorship for Partch's later productions at the University of Illinois, and in his own compositions he would extend Partch's theories of just intonation.

Health problems forced Partch to leave Gualala in the spring of 1951, and he relocated his studio in Oakland, California, in preparation for the production at Mills College of *King Oedipus*, directed by Arch Lauterer. The performances on March 14–16, 1952, received extensive news coverage and national reviews. But after the success of *King Oedipus*, two disappointments followed: a recording of the work could not be released because Yeats's agent refused permission to use the translation; and in the winter of 1952–53, a proposed collaboration with Martha Graham in New York failed to materialize.

Forced to give up his studio at Mills College, in February 1953 Partch established a studio in a long shed at Gate 5 of an abandoned shipyard at Sausalito, north of San Francisco. During the next three and one-half years at Gate 5, Partch formed an ensemble, composed, built instruments, and presented performances of *Plectra and Percussion Dances* and his revised *Oedipus*. A Harry Partch Trust Fund, established by friends and supporters (including Alan Watts and Jean Varda), organized subscriptions for recordings of both works (released in 1953 and 1954, respectively). These subscriptions and later Partch's own Gate 5 Records were sold by mail and became his principal source of income for many years.

In January 1955 Partch completed *The Bewitched* and began circulating the scenario to friends in hopes of obtaining a production of it. With assistance from the Fromm Foundation, Johnston secured its premiere at the University of Illinois, and Partch moved to Urbana-Champaign with his instruments in September 1956 to train an ensemble. First performed on March 26, 1957, and presented the following night at Washington University in St. Louis, *The Bewitched* received national reviews. But for Partch the production was marred by what became a public dispute between him and choreographer Alwin Nikolais over the liberties Nikolais took in interpreting Partch's scenario.

Bitter over the experience with *The Bewitched* and believing he had found collaborators for a film of *U.S. Highball*, Partch moved in June to Yellow Springs, Ohio. But efforts to find musicians willing to devote time to an ensemble proved futile, and no concert or filming ever took place. So in December, Partch settled again, now in

Evanston, Illinois. Earlier in 1957 he had met the experimental film-maker Madeline Tourtelot; with the film *Windsong*, for which Partch composed and performed the sound track, they began a series of collaborations on six films.

Partch returned to the University of Illinois in January 1959 to prepare another production of *The Bewitched*, sponsored by the university in collaboration with the Alice M. Ditson Fund of Columbia University. This production, with University of Illinois musicians and choreography by Joyce Trisler of New York, was presented at Columbia University on April 10 and 11, 1959, and repeated at Illinois on April 24, 1959.

Partch remained at the University of Illinois for two and one-half years. As at the University of Wisconsin, most of his appointments and commissions came from outside the university's music school—from the Graduate College, Department of Speech and Theater, and the Activities Board of the Student Union. In many ways, the conditions here were ideal for Partch and his work: he had broad support from across the university and community as well as large music, dance, and theater departments from which to recruit performers. At Illinois two more major theater works were produced: *Revelation in the Courthouse Park* (April 11, 1961) and *Water! Water!* (March 9 and 10, 1962). But exhausted from preparing these two works, faced with continuing hostility from the music school, and without further appointments or plans for productions, Partch returned to California in the fall of 1962, where he hoped to find further support.

In the office of a former chick hatchery at Petaluma, about forty miles north of San Francisco, he established another studio, where he began *And on the Seventh Day Petals Fell in Petaluma*. After two and one-half years, he was forced to abandon the hatchery and in June 1964 left for southern California. Here Partch spent the last decade of his life, successively living or establishing studios in Del Mar (1964), Van Nuys (1964–65), Venice (1965–66), San Diego (1966–67), Solana Beach (1967–68), Los Angeles (1968–69), and Encinitas (1969–72).

Except for teaching one course in the fall of 1967 at the University of California, San Diego, Partch had no institutional affiliation during these years. He was supported by record sales, the generosity of friends, grants and commissions, and the Harry Partch Foundation (established in 1970), which assisted with studio rental, assistants, and expenses. Until 1972 Partch actively continued to compose, build instruments, and organize ensembles for concerts and recordings. His final theater work, *Delusion of the Fury*—the culmination of his concept of corporeality and of fifteen years of evolving ideas about an integrated ritual theater—was produced at the University of California, Los Angeles, January 9–12, 1969.

Partch acknowledged that little of his creative work in this decade was possible without the friendship and assistance of Danlee Mitchell. A percussionist who as a student had performed in all of Partch's Illinois productions, Mitchell began teaching at San Diego State University in 1964. Without his knowledge of Partch's music and instruments, the preparation of *Delusion of the Fury*, concerts, recordings, and the enlarged, second edition of *Genesis of a Music* would have been impossible.

Belatedly, Partch received recognition for his music and creative achievements: grants and awards from the Pasadena Art Museum (1965), the National Institute of Arts and Letters (1966), and the San Francisco Art Institute (1966); a commission from the Serge Koussevitzky Music Foundation (1966); and a command concert for the Sixth International Music Congress at the Whitney Museum, New York (1968). And most important for bringing his music to a wider public were the first commercially released recordings of his music.[2]

His last composition was *The Dreamer That Remains*, commissioned in 1972 for the film produced by Betty Freeman, a patron and promoter of Partch's work from 1964, who had established the Harry Partch Foundation and secured the production of *Delusion of the Fury*. In failing health and to be closer to his instruments and Mitchell at San Diego State University, Partch retired to San Diego in 1973, where he died suddenly of a heart attack on September 3, 1974.

Like other composers of his generation in America, Partch suffered from two compounded prejudices: one against contemporary, experimental music; and a second in favor of European musicians, repertoire, and traditions. The latter became even more pronounced from the 1940s onward as the work of those American composers who sought to develop a native idiom was eclipsed by the international modernism of Stravinsky or Schoenberg and his disciples. And Partch, of course, increasingly suffered an additional disadvantage: his compositions could only be performed on his own unique instruments.

Faced with indifference, incomprehension, or hostility toward his work from most musical institutions, Partch spent great time and intense energy at the typewriter conducting polemics against the Western music tradition, writing about his own music, and fighting to gain hearings for it. His published writings consist of a book, *Genesis of a Music,* and a number of brief essays, lecture texts, and program notes; his unpublished writings comprise a wide array of essays, lectures, prefaces or introductions to compositions, prospectuses, journals, instrument manuals, and draft librettos or scenarios (some to works never composed).

Despite this large body of writing, full appreciation and understanding of Partch's life, music, artistic ideas, and creative accomplishment have been hindered: in part because, with the exception of his book, his published writings are difficult to obtain, scattered as they are among obscure small magazines and newspapers.

The present anthology, planned as a companion to *Genesis of a Music*, collects Partch's published and unpublished biographical and critical writings of substantial length and importance, and provides sources that now allow a more comprehensive understanding of his life, compositions, and ideas about music.

Because of the odyssey of his life—in which he lost even instruments and musical scores—and the scarcity of documentation, little will ever be known of the first forty years of Partch's life. We are fortunate that "Bitter Music," a journal that Partch destroyed or believed lost, has been recovered. This journal documents two formative experiences of Partch's early years: his research trip to England and meeting with W. B. Yeats in 1934–35 (recalled as a flashback), and the eight months Partch spent in California, Oregon, and Washington as a transient between June 1935 and February 1936—part of his years of Depression wanderings among the itinerants and hobos of the American West.

"Bitter Music" records Partch's disillusion at the collapse of his hopes to further his musical ideas after returning from Europe. His reaction arose from the irony that—having finally won institutional support and recognition for his work—he was beginning what would be eight years of a nomadic, hand-to-mouth existence on the margins of society. For like ten million men, Partch could find no employment, and like hundreds of thousands of them, with no home and savings exhausted, he was forced to go on the road as a transient seeking work in federal camps. But from these experiences as one of the "wayward," Partch drew texts and ideas that became the material for his later Americana compositions.

Beyond its great importance as a biographical document, "Bitter Music" is Partch's contribution to American Depression literature of the 1930s and early 1940s. Closest in tone and content to "Bitter Music" and the related Americana compositions (*U.S. Highball, The Letter, Barstow,* and *San Francisco*) are other autobiographical accounts of transient or hobo life, such as Tom Kromer's *Waiting for Nothing*

(1935), Edward Newhouse's *You Can't Sleep Here* (1934), or Nelson Algren's novel *Somebody in Boots* (1935). Partch's "Bitter Music" and especially *U.S. Highball* share with these works strikingly similar themes: the constant hunger, filth, loneliness, and despair of the transient or hobo; the brutality of railroad police; the dangers of hopping and riding freight trains; the shame of begging and the hypocrisy of accepting relief at Salvation Army missions; the suicides and homosexuality among transients and hobos; and throughout the failure to achieve any real human intimacy.

But unlike other Depression literature, "Bitter Music" and Partch's other Americana works do not indict capitalism or the American political system or urge the correction of social and economic inequities through organized political action. It remains an intensely personal—though unself-pitying—document of Partch's experiences. Partch's bitterness results not from a realization of a failed American Dream or what the Depression might foretell about the survival of American values, but rather from the acutely felt despair of an artist unable to further his creative work. While "Bitter Music" avoids the unmistakable socialist, communist, or even anarchist sympathies of much Depression literature, it does share its naturalism and experimentalism. The basic structure of the work is conventional and realistic enough: a first-person narrative in the form of a diary that includes fragments of external dialogue and interior monologue. But distinctive is Partch's use of music to heighten the realism of dialogue and events.

Partch occasionally listed "Bitter Music" among his musical compositions because of the music he incorporated into it—musicalized fragments of the hobo speech he had heard daily around him. Partch intended the work to be read and played at the piano, and he uses musical settings in several ways to heighten the experiences he presents. Primarily, Partch represents speech by notating its melodic inflections without fixed rhythm. Occasionally he introduces folk- or popular songs in full piano settings, and less frequently he provides a piano accompaniment to enhance the dramatic mood of a situation. His most virtuoso achievement is in the November 15 episode driving south from Santa Barbara: here the Filipino driver's singing of "Rock of Ages" is presented in counterpoint to the notation of Partch's interior thoughts.

Many episodes of "Bitter Music" reveal Partch's exhilaration at being amid the vast, natural out-of-doors, a feeling that no doubt evoked his childhood growing up on the deserts of the Southwest. The long, rugged coastline north of San Francisco was a part of

California that had long fascinated Partch, and "End Littoral" is the unpublished journal he kept about a fourteen-day hiking trip along this coast in 1947. Although not related to any of his musical work, "End Littoral" serves in this anthology as a pastoral-relief pendant to the nonheroic epic of "Bitter Music" — in much the way that Partch was conscious of following Greek practice by composing the satyr-dance music of *Plectra and Percussion Dances* as a form of catharsis after setting the tragedy of Oedipus.

The indispensable introduction to Partch's instruments and theories of just intonation, monophony, and corporeality remains *Genesis of a Music*, first published in 1949 by the University of Wisconsin Press. The substantive additions to the enlarged, second edition (New York: Da Capo Press, 1974) are background discussions of six major works, as well as updated descriptions of Partch's instruments, a bibliography, and lists of works, instruments, recordings, and films. But even in its enlarged version, *Genesis of a Music* leaves many aspects of Partch's ideas unexplored.

The biographical and critical essays presented in part 2 of the present collection trace the development of Partch's ideas about music and society between 1940 and 1967. "Patterns of Music" (1940) is an attempt by Partch (apparently never repeated) to explain — with the analogy of a painter using color — why as a composer he needed to use more than the usual twelve tones to the octave. "W. B. Yeats" (1941) and "The Kithara" (1941) report on episodes from Partch's 1934–35 trip to Europe. The remaining essays, all written in the two decades after *Genesis of a Music*, embody Partch's vigorous and still timely and provocative critique of contemporary musical life — its institutions, educational philosophy, specialization, veneration for absolute music, and unwillingness to explore the full range of musical sound — and what Partch saw as the stifling effect it had on the musical creativity of both composer and performer. These essays starkly expose those aspects of the Western musical tradition that Partch so fervently rejected and reveal the impulse behind his artistic ideals and compositions that sought to recapture the magic, mystery, and ritual of music.

To gain performances and understanding of his music, Partch often drafted detailed arguments and explanations of compositions, which he circulated among friends, delivered as lectures, or printed as program or record liner notes. The most extended of Partch's descriptions for eight major compositions are collected in part 3 of the present volume.[3] These help elucidate the background and context of these works and complement the complete librettos or scenarios to *U.S. Highball, Oedipus, The Bewitched, Revelation in the Courthouse Park, Water! Water!* and *Delusion of the Fury* given in part 4.

Although we have Partch's own precedent for circulating among friends librettos and scenarios to works in progress, in an important sense extracting readable librettos from his full scores violates Partch's own ideal of integrated, corporeal theater. Partch himself recognized the limitations of scenarios or librettos and prefaced printed scenarios to *Delusion of the Fury* with the statement: "Words cannot proxy for the experience of knowing—of seeing and hearing. The concept of this work inheres in the *presence* of the instruments onstage, the *movements* of musicians and chorus, the *sounds* they produce, the *actuality* of actors, of singers, of mimes, of lights; in fine, the *actuality* of truly integrated theater. . . . I feel that the only investigation which has genuine integrity is the seen and heard performance."

Since few readers will likely experience Partch's dramatic works in theatrical realizations, however, the printed librettos of his theater works presented in part 4 fill a long-standing need for a text that can allow readers imaginatively to construct—with the aid of recordings—these works in their entirety as corporeal theater. Moreover, the librettos are crucial for another reason: they serve as an indispensable source for understanding and interpreting Partch's life and artistic personality. *The Bewitched, Revelation in the Courthouse Park*, and *Water! Water!* are clearly period pieces; the topics, dialogue, characters, and objects of Partch's satire in these works—the phenomenon of the rock-and-roll idol, jazz, beatniks, small-minded civic and social leaders—can convey to readers and students, now at a thirty-year distance, a sense of that contemporary American experience as Partch witnessed it, but mostly lived apart from.

A Note on Editorial Principles

Like many writers, Partch occasionally borrowed from himself or elaborated an idea in several ways in different places. Readers may note similarities between, for example, passages in "The Ancient Magic" and in "Some New and Old Thoughts after and before *The Bewitched*," between "Delusion of the Fury" in part 3 and the preface to the libretto, and between discussions of compositions here and those in *Genesis of a Music*. Retaining such duplication seems preferable to omitting the pieces or destroying their unity by presenting only excerpts of them here. But in all such cases, the pieces included in this volume are important sources because they present earlier or expanded versions of an idea developed elsewhere or descriptions more contemporary with a work's initial composition and performance. (The account of *Revelation in the Courthouse Park* is reprinted from *Genesis of a Music* to provide a convenient introduction to the libretto.)

For a composer who had worked as a proofreader and who attempted to create a music arising from the spoken word, it is not surprising that Partch was fastidious about verbal expression and developed an economical yet vigorous prose style. Fortunately, the unpublished journals and other writings printed here survive in fair typescripts, allowing Partch to speak in his own voice with minimal editorial interpretation.

Given that the texts reprinted in this volume span thirty years and range from typescripts to articles printed in small magazines or newspapers, some regularization of spelling and punctuation was necessary to bring consistency to these diverse sources. Spelling and formation of possessives have been regularized to conform to current usage; and obvious typographical and grammatical errors (such as subject-verb agreement) and lapses in punctuating items in a series, compound sentences, and parenthetical and introductory elements have been silently corrected. However, many characteristic features of Partch's punctuation (such as excessive use of commas and dashes) have been retained. Occasional editorial clarifications are given in square brackets.

The musical examples for "Bitter Music" required considerable editorial reconstruction. The examples, often with the text only faintly penciled in, were microfilmed on separate sheets preceding the typescript journal but have been set in their proper places in the printed journal entries. For the sake of clarity and consistency, beaming, stemming, treatment of accidentals, and other aspects of notation are normalized, although Partch's setting of text above the notes it accompanies, his unorthodox placement of meter signs, and his omission of concluding barlines in most examples have been retained. Editorial clarifications are signaled by square brackets.

Partch's recorded lectures have been transcribed as literally as possible. Punctuation in these transcriptions is, of course, editorial; occasional false starts or misspoken sentences have been rectified. Partch's public introductions to his works usually concluded with musical excerpts and introductions of performers and instruments. For obvious reasons, these are omitted here.

The librettos for *Oedipus, Revelation in the Courthouse Park, Water! Water!* and *Delusion of the Fury* have been derived as closely as possible from Partch's final full scores. The overall format of the librettos follows that used by Partch for his own preliminary librettos to *Revelation in the Courthouse Park* and *Water! Water!* The text for *U.S. Highball* and the scenario for *The Bewitched* reprint texts prepared by Partch.

The principal authority for the libretto texts (including introductory material and stage directions) is always the final score; obvious typographical errors have been corrected, and punctuation and designations of characters have been made consistent. Lists of instruments are for the final version. The format of time and place and listing of characters and instruments at the beginning of a libretto have been made uniform for all librettos. Where stage directions in earlier scores or in Partch's preliminary librettos are more descriptive of action, lighting, incidental music, etc., these directions have been incorporated into the text and distinguished by angle brackets and braces. Occasional editorial clarifications appear in square brackets. Full identification of sources used for each libretto is provided in "Sources and Notes" at the end of the book.

In the texts of his scores, Partch tended to use dashes of varying length for sustained notes and to separate most repeated syllables with hyphens. For clarity and consistency the librettos use a single em dash to indicate sustained or glided syllables; hyphens have been avoided except to indicate spoken emphases or where necessary to indicate repetition of syllables in words.

There are occasional discrepancies between the spoken or sung texts of the librettos printed in part 4 and the recorded performance. No attempt has been made to reflect these—intentional or inadvertent—departures from the full score that occurred during the performance and recording.

NOTES

1. This biographical sketch corrects details in other published accounts. The first portion is based on Partch's description of his youth in the preface to the enlarged, second edition of his *Genesis of a Music* (New York: Da Capo Press, 1974). Additional sources used include Partch's correspondence and other documents that are still being located and recovered—often in the papers of friends whose own collections are being deposited in public libraries and archives. The principal collections containing significant Partch material include those of Otto Luening (New York Public Library); Douglas Moore and Jacques Barzun (Columbia University); Lauriston C. Marshall, Robert Kostka, Betty Freeman, Broadcast Music, Inc., and Barnard Hewitt (Harry Partch Archive, University of Illinois Music Library); Peter Yates (Mandeville Special Collections, University of California, San Diego); the John Simon Guggenheim Memorial Foundation, New York; the Institute for Interna-

tional Education, New York; University of Wisconsin Press, Madison; University of Wisconsin Archives, Madison; University of Illinois Archives; and the Moldenauer Archive, Harvard University. Photocopies of many of these collections have been gathered at the Harry Partch Archive, University of Illinois Music Library.

2. *From the Music of Harry Partch* (1964), Composers Recordings, Inc. CRI 193; *And on the Seventh Day Petals Fell in Petaluma* (1967), Composers Recordings, Inc. CRI 213; *The World of Harry Partch* (1969), Columbia Records MS 7207; *Delusion of the Fury* (1971), Columbia Records M2 30576; and *The Bewitched* (1973), Composers Recordings, Inc. CRI SD 304.

3. For briefer comments by Partch about these and other compositions (drawn from prefatory notes to scores, record liner notes, and program notes), see Thomas McGeary, *The Music of Harry Partch: A Descriptive Catalogue,* I.S.A.M. Monographs, no. 31 (Brooklyn, N.Y.: Institute for Studies in American Music, 1990). This volume includes a detailed chronological outline of Partch's life, a bibliographic catalogue of Partch's scores, an extensive bibliography, and a discography.

PART 1

TWO JOURNALS

Bitter Music

Preface

BITTER MUSIC is a diary of eight months spent in transient shelters and camps, hobo jungles, basement rooms, and on the open road. I wrote each of the diary entries on the day indicated or the day following, and notated the music of the spoken words in a rough way without instruments, in most cases, very soon after the words were actually spoken. I sketched the original pencil drawings—used as suggestions for the present illustrations—on the scenes described.[1]

Just previous to this experience I had returned from seven months in Europe, where I had done research under a grant of $1,500, made to promote my seemingly revolutionary ideas in music. I say "seemingly" because the fact of "revolution" was determined for me by non-understanding musicians. I had never thought of my work as revolutionary, but only as evolutionary.

Now, however, my "evolution" seemed to demand a sudden descent into hobo jungles. Why? Perhaps the diary will tell, but if it doesn't the reasons are too psychologically confused for me to articulate.

At any rate, there was a dull shock of contrast in the descent. I was walking off a plank from an ordered ship of adventure into a sea of chaotic humanity. But my music still comforted and sustained me, especially because I suddenly realized that I had an inspirational and creative use for it even in a hobo jungle.

I heard music in the voices all about me, and tried to notate it, and I tried to enhance the mood and drama of such little things as a quarrel in a potato patch. The nuance of inflection and thought of the lowest of our social order was a new experience in tone, and I found myself at its fountainhead—a fountainhead of pure musical Americana.

In retrospect the experience has a glow of attractiveness, but five years later there is still something underneath that is not so attractive. I remember each new fragment of music as an essence slightly bitter— bitter at its source, bitter in its sound to me, bitter—though unheard—to our culture.

Thus, BITTER MUSIC.

The urging present is not always sober. It would have been easy and perhaps natural to temper passages in the text which even a little deliberation would judge to be too self-revealing, rash, unjust, and possibly absurd; but this was not done.

Only such changes have been made as would clarify, not destroy, the spontaneity of the instant. Because of the resulting frankness all persons mentioned are cloaked in fictitious or semi-fictitious names or are left nameless.

Musical notes are given roughly as the words of critical passages were or might be spoken, and a piano accompaniment occasionally added. The accompaniment is designed to heighten and to reconstruct the original impression or emotion, which is now secondhand to all concerned.

If possible, the book is to be read at the piano, and the fragmentary music, on passages requiring emphasis and intensification of mood, occurs much as the incidental music might occur in a talking picture. The fragments are in no sense "performers' music"; they are readers' music.

If the reader is not piano-minded, he of course will ignore the music entirely. If he does play the piano, even poorly, the musical passages may be something of an excursion into an art form as old as history, but one which, because of our present preoccupation with music in the mass, is all but lost. It is an individual form—the expression of one individual to another.

The words are always directly above their respective notes, whether in bass or treble. When the intrinsic rhythm of the spoken words is too complicated for notation, stems are omitted from the notes. To reproduce the original effect, the words should be spoken quickly, on the tones indicated. They should never be sung.

The quotations from Lao-tse, Chinese sage of the sixth century B.C., on page 36 and pages 44–45, are from the versions by James Legge (Clarendon Press, Oxford); the two lines of verse on page 41 are from "Hymn to the Sun and Myself," by Ogden Nash (*Hard Lines,* Simon & Schuster, New York, 1931); the passages from the "Song of Solomon" on pages 52–57 are from the King James version of the Bible; the fragments of Sapphic verse on page 85 are from *Sappho of Lesbos* by Arthur Weigall (Butterworth, London, 1932); the Henrik Ibsen quotation on page 104 is from *The Wild Duck;* and the fragment of verse on pages 117–18 is from "Wilderness Song," by Everett Ruess, who disappeared in the desert in 1934. The fragment does not quite agree with the "Wilderness Song" which appeared in *Desert*

Magazine for September, 1938, although I took it from a sheet which Ruess himself had typed.[2]

The songs beginning "Hand me down my walking cane," "I left my gal in the mountains," "Stand up, poor boy, stand up, stand up," "And I'll tell you my story, kind mister," "Rock of ages, cleft for me," "He walked up to the queen of Spain," and "Adieu, kind friends, adieu, adieu," are my own arrangements of the tunes, for the most part as I heard them sung on the road. "Standin' in the need of prayer" is given without accompaniment as I heard it sung, and the melody of the Chopin F♯ Major Nocturne as I sang it myself.

In late October, 1935, walking down the unfinished mountain road along the coast south of Big Sur, California, with a pack on my back, it seemed that mood, sky, and circumstance had come to a sure coincidence, so sure that it brought from this confirmed wanderer the declaration, "Here would I choose to abide."

Convicts were working on the road, and I timidly approached and entered their little camp, huddled like a frightened animal between the beating sea and rising mountains at Anderson Creek. I walked through both timidly and boldly, because I had been told that coast residents only were allowed by. Once beyond the high creek bridge, I made a hurried pencil sketch of the camp, and went on.

I went south toward any god who softly whistled, and in early November the one spot where I would "choose to abide" was already far behind.

Now, the fall of 1940, I am back. The little house on the ledge — beside the lilac trees at the edge of the cliff — now has other occupants, but I am invited to lunch, and lunch conceives days, and days months.

The road is finished. The Convict Camp is now not a frightened animal but its ghostly spirit. The many gone houses make a vacant hole in the little flat, and one of the lonely bunkhouses is wrecked by a winter storm. But the offices remain, and through the generous interest of others who here choose to abide, I am living in one of them — formerly the camp superintendent's office — brief yards from the ceaseless impinging of earth and sea, life and death.

I am in the debt of old-old friends in Glendale, La Crescenta, and Covina, California, for the use of their homes and pianos in January, 1936, for notating of the music. And, finally, I am in the debt of those ever more illusory figures who were the manuscript's cause, excuse, and — more important — its life.

H.P., November 22, 1940,
Old Convict Camp, Anderson Creek,
Coast of Magnificent Descendings.

JUNE 11, 1935—Santa Rosa, California

JUNE 12—Federal Shelter, Stockton

I neither leave nor arrive on the midnight train; I come on the scorned-by-true-bums highway. But all my sins of futile ambition are taken away, for I am now a grateful itinerant ward of the United States government.

"How long have you been in California?"

The old, old question. My inquisitor is neither very bright nor interested. If he had been, he would have seen an expression of strained patience before him.

It is three years since I have done any undirected wandering— September, 1932. September 21, the date of my escorted exit from the San Luis Obispo jail, where I was an overnight guest, marked my reentrance into respectability after a spring and summer of roaming. I have forgotten how to lie. My very existence in these three years depended on the fervor, the intensity, with which I told the truth as I sincerely saw it.

This fervor is meaningless now.

"Just a month and a half, but I was born in Oakland and have lived in California most of my life."

"Bed tonight and breakfast tomorrow is all we can give you," he says.

"That sort of induces one to lie," I say, smiling.

"Yes, it does," he says.

I am bewildered, not knowing whether to protest or deny California residence. I am sent through a door into a dressing room.[3]

I have only the clothes on me.

The attendant smiles as he looks at the knifelike crease of my blue serge trousers. My tan shoes are polished: they, my plaid tie, and blue polo shirt are from the tiny isle of Malta. Everybody notices the boots.

After a shower I am given a "monkey suit," a pair of tan coveralls, to wear tonight. My clothes come back tomorrow.

I go to a large dark room with double-decked bunks, and pick one out.

Strange conversations come out of the dark—strange and quondamly familiar. Not all of me listens.

What listens—

". . . an' he says, 'Go to bed or check out,' he says."

"A guy can't even take a proper piss."

"They sure don't give you time to shake off no drops."

". . . (from another direction) why, you can look in his eyes, and they say, 'Come and get me daddy.' "

"Aw, you're crazy."

"Crazy! If he had as many things sticking out of him as he had stuck in him, he'd look like a porcupine."

". . . (back to first direction—a voice is addressing the attendant, who has just entered) how about getting some aspirin—had a bloody headache for two days."

"See the doctor in the mornin'. "

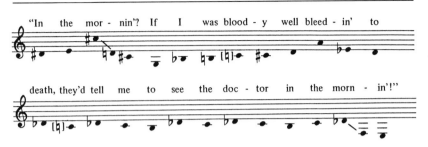

"In the mor - nin'? If I was blood - y well bleed - in' to

death, they'd tell me to see the doc - tor in the morn - in'!"

On and on and on, wisecrack ascending on wisecrack.

What doesn't listen—

Here I am being fed and sheltered and cared for—and I am glad. By bureaucrats? perhaps, but this body is having those things that it must have, and with least exaction on the mind—the mind that wants a brief repose from seemingly endless futile effort—and if it comes by bureaucrats, it is better than no repose at all.

Conversations stop and multifarious snores arise and undulate over the hours. I wonder which is more distasteful.

JUNE 13

I check out and go to the State Relief Bureau, as directed. There I deny that I ever forfeited residence in California, but I might as well have been dumb. After some hours of waiting they send me back to the Federal Shelter with a note. I present the note and smile my petty triumph.

Again I strip and bathe—the same clothes are again garnered for "delousing"—again I have a "monkey suit" to wear all day and night.

> *Hallelujah, I'm a bum—*
> *Hallelujah, bum again—*
> *Hallelujah, give us a handout*
> *To revive us again.*

This is as lusty singing as I ever heard—with bellies full of braised beef, beans, coffee, chocolate pudding.

American folk and popular songs have one of their greatest bulwarks in bumdom. These songs are heard over the world—and yet continental Europeans and upper-crust Yankees are often heard to say: "America is not a musical nation."

One dreary November night, in 1934, I walked down the main

street of Portsmouth, England. It was Saturday, and the many people overflowed the sidewalk onto the bicycle-ridden pavement.

A thick, cold Channel fog seemed determined to steal under my upturned windbreaker and into my marrow.

From a pub came a clear baritone—

> *Where there never is heard*
> *A discouraging word —*
> *And the skies are not cloudy all day.*

My heart beat fast as I strode through the fog and walked in. It was a young Scotch navy sailor, with a mouth organ in one hand, a glass of beer in the other.

Sailors and sailors' women, and barmaids crowded around.

said young Jock. He was a very clever entertainer and confided that after his twelve-year enlistment was up he was going to Hollywood.

I gave him an address. "Be sure to look me up when you come.

Also apropos of the America-is-not-a-musical-nation untruism was my first conversation, last year, with the director of the organization which guided the execution of my research and experimental projects in Europe.[4] He had not been introduced to my work before meeting me, and as a result the interview was a shock to both of us.

His part of the conversation was beautifully put together. I am abridging it because it is impossible to do it justice in a reconstruction. My own, after nearly a year of thinking about it, has undoubtedly improved.

I explained that I hoped to execute my projects in England.

"It is curious, your desire to go to England. Music students never go to England. Germany and Italy are the musical countries, whereas England and America are not musical."

"If you mean, when you say that England and America are not

musical, that they respond less completely to eighteenth-century German abstraction, I agree with you that they are not."

"If you mean, by eighteenth-century German abstraction, Beethoven, I think it's a pity."

"If you mean that Beethoven should become our one musical standard, I think it's also a pity. This sort of music has only the feeblest roots in our culture, and those mostly among a class of people that thinks of concerts as social occasions. And that's the way concert managers want them to think of concerts. It's a vicious circle. And this music has almost no roots among the people who—if we *do* have a contribution to give in music in this country—are giving it. It was the lowest of the social order—sailors, soldiers, criminals, and all their kin—who gave England one of the richest of musics. But whether given by the lowest, or by a higher class of people—it has to come from the people, just as Beethoven came from the people. But this isn't Germany, and this isn't the eighteenth century, and I'm trying to give myself, and others, a good basis for a new and great music of the people—not just for this country but regardless of country. And that's why I work with words, because they are the commonest medium of creative expression. And words *are* music. Spoken words. Spoken words were music to the ancient Greeks, to Gregorian chant (at its conception), to the troubadours of Provence and the Meistersingers of Nuremberg, to the hillbillies of Tennessee. Yes, even sometimes to the tune peddlers of Tin Pan Alley. Wagner had the idea, too, but then he threw it to the mercy of a ninety-piece symphony orchestra. Nothing could survive that. These others all used words in music in a way that retained some vestige of their spoken vitality, and they produced a vital, living art. An art that simply aims at rehashing Beethoven is no art at all. Not that the abstract music of Beethoven is not a legitimate art, and great. It is. But because it is legitimate, do you have to make it a cult of high priest and pharisees?

"And that isn't all," I continued. "There can be no growth in musical art with the present worn-out system of music, limited to twelve tones to the octave. That isn't the people's fault, and it isn't the composers', either, except indirectly. They were simply handed the system by their fathers and took it. But I'm going to hand them something else. I'm using forty-three separate tones to the octave— and I'm not just theorizing, lying on my back in the sun dreaming. I'm building instruments to play them—one, a viola, I have been demonstrating for four years—forty-three *true* tones, I might add, instead of the twelve false tones of the piano. For that is what the piano is—twelve black and white bars in front of musical freedom. Twelve black and white stiflers."

The learned doctor was somewhat taken back by my vehement dissertation, but he finally said, "Very interesting, very interesting—especially your reviving the Greek idea; but you know, Goethe and Schiller were an eighteenth-century German expression of the Greek spirit."

"But they had no equivalent in music."

"No. Well, I am wondering what response you will get here or in England. It is really pitiful to see Americans get together and then turn on the radio for their music."

"I think you are only familiar with the least interesting stratum of American life. I know the music of American hoboes, and of American seamen, and—"

"Seamen who were Americans? I didn't know there were any."

"Indeed. Well—"

"Well, you look intelligent," he concluded, and I detected an almost imperceptible emphasis on the word *look*, "and I wish you every success in England."

This man was very charming, and very erudite, but what can the academy know of the music of everyday people? That it isn't like Beethoven.

In the early days of presenting my music, the mere mention of the words Bach or Beethoven, twin gods of classical musicians, turned on a faucet of revolt in me.

Almost always I slightly overstep myself when talking earnestly about my music. As a matter of fact I love the piano, but I feel that the great music that has come out of it was not entirely due to its virtues—there is also the matter of beauty coming to life *despite* faults.

Music is not a desire—it is an omnipresent condition. Tones, like the colors of the sky, mountains, trees, and the body, are inescapable, and not all music is man-made. Some respond—some don't.

Much of that which *is* man-made we ignore, such as the music of speech. Well, I'm not ignoring it.

Hallelujah, I'm a bum —

Supper is another good meal. I think of the bread lines of my San Francisco days, the first year of presenting my music—crusts of bread, dishwater coffee, the Salvation Army.

After supper we have short-arm inspection. We line up before a man who sits in a chair with a magnifying glass. "Milk it out," he says, as each man steps forward with his pants unbuttoned, and when he satisfies himself as to the absence of gonococci, he then probes around each tuft of hair with his glass, looking for crabs.

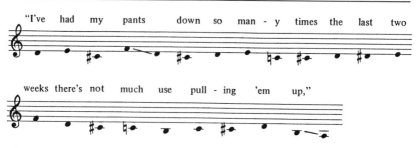

pipes one boy.

Concern for one is the welfare of all. Perhaps he knows what a lucky boy he is—but the true bum seldom ever admits it.

Another day is done, and I am lulled to sleep by the incessant periodicity of multinasal snoring.

JUNE 14

No one is allowed to stay in a shelter more than three or four days, except those necessary to its maintenance. We must go to "camp," and I decide to go immediately.

We are to work six hours a day, five days a week, tobacco and work clothes furnished, and four dollars a month besides.

Pablo's upper lip arches wistfully. I have seen his face in many old masterpieces—it is the oval of a mandolin. He is from Kentucky. One of his grandfathers, I believe he said, gave him a Spanish strain.

Anyway, he is the one sensitive person I have met and the only one I can bear to talk to.

There are three camps we may choose from—two in the mountains and Harrington Ranch, in the Delta.

Pablo tells me that Harrington Ranch is the best—he has been there before—with real farm chow—milk, fresh vegetables, fresh-killed meats. He is going back, so I decide to go, too.

We have a physical examination, a second short-arm inspection (where were we overnight, my dear doctors?), and I am vaccinated.

We arrive in time for noon dinner, and the food is everything Pablo claimed for it. It is Friday, and we dig spuds in the afternoon.

My company is barely tolerable.

We have had one or more days of idleness in shelter, and tomorrow (Saturday) and Sunday there is no work. One short afternoon's work for three or four days' keep.

Bums are miserable when they have no cause to complain, and continue it from pure habit.

"Somebody gets plenty from the work we do."

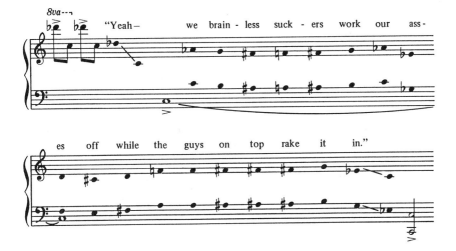

The afternoon's work is finished.

There is the supper gong. I hear a monotone—too dead for
notation: "Why do they put the mess house so far away? It wears a
guy out to go down there and back."

Almost too lazy to go and get it.

JUNE 15—Harrington Ranch, San Joaquin Delta

There are about two hundred men in camp, quartered in five
barracks transformed from barns.

I try to be friendly, but no one even looks at me, let alone answers
me when I venture to speak.

I overhear "the big house" frequently, "the Columbus riot," and
other phrases like them. I have read of "prison stupor"—"stir-bugs,"
the men call it. Now I see it.

My simple "hellos" do not penetrate their dream worlds. Vacant
stares say: "How dare you try to insinuate yourself into this consciousness?" I decide to insinuate myself no more.

This is mostly a middle-aged man's camp. The few very young
fellows present are those that were unable to get into C.C.C.[5] for one
reason or another, or who are simply seduced by any fateful wind
that catches them. Pablo is in this class.

My days as a proofreader made the following inscription on a
toilet wall highly amusing—

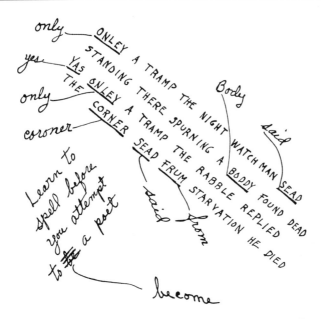

The corrections of the verse by the second bum, of common education, and, finally, the restrained correction, "become," in red pencil, by the third bum, the grammarian, without any derogatory admonitions, make this a priceless bit of tramp-lore.

JUNE 16

Pablo talks to me from his mandolin face most of the afternoon. How many women have played upon those tooth-fretted lips?

He shows me their pictures. They are obviously of the hustler type, and I say so. He seems hurt.

What chance has a refined and sensitive bum like Pablo really to possess a woman worthy of him? About as much chance as that such a woman will move in his orbit.

If the homosexuality in prisons, navies, and in any other circumstances which segregate men is similar to such tendencies as I have seen in this camp, it is mostly pure lust. Few of these men desire tender affection. A female sheep would often prove satisfactory.

Pablo is popular here—he has a cheery word for almost everyone, but it is mostly leg-pulling. With me he is always serious and wants to confide.

Now he talks of his buddy in camp, and shows me his picture—

his buddy, who left a month ago. They loved each other without knowing it.

Then one night they were both a bit heady with wine and boisterous. The buddy put his hand around Pablo's neck and said to him, in a mocking way: "Kiss me." And Pablo, mockingly, kissed him. But this mocking little kiss was a spark to tinder and simply led to a second which was consummated in all seriousness and with full cooperation.

And so the evening ended with music on the mandolin.

says Pablo.

Die for a few unchartered kisses? Pablo, you are young.

Still, he is worried that he should ever have loved a man. Pablo is twenty-four, and should know his feelings, without concern. He does not ask my opinion, but — "Any real love is a beautiful experience," I say, "and real love is apt to fluctuate over the whole idea of sex, and beyond, too. I wouldn't give it another thought."

"It is women who fill my thoughts," he says, and I only doubt the percentage of fullness—there are other absorbing things, too.

Who cares who loves who? It doesn't matter, anyway, so long as the music is good music.

Night has long since enfolded us. We are walking on the river levee.

Pablo raises his chin and turns it away from me:

he says, looking at the moon. He doesn't even know my name.

The barracks are sleeping quiet.

How warm it is—in this summer darkness—to have a "goodnight" wished for me, so sincerely.

It is late, and we tiptoe to our bunks opposite each other across the aisle.

I hear him moving restlessly on hot blankets. But I do not think— I am carried into sleep by the sequential snorgles from forty human exhausts.

JUNE 17

Today I have seen a beautiful face. If I could look like it, I would not mind being old.

A luxurious beard with pagan curls! It is worthy of Solomon.

I feel the thirty-seven pig bristles on my chin, and laugh.

I know nothing about him—I don't want to—for the looks of him are complete. They are like exotic musics.

JUNE 20

The ignorance hereabouts is of two kinds—hopeless and irremediable.

The hopeless kind reposes in those with capacity for betterment but who probably won't get it for so many reasons that they would fill a book.

I am trying to immunize myself to the second kind, but it is difficult. For example, this morning there is a long heated argument on whether North and South America are one continent or two. Ordinarily I would simply walk away. Now I have to listen because I am working with the arguers.

On this, and also on two other occasions when I can hold my exasperation no longer, I sing, with great deliberation, at the top of my lungs—

It has worked all three times—the subject is dropped immediately. They look at me as though I were a voice from Mars, and well I might be, for all I mean to them until I explode.

Some day I'll get smacked and then learn my correct place in these wretched conversations.

Carousals and episodes on the road are topics for endless talk. Unhappily, they are almost all Pablo and I have in common. He is in the hopeless class, having been on the road since he was fourteen. But he is beer in my gullet for he does not trouble to show his ignorance. He knows modestly and disclaims humbly. There is a germ of wisdom.

But we are not good company for long—and I am desolate.

Dinner.

It is a spasm. Arms reach out from, and going to, every direction, like traffic in Piccadilly Circus. These men work at dinner as though they thought it would end in an orgasm.

When a man can live through ten years of animality, inconsideration, bragging, stupidity, and still eat slowly, calmly, ask others if they will have food before he helps himself, be gentleness itself in requesting service—I say that when a man can munch a hunk of bread and a gob of peanut butter hesitating on top, in such surroundings, with the calm, grace, and deftness of a British statesman guiding a crisis, as Pablo does, he displays a source of serenity no less than divine.

Supper.

I sit opposite Solomon. I hardly eat from gazing—but the beautiful one does not deign to notice me.

He is attendant in the checkroom.

JUNE 21

There is a large meadow between our camp and the slough. It is in no way like Wimbledon Common—it has no heather and low rolling hills—but as I wander across it this evening, an echo of thoughts from across the sea comes back—for my forty-three-tone-to-the-octave organ came to life just three months ago, near Wimbledon Common.

A grass with seed heads as soft as down covers this deltic meadow. I take off my shoes and walk in caresses—up onto the levee. It is not like the embankment of the Thames at Twickenham—there are no swans here to define the surface of the river: it is lined with wild reeds and willows—but I can see a breeze from Cornwall rippling over the water.

JUNE 23

Intense casualness—this is the reaction of bums to everything in life—friendship, love, hate, death.

Today a fifteen-year-old boy drowned in the slough near us. We mostly go down—some to help grapple for the body.

One hobo laughs because many of the drowned boy's relatives were there, seeing him go. But I hear no comments.

The misery of this mother makes me breathe: "Oh, if we could only come without parents and live as alone as any homeless hobo. The only horrible thing about such sudden endings is the anguish of you who care."

The going of few of us here will be accompanied by the beating of breasts. Is this the reason for your strange laughter, my friend?

JUNE 24

Today is my birthday. I am thirty-four.

There is not much to do here but listen and think. Today I am in no mood for listening. I am too deep in my own thoughts. I am thinking of this same day a year ago. And day follows day in my mind until I come back to today—to myself, at Harrington Ranch—at thirty-four.

Some of the days of this year gone for good I see as clearly as I see this morning. I never had time to talk about them, or write about them, even in letters, before. I was too busy with my work.

Today I have all the time there is in the world.

A farm at East Chatham, New York, where I am working for my board and room—June 27, 1934. A letter comes: ". . . We are happy to inform you that . . . has made a grant to you of $1,500. . . . The fund is to be made available over a period of one year and the stipend will be paid in four installments. We should be glad to discuss with you your plans of research in order that we may co-operate to the fullest extent to the end that this year of research in your special field may yield as much benefit as possible. . . ."

This is money and a consummation in the recognition of my endeavors that have been long coming—eleven years of effort and three years of begging are behind it—and I wonder if I still have the energy, having spent so much in winning the award, to execute my projects.

I have committed myself to three. I did not promise to complete the three in a year's time, but I said I would at least try to lay the groundwork.

Project 1: Completion of my *Trails of Music,*[6] the theoretical basis of my work. I had rewritten this manuscript almost every year since 1926, but the historical background was still woefully deficient, and I proposed to prepare histories of intonation, and of the spoken word in music, at the British Museum in London.

Project 2: The building of a true chromatic organ, or, if this is a misuse of the word *true,* an organ at least three times as chromatic as the piano. The keyboard of this instrument I had already constructed, as a model.

Project 3: The setting of the entire drama *King Oedipus,* version by the Irish poet William Butler Yeats, to my music, preserving throughout the vitality of the spoken words. For this project I would require the completion of my chromatic organ, and I would hope to have the assistance of Yeats in its interpretation.

I could spend the whole sum of $1,500 on my chromatic organ—my beautiful dumb keyboard—in a single disbursement, and waste no part of a penny. After all, people spend a thousand dollars on a piano, which is standardized in mass production, and think nothing extravagant in it. And yet for my keyboard, only one of its kind—parts for which have to be specially made—I can spend, at most, half that much. For my $1,500 must cover all expenses—traveling, living—for a year, and instrument building. In that case it will, by gollies.

As for Project 3, last January I received a letter: "Dear Mr. Partch: I am overwhelmed to find that I never answered a letter of yours dated October 27th. . . . When it reached me I put it into an envelope with some other letters as I was starting for London. I intended to give it to my agent . . . and ask them to write to you. I got ill and forgot it. I only discovered it this day. I give you permission with pleasure (to set *King Oedipus*) subject, in case of performance or publication, to the usual business arrangements. . . . What you say in your letter is exceedingly interesting and has, so far as I can understand your methods, my complete sympathy. Yours, W. B. Yeats."[7]

New York, July, 1934. I am introduced to the president of the organization which made the grant.[8]

Dr. President: "Young man, you will do well to find a place for yourself in this country's economic system. You owe it to yourself to find it, because you can't go on year after year winning awards of this sort."

Me: "Dr. President, I have never had a grant before in my entire life, and I have been working eleven years for this one."

Dr. President: "Hm. Well, this is just a warning. We don't want to do to you what we did to Roger Sessions. He kept winning award after award, scholarship after scholarship, until we finally had to throw him off the pier."[9]

Me: "Dr. President, I have been off the pier my entire life. If you throw me off it won't be new."

Dr. President: "Well, it's up to you now. Good luck."

New York, August, 1934. Another letter. "I shall be here (Dublin) all summer with the exception of the month of October. I would of course see you with pleasure, but doubt if my unmusical mind would be of much help to you. Your work interests me very much but I have no knowledge of music. . . . I made no attempts to carry out my theories (setting spoken words to music), nor have I done so, since Florence Farr died. . . . Yours, W. B. Yeats."[10]

New York, August, 1934. My inquiries to American organ builders regarding my chromatic organ cause reactions of indifference or downright antagonism. Well, my tight little imaginationless businessmen, you have lost your opportunity. I apply for a passport, and get an English visa.

Aboard SS Gourko, *British ship bound for London, September, 1934.* "Where is the other passenger?" asks the purser. I didn't know there was another—I didn't see him. I have spent $75 for passage on a freighter direct to London.

Now I meet the other passenger, and she is immediately my friend.

London, October, 1934. I have barely gotten off the boat, have taken a bus, and have alighted from it in the vicinity of the British Museum. Walking down a side street, I pass a bobby rapidly clearing the street of traffic. A moment later King George and Queen Mary pass before me. All the men on the street remove their hats. I wear none, which is well, since I am too astonished to remove it.

I am looking for the so-called "university union." I have been given a letter to them, and they are supposed to assist me in my work in London.

"Well, what can I do for you." It is the secretary in the "union" speaking, in a voice clear and hard like glass.

I show her my letter of introduction.

"Oh. The first thing you will do, please, is register."

She hands me a book.

"Put your name here, and your degrees here."

"I have no degrees," I say, and there is a pause.

"You have no degrees."

There is no query at the end of the lady's sentence. It is a plain repetition of what I said as a fact. To say that she is appalled is a very mild statement. What is this business of grants coming to? My, my! giving money to people who have no degrees!

"Well, write your name here," she says impatiently, and I sense a feeling in her that I might not be able to do it, "and leave this space blank, please—you have no degrees."

"Who did you expect to study with here?" is her next utterance. That anyone with "no degrees" could be doing original and creative work was plainly incredible.

When I explain that I plan to study with no one, both the subject and I are dropped as quickly as possible, and I am handed a list of the most expensive boardinghouses in London, as I later learn, at one of which I might live.

However, she does hand me a slip of paper, some days later, which reads: "The Director of the British Museum begs to acknowledge the return of Mr. Partch's ticket of admission to the Reading Room; and to state that the ticket may be renewed, if again required, on written application to the Director."

British Museum, London, October–November, 1934. Day after day, from the reading room's opening hour to its closing hour, I go through ancient and modern volumes on music, and I call in a photographer for pictures to illustrate my new book. With my stacks of notebooks it is emerging into the grandeur of its conception. Another book! and the world is choked with them.

Thus begins Project 1.

Liverpool, en route to Dublin, November, 1934. My round-trip ticket to Dublin costs $10—bus and boat. I rush aboard at three minutes to ten, out of breath. The boat is scheduled to leave at ten. But I do not see a dark blind form crawling up the Mersey.

"Sailing postponed twenty-four hours—tickets refunded if you wish." I don't wish. I go to my bunk and to bed. Next night the fog is lifting.

Riversdale, Rathfarnham, Dublin, November, 1934. I phone Yeats immediately, and I am invited to tea. When I arrive I feel that his cordiality is perfunctory, and I sense worry and uninterest in his voice. But I insist on playing "By the Rivers of Babylon" on my viola, intoning the words to its music.[11] I feel fairly wretched.

I draw my last bow, and there is silence. But I am not uneasy for long. All the things that I have been trying to get across to Yeats in letters and in talking suddenly become significant to him—and, in a way, the flood of comment that finally comes, in his deep measured voice, epitomizes the total comprehension that I have striven for so long.

"I don't care for your voice," he says, "but a play done entirely in this way, with this wonderful instrument, and with this type of music, might really be sensational."

He shows me his book of Irish legend plays,[12] and gives me a copy, and talks whimsically about the things that might be done with them in music.

"Perhaps Mr. Partch would like to set *Fighting the Waves*," says Mrs. Yeats.

"That's a producer's play," says Yeats. "It isn't worthy of Mr. Partch's music."

From this time on I am speechless, and in the ten days or so that remain of my Dublin sojourn, I am invited to tea and dinner, to the Abbey Theatre, to the Gates Theatre, and to hear actors from the Abbey recite speeches from *King Oedipus*.

Yeats himself intones the choruses from *Oedipus* for me, and I graph his inflections on a blank page as he speaks. He tells me of someone in London who might intone the words for me, professionally, and of a theater for the performance of the final product.

Thus begins Project 3.

I leave Dublin with two letters of introduction to persons in England, and a blessing: "I am interested, but I must say, my letters didn't show it. You are one of those young men with ideas, the development of which it is impossible to foretell, just as I was thirty years ago."

Although he is ill, and weak from long confinement, he insists on escorting me to the bus. He stands in the middle of the road with his hands upraised, his huge figure physically blocking its passage. And this is my final picture.[13]

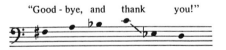

"Good - bye, and   thank   you!"

That is all I can say.

London, November 29, 1934. A card comes: "Dear Mr. Partch: Mr. Dolmetsch[14] (one of Yeats's introductions) will be very pleased to see you. . . . Your letter was considerably delayed as 'Hazelmere' is in Bucks and in Cumberland, but 'Haslemere' is in Surrey."

Haslemere, Surrey, England, December, 1934. Dolmetsch, maker of fine ancient instruments — clavichords and Irish harps — is talking —

". . . but the instrument that is illustrated in Mersenne's *Harmonie universelle*—"

"Excuse me, but which edition do you refer to, Mr. Dolmetsch, that of 1636, or—because—"

"Which edition! Which edition of Mersenne! You say which edition of Mersenne! For *twenty years* I have been talking Mersenne, and nobody even knows who I am talking about. And now you—you ask me which edition!"

He is pleased because I appreciate his passion, and I am pleased because he appreciated mine when it coincides with his, and I leave very happy.

Wimbledon, London, December 18, 1934. Although a canvass of London organ builders at least brings courteous and interested answers, I find none who will build even a three-octave model for my paltry hundred pounds. Finally, I visit one who has an idea to simplify the mechanical difficulties, and offers to produce a three-octave instrument this winter.

Shall I gamble? If this idea fails it means I will have no chromatic organ. But on the other hand if I won't gamble I won't win, and I so hate the idea of going on with only my one little viola to prove all my work.

I gamble, and I am handed a paper: "Received of Harry Partch Esq £60 on account for organ to be built to specification at £70. With thanks . . ."

Thus begins Project 2.

London, December, 1934. My work at the British Museum can't go on until my notebooks, which have piled up phenomenally, undergo consolidation and organization.

Loneliness—darkness at 3 P.M.—I decide I must have sunshine to effect this organization, and I buy a third-class ticket for Rapallo—$25—on the longer but cheaper Channel crossing, Folkestone–Boulogne.

Rapallo, Italy, January, 1935. From the high mountainside I gaze down upon the harbor of Rapallo and upon Portofino in the distance. Tall, slim cypresses march upward toward the heights. They are young gods—wistful, melancholy.

A road winds up below me, and as it comes to a sharp curve, a large sign reads: "Adagio." When Italians see this they think of brakes. When Americans see it they think of Beethoven.

I work on my book, in my room—a front room, in a Dutch woman's *pensione.* I work on my book despite lurking *carabinieri,* my exasperating *biglietto di sojorno,* cold tile floors, cracked houses, cold fires, short change, but at last it becomes unbearable. I buy a third-class ticket for Malta, blood oranges, and the Union Jack—$20.

In the harbor of Naples, en route to Malta, January, 1935. I find myself in the steerage compartment of a small Italian passenger ship. The men I see about me are all Italian—not one speaks a word of English, and my Italian is pitiful.

After much waving of arms I discover that—although meals of a sort are furnished—you are expected to provide your own dishes, if, indeed, you anticipate this refinement in eating. I finally fainaigue a tin plate out of the mess department, for which I am required to give two lire. I grasp the idea—in the flood of words that follows— that if I will return the plate when I get off the boat, I can have my two lire back. Eventually, I find a place where I can wash my plate, so that I can use it for drinking the black coffee that follows the food.

Thoroughly miserable, with the ship now under way, I stagger about the compartment looking for a good bunk, and something which I had noticed before suddenly registers—the bunks have no bedding! They do have mattresses—but, after all, this is January. It's cold today, even at high noon, and what will it be like tonight?

So you are expected to supply your own bedding! Your own dishes—your own bedding. I wonder why they didn't think of expecting you to supply your own boat?

I disgustedly throw my luggage on one of the mattresses, and then I realize that someone is trying to tell me something. Before me is an Italian sailor in uniform. He is obviously a passenger, since this isn't a man o' war. And he has a huge blanket in his hands. It is twice the size of anything like a blanket that I ever saw before.

And even as I see the blanket, I see that he is smiling, and talking good-naturedly, and rapidly.

Then, with utter spontaneity, he throws the blanket over my shoulder, retaining half of it himself.

he exclaims—("You see, it is big enough for two!").

I take back most of the nasty things I am thinking about Italy.

In the course of the evening, I gather that this group of men is from North Italy, and that they have the utmost contempt for the Napolese, as a whole. "Cheats," they call them, and are quite indignant when I tell them I paid a Napolese ten lire to get my things onto the boat.

"Ma donna! Two lire is twice too much," says my sailor friend. Mario is his name, and he is on transfer to Tripoli.

Now, with a wicked look in his eye, he motions to my two instruments—my viola and guitar.

"Musica!" he exclaims, and all through the steerage compartment the cry is taken up: "Americano! Musica! Musica! Musica! Musica! . . ."

In my long hours at the museum, I got thoroughly out of practice on my viola. Then, too, everything I do on it is bound up with words—in English! I can't see Italians responding to this. To a lilting melody over strumming chords, yes—but not to this. As for my guitar, I had only bought it before leaving New York, and in between hours at the museum I had been experimenting with forty-three frets to the octave. But the experiment as yet had not worked out, and I knew only two or three chords that were at all resonant, or even possible.

Finally I see I am cornered, and take out the guitar, singing, very softly, a melancholy Virginia folk song, in a minor key.

"Forte! Forte! Ancora forte!" shouts my sailor pal, jumping up and down like a college cheerleader, and so I try again, this time the same thing a little more *forte.*

Mario looks at me pathetically. No one claps. "Povero artista," he says softly, and everyone walks away.

That night something happens that is so natural it is ignored by everyone present. In any group of American men it would never have happened, because Americans know it would be ridiculed to extinction—the American male, with his straightjacket fear of what the next American male will think.

The Italian sailor and I snuggle together in the same bunk, under the same blanket, and sleep warmly and soundly.[15]

Valletta, Malta, February, 1935. I am working on my book—why?—for eleven years! Now I am using my only money to bring it to completion. I darkly wonder if anyone will try to understand it when I do.

A letter comes from the one who raised money to carry on my campaign for a grant in New York—she had provided thirty-five dollars a month for eight months.[16] She has crossed the broad Atlantic with an I-just-dropped-in-for-a-cup-of-tea air of nonchalance, and is now in a tiny fishing village near Gibraltar. It is too late now, being utterly unwarned, to see her on my meager funds.

A letter also comes from P., who is with her—sweet words: "You can't help but succeed because your results are emotionally compelling in the highest sense. That is, the aesthetic quality is not merely apparent, it actually operates. . . . You are bound to succeed because you have a vital message." He had heard some homemade phonograph records of my settings of Li Po poems, viola with voice.[17]

En route from Malta to Southampton, February, 1935. I share my cabin with an English army sergeant who gets up at an unconscionably early hour, leans over my bunk, and brutally sings: "California, here I come—"

I see the grandeur of the Sierra Nevada, on the southern Spanish coast, and the nearness of my friends—on the Mediterranean shore so few miles away!

Wimbledon, London, March, 1935. I walk up and down the streets looking for lodging signs. I finally find a place with a charming old lady who gives room, breakfast, and dinner for twenty-four shillings (six dollars) a week. After the first day I refuse to entertain any more calumnies on English cooking. Such Yorkshire puddings, salads, deep pies, and roasts! And every night when I come in late a voice calls to me from below: "Mr. Partch, wouldn't you like to have a nice haw-ut cup of tea?"

British Museum, London, March, 1935. I conclude final research for my *Trails of Music.* It will cover some three hundred typewritten pages, of a highly technical nature, and will contain more than one hundred illustrations, diagrams, and photographs. But I see no prospect of getting it into presentable typewritten form before my year is up.

Thus ends Project 1.

Wimbledon, London, March, 1935. The chromatic organ is finished!

But alas! the wording has a double meaning. I spend two weeks tuning the reeds, and in its intonation it proves all my contentions, and fulfills my finest hopes. It has forty-three tones to the octave over a three-octave extent, and 268 rainbow-colored keys in a practical analogy with tones.

But its mechanical workings—the ideas that made its construction cheap—are faulty. The action is extremely uneven, and so hard that playing a two-octave scale tires even this piano-trained hand!

But I cling to the hope that adjustments can later be made, and I find that it will cost only $40 to ship it direct to Los Angeles. I get an article and a picture in *Musical Opinion,* the monthly magazine, as a record.[18]

Thus ends Project 2.

Wimbledon, London, March, 1935. A letter comes: "Dear Mr. Partch: I am afraid, much as I would love to, I cannot go to see your instrument. . . . I hope, however, that we will have an opportunity, someday, not only of seeing it but of hearing it. Yeats is still in Ireland; I don't expect him till sometime in April. If you have a minute to spare, before you go, perhaps you will come and so to speak say good-bye. With best of luck to the chromatic organ and yourself, Yours ever, Edmund Dulac."[19]

Dulac, the artist and musician who worked with Yeats in his experiments with musicalizing spoken words, is the second of my two introductions from Yeats.

Wimbledon, London, March, 1935. Today I think of the plans for *King Oedipus,* and of the hopes for instruments, and singers, and a theater, which its presentation will require. And, of course, I shall not be able to go on in London indefinitely. My money is nearly gone, and I am prevented by very strict English laws from making any sort of a living, even if I had the opportunity.

All of which is provoked by a letter: "Dear Mr. Partch, I am very sorry that I have been unable to see you again. I expected to be in London before this but I am only just convalescent from a long illness. . . . My wife to whom I am dictating this adds her good wishes to mine. Yours, W. B. Yeats."[20]

Thus ends Project 3.

Wimbledon, London, March, 1935. I am talking about possible difficulties with the American customs over my chromatic organ.

"Just say to them," observes my organ builder, " 'Listen to this— this is no musical instrument!' "

He has no sympathy for anything post-Beethoven.

Wimbledon, London, March, 1935. For something like twenty years Kathleen Schlesinger[21] has been working on an exposition of Greek musical theory, and in the meantime has contributed many articles on musical instruments to the *Encyclopaedia Britannica.* It was at her home in Highgate, just this month, that I took measurements of an ancient Greek kithara she had had reconstructed from the design of an ancient vase. The man who read her gas meter offered to build it, and since it was during the last war and wood was scarce, he made it out of an orange box. I am going to have one too, by golly.[22]

Another letter: "Dear Mr. Partch: Please pardon my delay in writing to thank you for the photograph of your keyboard. I shall look forward to the pages of exposition of your theme in the future months! I have had great pleasure in meeting you, and shall always be glad to hear news from you, of the progress of your work. You are a worker after my own heart, and I wish you every possible success and a good journey across water and land, to your home. With kindest wishes, Kathleen Schlesinger."

"P.S. I have a great admiration for your beautiful diagrams!"

Wimbledon, London, March, 1935. Another letter. It is a simple little message, but with it the already sinking pit of my stomach goes to its nadir.

It reads: "Dear Sir, With reference to your enquiry we have the pleasure in quoting you three pounds, two shillings and sixpence for collecting organ . . . packing same in case for export and delivering to King George 5th Dock. Awaiting your valued instructions. Yours faithfully . . ."

I don't want to go.

Wimbledon, London, March 26, 1935. I leave for my point of embarkation in Cornwall tomorrow morning.

A card comes in the mail: "Dear Mr. Partch, Could you possibly come with us to see my friend. . . . I hope that AE—Dr. George Russell,[23] the poet and friend of Yeats—will be there. Utterly informal clothes of course. Bring the photo of your instrument if you can. Hope you can manage it. Yrs. O. Edwards." (Edwards[24] had done a book on Yeats.)

I go, and AE is there. When he hears that I have been working with Yeats on *King Oedipus,* he says to me, "Did you know that Yeats is utterly without feeling for music, that he doesn't know one note from another, and that he can't carry a tune?"

I want to make an answer to this provocative observation, but I am vacuous and distraught by so many things—my leaving, my mental confusion, my momentary frustration in my work, and I am tongue-tied by the smart sayings of the salon people around me.

I want to say that neither the fact that Yeats doesn't know one note from another nor the fact that he can't carry a tune is any indication of a lack of feeling for music. The epic answer of Yeats to the musicians who quarrelled with him comes back to me—*"I hear with older ears than the musician."*[25]

Those are my words, too. *I hear with older ears—*

And the fact that he can't carry a tune is more an indication of extraordinary sensitivity to tone. Such a person hears all the tones of the gamut. People try to confine him to seven or eight, and he is confused, jumping about all over the scale and being ridiculed until he has a tonal inferiority complex. Until I trained myself to sing in many tones to the octave, which was far past my twenty-first birthday, I couldn't carry a tune either.

AE reads some of his poetry, after much coaxing. His voice is soft music.

"I often have the feeling that the Irish poets finish reading a sentence on a major triad," says an actor present.

"A-ha! my boy," I say (speaking almost for the first time—such opportunities come all too infrequently), "what they do sometimes finish on are the root, fifth, and seventh of the so-called dominant seventh chord, the last three tones in that order, which naturally resolve to a major triad. Although only one of the triad tones is heard, you finish the resolution in your mind." (In key of C):

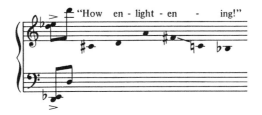

he says.

It is like life-after-death. We don't actually see it, but many of us expect the death of a good man (which we see) to resolve into the major chord of a perfect, harmonious, serene, and eternal hereafter (which we don't see). Then sometimes we get worried and wonder whether the resolution will be to a major chord or to a Schoenberg chord of the eleventh, in which case we probably throw up the whole God-damned idea.

Fowey, Cornwall, March 30, 1935. I am the only passenger on a freighter loaded with china clay, bound for Portland, Maine. This crossing costs just $55.

I say good-bye to ginger beer, yellow primroses, general civility, unfailing courtesy from the powers that be. I do not want to go.

New York, April, 1935. I am in the office of the organization that handled my grant.

"Did you see my six-months report, which I sent from Malta?"

"Yes, I did, Mr. Partch."

"What did you think of it?"

"I'm afraid I didn't understand it."

"Do you know what has become of it?"

I am referred to another office.

"Did you see my six-months report, which I sent from Malta?"

"Yes, I did, Mr. Partch."

"Did you read it?"

"Yes, but I didn't understand it."

"Have you submitted it to anyone who might understand it?"

"No."

Other things are said, too, but I don't remember them.

I walk out, a hollow shell, with nothing inside—just a vacuum.

Indianapolis, April, 1935. I have hitchhiked from Portland, but it has taken seven humorless days. I talk to some boys in a transient bureau—the new institution for homeless men that was established by the New Deal while I was in Europe: "Why don't you ride freights and stay in shelters—why throw your money away?"

The chromatic organ will soon be in Los Angeles. I must be there to clear it and thereby avoid difficulties and storage, so I buy a bus ticket to Los Angeles—$32.50.

St. Louis, April, 1935. It is good to be alive today. I have seen Merle, my San Luis Obispo jail pal. He is so glad that he puts his arm around me and dances about like a seven-year-old. He is a bum no longer but living at home, working, and expecting to be married.

"Be sure to write me if you ev-er need mon-ey, Har-ry,"

he says, and he means it—poor kid, he has had so little of the fruit of full living and deserves so much.

Los Angeles, April 30, 1935. My entire expenses from Malta to London to Portland to Los Angeles have been $150—food and transportation. I have 1 percent of my $1,500 left.

I spend a week persuading the customs officials to admit the chromatic organ without duty. And, through friends, a way is ultimately found. Its godmother, in Santa Barbara, has offered to keep it and pay for its transportation there. Off it goes again, direct from the dock.

My greetings in this, the one city that really encouraged me, are very various. There is nothing to do here. I feel that the former friends of my music are not cordial, so I head north.

Santa Rosa, May, 1935. My last two dollars buys postage for the story of the evolution of my music. I am sending it to my SS *Gourko* shipboard friend in London, who wants to do something with it among publishers.

My beloved Santa Rosa prune orchard, of bygone dreams, is all but uprooted. "I'm afraid I am imposing." My friends are very kind, but there are only two things to do—return to Los Angeles and resume begging under the apology of my music, or, wearying of begging, with a whoop and a holler go on the road. I think of the five days in 1932 I lay on Imperial Beach without food—because I was determined to have surcease from continual begging for my music.

Still, I do not hesitate.

Harrington Ranch, June 24, 1935. Today we hoe weeds in the potato patch—about a dozen of us. Mechanically my hoe goes up and down, and now and then I stop to roll a cigarette.

And when I stop I hear music everywhere—in the willows by the slough, just over there, and in the voices about me. Because I record this music doesn't mean that it belongs to me. I give it freely

to anyone who asks it. That's the only way it has much value. But
that isn't the way of the world. What we make is ours, in theory at
least, and it's up to us to make something that has an immediate
dollar-cents value.

And so, it might be said that I am a fool for spending my effort
and my spirit on something beautiful when I might be spending them
on making money. But I think not.

For have I not found my place in the American economic system,
as the learned Dr. President advised me to do—in a camp for transient
bums?

Said Lao-tse, Chinese sage of the seventh century B.C.—

> . . . *all things shoot up (in spring) without a word spoken,
> and grow (in summer) without a claim for their production.
> They go through their processes (in autumn) without any dis-
> play of pride in them, and the results are realized (in winter)
> without any assumption of ownership.*[26]

JUNE 25

There is not a man whom I have really talked to who has not
"made the can" for at least ninety days, Pablo included.

Idly I thumb a magazine. A young fellow lies on the table beside
me—it is the recreation room. I catch half of his mumbling—

"Is this your first bumming?"

"It's my first chance. I've been locked up since I was sixteen. I'm
twenty-two now."

I gaze deeply into the blue of his eyes. There I see him hugging
his mother's legs and shyly hiding his face behind her rump.

JUNE 26

I am sure that in time I would develop an affection for them,
something like Pablo's. They do not understand me, and I seem to
ignore them, but I am not ostracized for it.

They are really very tolerant of my little impatiences. They sometimes mock my inflections—

—and mimic my ways, that are none too rough. A less sober person would be insulted. I cannot be, because no malice is meant.

Their whole lives are a continual escape—they try to escape their boredom in trivial arguments, they try to escape their impotence in alcohol, they try to escape the necessity of continual effort in crime, in begging, in institutions such as this, and they try to escape reality itself in a crazy dreamworld.

I am myself almost exactly like them. I am escaping the meaningless, the stupid, the banal, in conventions, art, music, in a fantastic order of my own creation.

But is mine so blind? I don't know.

JUNE 27

It is bedtime. I am lying—gazing abstractedly at the ceiling. The delicate structure of my thoughts is demolished by the man next to me, who loudly calls to someone near him:

"Go out and do it now, so you won't do it in your bed like you did last night."

Pals—all of us.

JULY 4

He is from the home state of Abe Lincoln. Kain-tuck, the fellows call him. He is six feet plus, angular, and uncontrollably playful.

His mother abandoned him and his father when he was less than a year old. At seven he was farmed out to work for his keep. A year later he stole some money from his employers and ran away.

In time he was again living with his father and a sexually wanton stepmother, recently acquired. At eleven, after several petty crimes, she turned him over to the police for reform school.

Two years incarceration added similar ingredients to the accu-

mulation that is Kain-tuck. It was ended in a turnip patch one day
when he saw an opportunity to escape and took it.

From that time, when he was thirteen, to the present, when he
is twenty-two—nine years—he has surveyed the world from jails
coast to coast, jungles, and chain gangs.

A pound of coffee pilfered from a grocery for his jungle larder
brought sixty days in hobbles and sixty nights in chains—in Florida.
Sweet corn ripening in a Negro's garden caused ninety similar days
and nights in Alabama for Kain-tuck. Tumbles from fast-moving
freights and bruises were the rewards of resistance to bum seducers.
The ecstasy of morphine followed a lockup in the county jail of the
great, generous city of San Francisco. Every large city in our country
has been graced by Kain-tuck's charming panhandle.

He is now an incipient dipsomaniac and a marijuana addict.

A bleak recital.

On the credit side he has these: wit, a smile, a frank way, and
evidences of loyalty.

The stories of many of the others in camp differ only in the
degree and arrangement of the elements. Come, Ubiquitous Col-
umnist, and deny that they were born to be anything except exactly
what they are!

Kain-tuck seems devoted to me—why?—perhaps I don't know.
He waits for me at the mess house door at every meal gong.

This evening we walk along the levee looking for a place to fish.
One of a group of fellows celebrating the Fourth and their own futility
in alcohol tries to insult me as we pass.

"Fruit," he says.

Kain-tuck wants to fight. (There is the intendedly implied slur
that he associates with such a person.) The incompetence of liquor
added to his congenital incompetence is abundant excuse for the man.
I laugh it off and walk away, and Kain-tuck finally follows after the
insulter partly retracts.

"Well, maybe I'm wrong," he says.

I am a coward because theirs are physical standards.

Time flashes back twenty years or more. I am standing grimly
with my back against a wall—unmoving from terror—while a group
of my schoolmates—always groups—pummels me and taunts me with
"Sister!"

But these things have never failed to win for me in the end: an
insistent attitude that denies the right of others to disrespect; an intense fervor in the justness of my life.

Have I won?—I, who am languishing in nominal hopelessness, however tacit?—a camp for transient bums?

Criteria differ.

Kain-tuck gets drunk too, on a borrowed four bits, rails against all and sundry in his turn—wildly swings his fists.

I try to pull him away from the levee, but he staggers up to a group of holiday-makers: "How about a match, mister?" He hasn't even got a cigarette.

I forcibly take him while the strangers titter: "I've got matches!"

Suddenly I drop him and walk away.

"Har - ry!"

he calls to me.

Poor, wretched boy!

"Are you disgusted?"

"I don't know—I'm disappointed."

"Please forgive me. It's my first chance in months."

He collapses. I drag him to a clump of weeds where he can sleep before I abandon him.

JULY 5

Mandolin-face of the tooth-fretted lips left today. Last night he was sick drunk. One of the directors happened to see him lying in a stupor on the levee. Foxtails decked his denims and wildly his hair.

Had the director gone farther he could have seen more.

This morning the boy claimed the advantage of checking out before they could expel him.

No music is in our farewell. We are both vacuous: he for reasons to be imagined—I because of this helplessness before an all-encroaching stupidity. My heart freezes.

"Good luck."

"Adios."

Good luck to you with your liquor and your women, and may they bring fewer sorrows entrained.

Our barracks are empty without you, Pablo.

JULY 13

Days—daze—days impregnant.
Our too-gazed ceiling suspends the hours of our gazing.
The look of eye says, "Flats for Rent."
The lead of arse says, "Let the Dead Rest in Peace!"
Our behinds go to their rests on broad protuberant bases like
irons to magnets.
"What! More bunk fatigue?" Kain-tuck jibes.
Nothing to hear but functions. Nothing to read but purchased
words. Nothing to do but attend this painless existence gazing deeply
into vacuity.

JULY 14

Kain-tuck and another young stiff inveigle some catfish out of the
slough, stab, and clean them. I build a fire and help to spit and broil
them over the coals.
We joke unceasingly. We are ribald.
We lack beer. We lack a boat. We lack women. And we laugh
coarsely over each facet of suggestion.

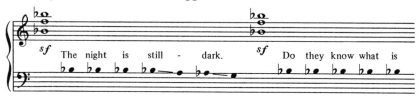

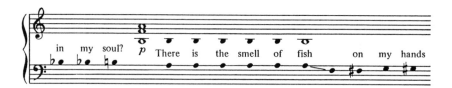

JULY 15

Today after dinner Kain-tuck sits on my bunk softly singing:

The written notes convey nothing of the charm of the casual, half-spoken manner of Kain-tuck. It is full of softly nuanced gliding and subtle stresses.

There is no grand audience here—no applause. In my mind I see an orchid on a packed bosom and hands fluttering in front. The tenor has concluded his masterful Oh— Ah—. A sycophant stiff shirt constitutes the background.

Indeed, America is not musical.

I come back to Kain-tuck, and I am flooded with warmth. Let others wallow in careless gluttony! We will still hunger for these morsels that fall to us!

It is good to live for these little things.

Like Ogden Nash, I can sing:[27]

JULY 16

There is a strange alliteration in the three principal desires of bums. Food and flops are the two most important, but they get the least attention in conversations.

"They go to bed at night talking about it, and they get up in the morning talking about it."

Right you are, my lad.

One well-made chap, with a pair of statuesque "shoulders," "featherless," as the 'bos say, gets endless ribbing. It is especially brazen in the shower room.

"Don't you wor - ry, hon-ey, I'll fix you up to-night!"

He accompanies the words with a well-directed pat.

Horseplay and wild repartee follow. They are a safety valve.

Another subject, which runs a close second in popularity, concerns the gifts and instincts of various farm animals.

Tonight I say, I believe without any tinge of morality: "An eighteen-year-old boy in colonial Massachusetts was hung for that."

"Well, boys, they can't hang you for the old stand - by,"

is the reply.

Another big palooka cups his hand out in front of him:

"Yeh— Meet the wife!"

he grins.

JULY 19

(Oh, to get drunk on a brew of jasmine tea—or a smile from unstubbled lips—or an uncurse-strewn colloquy—or a random tone from my rainbowed organ!)

Because all my sins of inexcusable functionism are taken away in an irrepressible desire to go on.

I am taking the broad highway running along the east levee of the Sacramento River, heading toward the capital city.

Behind is Mount Diablo, the lone sentinel of these perceptions, sinking beneath the horizon.

Kain-tuck is also there, behind the horizon, and it is hardest to think of that. And there, too, are Solomon, Wimbledon Common, the embankment of the Thames at Twickenham, and a breeze from Cornwall over the water.

JULY 20—Heading north, between Sacramento and Redding

On my way. But where am I going? To what end?

I fly from twelve years' frustration of my dreams. I fly from the humiliation of begging. I fly from the present-day insecurity of a true bum existence. I fly from the functionism of aimless security when I do find it. And now I am flying to what? Another revolution of the cycle?

"Oh, what a fool I was to ever try to bring beauty into the world," said Isadora Duncan in her later years.[28]

The words revolve and pound my brain like hammers on a wheel as I wander along.

But I will not claim them, as I am sure Isadora would not have in a soberer moment.

The beauties which we mothered are our abundant solace.

I, like Isadora, began my apostasy and my zealousy in the great, generous city of San Francisco.

I, like Isadora, was driven out of this great city by two hungers: hunger for bodily sustenance and hunger for understanding.

I, like Isadora, described a continuous migration eastward, seeking greater understanding, both from within and from without.

I, like Isadora, found both.

And yet did the intransigent Duncan live to mutter—

And my own efforts to bring beauty into the world have come to aimless wandering.[29]

Redding.

A man is standing on the curb.

"Will you please tell me where the transient shelter is?"

"Transient shelter? What's that? I don't know. Never heard of it."

"If I could see a bum in blue denims, I'd soon enough find out."

"Bum? Did you say? The place where the bums stay? Is that what you're looking for? Why the hell didn't you say so? Go down six blocks and turn left. It's all lit up. You can't miss it."

"Lit up" sounds correct.

JULY 21 — Nearing the Oregon state border

A pink-haired human brings his car to a stop in the red hills.

"I'm going to Seattle," I say through the open door.

"Well, I'm going to Klamath Falls. Why not come up and look it over? You might find work."

It is only sixty miles off the road.

"Why not?" I echo.

"Well, suppose we have a drink first."

There is a roadhouse across the way.

"Straight whiskey," says Pinky.

"Beer," say I.

I am a thorough fatalist. I will forgive Pinky all the straight whiskeys he wants so long as he is not bad company.

Yesterday a very old gentleman picked me up in Orland. Immediately after getting in I called his attention to a lovely shelf of mountains. He looked.

The next thing I saw, we were heading up the wrong side of the road and into an almost certain collision with an oncoming car.

I grabbed the wheel, the first time in all my hitchhiking experience that I have done such a thing.

My host said: "You see, I am blind in one eye."

"Oh, I'm sorry!"

Having only one light eye he could not divide his vision, keeping one on the road and lending my love of beauty the other. It was a high compliment, giving me his only one.

Later something got in it. He rubbed it as we swerved drunkenly.

My benefactor took me sixty more miles, and although scenery was propped up all about us, we didn't much look.

Pinky gives me a bright yellow sweater and a white starched shirt. "They'll do things to you and get you rides," he says.

He knows the resorts and stops at each one on our one hundred-mile trip.

After three beers I lose all interest,

JULY 22—Jail, Grants Pass, Oregon

There are some twelve men in a room about fifteen by fifteen.
The floor is laden with bums' bodies, and the air with their smell.
    I find a crack in the one open window and stay there all night.
    The bunks are triple-deckers and of strip iron. There is no bed-
ding or mattresses.

JULY 24—Federal Shelter, Portland

The various manners of shelter reveille range from the comical
to the heavenly.

In Stockton a man walks about through the aisles tapping a sweet,
soft gong. The transition from the luxury of sleep to the garish day
is gently provocative. He walks about for approximately ten minutes.
He seems to be the impersonal augury of better things. He is persuasive.

This reveille is paradisian.

In Sacramento the agent of awakening whacks each bed with a
stick, unceremoniously. The result is not even impudent. But it is in
harmony with 'most everything else about the Sacramento shelter.

It is disgusting.

In Redding an old man gently taps each somnolent protuberant
behind with a broom handle. I was very sorry to be awake when I
discovered this. I couldn't help wishing to experience the sensation
of such an awakening.

This is a highly paternal reveille.

In Portland an attendant who is a stupendous basso profundo
comes to each tiny room (four bunks to a room—the men are not
in large barracks, as in the other shelters), stands in the door, and
roars:

"Time to get up! Oh, it's time to get up! Oh, it's time to get up!"

This agent is not only profound—he is the essence of modesty.
He assumes that his voice alone is not enough to wake the dead (bums
sleeping after coming off freights can only be described as dead), and
carries a club with which he delivers one Herculean crack on each
bed.

It shudders.

I cower: "Well, that's over!"

The words have hardly sounded from my lips when he reappears.
As though every man there were not now as wide-eyed as he ever
hopes to be, De Profundis repeats the performance.

I get up quicker than I ever did in my life and stagger out. I
take no chances on his coming back. On my way to the dressing room,
I hear more reverberations from hell:

Those who don't know it now never will.
My only word to describe this reveille is demoniacal.

JULY 25—Blue Ox Lodge, Seattle, Washington

"Partch, Harry, Oakland, 34, 5' 10", 145, Blue, Brown, Physical defects none." I rattle it off without prompting, and the registration clerk smiles.

Today I have bitter thoughts as I wander from one line of red tape waiting to another. (Poor man! he is impelled to defend his processes.)

He does not know ecstasy who does not also know bitterness.

Seattle: Here is another city built by marauders. The huge black stumps stretching hundreds of miles in every direction are epic testimony. The gluttony in the Yukon also helped to develop Seattle.

The blood of the proud '49ers flows through the other city of despoilers on this coast. Much of it belongs to persons who run to excitement like dogs to a fight. How little of it is admirable!

Recently, I read a magazine article on music in America lauding San Francisco as one of the most active. It said, as I remember: The pioneer spirit of the '49ers is leading their descendants into new paths of the arts and music.

To demonstrate this neo-pioneer spirit, they build a four million-dollar opera house which allows descendant '49ers to repose their fulsome fundaments in a diamond horseshoe, from which they support "American" music—

"Ah, Si, si, Ah! Si, si, Ah! Si, si, Ah! Si, si, Ah! Si, si, si, si, si, si, si, Si! Ah! Si!—— Ah!———— Si!——————— (much sforzato and tremolo).

scream our young Yankee pioneers in the arts.

As a further demonstration of matchless artistic courage, these pioneers invest any required amount of capital in infancy.

This infancy interprets the masters, and its left hands pick the strings with swift, easy skill.

Of the several prodigies extant I can think of not one who does not have his residence on the shores of San Francisco Bay.

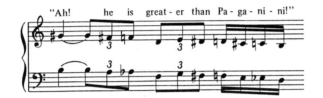

cries packed-bosom-of-the-orchids.

adds Daniel Boone in the background.

As a final demonstration of pioneering (in this, Los Angeles is also guilty) persons with shattered English and long noses are engaged to conduct something like ninety-piece orchestras. We are implored to save "American music!"

"Scho-o-o-olchildren, gi-i-i-ive your pennies! Re-e-e-escue us from the disgra-a-a-ace of only ei-ei-ei-eighty-nine pieces, go-o-o-od English, and a short nose!"

. . . It is during one of my first days in New York. I am walking down Thirty-fourth Street depressed by many things—the noise, the long dark faces, the commercial cackle, the gluttonous light of the eyes. My attention is suddenly arrested by a man coming toward me. He has a pleasant expression.

I cry, and as he passes, and finally sets behind the dark swarm, sotto voce:

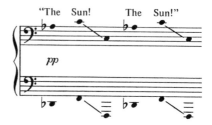

I stride swiftly into the William Sloane House, where I am staying, and drench myself under a shower. Oh, the goodness of water!

Seattle: Tonight I am standing in line waiting for a bunk. Many of us have stood in line more than eight hours today.

I lie in my bunk sleepless because my arm has a typhoid inoculation that hurts.

I do not sleep all night, and there are snores unending, invading, repelling.

The voice of my music —

Stay me with flag - ons, com - fort me with ap - ples: for I am

sick of love. His left hand is un - der my head, and

his right hand doth em - brace me.

From a long memory—

As it might have come

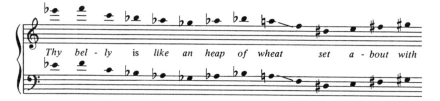

—from the rainbowed organ—

Is my anodyne—

That hovers over the bunk and feeds me on this wakeful night —

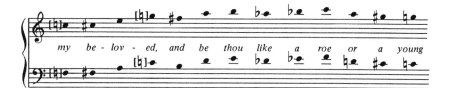

Until the shadows flee away.

JULY 26—Camp Milan, Cascade Mountains

In camp again. This is smaller than Harrington, much better situated, prettier, and more livable. But the same dings and their conversations go on forever.

Today, soon after we arrive, one of the directors offers me an incivility. I draw myself one hundred miles away and gaze back at him. My throat is constricted, and I do not speak all day.

I walk out among the huge blackened stumps all around us. Rainier rises to the south above the greed-reeked hills. Would this splendor, too, have been demolished, had there been a money gain to man in doing so?

JULY 27

Members of the fraternity: Itinerants, Tramps, Hobos, 'Bos, Bums, Stiffs, Dinos, Dings or Dingbats, Gorillas, Airedales.

There are a few qualifying niceties. Bindlestiff means a stiff who carries a bundle; rubber tramp, the wanderer in a battered car; two-bit bum, one who would steal the shoes from his drunk pal; airedale, a stiff with a beard; and there are many more that I don't know or recall.

JULY 28

> Camp Milan, Wash.
> July 28, 1935.

Dear Kain-tuck:

They give you real butter here, and the pie isn't filled with corn-starch. When I saw bread pudding, I thought: Oh, Oh—the old stand-by, but it proved to be okeydoke, the best I ever ate.

Also, they pay every Friday, one buck. There are things I don't like. We are on ground of the Seattle water system, and you can't take a piss, except in the can, without being liable to thirty days imprisonment. And there are only two places they will let you even walk. Besides, these gorillas are not very friendly.

They haven't taught the dogs to use the can. They seem to think that the good people of Seattle are not too good for dog piss.

There is one of the prettiest little camps you can ever hope to see on the Rogue River six miles east of Grants Pass, Oregon. The Rogue is one of the most beautiful rivers in the country. There is a dam on it just below the camp, and they say the fishing is great. The camp buildings are made of logs, and they're hidden back in the woods away from Highway 99.

Of course, I don't know how it is in other ways, but I'd like to give it a try. I expect to be there about the middle of next week (about August 7th). If it sounds good to you, come along—I'll meet you there.

I don't know the name of it, but I think they send you out from Medford. Remember, six miles east of Grants Pass on the Rogue River and Highway 99.

> Happy landings!
> Harry.

JULY 29

Today I clean ditches.

If there is a sensitive man in this camp, he is successfully disguised as a gorilla. This sack of bones has hardly spoken in four days. It moves like a storm cloud—silent, melancholy. On its face are written ten thousand tragedies that never happened. Beyond the horizon it mutters senselessly.

JULY 30

A complete set of work clothes is issued to each new man. I have a set, all but a pair of shoes, that was given to me at Harrington Ranch. I don't want another. I would like shoes, but I discover that the one who was uncivil is issuing clothes. I do not go.

It is noised around that Blue Monday has refused clothes. This is unheard of.

asks one.

Many tramps refuse nothing that they can sell for two red cents. They take all the clothes they can get and peddle them from shelter to shelter. They glut the bum market, so that a new pair of shoes can be gotten for as little as fifty cents, and take articles to Jews on the skidways who give them ten cents and sell for a dollar.

These, who are more or less continually at the mercy of others' generosity, are themselves avaricious bargainers. They haggle like Genovese.

The uncivil one avoids my glances. Do my reactions confound him? I neither know nor care.

And all his sins are taken away.

Today, another gorilla and I clean the drain ditch from the bath-house and kitchen. We are covered with muck, and we radiate smelly splattered batter.

I recall the time Kain-tuck, the other stiff, and I broiled fish — *Do they know what is in my soul?*

Do they know what is in my soul? They make a rough guess and then put me to work in a sewer.

Damn their souls!

AUGUST 1

All day the other gorilla and I bend over the odorous drain ditch. Night before last I was delirious.

declares my companion.
All-obliterating humility!

AUGUST 2

I have heard a great deal about the various passion dampeners used in the food, but none of it has come from a reliable source.

If an eroscide is used, it seems to have little effect on the young-sters. Most of them sleep naked, and in the morning they throw back the covers and naively gaze down at their nocturnal potential.

They are pagans, poised, and all-equipped to jump onto a Greek vase and chase maidens around it.

AUGUST 5 — Toledo

I do not try to check the flood of tears in my eyes as I walk away from the house of a woman who has fed me.

She gave me a plate with two fried eggs, creamed carrots, jam and bread and butter, and a large cup of tea.

It has been three years since I did this sort of thing, and I never did it more than three times before. Starting again, the pain of humiliation is just as intense as it was the very first time.

When a man gives a ride to another on the highway, he is giving something that would go anyway, whether the hiker is in it or not, that is, the seat. It is very generous of him to take the risk of trouble so that the seat isn't wasted, but he is not giving out something that is money value to himself. I am grateful for transportation, which might be money value to me, but for the above reasons I am only a little reluctant to ask it.

On the other hand, when good people in a house by the road

give supper to a 'bo, it is something which they are definitely out. It is not a value that is going anyway, like the empty seat.

It is this fact, that I must ask strangers by their own efforts to sustain and warm this body, which is of no significance to them, that makes it painful to beg food.

Is a charming panhandle on the street the next step? Already I see the insidious quality of the disease.

Is not the next step to beg money for nightly flops? Oh, it would be so painful to start and so easy to continue!

A man must satisfy himself as to the justness of his requests. That I have done, and if I deliberately inoculate myself with the disease, it is a sober act.

I do not speak of my justification because it would be difficult and indiscreet to do so, but it is my dumb solace. I speak as a human being in need for his body.

I say: "I'm hungry. I'd be glad to work for something to eat."

Now suppose I were to invoke my justification and say:

"I am doing an invaluable work in the arts. It is not as yet widely recognized because there are so few people that I can meet with the ability to see, and because I can meet so few in my lifetime. I am sure that as far as value delivered to the world is concerned that I have paid for the food and blankets of these little emergencies. I'm hungry. Recognize just a tiny part of what I say as true and give me something to eat."

Upon the delivery of such a speech, our good people by the road would think one or all of three things, given here in the order of probability—

1. He's a nut. The quicker we get rid of him the better.

2. He thinks he's smart. What's he doing on the bum, then?

3. Maybe what he says is true, but how are we to know?

The second approach is the one I believe in, but why should I deliberately throw rocks at myself?

After all, it is less painful to ask a total stranger by his effort to warm this body than with weighty introductions to ask a human power to promote this musical passion.

And for two good reasons: (1) a need of the body is a fraught possibility to everybody in this world—"There, but for the grace of God . . ."; (2) the chances of success are ten thousand times greater.

In the first case there is understanding. In the second case, there is, ten thousand to one, none.

And to what end is this body sustained when it is thwarted in its reason? Women hold a keen sympathy for the physical needs of men, but it is blind instinct.

It was this blindness that maddened me in Pasadena. They recognized and guaranteed my body for a time, but, having done so, dropped it into a pit. Its purpose in being was not within their ken.

Human life is plentiful. Everywhere it cries for sustenance. Why pick on me?

Thoughts revolve and ramify. I have made my bed in a hay mound by the road, and the straws tickle.

I do not sleep because it is cold and there are too many cracks.

AUGUST 7—Between Grants Pass and Klamath Falls, Oregon

Supper.

It consists of roast beef, green beans, sweet pickles, bread and butter, and three cups of coffee. It is of the substance of an old couple living in a cottage by the Rogue River.

It is eleven and very dark. I am beyond Ashland and reconciled to walking all night, hailing no one. A large lumber truck stops.

"Klamath Falls!" I shout above the motor.

"Get in!"

He wants me to drive. Never in my life have I faced the hazards of driving. I excuse myself. He slaps his face, shouts and bounces himself in the seat, trying to keep awake.

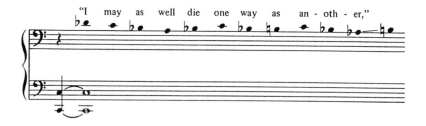

I mutter, and take the wheel.

As a teacher the man is a genius.

I have driven a total of less than twenty-five miles in my whole life, and now this person entrusts to me, a perfect stranger, his valuable truck, for me to drive fifty miles over curving mountain roads in the blackness of midnight, and he promptly goes to sleep!

I come to a stop on the main street of Klamath Falls some two hours later and awake my host.

"That sleep saved my life,"

he declares.

Perhaps you are right, inspiring preceptor!

He invites me to apple pie and coffee.

I have come 464 miles in twenty-two hours—very good for Depression bumming, and making up for yesterday when I made only 120 miles.

The transient shelter is closed after ten o'clock, so I go to a vacant lot and snuggle in between some pine logs. Their sweetness is perfume.

If I had listened to what my mama said —

Oh, hell!

AUGUST 8—Klamath Falls

Kain-tuck was not at the Rogue River camp, nor has he checked in at the Klamath Falls shelter, from where he would be sent, and not from Medford, as I had thought. I decide to go on to Redding.

Kain-tuck may not have been present to receive my letter, and I know he never leaves forwarding addresses, since he never expects mail.

We had planned to leave Harrington together, but at the last minute he insisted on getting drunk first. I refused to join him, and in his absence from camp I quickly decided to go alone.

Yesterday I ran into Pinky, and he pulls me out of bumdom for twenty-four hours. I fill up on everything I've been missing.

"Aren't you having a rip-roaring time!"

Pinky cannot conceal his disgust because, everytime he orders beer, I order ice cream and chocolate milk shakes, and over the same counter.

He gives me a jaunty brown felt and a verdant shirt to go with my yellow sweater.

I shall blush walking into a transient shelter in this rig-out.

I can hear the lilting scorn:

"You should go to Lol - ly - wood!"

—with tongues sticking out obscenely on the *Lol*—

Dunsmuir, California.

I ask the man who brought me here if I may sleep in his garage. He puts a bedspring and plenty of blankets under the pines on the precipitous bank of the Sacramento, hardly bubbling from its source. Here it is a brook of rapids. Sixty miles below it is a deep, silent river.

AUGUST 9—Federal Shelter, Redding

The outside world has few smiles for the transient stigma.

In the shelter towns, I have frequently walked into the business districts in the shelter denims that we have to wear while our own clothes are being "deloused." These denims often have "U.S.A.—S.E.R.A."[30] splotched over them in large white letters.

At first I walked about with native unconcern—but not for long.

This evening I ask a simple question of someone on the street—"Will you please tell me where the post office is?"

"Don't come too close—you might have halitosis. And please go away quickly before someone sees me speaking to you."

His lips direct me, but his manner talks.

AUGUST 11—SERA Camp, Ingot

The flotsam and jetsam of my beloved California is gathered here—it is a state camp (admitting those with established California residence)—and, dispassionately, I say that it flottles and jettles with better manners than the riffraff of our Eastern hinterland.

My first hour in camp I am asked by three men if I care to read, and offering to lend me books, and at my first meal I am continually being asked what I wish.

In Stockton they refused to admit that I was a California resident, while in Redding they refused to admit I wasn't.

Ingot is thirty miles northeast of Redding. A little brook washes its rocky bed through the camp. The water runs in and about clusters of sweet cold cress. Across the brook there is a little flat corralled by towering mountains. A group of trees is growing there, with just now reddening apples weighting its boughs. The men have built a rustic bridge over the creek, leading to the flat. The apples beckon:

Stay me with flagons, comfort me with apples —

AUGUST 12

Several men ask me if I like the camp. That shows that they want me to like it. Ergo, I like it.

The personnel has charm, the spot has beauty, and the cook has imagination.

AUGUST 14

One time when I was six and in the first grade I sat at my desk drawing a stallion on my tablet. I took great pains with it, and drew his symbol of fertility as I had often seen it, long and portentous.

It didn't occur to me to be ashamed of it. I didn't reason, of course, but it meant something elementally right.

I then showed the drawing to the little girl sitting in the double desk beside me. She banged me on the head, cried "Shame!" and with her eraser vigorously rubbed the sex out of my horse.

"This is the way to do it," she said, redrawing a simple belly line, and leaving my once virile stallion presumably female or ambiguous.

I took my humiliation quietly. But my inward ferocity burned for days—in fact, never stopped.

Thus in early years did this Christian, abstract, female age cow me.

Wherever you are, young woman, long-deferred nuts to you!

AUGUST 15

Today my letter to Kain-tuck is returned. He had left Harrington Ranch before it arrived, and he gave no address.

Down in the country where I was reared, cottonwood trees line the dry streambeds, the rivers, and canals. For several weeks each spring they snow their tiny bolls of cotton down on the desert fields.

My friends and loved ones burst upon my consciousness like the cottonwoods' whitenesses.

all,   and   in   the   brief - est   mo - ment   they   are   a - way.

Others hesitate before my eyes, and tantalize them, then recede.

But they all float on, hesitate, go one way, then another, without seeming purpose, vanishing slowly from these perceptions, then forsaking this waking consciousness, and, in fine, growing ever more formless in this memory.

And I have only the empty pods that they have left.

How   can   I   i - mag - ine   that   they   are   here   when   with   these

eyes   I   have   seen   them   tak - en   be - fore   a   hun - dred

winds   be - yond   my   pow - er   to   con - trol?

AUGUST 18

Days—daze—days impregnant.

What is the sum total of these days of daze?

Is it the indescribable joy of work behind and love in the sooning dark hours?

No, it is the indescribable drunk of a sooning two-dollar payday.

Now we sit around on benches waiting for darkness. Now on our dreamless cots we attend the nine-thirty "Lights out." Now we gaze into the fantastic luminosity of our eyelids while surviving remnants of consciousness follow the rest into refrigeration.

Nights—nights—nights unardent.

The morning gong—we are oysters fresh from the ice.

We hesitate on the edge of our unhallowed beds with one leg in our underpants.

Do we look forward, this day, to the nameless fervor of evolving attainment.

No, breakfast.

AUGUST 28

This evening I walk past Tobacco Garden into the narrow tree-gorged canyon.

Thoughts, thoughts. Thoughts recharging, tormenting, consuming.

Time passes. How much, I have no vague idea.

I stumble back to camp through the black perfume of the mountains. It is for me.

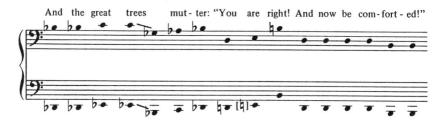

AUGUST 29

We ordinary bums in camp get $5.00 a month, or $2.50 every half month, provided we don't draw tobacco. There are several higher rates of pay—$8.50, $13.00, and $25.00 a month, among them. These apply to men with special jobs, such as cooking and truck driving.

In this camp, as in the other two I have experienced, those receiving more than $5.00 a month form a little bum aristocracy.

They have their meals at separate tables, they give their God-damns a patrician inflection, and they only reluctantly consort with us plebe bums.

I see one of them walking into the lavatory now. He has the $8.50 expression.

He is obliged to pull his peter out over the smell of five-dollar urine!

SEPTEMBER 1

Cisco throws himself out of his husky throat with all the fervor of a Negro Baptist—

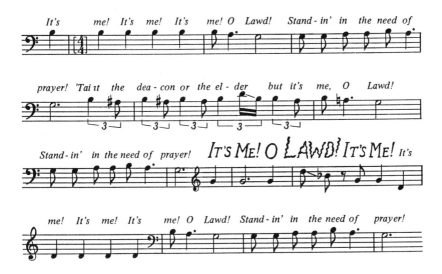

His voice resounds down the length of the Canyon of Reaching Blackness. Back it comes, to be reexploded with an even greater impetus.

Yesterday we got acquainted throwing horseshoes. "I'm not used to associating with people like this," is one of the first things he says. He does not curse while conversing, a very unbum-like habit.

Tonight we are walking up the highway toward the head of the canyon. Cisco alternates between singing and playing the harmonica. He makes it wail.

He seems hungry for company and wants to confide. Do I sport the manner of an absorber of secrets?

"I'm a bastard," he says, and his inflections and matter-of-factness would fit "I'm a Mason" quite as well.

When he was three years old, his mother placed him in a home. From there he was taken in adoption by a family living in the cow country of eastern Oregon.

Because of continual quarreling with his foster father, he started out on hobo trails. The five years since that time were spent as an occasional cowhand and as a wandering minstrel, playing guitar and banjo at dances and entertainments.

In my mind I see a room in which a radio cackles on, rudely oblivious to three or four groups of people conversing. Cocktails adorn or anoint every altar.

Indeed, America is not musical.

Cisco is searching the highway for a cigarette butt — we have run out of tobacco and have forgotten to bring matches. Cisco sees a lighted butt being tossed out of a passing car, and we race to get it before it goes out.

Again he is singing —

> I've counted the moments,
> I've counted the stars,
> And I've counted a million
> Of these prison bars —

It is not remarkable that many hobo songs are also prison songs, or that they contain a large element of so-called self-pity. This element is an essential manifestation of the ego, and is not indulged in by the dead body. The dead body is not an ego.

Self-pity is sometimes described as a mark of cowards and criminals. It is a mark of the living, a lack of the dead.

What are the thousand new yearly maunderings of disconsolate love on every American radio — "Dancing with tears in my eyes . . ."

"I wonder who's kissing her now..."—but self-pity. What of the cries of "Money! Money!"?—Self-pity without benefit of music.

I come back to Cisco because he is singing—

Stand up, poor boy, stand up, stand up, And dry a-way your tears— I've
sen-tenced you to a pris-on term Of nine-ty-nine long years— Miss
Jen-ny Lee was good to you. She nev-er done you wrong. But
with your knife you took her life. Get a-long, poor boy, get a-long.

Now we are back in camp again, Cisco to his bed—I to mine. This little cabin is brimful of feelings tonight—and yet, when sleep comes, it comes complete, like death.

SEPTEMBER 2

Now I know a little story which proves that my entry for August 29 was not risqué fiction.

Each camp employs a first aid man who is generally some degree of a doctor. Cisco is the first aid man's assistant here. They dress in white, and Cisco scrubs it every other day.

This afternoon he comes in and sits on my bunk. He rolls me a cigarette, then one for himself.

"Did the doc romp on my tail when I came in last night!

He thinks we're superior and doesn't want me to associate with any of you fellows. I never saw him so mad."

The "doc," a registered nurse, gets thirty-two dollars a month.

Cisco continues: "He said, 'Why do you hang around those (five-dollar) bums? (Cisco spent most of yesterday with me.) You're used to better things. Stay on your own level and look up! (How far could you look *down* from a camp for transient bums, doc?) Who are they? What are they worth? (Five dollars.) Do you want to degenerate into a bum?' "

(The doc refers to a five-dollar bum.)

"I'd like to at least keep my job until I get a better one," says Cisco. "I know he's wrong. I told him I could pick my own friends, but he's been good to me, so I guess I'll try to fix things up."

I realize that emotions in these circumstances come frequently to a climax, and that part, but not all, of the doc's anger is irritation and jealousy, although he himself probably doesn't know it.

It is four o'clock, my hour for supper duty as flunky in the dining room. "I'll see you at supper, Cis."

This life is a phantasm. Cisco has made his entrance and his exit in less than forty-eight hours.

It is in the after-supper twilight. He walks about as usual, but I have never met him.

SEPTEMBER 3

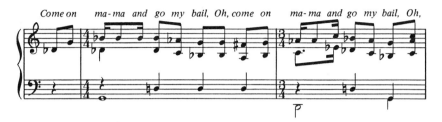

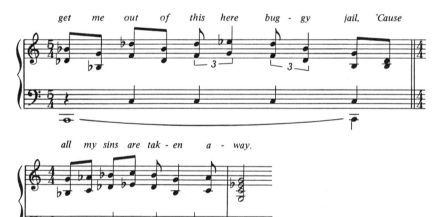

Come on, mother eternal, and get me out of this pervading stupidity!

Today I execute three preliminaries to an effort. One of them is a letter to him of the music discussion (June 13).

". . . I would like the evidence of my past year of work under grant to become the basis for an application for $1,000 from the foundation to complete my projects. I believe that they will want to

see them through to some logical end if they can be made to understand them.

"I cannot prophesy as to when the evidence will be ready. The
time now seems very remote. But it will be completed. Of that I am
sure. . . ."

SEPTEMBER 5

My Los Angeles postmistress forwards me a letter:
"———, Spain, August 12, 1935—

"Dear Music—Your letter of July 15 just received and carefully
perused, brought the usual mixed feelings—i.e., joy and sadness. I
thought of your birthday and wanted to send you something—now
I am almost as uncertain of reaching you but I will take a chance. . . ."

(A ten-dollar check is enclosed.)

There is also a letter from P.

"Dear Harry—

". . . I think the most important thing you can do is to put your
idea in a concrete form—printed, if possible—with photographs, etc.
of the instruments. Send these to a few libraries and archives—put
them on record—Library of Congress, British Museum, Dept. of
Fine Art in Moscow, etc. That is your main work.

"The only other thing to do is to try to publicize and gain a
hearing for your work—an activity which I think would be abortive
and a waste of energy.

"This is a time when changes in politico-economic ideas are taking
place all over the world. There are only two aspects of this struggle:
(1) the attempt to exploit other men for your own personal gain; (2)
the attempt to exploit nature for the just benefit of all. Now I am a
protagonist of politico-economic ideas which have as their objective
the realization of the second of the above concepts.

"I believe that art is cultural wealth—it ought to be available to
everyone because it is one of the sources of vital understanding of
ourselves and our environment. Now in a society where art is recognized as an essential cultural asset and where the objective of creating any kind of wealth is to benefit all of the people, you would
have been given every possible aid—instrument designers and print-
ers and librarians, etc., would have been at your disposal.

"You see what happened in a society based on doing the other
fellow. I say to hell with that kind of a social system. I am on a side
in the fight. You aren't even in the middle—like the silly 'liberals.'
You aren't anywhere. As far as the world of today is concerned, you
don't exist. . . ."

SEPTEMBER 8

"Dear P.—

"I think you know that exactly the thing that you said I should do, the exposition with illustrations (*Trails of Music*) has been striving for the light for seven years. Now it gathers dust in wrapping paper, and it can damn well gather.

"I will never jolt the leaders of music *with* it—but I will jolt them *into* it, eventually, by branding them as the idiots they are.

"I have been gentle and persuasive all too long. The time has come for combustion and contempt.

"I can see little hope for *any* social system so long as the present stupid breeding habits prevail.

"*Per contra, any* social system is good and workable when the mass of people is bred and inured in the common virtues of honesty, kindness, and understanding.

"As between the political practices extant I would claim the American as my own without a second's hesitation—but I am for beginning the evolution of a superior race right here and now. . . ."

SEPTEMBER 12—Between Ingot and Ohio Valley

Last night we were ordered to pack our belongings to be hauled 165 miles early this morning on a public works project authorized by Congress. We are promised $35.00 a month clear.

Since we received checks for half a month's work ($2.50) before leaving, most of the seventeen men in the van of the truck celebrate this chance to better themselves.

In a few moments we are due on a new job. Three of us might be described as dead.

At one of the swill stops a fellow collapses on the gravel. Some others try to help him up and carry him, and he mouths insults.

Again he strikes the gravel. His head and face are bruised and bleeding.

He is finally thrown over the side like cement. Blood smears the floor and baggage.

Just five or six of us have not been drinking. Cisco is one of these. He gets his medicine kit out in the joggling truck and washes the man's bruises with absorbent cotton.

Now I don't know which love is more gracious—the one for Cisco's gentleness, or this for the green perfume of the mountains that have swallowed us.

SEPTEMBER 15—Ohio Valley

It is Sunday, and I sit at the open flap of [a] tent carving pictures
on my belt.

Men pass back and forth. I mentally classify them by the figure
they cut in this morning's sunshine.

Some years ago a group of psychologists announced that California's children of promise were invariably broad-hipped and shoul-
dered.

I generally heap scorn on their findings, and I give them no credit
for this observation, since it requires an extraordinary genius to be
always wrong.

Now here is a man, just passing by, who is guided by a sterile
mind. He is flat behind. Indeed, the inferior man is often arseless.

Now here is another, with a recognizable rear protuberance.

"Ah,_____ In - tel - lect!"

I murmur.

SEPTEMBER 18—Headed for the Great Valley

Today I leave Ohio Valley. Yesterday I discovered I had trench
mouth and reported it immediately. I was rushed to a doctor twelve
miles away who confirmed my diagnosis.

"It would be better if you were not in camp," he says.

I, who have made $3.50 in four weeks' work, am supposed to
pay for a doctor's visit and for a prescription at a drugstore. I am
told that county hospitals will not treat me since I am refused the
status of a resident of any county.

The superintendent lends me $2.00. I am obliging, and so, after
expressing my feelings anent a system that shunts an important social
obligation onto someone else—anyone else—I shut my disease and
depart.

OCTOBER 22—Nearing Monterey

Now, for thirty-five days, I and all my sins have stalked the high-ways of California.

One of them searches for cigarette butts long enough to light without burning our nose, but seldom finds any.

Um - ah   Don - na!

Another curses when no one picks us up. Those unheard from are too frustrated for expression.

I am told that the transient camps and shelters are now closed. The powers that be think that they have not wholly served the purpose for which they were intended, I gather, and that they were abused, as they undoubtedly were.

I walk through the crooked streets of Monterey, and on up the hill into Carmel. I don't try to get a ride, enjoying the four-mile hike through the pines too much to want to hurry it.

In my pale blue dungarees, with a blue bandanna hanging out of my hip pocket, and with my yellow canvas-covered bedroll coiled over my shoulder—sweaty, dirty, and weary—I saunter down Car-mel's pine-shaded business street. Smart shops crowd each other on the little flat with a "Me too!" attitude, before the hill drops suddenly down. Late model cars pull up in front of them, many with uniformed chauffeurs.

I am passing a swank hotel. A taxi driver rushes up and accosts me. His mockery is devastating.

"Taxi, sir? May I carry your luggage, sir? Taxi, sir?"

"Ha! Ha! Ha-a-a-a!" roars the great-free-artist spirit of Carmel standing around on the sidewalk.

I come to the beach and drop my roll behind some of the bushy hillocks in the high sand above the surf. Since leaving Ohio Valley, I have not kept up my diary, except for a few desultory phrases and dates in my notebook. So, this afternoon, I lie in the warm sand and go back over these thirty-five days just passed.

They have not been unhappy—

Now I am spending the night in jail in Quincy. A boy lends me one of his blankets. In the morning the jailer opens the door.

says the boy.
He is not.

Now, in Sacramento, I buy a sleeping bag with my birthday present. In the willowed sands of the American River, within the city, I gaze up at the enthillion stars and bless the giver. And she shall be multiply blessed, for at every approaching dusk I shall thumb my nose at tomorrow.

Sacramento Jungle—I think of the hobo song I wrote in 1929, just previous to my great zealousy in the preservation of spoken inflections in song.[31] Still, this tune is no great violation of the words—

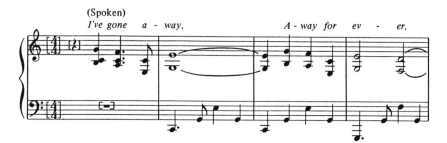

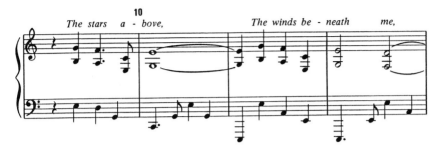

heart keeps beat - ing   time.   Cal - i - for - nia,

25

retard   *p*   *to time*

here's your ho - bo ba - by! Here   he   is   with - out   a   dime—

pp

Strum - ming,   a   strumming   on his   ba - by   u - ku - le - le While   his

30

heart keeps beat - ing   time.

retard   *p*   *pp*

to time

From a warm sleeping bag, in the willowed sands of the American River, I gaze up at the enthillion stars, and they seem to say—

"Why wan - der? Why tire your-self use - less - ly?"

There is noth-ing but e - ter - ni-

Stop and re - flect.   Rest.

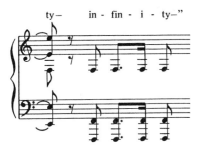

ty — in - fin - i - ty—"

And even while they are speaking, a cold wind stabs in the open bag and whines—

"So yuh can't take it!"

Now I am wandering in Madera County in the Great Valley. At night I trudge along until I find a row of fig trees and then lay my bag nearby in clumps of wild oat straw.

The trees are aching heavy, for it is late September. I put my hands into the black tresses of the boughs, feeling for the figs.

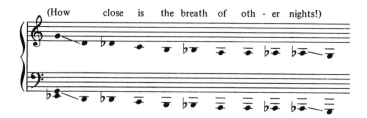

Sweet oozing drops drip from them.

Now I am working in the grape harvest. In two and a half days I make five dollars. I will not hurry. I consider hurrying a double desecration of the flesh—of the grapes and of myself.

They are yellow ripe, and they shatter like water on pavement.

> *. . . and the results are realized in winter without any assumption of ownership.*

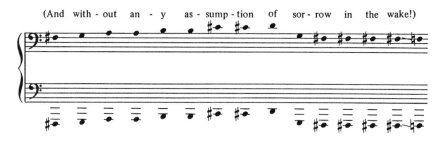

Now I am cleaning a clogged sewer for some kind people at Berenda who have taken me in in spite of my disease.

This job for the second time this summer is prophetic.

When I have cleaned clogged minds, then will I make progress with my music.

Conclusion: to be called up to clean a sewer.

The first time is a misfortune,

The second time is a prophecy,

The third time is a momentous consummation. (Later it becomes a legend.)

A letter comes from London like the sudden sun (October 8)—

". . . read your MS and returned it (alas) but with such a kind note and the address of two publishers who might consider it. We'll get that MS published yet. Don't talk about bottoms of trunks— nothing doing."

An American dollar bill is enclosed.

Echoes from Mandolin-Face of the tooth-fretted lips—

"———, Ohio,
"Oct. 2—1935

"Hello Harry,

"Gee! I was glad to hear from you, believe it or not Pal I just received your letter today it must have followed me all over the world, but it got to my wife at last and she broke it open and read it and sent it to me this morning.

"Well I came back east and run into a shot gun wedding, and I was the goat but thank God, I ditched the poor little innocent mother of my kid (or somebody else's) and back on the bum again, well Pal I had a swell time in Cincy, till my wife's father found out I was back, and then the little lamb was led up to the altar, so now I'm just out of jail, and feeling fine, and I think I have a job starting the 12th of Oct. as a clerk in the ——— Hotel in Cincy and I truly hope my dear little wife is dead by then.

"Well I hope you and Kain-tuck are having a good time together and wish I was with you would we have a time of our life just ask me.

"Give Kain-tuck my best regards and tell him I'm not doing so well, but looking to score before long in fact I've got to, or get in jail again for it is cold out here, and I'm not good looking enough to get by that way do you get the drift.

"So I'll say good night and good luck hoping to hear from you at once and tell me all the news.

"Your
"Pal
"Pablo."[32]

Near Lodi I cut the huge tokays one day at thirty cents an hour for ten hours. I suppose it is a necessary performance, but I detest the manner.

The whore pickers say to the grapes—

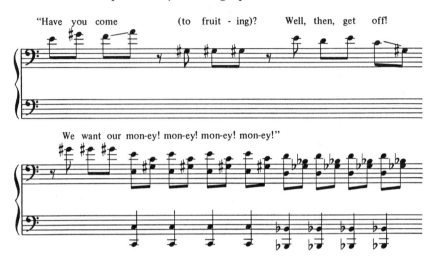

Our pittance from the whoremaster's "legitimate profit" then mostly buys the ferment of our prostitution and dutifully returns to Whoremasters and Company, not necessarily the farmers, but the exploiters of his product.

Who breed stupidity.

I stumble away and cleanse the prostitution from my soul in the jungle of the gentle Mokelumne.[33]

Music!

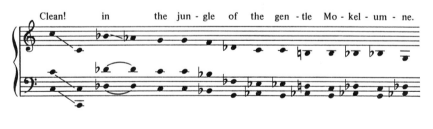

Toppin's, the tramps call pastries and pies. I reflame my jungle fire and make a brew of black Japan tea (October 14).

The stiffs nearby are beginning to prepare supper. It consists almost invariably of stew and coffee.

One of them wanders over, and I invite him to tea. Toppin's, he is called, because he loves them.

I pour from a gallon fruit can. Our cups once held evaporated milk. We also have chestnuts roasted over the coals, and toast with butter spread like the Rocky Mountains.

. . . and you shall be crowned with flowers wreathed about your head, and so you will come, sweet with the beauty with which you make me mad. And Praxinoa will roast us some chestnuts . . . sang Atthis, beloved of Sappho.[34]

My choice of refreshments causes long merriment among the bums around me. Butter is seldom on their menu, and tea and chestnuts are beyond their orbits of thought.

I try to be solicitous toward my guest, the evening passes happily, and Toppin's tells the story of his life.

Time passes painlessly in a sleeping bag, twelve hours out of twenty-four, and I am so willing to let it.

This morning (October 16), in spite of trench mouth, poison oak, and an aching back, carryover from my ten hours of work four days ago, I get up with every intention of asking for a job at the free state employment office.

But the day is long. An hour's siesta in the sunshine by the railroad track subtracted from a day's work will never be missed.

I find some black walnuts and pick them. Then I really start for the employment office. I have even taken my knife (a special one with curved blade for cutting grapes) as evidence of my intentions.

I linger for repletion in a vineyard on the way. When I tire of red grapes, I eat black or amber ones, and wine grapes with white or red juice.

As one grape leads to another, I walk a mile into the country. I eat white figs, then black ones, then white again, gigantic fresh prunes, walnuts, and I top them with almonds, sun-dried on the trees. When I can hold no more, I fill a brown bag to take back.

And so I lie under an almond tree and sleep.

It is now two o'clock, much too late to go to the employment office, so I loll back toward town, feasting and resting by turn.

I make no effort to hide my movements—all but the grapes have been harvested, and I am merely saving for myself what would otherwise rot—and all passersby ignore me (and as only Californians can!).

It is now seven-thirty and chilly October. I am weary, so I lay my bag in a vineyard and am in it.

(Tomorrow morning more sweet grapes than I can eat are within the lazy reach of an arm.)

I sleep in oat straw near Gilroy (October 21). It is in the mountains, and tiny ice crystals cover the top of my bag, when I awake—but I am warm inside.

Of my three preliminaries in trying to rise from bumdom (September 3), only one is answered and that perfunctorily.

And it serves me right! I deliberately plunge into it, and then I try to renege when it becomes onerous.

I have thrown the petty respectable life with all its comforts behind me after the effort to broaden and beautify it has destituted me and drained my stamina. All right—let me throw it behind without guile, without hoping either for a return to it or for a constant absence. After all, it did not request my efforts.

The normal live body hopes for the respect and love of others, and enough of the world to bestow largesse. He hopes and he abandons hope by turn. In the first there is fire to live, but in the second there is greater peace.

are weary sins. They crave peace.

down to the sea past Monterey (October 22).

Instead of hope I shall live for

simple things, for a good hamburger sandwich, sleep, a smile. Who will say that it is not a better life?

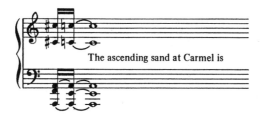

The ascending sand at Carmel is

dark white tonight.

And all my sins are tak- en a - way.

OCTOBER 23—Big Sur

Tonight I lay my sleeping bag under the bay and redwood trees at Big Sur.

The drenching redolence of the bay comes from this hand crushing leaves as I lie waiting for sleep.

There is no one about, but I am not alone. This is the sacred way where the ichor of Robinson Jeffers courses.[35]

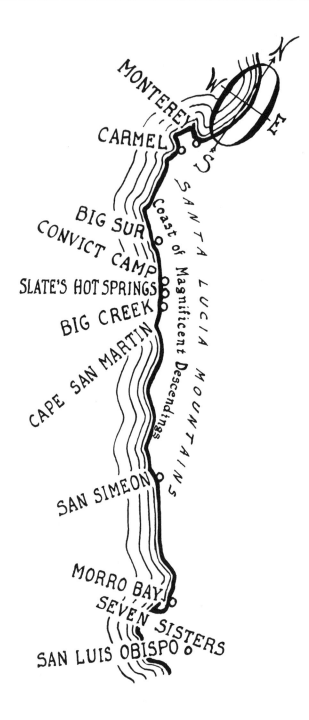

OCTOBER 24—Leaving Big Sur

I walk with my pack down the cliff-veering road past groups of convicts working under supervision of the California Highway Commission.

I do not know they are convicts when I first engage in passing conversation with two of them.

"Where do you stay?" I ask.

"In the 'con' camp, what d' you think?"

one says quietly but with a little sneer.

I try to make things right.

"How was I to know? Anyway, what of it? Maybe I'll be there someday myself."

He smiles. The others call him The Hoodlum.

On my way I meet others. I try hard to make my hellos casual and friendly.

There, but for the grace of God . . .

I hear one of them say:

"In fif - ty - four more   days I'll   be   a   free   man."

> *I've counted the moments,*
> *I've counted the stars,*
> *And I've counted a million*
> *Of these prison bars.*

They stay in an honor camp. It is on a little flat between the road and the sea cliffs. There are only four guards, who bother the men little, and after work they are allowed to stroll about a mile south, on the road, until nine o'clock.

This twilight I have dropped my pack a little way beyond camp. The Hoodlum and two of his friends wander down.

These mountains drop suddenly into the sea. Consequently, there are many sheer cliffs, and wide horizons everywhere.

This is quite opposite from our southern and eastern coasts, where the geography is uncertain whether it is land or water. Land slithers off in swamps and sand bars and then suddenly reappears as islands, unsuspected peninsulas, reefs, and whatnot.

Now, the bleak unbroken Pacific is on one side, and on the other are these down-coming mountains. They end, and they do so simply, directly, utterly.

The life that is earth comes to death that is sea—suddenly, violently, completely.

The Hoodlum talks of prison ways and of the conviction which sent him here.

He wants to give me tobacco, and before I can protest—

"No, I have everything I need, thanks a lot."

And so, as we sit gazing high above the twilight sea, The Hoodlum offers the story of his life.

OCTOBER 25—Near Slate's Hot Springs

A car stops beside me.

"Where are you going?"

"San Luis Obispo, but I don't want a ride, thank you, because you go too fast. I like to walk along the cliffs too well."

"Where do you eat?"

"I can cook."

"And you sleep in that?"

"*That's* a good sleeping bag."

"Why don't you get a job?"

"I'd like a job for my board."

"Get in."

And so I hoe weeds a few hours today for my meals.

The cottage of this couple is on another of the flats between the highway and the imminent cliffs.

On the very face of the next cliff north of this one are Slate's hot sulphur springs.

The original owner, who gave the springs his name, is long since dead, and the present owner has leased the property to the state for a highway construction camp.

Twin bathtubs stand on a little platform fully exposed to the great sun and Pacific, and to anyone who wants to look down from the tops of adjacent cliffs.

But he can't look intimately without glasses, the country is so immense.

There is a little trail—a miniature Bright Angel—leading from the flat to the baths, halfway down the cliff.

At the head of the trail is a board with the legend: PLEASE USE THIS SIGN. On entering, the bather turns the other side of the board, which says: BATHS OCCUPIED PLEASE WAIT.

Because the water is too hot for bathing as it comes from the spring, a cooling barrel is provided between the two tubs. The bather fills his tub with hot water from the trough, then dips as much cold water from the cooling barrel as he wants and refills it from the trough for the next bather.

The baths are free to what little public is present.

This afternoon after work I spend an hour scanning the horizon while lying in sulphur water from the bowels of the earth.

My host and hostess like it moonlight.

After dark I walk two and a half miles up the road to meet The Hoodlum. He has a thousand things to tell me, and I a thousand things to ask.

He knows that I am only a bum, but he shows his appreciation of my interest in him like a hungry dog, and it tears my heart.

"Do I!" he exclaims when I ask him if he likes it better here than in San Quentin. The convicts pay for everything—clothes, tobacco, and attention—out of their wages. The accumulation of the few cents a day which they earn above expenses they draw on going out.

In addition, they are on a "three-for-two" basis—they get credit for three days served on their sentences for each two days of work on the road.

The Hoodlum does not complain. He is always thoughtful and never arrogant.

Aha! someone will say, prison has done him good.

All right, I will reply, if prison is good for him it is even better for some other people I know who have committed no statute crime that I know of.

And including all symphony conductors.

OCTOBER 26

These San and Santed hills—these swerving piles of earth, rock, and redwood behind me, they are called Saint Lucy!

I would like to know the Indian names for this land, although it is useless to try to change them, since Californians are sublimely doped with the tradition of the people they hot-tailed out of here in the 1840s.

California! Land of oncoming Los-es and Las-es, Sans and Santas, Virgins, Conceptions, and Angels!

As for corruptions—

Ah, the glorious conquistadores!

Their imaginations ran the entire gamut from Saint John to Saint John.

OCTOBER 27

It is paradise—this coast—and here would I choose to abide.

Of course, it is not denizened by perpetually revirginizing damosels, Uriah bathed her beautiful young body in the sun from no rooftop here, the possibilities of being gypped and short-changed are practically nil, and although the weather is lovely it is neither *bon jour* nor *buon giorno* scented with garlic.

But from where I lie beneath my wild lilac tree at the edge of the cliff, neither a Trojan War nor an Odyssey could make it grander than it is.

OCTOBER 28

This is not the tempered past. It is the intense present under the wild lilac tree where I am sleeping—fragile and intense.

The roots of the lilac cling to the very edge of the 300-foot precipice that holds us from the bygone sea.

OCTOBER 29

I feel my way along the earthy ledge where I am to meet The Hoodlum once more. It is good to see him looming—coming out of the ambient black.

He gives me tobacco and the address of a friend he says can get me a job.

I give him my good luck coin.

"Harry, you've got to write.

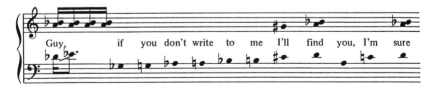

Guy, if you don't write to me I'll find you, I'm sure

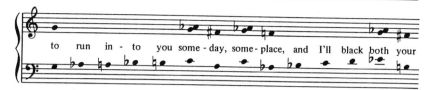

He laughs, but I know how desperate he feels, breaking the first
bond that he has had with the outside world in years.

"If I don'.t write, you can do worse than that."

We stand against the earthy bank, saying nothing—wind in the
chaparral, beating sea.

Something comes to me out of the void.

We shiver. He grips my shoulders. I feel the warm breath of his
whisper,

against my cheek.

I look at him, vague in the dimness, from far away—two inches.
I am abstracted.

OCTOBER 30—Big Creek

This Chopin hems my brain all day—[36]

It pounds. I accent it savagely. I care not how Chopin felt it. It is mine now. I explode it like the last act of my life.

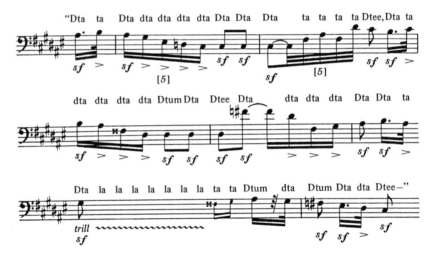

It parries eternity as these mountains parry the sea, and I, knowing well the mortality of everything I love, am defiant.

OCTOBER 31

Oh, if music were as simple to use as words, requiring but pencil and paper for a nickel or a dime!

Music is many things, but among others it is the stimulus of a vibrating agent acting upon the ear via the air. Ergo, if there is no vibrating agent, there is no stimulus.

Notes that are not heard are not music, and people who pretend to appraise music by studying the printed notes are those greatest of abominations—asses without ears.

The way of music is money, for instruments, and for a place to live to keep and repair them; and what is even harder, it is the way of people to play them whose souls are in tune with the expresser's.

NOVEMBER 1—Between Big Creek and San Simeon

Today I gaze long at the Coast of Magnificent Descendings. The ascending arpeggios of Cone Peak black the evening horizon at Cape San Martin. These forms have seared me till I die.

And now they are all behind me, and it is raining. I am camping in a little cove of the sea at San Simeon, and I have built a fire under an overhanging rock.

A hobo may be on the saucer edge of life, but a fire brings him back to the center.

NOVEMBER 3—Morro Bay

I come out from under the eaves of a deeply eaten stack of oat straw searching for a coffee site, and meet tatterdemalion nine- and eleven-year-olds. They help me build a fire hidden in the willows of the creek bottom this frosty morning.

Nine watches me roll a cigarette. I cannot bear it, and toss him the sack, one of The Hoodlum's presents.

His neat little fingers turn out a cigarette to shame me.

"Do you take sugar?" I ask as I pour coffee into a ten-cent tobacco can.

"He don't," says Eleven.

he says.

We linger by the fire, the Seven Sister rocky peaks line the southern horizon, and Nine and Eleven begin the stories of their lives.

San Luis Obispo.

Strong chocolate is brewing on my incense-of-the-gods jungle fire tonight. It is kindled from eucalyptus, oily, green-dry.

Since this is a division point,[37] I decide to sleep in the heated sand of the railroad sandhouse.

NOVEMBER 5

My forwarded mail includes a letter from P.—

". . . Your position on birth control and sterilization involves two elements or objectives: (1) a limited number of human beings alive at any one time; (2) improvement in the quality of those human beings.

"Both of these objectives are beset with insurmountable handicaps and obstacles. . . . Don't try to beat Nature on this heredity business, Harry. She has her joke, and if you try to act seriously about it, and change things, she kicks up an awful row, produces sterile offspring, albinos, all sorts of things, in her efforts to bring things back to what, as far as she is concerned, must be the only way.

"You may also be interested in the recently outlined facts on intelligence as measured by adequacy of reaction to problem stimuli— a far more just test than the old knowledge basis. These tests demonstrate that most differences in normal intelligence groups are derived from different educational and environmental pre-test conditionings. So environment and education are far more worthy and capable objects of idealistic attention than are the hereditary and eugenic sides of the question. . . . Environment and education are the things which need changing—not people. They will be changed for the better by a better environment. . . ."

NOVEMBER 6

"Dear P.—

"I don't suppose it's possible to breed a dog entirely without ears—however, it is possible to breed a dog with either large or small ears.

"But it isn't possible to educate large ears into small ones, nor is it possible to educate a skunk to smell like attar of roses.

"Intelligence, as it is measured by the academician, is not an index of human worth. I cannot believe that you meant to imply that.

"He cannot devise such an index, and the fact that he tries shows why he is an academician—he lacks the leaven that renders knowledge tolerable, i.e., imagination.

"The academy is a snare and a delusion for ductile minds.

"In New York I spent some three weeks being psychoanalyzed, interviewed, and examined, medically and musically, by Adjustment Service. At the end I was solemnly informed that my life had been wasted because I should have been a bookkeeper.

(A timid little tantalizer,
Typed in shame and sin—

O Mister Psycho-Analyzer,
What should you have been?) . . ."

NOVEMBER 12—Santa Barbara

Something to eat, a dry place to sleep, and sometimes a smile—
they seem like little things.

But they are not always easy. Five days ago I begged at fourteen
houses in San Luis—at fourteen sets of steps I mortified myself—

"Please,   la - dy,   I'd glad - ly work for some-thing to   eat"–

and when I was through I held a can of milk and a can of pea soup.
Not even these would I have gotten had I not insisted on my need
like a homeless please-eyes dog.

True, there was a Sally kitchen.[38] I went there twice, the limit of
meals allowed, since they want you to move on. It is always move,
move, move—where? Nobody knows nor cares.

They gave me beans and skimmed milk, and it tasted good.

A can of milk and a can of pea soup—not enough to satisfy that
night's hunger, let alone the accumulated hungers of the day, and the
day before that, and that, and that.

And not even enough misery of mortification to end it. And all
around me spirits.

That hover like humming birds over flowers. Is there honey for
the sucking?

Now I have been in Santa Barbara for four days and chromatic
organ's godmother's bountiful table has sated one hunger.[39]

"Has your ca - pac - i - ty   no   lim - it?"

asks Daughter.

I look at her sadly.

Wake over Chromatic Organ the First.

It is attended by Godmother, a few others, and myself.

The 168 keys of the organ rest. They will not speak because of
mechanical derangement. Their rainbowed colors are half chipped
off.

I listen to the funeral music—Brahms Opus 118, No. 6, which Godmother is playing—and gaze upon them. I am glad that no one notices me.

Today I dress the body—cementing the colors back on before leaving.[40]

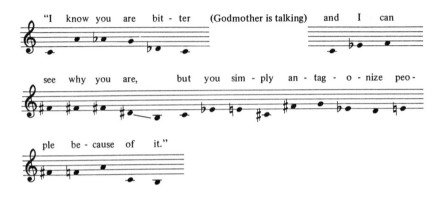

"I know you are bit-ter (Godmother is talking) and I can see why you are, but you sim-ply an-tag-o-nize peo-ple be-cause of it."

I continue her thought but do not say—"Work with them, as they work, and thereby deny your existence."

I wipe the dust from the body with my handkerchief. The mask fretwork smiles.

Tears weary, wither, and blow away.

NOVEMBER 14

I am walking about in the park and find forty-four cents in dimes, nickels, and pennies at a spot in the grass.

"How lucky," I say as I go away, but I turn to look back and see a fat man scratching in the grass on the spot.

Instinctively I start back, with the forty-four cents in my hand ready to present. Before I get to the fat man, I also see a stylish lady in a shiny car, its motor idling, waiting.

I turn and disappear quickly in the bushes.

NOVEMBER 15—Leaving Santa Barbara

"Please don't be bit-ter, Har-ry

(Godmother is talking as she drives me part of the way to Ventura),

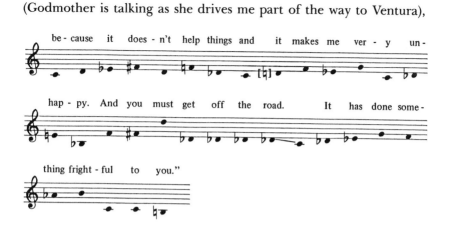

Sans home or hope—the wanderer still lives, does things, says things, thinks things. I am thinking that if I have done nothing more than show these I perhaps have done a service.

"It is only through the ferment of experience and bitterness that evils are corrected (I am replying). If all feelings were suppressed, there would be no voice.

She, who has courageously supported herself and her children for many years and is now debt-ridden, insists that I take a dollar.

We then agree that life is a siege of anguish, she smiles, and we part.

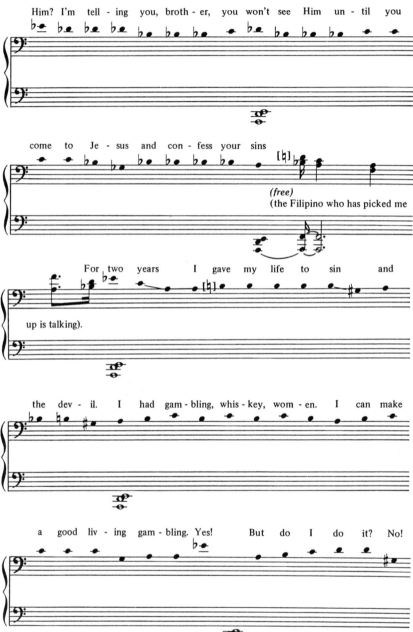

Him? I'm tell - ing you, broth - er, you won't see Him un - til you

come to Je - sus and con - fess your sins

(free)
(the Filipino who has picked me

For two years I gave my life to sin and

up is talking).

the dev - il. I had gam - bling, whis - key, wom - en. I can make

a good liv - ing gam - bling. Yes! But do I do it? No!

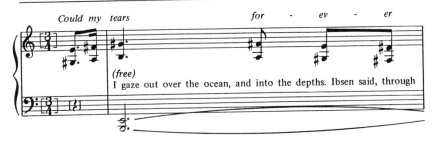

Could my tears for - ev - er

(free)
I gaze out over the ocean, and into the depths. Ibsen said, through

flow These for sin could not a -

Hedvig, "Why do you say 'depths of the sea'? You could say 'the bottom of the

tone— Thou must save and Thou a -

sea.' . . . it sounds so strange to me when other people speak of the depths of the sea."

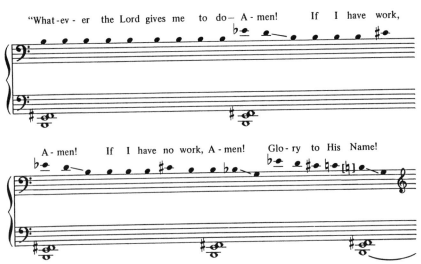

"What - ev - er the Lord gives me to do— A - men! If I have work,

A - men! If I have no work, A - men! Glo - ry to His Name!

"May God bless you," I respond softly.

NOVEMBER 16—Ojai

Last night I laid my bag on the dry leaves under a pepper tree in Ojai Valley. The berries are dry and red now, and sweet to taste.

Tonight I am camping under a live oak tree with a heavy roof of leaves.

I take off all my clothes, as I always do before crawling in, and gaze down at a body pale in the blackness. It is beautiful.

My hands stroke its belly, and I am very happy this November night looking up into the inky O-high oak.

Back be - hind the ink - y oak.

Since I may wan - der ev - ery - where

I will draw there what I will.

. . . I don't want your body. Jesus doesn't want it. . . .

But I do, and I think it is beautiful.

NOVEMBER 17

About two o'clock this morning it has started to rain, so I take refuge in an abandoned house nearby. Although the cover to my bag is waterproof, I dislike smothering myself beneath the canvas.

Now the rain has abated somewhat, and I have blow-nursed a fire of soaking wood for an hour before it becomes vigorous.

Some Mexican children wander by and watch me drink coffee. Bless their charming smiles!

There is a tradition among hobos that a Mexican will never refuse to share his food, although it may consist only of tortillas or unflavored frijoles. In fact, it is a tradition that extends to all those of the Roman Catholic faith.

My only feelings are a fervent wish that they attain their promised heaven.

It has begun to rain hard again, and still the children stay and laugh and talk to me. I have nothing in which to offer them coffee, and they insist that they have had their breakfasts.

It is great to live this life of abundant beauty, I reflect, as large descending drops splatter coffee in my face.

NOVEMBER 23—Los Angeles

My old-old friends welcome me again to the vicinity of El-lay—this one with a broken back from an auto accident and still raining wisecracks and explosive mirth on all within earshot.

A letter awaits me—

". . . informed me that, in making the grant, the foundation had no intention of renewing it and that attitude has not been changed. . . . May I express the hope that you will be able to present the report of your year's work under the grant at an early date. . . ."[41]

NOVEMBER 28

My postmistress has provided me a little basement room with morning sunshine near the center of downtown El-lay rent free, and old-old friend has sent me a large box of groceries. There is a gas plate just outside my door. It is also used by other young fellows living in the basement.

I decide that suppressing my feelings will accomplish nothing—

". . . I do not understand why I have seen so little evidence of any measure of appreciation of my efforts. I can generate no enthusiasm in sending a compendium of twelve years of intensive thought when I must anticipate being told that it is not understood (entry for June 24). If disconcern with results *is* the policy of the foundation, it is my opinion that there is a serious fault in the organization of the foundation. If the above is *not* the policy of the foundation, then I am forced into this generalization—that a foundation for the promotion of culture that is incapable of commanding a project simply because it is unorthodox shows a most unfortunate lack. . . ."[42]

NOVEMBER 29—Banana Center, Central Park, El-Lay

This became Pershing Square in the war-mad days, but it is still Central Park to me and still "Cannibal Island" to the skidway.

"May I speak to you?"

"Surely."

"Have you been saved?"

"I'm sorry, but your subject doesn't interest me."

The young man bows and walks away, and I mentally collapse from astonishment. Such passivity before pagan resistance is unlike evangelical votaries.

Endless, endless movement. Loitering figures—lingering, lurking.

Some have been heard to say that no respectable person would allow himself to be seen in the park after dark. Huh! I walk about under the thousand shadows of the bamboo and banana trees with utter unconcern.

Here, Saint Francises tempt birds by day.

Here, Saint Pauls tempt God by night.

DECEMBER 4

Light from the Road of Reaching Blackness—

". . . You can't imagine how different this place is in comparison with the joint (San Quentin). I am practically a free man, what makes it so extremely wonderful, the camp is located on a beautiful spot. (In my mind he is one with the Coast of Magnificent Descendings.)

". . . it will only be a few short months before I will be a free man, and incidentally, I am going to continue on being a free man. . . . As ever a Pal. . . ."

On the flap of the envelope are the prerequisites for censorship, that is, name and number of the writer, and the relationship of the addressee, thus—

M_____

_____

Friend.

_____

I am looking for a hobo acquaintance in the flophouses of East Fifth Street. Here is one run by a Japanese. A large sign greets me as I ascend the stairs:

NO GIRL HERE

DONT ASK FOR IT

DECEMBER ?, 1935

Night.

Four black walls—I don't like them after all the lacy heavens that I have slept under so much before this.

Four black walls surround a month that is marked by turmoil.

When a friend who has lived with me has suddenly gone, he is still present in my mind—he is in the feeling of the rug under foot and between the leaves of my manuscripts, and I cannot shake him out overnight.

And so with this December.

A few nights ago whistles shrieked, and I hear that this is another month and another year; but in this little black room, it is still the chaos of December.

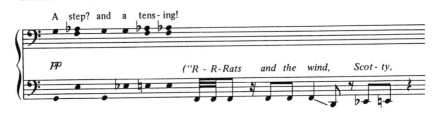

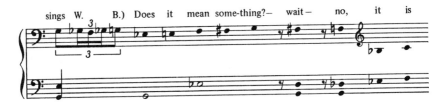

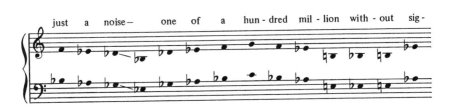

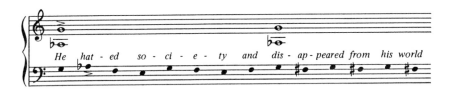

He hat-ed so - ci - e - ty and dis - ap - peared from his world

in Ar - i - zo - na. I find a sheet of pa - per toss - ing a -

and I

bout the house on which he has typed some vers - es,

see him from the be - gin - ning—

"Say that I starved, that I was cold and wea - ry.

That I was burned and blind - ed by the des - ert suns . . .

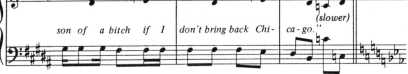

gets fi - nan - cial back- ing from man - y pa - tron - ess - es,

and he is best hung of an - y man I ev - er saw.

"Con - sid - er - ing the con - sti - tu - tion of our so - ci - e -

ty I feel that an art - ist might as well give up

who is - n't blessed ei - ther with a sub - stan - tial de - pend - a - ble

in-come   or   a   sub-stan-tial   de-pend-a-ble   ring   dang   doo."

Oh! Su - san - na.   Oh! don't you   cry   for   me,   For I

(vigorously)

come from Al - a - bam - a   with   my   ban - jo   on   my

knee — Now   don't   you   cry, Don't   cry   for   me,   Su - san - na

ff

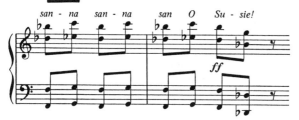

san - na   san - na   san   O   Su - sie!

ff

"Have you confessed your sins to Jesus?"

FEBRUARY 1, 1936—San Bernardino

"Do you drink?"
"No—that is, I don't make a habit of getting drunk."
"Well, I feel sure, after talking to you, that

what you say you are, a practical newspaper proofreader."
"Huh— (I smile as the years crowd around) that I am."

"If I continue to feel as I do now, you will hear from me definitely, and as to when you can report for work, within the next week."

"Thank you. Good night."

Wind-maddened rain strikes the sidewalk. It is after dark.

Then abandon hope! (try and do it, I think to myself) *because these are weary sins. They crave peace. From high hills the pines march down to the sea past Monterey. . . .*

I plunge into the nerve-exciting downpour, then into the inter-urban station.

Someone notices me.

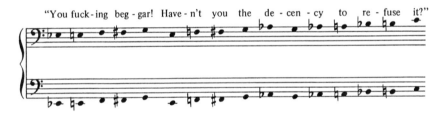

"I'm glad for you," he says.

We talk—what about I don't know.

We are going to part.

"I have a job, and you aren't working yet," he says, putting fifty cents in my hand.

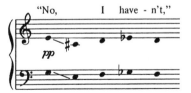

I say to myself.

I answer myself weakly as I think of the six meals I've missed since day before yesterday.

He is a marine in mufti. He only makes thirty dollars a month. I have an idea.

I think, as I copy what he tells me.

I sneer back at myself and think of the hundreds of people whom I can never hope to repay.

  Thoughts wrangle around me under the deluge—the only trouble with hoboing is the continual uncertainty of bodily sustenance and of its quality even when available.

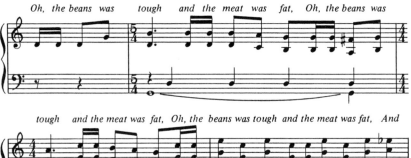

Someone pans it on the piano of a poolroom I have barged into to escape a new impulse of heaven, and I supply the words.

The moon—apart from the life of civilized man—is taken away from me, along with the inky oaks, the canyons of reaching blackness—

This conglomeration will have a weekly wage and enough unobligated money to buy a suit of clothes for the first time in five years. Perhaps it should be pleased. It isn't sure.

This body wants tender beans, and this spirit wants the moon. Both can't be satisfied. There is no compro——

The heavens are raining the color black.

"Have a shot." A man offers me a drink from his bottle of gin where we stand urinating under some eaves, and I accept.

Rain is beating on the highway.

"It'll warm you up," says the man who has swished me into his car. I take his word for it and finish his bottle of port. But he doesn't go far.

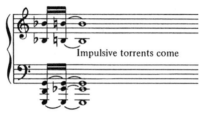

Impulsive torrents come

with increasing ferocity.

I stop running away from them and thrill when water runs down my leg.

It is miles out on Foothill

Boulevard and the sixty-mile road to El-lay.

I signal all the cars and laugh when they pass, just as though I were playing a joke on them, and didn't want a ride.

THE END

End Littoral

The Journal of a Hiking Trip

Written Frivolously, yet without Scientific
or Literary (or Musical) Observations

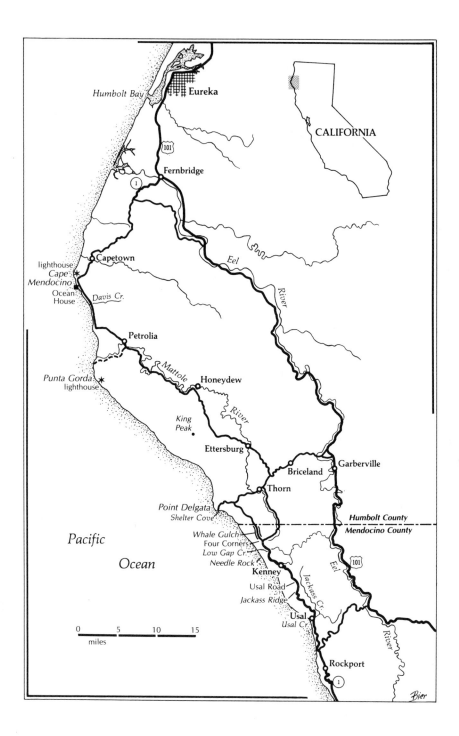

Humbolt Bay

Eureka

101

Fernbridge

1

CALIFORNIA

lighthouse
Cape
Mendocino
Ocean
House

○ **Capetown**

Davis Cr.

Eel

River

○ **Petrolia**

Mattole

Punta Gorda
lighthouse

○ **Honeydew**

River

King
Peak

○ **Ettersburg**

○ **Briceland**   ○ **Garberville**

○ **Thorn**

Point Delgata
Shelter Cove

Humbolt County
Mendocino County

Whale Gulch
Four Corners
Low Gap Cr.
Needle Rock

○ **Kenney**

Eel

101

Pacific

Ocean

Usal Road
Jackass Ridge

Jackass Cr.

Usal
Usal Cr.

River

0   5   10   15
miles

○ **Rockport**

1

Bier

TUESDAY, SEPTEMBER 9 (ADMISSION DAY), 1947—Rockport, California

Arrived Rockport last night from Jenner—one bus a day. It gets here after dark, about seven-thirty. No choice.

This place is not for a claustrophobic. Although the ocean is only about 200 yards away, it is reached by a narrow pass, and mountains close all around, their steep slopes covered with redwood and fir. Rockport consists of one general store, one post office, one rather large logging and sawmill camp, one hotel, and one population. One tavern is a mile away.

I try to get information—all I've been doing the past week. Is there a beach? Yes, but the log-pond and sawmill block the way.

A friendly logger, half-Mexican–half-Irish, I learn later, calls the bullcook. "Here's a guy on the road, and he wants a place to sleep." The bullcook takes me to a shack with two unoccupied single beds with mattresses. (Some way, that qualification "unoccupied" seems unnecessary—after all, this man is a bullcook.) I throw my knapsack on one, my sleeping bag on the other.

I offer to buy the bullcook a bottle of beer for his trouble. "You'd buy me one, then I'd buy you one. That could go on all night," he says.

So I sack in. The Mexican-Irish tells me to come to the cookshack for breakfast. It won't cost me anything.

I wake up this morning about eight, nine, or ten. I dunno. I carry no watch. Breakfast is over, but I manage to bum a large cup of coffee at the cookshack.

(Three weeks later I really have breakfast in this joint. I hear the girl call to the cook: "Fry four over easy. Fry six straight up. Scramble ten." Then when I get to her, she asks: "How many, and how d'ya want 'em?" "Does one man really eat ten?" I say. "Yes, really," she says. When I tell her I only want two, I hope she won't yell it out. But she does: "Fry two straight up," she calls in a loud, clear voice. I imagine that everyone is looking sidewise at me.)

More questions. Roads or trails up the coast? Yes, an impassable road to Shelter Cove but no trails. Or—maybe there are trails, who knows? Maybe yes, maybe no. Know we don't; no, we don't know.

The woman at the store says: "You must be queer!" Some of these folks have lived here all their lives, yet can give no information about the coast ten miles away. Queer people!

At the tavern I find someone. At last! The proprietor talks with authority. Sheer sea cliffs, going straight into the sea, prevent anyone following the beach from Rockport to Shelter Cove, about forty miles. But the dirt road, such as it is, runs along the top of the ridge of mountains lateral to the coast, dropping down to the rivers that cut across, occasionally.

And he once knew a man who walked from the mouth of the Eel River to Shelter Cove, going generally south (I'm going the chilly direction—north), *right on the beach*, waiting now and then for low tide, so that he could get around points and over rocks. He said this guy claimed to have walked the entire California beach (some thousand miles) except where there were cliffs, and this particular section was the last gap. (Understandable. His last gap and very possibly my last gasp.)

The tavern prop gives me a lift about a mile, to the place where the Usal Road branches off from State 1, some three miles north of Rockport. Almost the only evidence of a road is a large highway sign which says: "Road Beyond Usal Not Advisable," or something similar.

Now my trip into the wild littoral really begins. The "road" isn't numbered.

For years this project has been in the back of my mind. The section roughly from Rockport to the mouth of the Eel is the only uncivilized coast left in continental United States where there is no paved road or no road at all. The reasons are pretty obvious: steep, irregular mountains, heavy rainfall in the winter, and consequently deep forests and dense brush. Almost no one (except the "queer") sees any point in battling the difficulties.

Road building is a challenge. To go ten miles as some one-track-minded bird flies it, almost anyplace around here, you find it necessary to wind about, up and down, back and forth, for about forty. (And that's a paragon of understatement.)

Were there a constant, concentrated, and valuable natural resource a road would of course be built. But logs aren't such. Sawmills are set up only for a few months or a few years, depending on the supply and the price. The settlements they engender disappear, and aren't reestablished for fifty years, if ever.

Also, the scenic grandeur resulting from the impact of mountains and ocean might make a road worthwhile from the tourist angle but for one difficulty. Fog, the unpredictable, would bring curses upon the designer of such a road a good part of the year. To the newcomer there is nothing with less scenic grandeur than fog (only the native feels joy in the half-seen–half-assumed fog forms), and he would probably never try the same route again.

With my forty-five pound pack on my back, it's that "up and down" ingredient of the present route that gets me. The poundage is distributed among the following items, most of which I picked up at war surplus stores in Santa Rosa last week:

Two wool sleeping sacks......................... $3.86
One rubberized cover........................... .96
One knapsack................................... 3.86
Canteen .... .48
Mess kit .... .29
Marine jungle knife 1.95
Air pillow .... .29

And about twenty pounds of dehydrated food.

I can see the road to Usal taking flight up to the ridge ahead of me. First it goes across and through a creek, as though to get a fresh drink before the ascent.

About a quarter of a mile up, I see clearly what the tavern prop meant by the advisability of taking the ridge. Some five or ten miles above the dip in the mountains, that I assume indicates the location of Usal, is a huge bluff. It looks to be 1,000 feet high, with a precipitous rock face, and no beach whatever—just the bygone, doggone ocean below. It might be 40,000 feet high! (For all I know.) I'm sure it's more than ten, and I'd hate to be clinging to the bottom with a tidal wave staring me in the face.

Beyond the bluff, hazy promontories and mountains.

So up I go. The ascent is terrific. With a good low gear it would be nothing. But what with a forty-five pound pack, including twenty pounds of uneaten food, my low gear is somewhat overawed.

Up the road goes for about twenty-five miles. (The scientifically inclined might say that the map shows the ascent to be about a mile and a half, but maps are only half-emotional. The only true picture of the effort involved is twenty-five miles.)

At the top is a sign: "Danger—bear traps on this place."

Only one car passes me—going my way—all day. And I was fondly gazing at the ocean when it passed. I wasn't even noticed.

In the evening, after walking the seven miles from the junction

with State 1 to Usal, I camp by a little creek filled with the tallest
alders I ever saw. The creek is swift, running over rocks. Each rock
has a clump of watercress against its upper part. I eat several bales
of the cress before making a fire, getting supper, and bedding down.

WEDNESDAY, SEPTEMBER 10—Usal

Slept warm and wonderfully well. But I ache at all my junctures
from yesterday's mountainous climb. Think I'll go to the beach, about
a quarter mile away, and get de-junctured.

I walk down a meadow past what looks like an old abandoned
hotel. Sheep look out at me through the second story windows. (People
walk around meadows, and sheep stare at them from windows. What
a wonderful country!)

Crossing two stout fences, I arrive at the beach and pick a secluded
little nick in the cliff. Take off my clothes, build a barricade out of
driftwood against a possible northwest wind, and walk a half mile to
the south end of the beach, a rocky point, naked. I find a life jacket
stamped with "S.S. Peter—— N. Daniel."

I also see a sunset naked, for the first time in my life. What a
thrill! Three or four of the important things all visible at once.

Went swimming this afternoon but hardly more than got wet.
The beach descends too rapidly for comfort, and the breakers are
savage.

Built my barricade against the cliff, well above what seems to be
the ordinary high tide line. An exceptional high tide, driven by a
wind, would flood me, so I'm ready to move at a moment's notice,
up the climbable cliff.

THURSDAY, SEPTEMBER 11—Usal Beach

No, the night's tide didn't even come close. I wake up lazily about
mid-morning, when the sun finally rises over my little cliff. I wear
clothes at night for added warmth. And so, this morning, I take off
my clothes and start breakfast.

(Night, or covering of the earth, is for the unconscious. Daylight,
or uncovering, is for the conscious. All very sensible.)

I made two fires last night, a little one between two flat rocks for
cooking, and a big one for hell. The big one, made against a huge

driftwood stump, is still burning this morning, so I cook breakfast over the coals.

Typical breakfast:
   Dried lemon juice (gotten at a health food store in
      Santa Rosa), dissolved in a cup of water
   Thin slice of fried salt pork
   Drop cakes made half of prepared flour and half
      of Pablum (Wonderful!)
   Coffee (made in a two-pound coffee can)
   Dried prunes (I also crack the seeds, eat the kernels)

Typical lunch:
   Dried prunes, plus anything left over from breakfast

Typical supper:
   Beachcomber's daiquiri
   Smoked herring
   Watercress
   Dry Pablum
   Wet chocolate

The beachcomber's daiquiri is made from equal parts of fresh water and dark rum (I brought along a pint), a nub of dried lemon juice, a dash of seawater, and a sprig of floating kelp for a decorative touch (may be eaten or not). It should also have a bit of sugar, but my only sugar is in my sweetened condensed milk.

The mountains on each side of this little cove are steep and forbidding, even though the tops are forested. The beach is desolate, lonely, and I love it. It has the blackest sand I ever saw. Clean but black.

I had thought that fresh water might be a problem, but there are a dozen little springs in the cliffs around me. None of them really run, this dry time of year, but I can get a canful of drips in an hour or two. Some of them stop running when the sun hits them, start again at night.

Tried to clamber over the rocks at the southern point this morning. Couldn't make it: rocks too steep and sea too vicious. If I find places like this between Shelter Cove and the Eel, I'll have to change my strategy. Even the lowest tide, which doesn't come till December, would be no help here.

Haven't seen a soul down here in twenty-four hours. Of course, the local source is not very soulful, since Usal consists of just a few fishers' huts at the north side of the creek opening on the beach, and a cluster of three or four houses inside a protecting arm of mountain three or four hundred yards up the creek, also north side.

No one is around the fishers' huts, though they seem well kept, and one has a nice little vegetable garden. I knocked and halloed, but such souls as may have been around probably saw me coming. There is evidence of the army or navy, some kind of amphibious craft being abandoned in front of the huts.

A few wisps of fog are coming in this afternoon, partially obscuring the north mountain occasionally. But I refuse to put on my clothes as long as I make a shadow in the sand.

This is the fourth day without a cloud in the sky, but now I guess they're over. It's about four o'clock, and the fog is billowing in for vengeance.

I put on my clothes, pack my things, and return to my camp under the alders. The fog is here too, but it's not so dismal as on the beach.

The alders drip all night. They drip drops and trouble for my sinuses, too, dammit.

FRIDAY, SEPTEMBER 12—Usal

Today I head for another long climb up and another ridge road, on the twenty-five- to thirty-mile stretch to Shelter Cove. I figure it will take me three days by easy stages. If I simply wanted to get someplace, for some obscure reason, I wouldn't be walking. I'd evolve a carburetor in my left armpit, a propeller in my cowlick, a rudder on my tail, and take off.

After a good stiff climb I am above the fog, and now, a mile or two farther on the ascent, I am 500 to 1,000 feet above it. Huge firs and redwoods everywhere, but almost no vistas.

Mountains often seem to hem you in because of this absence of vistas, although actually you are fairly free in them. You can scramble off in nearly any direction, like a goat, if you envy goats.

The beach does not seem to hem you in, because of the tremendous sweeps of geography before your vision, although it does hem you in terrifically. On the beach there are only two ways to go, forth or back.

This road is fair only in spots. It is frequently overgrown with a green ceiling, making in effect a tunnel, and it is at times deeply rutted, so that a modern car, unless expertly straddled, would be stranded, a modernistic ornament perched on a ridge. Where you turn on the motor to watch the wheels go round.

No one passes me all day, going either direction.

Some five to eight miles beyond Usal I come to a fern-encompassed spring, with a pipe leading out to a hollowed-log water trough. And a little farther on the road crosses a creek and comes upon a little camping spot under five huge firs.

The sun is low, so I make camp, using the fireplace of previous campers. It is well cleared of brush and debris; I don't need to worry too much about starting a forest fire. I make my bed on a little shelf between a large fir and a small huckleberry. (And feel even smaller than the huckleberry.)

SATURDAY, SEPTEMBER 13—Five Firs (Jackass Creek)

After Thursday night's fog-drip experience, last night was wonderfully warm and dry.

As I get breakfast two men come by in some kind of small truck. They have business in my vicinity which they do not choose to state. But they are the first persons I've seen to talk to since leaving Rockport on Tuesday. They are friendly, and I state my business.

They tell me that I've come just a little over five miles since leaving Usal (each of those first two miles of ascent was equal to three or four on the level!), and that some seven miles beyond this spot I will come to an old highway sign near which is a spring, an ancient orchard, and a good camping spot.

The road goes up and down, in almost perpetual shade; just a spot of sunlight here and there. It is like a small child, insisting on climbing to the top of everything in the vicinity of the direction it's going. And sometimes I wonder whether it *has* a direction. If there were a view to be attained, it might be different, but the tops of the mountains are invariably submerged with the perpetual twilight of deep forests or as thick with tall brush as the sides.[1]

For more than a day I had occasionally seen a long forested ridge blocking my direction to the north. Today I finally reached it and crossed it, only to find another forested ridge that looked exactly like the first one, and about the same distance away as the first one was when first seen. You can't win.

I gorge on huckleberries that line the road, and discover the two men cutting fronds, gathering them (huckleberry fronds) in large bunches for the florists. They put them in refrigeration, they tell me, till time of shipment.

Three boys in a car pass me going south. Turned a sharp corner and there I was. You could see the car jerk back with astonishment. I had the advantage, hearing their motor before I saw them. They are hunting. Seemed amazed that I am walking.[2]

He's walking! No, you're kidding! He *is* walking! My God! Walking! Imagine that! He's really walking! Hey, fellows, here's a guy walking! Honest? Yeh, honest! Walking!

They say it with an inflection that would suggest that the human race had suddenly evolved—in the memory of living men—without legs. And here, before their eyes, was a specimen who still managed to walk despite the absence of legs!

I gaze back at the expostulators with the air of a veteran exhibit in a circus tent. Yes, I'm walking. It's free, boys, so enjoy the show. No one asks me to demonstrate, thank heaven! That I couldn't take.

Arrive at Kenny's, as the huckleberry-frond men called the place with the old orchard, and find it charming. A campground in a redwood circle (small redwoods growing around the stump of a redwood cut off some fifty to seventy-five years ago), an old springhouse with wonderfully cool water, a dozen apple trees of various types, loaded with fruit, a blackberry patch.

I decide to stay for the night. I am now ten miles from Usal, according to the California Auto Club sign nearby (and by addition twenty miles from Rockport, my starting point).

Five friendly fisher folk from the Noyo River fleet dropped in while I was getting supper. One of them said that on his last trip he fished so far out that the albacore had slant eyes.

Another gave me some new dope, and knows even the names of the gulches. At Four Corners the road left goes down to the sea at Needle Rock. I shall forego that pleasure—a long hike down from a ridge two to three thousand feet high *and back*—since I can't follow a beach there either; there isn't any. Beyond Four Corners is a junction, and the road left goes to Shelter Cove.

Two hunters dropped in at dusk to camp here with me.

SUNDAY, SEPTEMBER 14—Kenny's

The hunters have had breakfast and are already taking off at my first stir. They leave all their gear and chow and tell me to help myself in their absence.

I slept well, but awake tired. Those forty-five pounds on ascents are beginning to get me.

I have an egg and toast with huckleberry jelly and coffee for breakfast (on the hunters), a nice relief from my usual fare.

Shelter Cove is still some fifteen miles away, and I won't make it in any three days from Usal, unless I get a ride.

They tell me that Kenny's, fifty years ago, had a hotel, post office, livery stable, and a dance hall, being a big logging camp. And that the road I am traveling was once the stagecoach road from Fort Bragg to Eureka.

I leave a note of thanks for the breakfast and start out. At first the road wanders up and down, as usual, in perpetual twilight.

Two or so miles beyond Kenny's there is a magnificent view of the ocean headlands to the south. Now, from the north, I see the rocky face that I saw from the south on my first day out of Rockport. Today the ocean is completely obscured by fog. I am standing a good thousand feet above it, yet the rock face, topped with pinnacles and redwoods, still rises several hundred feet out of the fog.

Three of the fisher boys pass me on the way back to Noyo.[3] They have their buck, a pathetically small one. He had only one horn, a club foot, and already one eye had been shot away by another hunter. (Why not require the hunter to capture his animal alive, then gas him to death?)

I drop down to the streambed camp, farther on, of the two remaining fisher people, Mr. and Mrs. Hugh Miller. They both fish, each having a boat. She is one of two women fishers on this coast, says Miller. She is her own engineer, navigator, and fisher.

She studied painting, fresco, etc., and taught art in S.F. and Portland public schools. She still paints when fishing is slack, and has some paintings hanging in the Noyo Cafe. And her thirty-foot boat, the *Ellinart*, has the only painted sail in the Noyo fleet. She invited me up to see her, in her house overlooking the bay, next time I'm in Noyo.

Said good-bye to the Millers and trudged on out of the twilight into a large burned-over section. But you can't kill the redwoods, apparently, either by saw or fire. They sprout right out again, as though these were just other incidents in other 2,000-year cycles.

Come to Low Gap, or Champagne Gulch, as Miller calls it, a possible camping spot. But it is early afternoon, much too early. Three people are here gathering huckleberries, which are especially large and plentiful in the burned-over section. They offer to give me a ride to Four Corners, and I gladly accept. My weariness with these mountains is in direct proportion to my desire for a view.

Four Corners. It is exactly what it implies: the road "west" goes every direction of the compass down a precipitous decline to Needle Rock, on the ocean; the road "east" ditto to Thorn, Briceland, and Garberville; and the road "north" by uncounted blind turns and ascents to Shelter Cove. An old yellow highway sign, the kind used by the auto club in the early twenties, at the junction, gives only part of this info. An old shack on the NE corner, the first house I've seen in days, is occupied by an Indian family.

My friends the huckleberriers decide to give me an extra lift, take me up the next incline to a spring where I can camp. But it is still early, and I decide to go on, starting on the long ascent of Whale Gulch grade, on foot. Over the top of this grade, I understand, is the junction with the road down to Shelter Cove.

Maybe it's because I'm beginning to tire, but I swear that the road rises 1,500 feet on Whale Gulch grade. And the man who picked me up says he understands that this ridge road wanders up to 3,000 feet above the sea. He expressed disgust that all the geodetic survey markers through the mountains say: "Elev. _____ Feet" (which I had noticed too). They put in the markers for elevation, many years ago, but never bothered to ascertain, or, at least, *mark* the elevation.

Undoubtedly a dirty Republican, Democratic, Socialist, Communist, or Bureaucratic trick. Take your choice. (I later learned that you can write to Washington, giving the number of the marker and enclosing a stamped, addressed envelope, and obtain the information, if you're that interested. I wasn't.)

He (the huckleberrier) confirms my understanding that sheer rock cliffs prevent any passage along the surf in this section. And he says I don't know the half of it. He drove a Mack truck over this road when he was fourteen—knows the country well.

Whale Gulch grade is a whale of a job, but when I get to the top, finally, I get a view. I see to the south the country I've been through for three days. Ridge after ridge and forested ridge, and uncountable deep ravines. No wonder I'm pooped!

Although these mountains are not so high as the Santa Lucias, south of Big Sur, they are much wilder. Here, the ridges run off in any and every direction, patternlessly, in a jumble, and every slope, unbelievably steep, is forested, except now and then right over the ocean. The Santa Lucias have a high spine, and hogsbacks running down to the ocean from this spine, fairly regularly, and they are wooded only in the canyons and along the spine. And they have no

1,000-foot rock faces falling into the sea. Still, I like the Santa Lucias, because the fewer forests make for frequent expansive views.

I sit and gaze southward from the ridge, but the sun has already dipped below the hulk of the west mountain, that hides Shelter Cove, so I must go on to find a campground.

Some two miles beyond the ridge is a place that might be a beautiful one, under high fir and bay trees. There is a table with benches and a stove, but also papers and cans scattered about in a filthy fashion. Strangely, there is also cut wood, ready for use, and this is true of every campground I've been in. I don't understand the person who inconsiderately dirties a campground but considerately leaves cut wood for the next comer.

There is also a dry fern-leaf mattress on the ground that someone has carefully prepared. I decide to stomach the filth, for the sake of that mattress.

I have salt beef, sweet Pablum, and an apple for supper. I am too tired to build a fire — hiked some seven miles, rode some four (by the map).

But after supper a few mosquitoes bother me, so I build a fire out of rotten wood. It is wasted effort. It is dark now, and the mosquitoes have already vanished.

These coastal mosquitoes are extremely lackadaisical. Just a swish or two discourages them, and I have rarely known them to attack after it really gets dark. I don't know where they go, but presumably they say, "It's time for bed and to hell with you."

The fern-leaf mattress is wonderful!

MONDAY, SEPTEMBER 15 — Fern-Leaf Mattress Camp

I rise groggy, from a sleep of the dead, and after breakfast I unconsciously let out one of my whoops, the kind that used to rock the Gilson piano.[4] And am I startled to hear it resound down this little valley, echoing and reechoing! And then an owl starts hooting, at a time of day when owls should be deep in sleep. I guess I woke him to the belief that he had at last found his long-lost brother!

I pack up and leave, late in the morning, fill up on pears, blackberries, and watercress at Burnt Ranch, an abandoned place recommended to me as a campsite, and arrive at the junction with the Shelter Cove road.

Up another ridge! But here I get a ride, from three fellows in a car, one of whom operates a little resort for hunters and fishers.

And so, after four days of wandering in the mountains for no reason except to get to a place where I can stay with the sea, I finally *get* to the sea. And what a pass!

Shelter Cove. It is so foggy I can't even find the cove, so I look for shelter. I rent a cabin, reconnoiter, and come to a number of conclusions, the sum total of which is very sad, viz., I cannot take my long-planned trip along the beach.

The reasons are fog, low supplies (and no store here), an annoying sinus infection, and the beach itself.

To amplify, the fog that drove me from the beach at Usal is still with us. That south, south wind, and heaven knows how long it will continue! I came to see the country, and this fog blots out all values. I might as well be in the middle of New York City—I'd be just as depressed. How ironic that some of the most beautiful country I have ever seen suffers from this fog curse so much of the year!

I had planned this trip in September because it is generally both fogless and rainless. I see now that I should have waited till October. The early rains are not long ones.

Finally, the beach. I walked west along low sea cliffs about a mile to the place where the beach really begins, and it is extremely impressive. Only once before, at the Waimanalo Beach of dazzling white coral sand on the island of Oahu, has a beach done this to me. This is a series of circular beaches, not of white sand, but something of a slate blue color. And when the savage surf recedes, it makes a sound like steam out of a jet.

After climbing down the cliff to the beach, I saw that it wasn't sand at all, nor blue, but tiny pebbles, black when wet, gray when dry. I suppose the fog, white surf, and eroded yellow rock-and-earth palisades above created the illusion of slate blue. Anyway, I shall call it Slate Blue Beach.

Of course this is effrontery, but not unusual. The Indians already had names for every geographic feature worth naming, and then the Spanish and the English came along and imposed their Sans and Santas and their towns and burgs all over the lot. And so, to me at least, this is Slate Blue Beach.

But the disheartening aspect of the beach is that the feet sink in three or four inches, even in the wet part, at every step. It doesn't pack hard like wet beach sand.

And!—the resort prop tells me it is just like this all the way to Punta Gorda, some thirty miles! He tells me, oh, you can make it all right, but it's tough going!

I walked a ways on it, without a pack, and felt as though I had just climbed Whale Gulch grade with a pack. You need snowshoes to walk this beach.

It's just no go, so I shall return to the viewless mountains tomorrow, where, in between the forests, it is at least warm and sunny. Perhaps I can take the road (hitchhiking this time!) through Ettersburg and Petrolia that finally comes out near the mouth of the Mattole. That Gunga Din who walked the beach from the Eel to Shelter Cove is a better man than I am.

TUESDAY, SEPTEMBER 16—The Land of Old Man Blotto

The old horn is still moaning off the rocks this morning, about one moan a second, and Old Man Blotto is still with us. He has lifted about fifty to one hundred feet here and there, but that south wind, his trusty steed, still carries him billowing in.

I'm through. I pack up my handful of "sand" from Slate Blue Beach, my gear, and depart, up that long, *long* ascent to the ridge (O Lord, how many ridges? *How many?*).

The prop takes pity on me, and carries me in his jeep back to the junction where I started out to Shelter Cove—and back to sunshine. We surely go up here 1,500 feet to the ridge. But I have still another ridge to climb—on foot—not so terribly much higher, thank heaven.

The face and form of Old Man Blotto are very beautiful, as I look down from the ridge, but his digestive organs are damp and nonperistaltic!

All day I hear guns popping off. This is the first day of deer season in Humbolt County, the legal confines of which I am now within. The hunters go around drinking beer and whiskey and shooting at each other, the wardens go around drinking beer and whiskey and hunting for the hunters, and the property owners with No Trespassing signs go around drinking beer and whiskey and letting the air out of the hunters' tires.

The beer and whiskey drinking is only assumption on my part, but the roads are strewn with empty beer cans and whiskey bottles, and I feel morally certain that the deer never touch the stuff.

Trudged up over the second ridge (a tremendous view of seemingly endless mountains to the south from the top) and down into the sawmill settlement of Thorn, getting a ride the last three miles.

Had a good dinner at the restaurant, and watched some men shoot craps on the ground in front (they speak a foreign language), then spent the rest of the afternoon watching at one of the sawmills. They turn a huge fir into two-by-fours in virtually the flick of an eyelash.

I am introduced to a man who is going to Ettersburg, fifteen miles down the road I want to take, after work, and he offers me a lift.

We arrive in Ettersburg (it consists of one building, a combination store and post office about ten by fifteen feet, and a few ranch houses scattered about) just barely in time for me to find a campsite, in the rocky bottoms of the Mattole.

WEDNESDAY, SEPTEMBER 17—Mattole River Camp

It is already mid-morning when the sun rises above the tops of the firs lining the river. I have had breakfast—red lima beans and salt pork (a pot of which I cooked at Shelter Cove) and coffee—after a cold and restless night.

The first thing I notice is a tiny cloud or two moving down from the northwest. Hurrah! Maybe now I can get down to the beach and find a little warmth. Don't ask me why, but at this time of year south wind equals fog, and northwest wind equals sunshine, except that sometimes northwest wind also equals fog, especially in the late evening. (For all I know east wind might equal a new glacial age, but I ain't never seen it.)

I like mountain streams. They are doing something, with certainty and a good deal of direction (I come to this last conclusion only from an examination of the map). And they chatter, in a comforting way, while they do it. The Mattole is like that.

Back to the road. I discover that the road from Ettersburg to Honeydew, where it gets back to the Mattole again, is one of those ridiculous affairs that wants to get on top of everything in sight.

In my ascension to heaven, today I snake over thirteen miles, up and down, back and forth, east, west, north, south, and all their conceivable combinations (but there are some swell views here for a change, e.g., the great mass of 4,000-foot King Peak, just west).

My idea is to hitchhike. That is *my* idea. The road has no such understanding of the situation.

For I discover that it is a one-way road. All day, in my wanderings over these infernal ridges, thirteen cars pass me, *all going the wrong direction.* Not a single car comes along going *my* way.

There are no signs, along this Rideless Road, saying that it is a

one-way street through heaven. Perhaps there is simply an understanding among those who have made the ascension that there is no
going back. That *you only go* one way here. A sort of higher, unwritten
law.

That whenever you get to the appointed place in heaven you just
stay there. Obviously, no one ever comes back. I think wryly that
wherever that place is it must have a terrific overpopulation.

I am thoroughly disgusted with the direction this trip is taking.
I do not want to go to heaven. This is not the way I foresaw it at
all—*at all.*

I foresaw warming my feet in idle hours on strange beaches.
Instead, I am getting sore dogs in man-killing hours on strange ridges.

> Hallelujah, I'm a nangel.
> If I were a cockney I'd be a hangel.

I stumble into Honeydew (God knows where it ever got that
name) long after dark. But the little store (the only, and—I might
say—doubtful, evidence of Honeydew) is still open, and somewhat
reluctantly I am directed to a campground across the river.

I make tea, reinforce it with a bit of rum, have a bit of dried
beef, and go to bed. (I also beef like hell.)

THURSDAY, SEPTEMBER 18—Honeydew

I get out of camp very early, just as the sun is coming above
whichever of the thousand and one ridges it comes above this time
of year. I am only twenty-four miles from the beach, and I shall
hitchhike my damnedest to make it today, for it looks crystal clear
out that way.

But I might as well have stayed in bed. No rides at all. I have
walked ten miles, along the banks of the Mattole, where the road
now runs—it has given up climbing the ridges, hallelujah—when I
find a pretty little hunters' camp overlooking the river, about middle
afternoon.

I make camp, wash my clothes, hair, and bathe, and go swimming
in a rocky pool which is away over my head. And decide that this
isn't such a bad route after all.

One of the peculiar things about the Mattole Valley is the absence
of redwoods. All the big trees are firs. I see neither young redwoods
nor the huge blackened stumps (evidence of previous logging) that
have been so frequent before. I ask about it, and am told that redwoods

never grew here, while just a few miles to the east, on the Eel River, which roughly parallels the Mattole, are the tallest and oldest redwoods found anyplace. Strange, a fir island in a redwood sea.

A hunter drops in after dark to camp with me, fries some trout he has just caught, and insists that I join him in his supper. I don't need much persuading.

FRIDAY, SEPTEMBER 19—Mattole River Camp No. 3

My hunter friend asks me to help him eat up his provisions. All these hunters bring the comforts of home with them: cots, sleeping bags, grates, coffee pots, and virtually the entire contents of the kitchen cupboard. He makes a cheese and onion omelet that is perfectly delicious, and with this we have toast, jelly, and coffee.

Now he is gone, and I've run out of tobacco. So I try various dried leaves in my corncob. Madrone makes the sweetest smoke, and mixed with a little tobacco is quite satisfying. Redwood needles are next best; quite mild. Eucalyptus leaves give me visions, and a pipeful of bay leaf is almost equal to a knockout drop.

When my clothes are dry I start out, but disgust rides high with me again. This is the third day of a northwest wind; I can see that it is beautifully clear out on the coast, but again, all the cars are going in the wrong direction. What is this? The Great Circle Tour? In which I am the Famous Minority of One?

I walk the remaining six miles into Petrolia, and at last my luck changes. Mrs. Adams, in the general store, hears my story and takes an immediate interest. She tells everyone who comes in: "Here's a gentleman who wants to see our country. He's walked all the way from Rockport. Now he wants to get on the beach. Please do anything you can for him."

She gives me papers and magazines and introduces me to some Coast Guardsmen who offer to take me to a good camping spot. We drive in their truck to the north side of the Mattole's outlet to the sea, where there is a spring. Here they change from truck to team and wagon, with which they go along the beach four more miles to their station, beyond Punta Gorda. This is the only such station in the country, they tell me, the only one that can't be gotten to by truck.

They also offer me the room where the horses' hay is kept to sleep in. And since the nights are getting colder, I happily accept.

(Last night I was glad to see daylight come, so I could get up and build a fire.)

SUNDAY, SEPTEMBER 21—Mattole Mouth Camp

After two days of lying naked in the sun, I am still exhausted from my strenuous and heavenly sojourn. But this is more like what I went after! I am living in a beautiful arc of beach that ends to the north some twelve miles away at Cape Mendocino. Three huge head-lands, separated by canyons, front it.

Driftwood covers the beach everywhere above the high tide lines—its fantastic forms sand-scoured, salted, bleached. The driftwood I have encountered on this trip alone would provide fireplace fuel for the whole state for at least a winter. After soaking in the sea and drying in the beach sun, it makes colorful fires, with flames that range from the usual yellow to a deep chrome yellow, pale lavender, and pale green. But it cannot be used in cookstoves, I understand; it ruins grates.

The people around Petrolia seem extraordinarily friendly. I felt a slap on my back in the store, and—half expecting to turn around to face some chum of long-gone school days—found the man who had gotten me a ride to Ettersburg from Thorn. And last night, walking up to the spring, in late evening, without a shirt, a man came along in a truck, offered to take me to the store. I jumped in, because, in my weariness the day before, I had forgotten a few items. But it was getting chilly, and this man tossed me his wool jacket. "You can leave it at the Coast Guard station when you pull out," he says cheerily.

He introduced himself as Ernie Lanini, and owner of the property where I am camping.

In the store I met two Indian families living near the mouth of the river. And an old one-eyed Indian, Weaver Denman, invited me up to his mountainside shack to hear Klamath tribal songs.

Then this morning Lanini and his wife came by in their truck, passing a half gallon of muscatel back and forth between them (and me) while they were talking, and invited me to inspect their ranch, on the bluff overlooking my campground.

They have a cabin two or three hundred feet up, by a very steep and rocky road, which they occupy only when lambing (they are sheep and cattle raisers). It has a linoleum floor, wood stove, well-stocked cupboard, sink with running spring water, Aladdin lamps, and a big bed.

"Come up and camp here," said Lanini. I am bent on going north tomorrow, so he added, "Come up and stay here anytime!" Then, "You ought to be able to write Waltz of the Sea Breezes here!"

It has a tremendous view of Cape Mendocino and the whole of the lower Mattole Valley, with its backdrop of peaks.

I had asked the Laninis when they would bring me back to the beach, and they replied, "Right away." But these are easygoing people, and I should have realized that "right away" means sometime before next week. We arrive back much too late for me to climb the mountain road to hear Klamath songs.

I have been on or at least seen all the coast I intended to see except that between Shelter Cove and Punta Gorda, because of fog mostly. My curiosity urges me southward around Punta Gorda, at least to see this coast. But my wretched sinus urges me back to warm rooms and warm beds. "I feel for you, but I can't quite reach you," I say to Punta Gorda in glass eye language.

This one section of coastline, and the Klamath songs, I shall have to postpone to a more auspicious occasion.

MONDAY, SEPTEMBER 22—Mattole Mouth Camp

I get started fairly early. The tide is already flowing, and, as I reckon, will be high about eleven. This is not the best beach-walking time, but I anticipate no great trouble, looking at the coastline ahead.

I wade across the Mattole at the bar, and at the first rocky point north I suddenly come upon a beached whale, about forty to fifty feet long, yellow and almost mummified with salt and sun. Surprisingly little odor. I had seen the yellow something at the point from my camp, but myopia stymied ascertainment.

The beach is pretty fair walking on the wet sand. I play tag with the surf, but the way I play it the surf is always It. Now and then It gets me, and I have to race around two or three points when breakers recede, not always too successfully.

The beaches are mostly broad, but quite dark, with pebbly or rocky sections frequent. And black rocks, some with guano frosting, dot the near ocean.

This is the way I planned it! And the first day I could really do it. It is cloudy (not foggy) all day, but I don't mind, after so much sunny weather.

About noontime I come upon a shallow cave, and at the entrance to it are seventy-five to one hundred hornets' nests, or some kind of flying-animal nests, huddled together like the mud huts of Inca peasants. Each has its central "smoke hole." Also, farther on, a beautiful arch of rock, through which I triumphantly pass.

I arrive at what I presume to be Davis Creek (I had been told about it) after walking eight or nine miles. The road from Petrolia to Capetown comes out on the beach near here, and under the bridge over the creek I find a campground. It is not the prettiest in the world, but here is water, and the bridge will give me some protection in case of rain, which is certainly threatening.

(Just saw four legs walking on a hill. Saw them beneath the lower line of the bridge, but couldn't tell whether they were two men or a cow. It certainly is getting misty.)

My marine jungle knife hangs on my belt. I almost never use it except in cooking and to sharpen pencils. Some way, every time I get it out, I feel like an amateur Macbeth drawing his sword. (Careful, pal. That comes awful close to a literary observation!)

Had hotcakes, cold Pablum (will this Pablum never end?), bacon, tea, and cucumbers for supper. I hadn't had a green vegetable in days, and the cucumbers tasted grand. They were manna from heaven. I dunno where they came from. Just fell over the side of the bridge. Mebbe they fell off a truck, although I didn't hear one. (Sermon of the Open Road No. 1—Camp under a bridge and ye shall receive!)

TUESDAY, SEPTEMBER 23—Davis Creek

Feel like my back was broken. I dreamt that a gopher was digging a hole, and that it was pushing the dirt in various places up under me. My bed was that rocky.

But I have a breakfast of crisp bacon and limp Pablum (there it is again!) and strong coffee long before the sun rises (which isn't as ambitious as it sounds; these eastern hills are high), shave, pack, and depart. I am not sorry to leave this stony pallet.

No, it didn't rain, and, except for fog on the western horizon, it is beautiful.

But I get out on the road and change my tune. It turns out to be an ugly day. The wind whistles on points of rock, not at all seductively, and Old Man Blotto lurks no more than a hundred yards away. At the turn of the fog, above the cape, the sun makes it a snowy cloud bank, the only nice thing about this scene.

At Lanini's suggestion I call at Ocean House, just south of the point (at the cape), and am invited to lunch by Mr. and Mrs. Joe Russ.

They say lunch, but it turns out to be a very large meal, topped off with homemade chocolate pie. (Joe Russ makes me feel no better — tells me I missed the most scenic part of this coast, between Shelter Cove and Punta Gorda.)

The Russes advise me to call at the old lighthouse, which I proceed to do, high on the next grade. Here I meet Roy Crockett and his wife and baby, and have coffee, cake, and ice cream (and talk about Schoenberg and the atonal scale, at Crockett's prompting) on what is described by some maps of California as the "Westernmost Point in Continental United States."

It is perhaps a matter of incidental interest that I have also seen maps of Oregon that give the same information in regard to Cape Blanco, and maps of Washington indubitably the same in regard to Cape Flattery, on the Olympic peninsula.

Well, they could all be right, I suppose. Perhaps the "Westernmost Point in Continental United States" ends in a westerly dead heat — Blanco, Mendocino, and Flattery.

But mapmakers might be more specific. That is: "One of *Three* Westernmost Points in Continental United States," but this would be ambiguous, and it would remove the fascination of *the one* "mostest." Or, being less specific, they could simply put it, "A *Superlative* Western Point in Continental United States," but this would be subject to misinterpretation, as Livia[5] at the proper occasion might remark.

It's hardly important. Still, this simple claim, "Westernmost Point in Continental United States," encountered in three different states of these United States, is slightly annoying.

Of course it could be that Cape Blanco is seven-tenths of a foot farther west at low tide than Capes Mendocino and Flattery at low tide, but also that once upon a time a low tide was recorded at Mendocino which made it three-tenths of a foot farther west than anything recorded at Blanco. And, further, that Washington, not to be outpublicized, dumped a carload of granite at the tip of Cape Flattery, which nosed out the daily claim at Blanco by a full tenth of a foot.

The subject could induce hysteria.

"We're farther west than you are," say the Blancoques.

"Maybe you are, but you weren't," say the Mendocinese.

"Maybe you were, but you aren't," say the Flatterites.

"*Bul*-loney," say the Blancoques.

"*Mul*-larkey," say the Mendocinese.

"*Hog*-washey," say the Flatterites.

"We'll blast you off the map," say the Blancoques.

"There are roses in Picardy, but your mapmaking days are in jeopardy," say the Mendocinese.

"Capes may come and capes may go, and we know a couple that may go damn fast," say the Flatterites.

Boomaty-Boomaty-Boom!

Then, when the dust clears, and with the rocky tips completely gone from Capes Blanco, Mendocino, and Flattery, the respective claimants that have survived—the Blancoques, the Mendocinese, and the Flatterites—look off to the south and see poor little old Punta Gorda, which no one had paid any particular attention to before, but which is now, definitely, without a doubt and without a shadow of competition, the "Westernmost Point in Continental United States."

Then they all suddenly and remorsefully realize that they have been the victims of mapmakers' propaganda.

Roy Crockett says it is his recollection, looking through lighthouse records, that Blanco is several miles "farther west," and he doesn't know about Flattery. Enough of that.

The weather does not improve as the day wears on, and I can easily see that beyond the protecting point of the cape the coast is blotted out completely. Fog and wind in a perfect synthesis come around the point in a way to knock you frigidly flat. There is nothing to gain in continuing this trip, especially since I am approaching the beaches where Eurekans picnic. Crockett kindly takes me the four miles to Capetown (no longer with even a store), and here he gets me a ride the remaining seventeen miles to Fernbridge (with the schoolteacher at Capetown), across the Eel River on the Redwood Highway.

But the Redwood Highway is old stuff, and so is the Eel River. (And the place where the Eel runs to is older stuff still.)

PART 2

ESSAYS AND LECTURES

Patterns of Music

1940

He is an artist. Before him is a scale of colors, and in his mind he approaches the reds. For his brush's immediate use he sees a carmine, a vermilion, a scarlet, a crimson, a cerise, a garnet, a ruby, and verging off into other color values are an orchid and a magenta, a nasturtium and an orange, and a sienna, a rust, and an ochre.

He ponders leisurely. No, the exact shade he envisions—despite the great variety at hand—isn't here. With the assurance born of a life spent in being able to get what he wants, he then mixes—in just the right proportions—a bit of white, rust, and cerise to his vermilion, and—there! He has it!

Consider the writer of music. Before him is also a scale. It holds seven white keys and five black ones. In his mind he approaches C-sharp, one of the five blacks. He approaches it, and he lands on it. His action is direct, simple, predetermined.

There are no shades of C-sharp, no shades of red, for him. The one shade that his gods will allow him to use is before him. He is taught that that is enough; it is good, traditional, and proper, and he feels a vague sense of immorality in even wondering about those possible bastard C-sharps.

The present-day musician might observe: "If he doesn't like C-sharp he has D," which paraphrases: "He has yellow; why must he be so difficult as to also want vermilion?"

With the disquietude born of a life getting substitutes for nearly everything he really wants, the composer yearns for the streaking shades of sunset. He gets red. He longs for geranium, and gets red.

He dreams of tomato, but he gets red. He doesn't want red at all, but he gets red, and is presumed to like it. But does he?

Another picture. It is that of a poet in torment over a line, and—to particularize—let us conjure a vision of Hart Crane laboring over the handful of words which, referring to the ocean, end: "Her undinal vast belly moonward bends."[1]

There is no intention here to divine the thought processes of Crane in coming at last to this particular beauty of word cadence. But—were Hart Crane a composer of music—it would be exceedingly easy to unravel his processes, and, because his medium wouldn't allow him subtle and unusual shadings, he would never, never arrive at—"Her undinal vast belly moonward bends."

He would tentatively write: "The deep blue ocean moonward bends—"

Or: "With the moon rolls the boundless deep—"

Or, if he wanted to be modern: "Mooncalls sea-ocean bluedeep rolling—"

"Deep blue ocean" was and is used to excess by every writer of music since Palestrina. "The boundless deep" dates from Schubert and John Field, and is still widely used, and the last version is a fair literary paraphrase of most modern tonality—a cliché hash.

Before he ever writes a note the most brilliant composer is doomed to a system that is not capable of growth at his hands—or even of elasticity—and thus to a weary sea of worn-out forms, phrases, progressions, cadences, and chords.

Perhaps better than in any other way the two pictures above explain the reason for my musical heresy. The wayward trail began eighteen years ago, and, having traveled it all—inch by inch—I would not recommend it to others too heartily.

The great cathedral of modern music, erected in trial and labor and pain through most of the Christian era, is a safe and beautiful sanctuary. Its one sad aspect is that it seems to be finished—there is so little, if anything, that is significant that can be added to it. On the other hand, in the wild, little-known country of subtle tones beyond the safe cathedral, the trails are old and dim, they disappear completely, and there are many hazards.

The zealot driving into this wilderness should have more than one life to give: one to create instruments within the tyranny of the five-fingered hand, to play the tones he finds; one that will wrestle with notation and theory, so that he can make a record of what he finds, and give it understandable exposition; still another that will create and re-create significant music for his new-old instruments and in his new-old media; and, finally, another that will perform it, give it—as a revelation—to the general wealth of human culture.

It is not so simple as the few minutes' work of dabbing colors together from the already rich language of color. It is not so simple as combining a few choice words from the already rich language of words. It is the long, painful process of making less poor the pathetically impoverished language of tone.

The present book shows how the bonds of the composer might be, and are being, burst—how that which is too limited is being delimited. It is not a new trail in itself. It is only a survey—but a survey of all trails, both old and projected, and of one particular new trail.

Hence, *Patterns of Music*.

Bach and Temperament

1941

In kneeling before the tonal benedictions provided by a Bach festival, we are apt to forget that the blessings of this music so freely called "immortal" are not unmixed.

Johann Sebastian Bach casts two distinct shadows upon the historic screen of musical culture. One aspect orientates the tones he used — his system. The second delineates his music.

A musician said to me recently: "Why must you insist on music being a 'system'? Why not accept it as a God-given fact!" It may be a shock to some musicians, but our present "system" was not handed out of the clouds of Mount Sinai. It was born in the throes of labor and pain.

From the time of Gregorian chant it was inevitable that a Bach would one day appear. Music was veering away from the linear, becoming harmonic, and attaining a status independent of poetry and the dance. Consequently, instruments with harmonic versatility — keyboard instruments — became the intellect of the new music.

To musicians of ancient Greece and medieval times, the problem of dividing the octave into arbitrary parts was only a mathematical teaser. They conceived of scales in true acoustical relationships, as the human ear demands, in simple ratios to one fundamental.

The new music, however, demanded that any one of several tones of a keyboard be used as a fundamental. Tones were therefore deliberately falsified, or compromised — only a few at first; later, all. And the ancient idea of simple ratios was junked.

The modern musician doesn't talk in plain terms, such as the painter's red, purple, blue, but in a cant — an idiom peculiar to the genus musician. He talks of A-flat, B-sharp, tonic, mediant, dominant. And this strange language developed with and largely because of the above-described falsifications.

In meantone temperament, used before Bach's time, sixteen keys (major and minor) were fairly good, but the other eight were so bad that musicians compared them with the "howling of wolves." To render all keys equally bad, so that there would be no contrast, seemed the only solution. Having fallen into a sea of compromise, it was the most natural thing in the world for musical Europe to sink.

To Bach's patternistic intellectuality, the solution was a godsend. He could now put one of his themes through a dozen keys in a dozen variations and involutions—double-timed, quadruple-timed, half-timed, inverted, retrogressed—and it would still be the exact interval pattern of the original.

Thus have twelve equal tones become Mosaic law, and the *Well-Tempered Clavichord* the Arc of the Covenant.

The human ear is capable of a keen appreciation and classification of intervals, if it is given half a chance. Teachers frequently deplore the lack of "ear" in their pupils, but what strange judges they are, since their own "ears" have had a lifetime of training in falsity.

An examination of Bach's second shadow reveals the whole trend of music since Gregorian chant as a tangent to the main historic stream. The ancient Greek and Chinese conception—as old as history—that music is poetry has deteriorated until now; even when words are used, they are merely a vehicle for tones. The voice is just another violin, or another cello.

With this metamorphosis was the ancient conception lost? By no means. It was obscured, left to folk peoples—sailors, soldiers, gypsies. But it flowed on in a broad deep stream, in the troubadours of Provence, the Meistersingers of Nuremberg, the Japanese Noh and kabuki, the recitative of Peri and Monteverdi (not the vocal tour de force of present-day recitative), the folk music of England and our own southern mountains, the pure Negro spiritual (not "symphonized"), and a minor degree in both Wagner and Debussy.

The music of the symphony, the chorale, the oratorio, in which those contributing must submerge their identities to the will of a leader, is an art of mass-massed tones, massed instruments, massed voices, and hearers are transported by sheer mass and volume.

The music of the historic concept involves the greatest economy of materials, and hearers are transported not by mass, but subtlety.

The one is the true music of autocracy. The other is the true music of the individual.

In this sense, and also as one of the props of our tonal priests, Bach, however legitimate, is potentially as great a limiting influence as the twelve equal tones he helped to perpetuate.

W. B. Yeats

1941

"Many years ago," said William Butler Yeats, "I received a letter from a man asking permission to use 'The Lake Isle of Innisfree,' the theme of which is a search for greater solitude, as the setting for a song. I granted permission.

"Some time thereafter I received another letter from the same man, inviting me to a certain occasion, to hear my poem sung by 300 assembled boy scouts."

Yeats was discussing one of his great passions—and great disillusionments—the setting of his texts to music.

"I made it a practice, for some time after that, to refuse everyone," said Yeats. "Then, later, I decided that was a mistake, and granted permission without exception."

Throughout his life Yeats looked in vain for music suitable to the ancient feeling of Irish legend which he expressed so eminently in words. But musicians, knowing only one way to set words to music, in song or opera, had no ear for his pleas. They saw music only as abstract form, whether words were used or not, as in German lieder, and Yeats had no patience with this.

"There is something in the Irish soul that rejects abstraction," he said.

Looking for the exact opposite of the over-harmonized and complex symphony, he went on, "I am inclined to sympathize with the remark by Arnold Dolmetsch[1] that modern musical instruments have followed the Darwinian law of the survival of the loudest, and also with that Irishman who, in his rebellion against abstraction and symphonic complexity, wrote all his music for drum and tin whistle."

This was in 1934, nearly five years previous to the great poet's death. I had asked his permission to set his version of Sophocles' *King Oedipus*, in its entirety, which he had promptly given, and I had taken my viola to his house at Rathfarnham, on the outskirts of Dublin, to give a demonstration of my work.

I sensed guarded worry and disbelief, however, even when I went ahead with my exposition, chanting the words of the 137th Psalm to the tones of my viola.[2] Now, in the flood of comment that followed my playing, the feeling of disbelief was entirely dispelled.

Some six years before my meeting with Yeats, and after many years of dark groping, I had eventually come to his conclusions about music and musical instruments. Beginning with a single string, I had evolved a musical system much like the ancient Greeks with their monochords. My viola, with its long neck, was actually a glorified Euclid monochord, with the marks for forty-three true musical ratios indicated on its fingerboard.

My single instrument then became the basis for use of words after the ancient manner, with their inherent rhythm and tones preserved.

It was all intuitive. I did not know that this was a system, both of music and manner of creating music, that was the oldest in the world. And, finally, I did not know that a famous Irish poet had given some of his best prose to enunciating the same theme.

Yeats had been continually misunderstood on his attitude toward music, even by his Irish compatriots. The late George Russell, the famous AE, poet friend of Yeats, said to me, when he was told that I was involved with Yeats in an interpretation of *Oedipus:* "Did you know that Yeats has no feeling for music, that he doesn't know one note from another, and that he can't carry a tune?"

The calumnies of such observation, which are commonplace utterances, are manifold.

"No feeling for music" might mean several things—no feeling for the eighteenth-century golden age of European music, for example. Or, no feeling for Japanese Noh, or no feeling for American jazz and swing. But "no feeling for music" as an idea is literally an impossibility in the human animal.

And the inability to carry a tune is more like hypersensitivity to tone. Such a person hears all the tones in the gamut, instead of the seven or eight or twelve our musical fathers have insisted must be our limit.

In answer to such critics I like to quote Yeats's own words: "I hear with older ears than the musician."[3]

Indeed, the oldest music of the human race, in which the octave was an unlimited field for fancy, and in which there was no *bel canto* mockery of words.

"We require a method of setting to music that will make it possible to sing or to speak . . . in such a fashion that no word shall have an intonation or accentuation it could not have in passionate speech. . . . It will be necessary to divine the lineaments of a still older art, and re-create the regulated declamations that died out when music fell into its earliest elaborations," Yeats wrote.[4]

During my ten or so days in Dublin, I induced Yeats to assist me in interpreting *Oedipus*. This was not easy because he was continually doubtful, after years of attack that he was not "musical," of his ability to help.

He intoned the choruses, and I can still hear his reading of the line:

For Death is all the fashion now, till even Death be dead.[5]

I made diagrams of his inflections, but my memory of his vibrant tones is more accurate than my marks.

Yeats also invited Abbey Theatre actors to help me, and I outlined my plans and the instruments I would use, which he tentatively approved. I had with me a model of my Chromatic Organ, one of several instruments I felt I must complete to do justice to the setting.

The console of the Chromatic Organ, shown in the photograph, has forty-three tones arranged much like a typewriter. It is designed on a pattern of the hand (as in photograph), and a chromatic scale of forty-three tones is then a simple five-finger exercise over eight patterns, which is possible with great manual ease.

Console is only a model. It was given sound by a London organ builder, but the mechanical solution was faulty. Consequently, I was forced to abandon all but the keyboard idea itself.

Yeats gave me letters of introduction in London, among persons he thought might help and sympathize, and spoke of a theater and chanters for an eventual performance.

But Yeats was too early for me, and I was too late for Yeats.

He had been through many illnesses, he had already given a long lifetime to beauty as he saw it, and he had not the vitality to plunge into the problem that had baffled him in earlier years.

At the conclusion of my last visit to "Riversdale," though he was not well, he insisted on accompanying me to the bus which would take me back to Dublin.

"You are one of those young men with ideas, the development of which it is impossible to foretell, just as I was thirty years ago."

Then my bus came in sight around a turn. Yeats stood directly in the middle of the road, to bring it to a stop. We waved good-bye, and in a very little while I was on my boat headed for Liverpool.

But in my mind I still saw a large man in the middle of a road before an oncoming bus, his hands upraised, his huge figure physically blocking its passage.

That was my final picture, because I never saw Yeats again.

The Kithara

1941

It is one of those much-fictioned London days, gray fog in the shadows, silver in the light. I step from the busy street into a booth, drop my two big pennies into the slot, and call my number.

Someone answers. I try to be brief. I haven't much time left in London. Would it be possible for me to see the kithara? Yes. Then could I possibly come to tea that very afternoon? Yes, indeed, I could.

The "Tube" speeds me to Highgate, and in a moment I am knocking on a door. The maid says, "Miss Schlesinger is expecting you."

Kathleen Schlesinger, one of the greatest of English musical scholars, contributor of many articles on ancient instruments to *Encyclopaedia Britannica*, writer of a Greek musical theory through twenty years of devoted labor, greets me.

I do not need any letter of introduction. Nor anyone to bespeak me. For she is gracious and sympathetic, and, though I am a stranger, I need no further introduction than my interest in the kithara.

She is quite old, and she tells me she has been ill most of the winter. Will I have tea? It is brought in at that moment on a tea wagon, piled high with food and on the lower deck sweets, and there are the inevitable two teapots—one India and one China, each in its cozy.

Now, suddenly, on the piano bench, I see the kithara. The kithara! ancient mother of nearly all modern string instruments.

It is given to a few in this world to know the remains of the glory that was Greece through vision. But how infinitely small is the number who know the glory that was Greece through hearing!

Not for Kathleen Schlesinger are the dull theories about ancient modes, the ancient intervals, the ancient manner. For her the ancient things still live, because she makes them live.

All about the room are flutes and auloi, reconstructed from vase drawings, and from other data. And this zealot for the ancient things has actually determined in vibrations per second the "nete," or starting point, of the Greek scale.

Over tea she tells me the story of the kithara:

". . . it was on a vase in the museum: yes, the British Museum. I made a pattern out of brown wrapping paper, in the same proportions as on the vase, but of course much larger (the kithara is thirty-two inches high, twenty-two inches wide), as large as I determined it must be. But violin makers wouldn't handle it—no one would make it for me. Then one day while I had my pattern out, pondering what to do with it next, a man came in to read my gas meter. He looked at my pattern and said, unhesitatingly, 'I'll make it for you, Miss Schlesinger.' And so he went to work, but it was during the last war, and wood was practically unobtainable. He finally made it out of a discarded orange box. . . ."

She walks over and touches the strings, and even though she touches them ever so lightly, deep vibrations fill the room.

". . . It has quite a lovely tone. Don't you think so? And it is a beautiful piece. . . ."

Kathleen Schlesinger leaves me alone for a little while then, and I examine and measure the instrument, and pluck the strings. The kithara was the lyre of professional Greek musicians.

Yes, it is a beautiful piece. (The reader may see it here in simple line drawing). I, too, must have one. . . .

Three and a half years pass. I am only now ready to build the kithara that I determined I must have that day in Highgate.

My design is not strictly ancient Greek. It is, I like to imagine, a development of the kithara that the Greeks would have evolved themselves had they remained culturally vital.

I had drawn the design almost immediately after leaving Kathleen Schlesinger's, and I had taken it to my sculptor friend, Gordon Newell,[1] in Los Angeles, to criticize.

"These lines are bad," he said. "They fly out."

"Make them good," I replied, and Gordon took a large sheet of paper and rapidly sketched lines. It took him perhaps fifteen seconds.

And the modern Kithara shown in the photograph is that quick sketch come to life. The body, of redwood, is constructed in the wood shops of the adult education classes in Los Angeles.

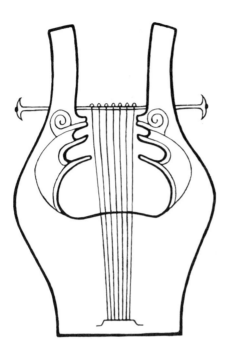

Three more years pass. Many ideas have to be changed. The inside structure won't stand the strain of my seventy-two strings, and the upper and lower parts are entirely rebuilt three separate times.

And now the instrument must have a base, since it is much too large to be held in the arm, after the usual Greek manner.

Rambling around the bottom of the canyon at Anderson Creek, at the old Convict Camp south of Big Sur, I find a huge block of redwood. It is evidently a remnant from the great redwood supports for the high bridge at Anderson Creek, built six years ago. But it has not rotted very much.

With a bit of planing, here is the base for my Kithara!

And now the instrument that had its conception in a little room in Highgate, London, in 1935, has come to completion in Carmel in 1941.

My interest in building this instrument was not theoretical. From the first I had a definite and important role for it to fill. I had already made plans to set the entire drama *King Oedipus*, the version by William Butler Yeats, to music. I had gotten Yeats's cooperation in interpreting the lines, and I was casting about, at the time I read of Kathleen

Schlesinger's kithara, for instruments with which to execute this setting.

With a noble quality, and with an extraordinary "sing" to its tone, the Kithara is ideal for accompanying and musically complementing the spreading paternal spirit of Oedipus, and for providing rational dynamics throughout the rise to the great denouement—"Oh! Oh! All brought to pass! All truth! . . ."

At this writing *Oedipus* is still the immediate objective in making the Kithara strings actually vibrate. But in the growth of the work of which the Kithara is only a detail, I shall doubtless find many uses for it, alone, in conjunction with other instruments, and with voice.

The obscure craftsman who delicately limned the outlines of a kithara on a vase 2,500 years ago started more than he could possibly imagine.

Show Horses in the Concert Ring

1948

The profession of music is lacking in horse sense, not only because the commonplace variety of horse is absent from its operations, but because parts of horses are noticeably present. The profession is indeed carried on by people, but by people who have forgotten the human ear. Its pattern of education denies the only logical starting point for a genuinely creative art of music—the ear, and the manifold delights and stimuli that the ear, in conjunction with the experienced mind, can find in the exercise of imagination. To spotlight this fault is necessarily a critical procedure: no service is rendered either to oneself or to music by minimizing clearly seen evidences of illness and decay, and suggestions for investigation and positive rebuilding can be only briefly touched. The matter of exact methods of correction and a detailed conclusion is a huge subject.

This diagnosis is largely concerned with the obvious, but let no one assume that to state the obvious in music is necessarily a dull and pointless procedure. Simply because of widespread neglect, the musical obvious is a field for extensive commentary and intensive speculation, revealing as to pointed particulars and broad in scope. It is a skeleton in a closet which, in true abstract style, has bred a whole race of skeletons in closets, without flesh, and conceived therefore without contact of flesh. It is an unmentionable, a *terra incognita* to musicians, for musicians have been educated away from the only attitudes that would make its exploration valuable or even recognizable.

The initial evidence [for] lack of curiosity is our interpretive age in so-called serious music. We learn to play music written by others, mostly long dead. We emphasize perfection of digital control, polish of phrase, "musical tone" in the voice. We accept without even a gesture of investigation any instrument, any scale, any asinine nomenclature, any rules—stated or implied—found in the safety-deposit boxes of various eighteenth-century Germanic gentlemen whom we and our immediate antecedents have been dragooned into idolizing. And we permit an industrialization of music on the basis of such parlous degeneracy: issuance of interpretation upon interpretation of the accepted limited repertory by the record companies; facture on an assembly line of the accepted musical instruments— required by that accepted repertory—by other companies; the publishing of the music of that accepted repertory—for the same accepted instruments and in whatever asinine notation and implied nomenclature they require—by still other companies, and so on, perennially sporting a bloom of pride over the magnificent spread of our culture. The "so on" stands for literally thousands of scholarly magazine articles, whole walls of libraries stacked with sciolist praise, ubiquitous classes in music appreciation, multiplex radio programs, all deliberately calculated to weight us permanently with the incubi and the succubi of an interpretive age; that is, with a factitious, noncreative art. The only real vitality in this entire picture is exuded by the men who are out to make money in the deal.

The house of music is freshly painted in a proper—that is to say, conservative—color, its front lawn is perfectly clipped, its flower beds scratched and banked. Its backyard is raked—not a leaf falls that is not dutifully snatched up and deposited in the proper receptacle. Its garbage can is sterilized daily, and well sealed. Inside the house everything is consonant with the outdoor department; one could eat his peas and chops off the floor. Alas! there is more than one trouble with this establishment, for it is not just obnoxiously and studiously proper. It reeks of stodgy, frustrated human beings.

Value of intrinsic content—value of human beings, of human works and attitudes—never enters this picture. It is never discussed by those who habitually beat their feet in the menage. Discussion or any inference of the basic philosophies of life is strictly taboo. The place operates by code, by formula. The house is a showcase—everything polished, everything perfect, everything correctly interpreted and reinterpreted ad infinitum, everything accepted in the terms of the will—a will that is taken as a *corpus juris* which sets forth all our ancestors' house rules and stipulates their furniture, but leaves their humanity somewhere else. To prove that we have lost their humanity, that to regain their humanity we must renounce the suffocating atmosphere of their house, one needs only to point to the degeneration of an interpretive age that the tenure of their house has led to.

Our honored ancestors were not averse to investigating the physical nature of music, yet our reverence for them is so excessive that many of us would prefer musical suicide to the harboring of even a suggestion that we might more advantageously work from other conclusions. The system of theory and usages which they evolved was once a bright plump fruit. It is now a lemon squeezed out of its last spot of juice, so wasted that chunks of the dissonant abstract are virtually all there is left—chunks of bitter, acrid rind. A little of the rind is tasty, but a little goes a long way.

The emphasis on polish—the papistical proscription of any physical investigation with a creative purpose—brings to music a mandarin artificiality that attracts too many of the wrong kind of poets. It need hardly be labored that music is a physical art, and that a periodic groping into the physical, a reaching for an understanding of the physical, is the only basic procedure, the only way a musical era will attain any enduring significance. Those musicians who say, "I am interested in music—what has music to do with physics?" gloss over the fact that they accept the piano and its despotic influence over the form and use of other instruments as their basis of music. These are physical things, brought to their present state by physical processes and philosophical modes of thought. They are an end, not a beginning. Were the musician able to create the actual sounds of music for an audience merely by thinking—by standing in the center of a stage, raising one hand to heaven, and pressing an auricular nerve with the index finger of the other—entirely without physical appurtenances aside from his own admittedly versatile anatomy, his attitude would be valid. Under the circumstances it is not only not valid but a dreadful commentary upon his particular vicious circle: a pseudo- (interpretive) art attracting misled (interpretive) minds.

Some very drastic remedies are called for in order to bring vitality to a body of theory that rejects investigation and a physical poetry that excludes all but purely metaphysical poets. A period of comparative anarchy, with each composer employing his own instrument or instruments, his own scale, his own forms, is very necessary for a way out of this malaise. With his compositions recorded the composer could continue to grow and develop, wasting no time on the preservation of a technique for continuous replayings, and leaving the mark of his efforts in a definite state of completion. With the age of recordings actually upon us, the whole body of interpretive musicians is very close to being an anachronism, thank heaven; we have only to guard against any untoward signs of vigor in the normal process of demise. The formal and degenerate concert system is close to kibosh, and the livelihood of critics whose sole purpose in existence is the weighing of one interpretation against another is propitiously jeopardized, thank God.

In a more vital era the creative faculties would be encouraged in babies, and not stifled, as they are now, in the acquiring of technique, and practice—practice—practice, through infancy, latency, puberty, and an indefinitely prolonged immaturity for the sole purpose of making an interpreter and a show horse. Perhaps no element of modern life is so stifling—so destroys a human being—as this idol of digital and laryngeal proficiency. I know; I experienced it, and had to die and find still another womb to emerge from.

The advice of our powers in music is one-track and repetitious: "Do not aspire to be a musician," they say, "a pianist, singer, a conductor, or a composer—unless recognized authorities affirm your talent." Wot whrot! In a world grown haggard from the keenness of competition between cyphers, it is hard to conceive of anything more idiotic than to worry about the development of some given individual as a concert personality; whether the authorities accept or reject him is inconsequential; in the face of historical fact it takes an unconscionable effrontery to assume that the authorities have ever been anything but timid, reluctant, flippant, or passively hostile when forced to rein up before truly creative faculties. It is too easy to throw prophets' robes on both authorities and creators after they are dead, and the pattern of musical education—which creates the authorities—is against any individualistic determination and, so far as my readings of history indicate, always has been. Civilized man pours his authorities from a pot in a cozy.

If I were to choose a single dominant adjective to describe human beings, that adjective would be *creative*. If we are human, we are also creative, unless—of course—we are educated into interprepoops— into show horses, and I for one would feel less apprehensive for a future world in which everyone would be a creator in realms artistic or intellectual. The banality that "We can't *all* be composers" approaches validity only insofar as we don't all want to be composers, and the noncompetitive spirit of an Aztec village, in which virtually everyone is an artist, begins to show what the human race is capable of. The current musical values, symbolized by the average good music student's prayer to be able to play or sing a scale more skillfully, smoother, and faster than anybody else, are exactly as ennobling as a competitive armaments race.

One does not fertilize the creative instinct by twenty-year plans of practice to play someone else's music, and the student would do well to carry the realization of that fact through all his classes in the music school. With a questioning spirit as his prompter, he will listen to all his teachers and read all available books on music and related subjects, but he will hold everything they say and write in abeyance until each assertion has had an individual seminar with his powers of concentration, logic, and perception. Very soon the critical faculties are sharpened, and he finds that most teachers can be dismissed with one lecture, most books with one chapter—often with a cursory glance. He may eventually come back to a very few teachers and a very few books, and he may even welcome back to his bosom some of the inherited instruments, but only after an individual investigation of the true nature—that is, the physical nature—of each, and—even more important—the philosophy of human living and idea that brought them into being.

He will get no help from the music schools in this attitude; after all, they are music schools only because they are virtually impervious to individualism. Ritual of classroom double-talk and creed of safety-deposit-box dogma have vested the high priests of the musical academy with a calcification the envy of every other bone of human endeavor. But if the student's expectations of the school are not too high, and if he can maintain a sane agnosticism, that small proportion of his time in a musical academy in which he learns to philosophize about the world in general and the music profession in particular is probably not wasted.

Another tentative diagnosis of a pathological condition in the body of musical usage—and not just musical either—is provoked by the phenomenon of super-specialization. It has been said that the animal that generalizes is more likely to survive because he is adaptable, whereas the animal that specializes cannot retreat, in a new and hostile situation, and becomes extinct. It seems logical, with certain reservations, to apply this observation to things of the art world. The musician sings, "Music has nothing to do with acoustics," and the acoustician joins him in the refrain. The musician carols (here translated from the *bel canto* Italian which in the original is rendered unintelligible by tasteful interspersings of *fioriture*): "Music has nothing to do with speech," and the phonetician also goes to the opera to hear music, not words. The specialists complement each other in their determination to keep their specialties hermetically sealed.

Musicians of the "good" variety are frequently heard to decry the electric organ, mostly—I am inclined to think—because it was not found in the safety-deposit boxes of the Germanic gentlemen aforementioned. Perhaps nothing can be stated with absolute certainty in hypothesizing history, but I think we can be fairly certain that the classic masters would have taken electronics in stride; I think it is quite possible that J. S. Bach, for example, would have written seven sets of preludes and fugues, one for each of the electric organ's characteristic tonal envelopes. It is not enough to criticize, but the stay-in-your-own-backyard torpor of the age of specialization reduces us to pubescent wailing. Let the composer who rejects the electric organ either inspire someone who is qualified or else qualify himself to produce something better. Indeed the spirit of the electronics expert trembles with indignation at the very thought of tampering with the scale materials chez-Bach-Haydn-Beethoven. Even if I had had no experience with him, I would still be certain of his reaction. The logic of his situation demands such an attitude. This is the age of special-ization, and the specialists of the various specialties must and will defend each other's mangers unto extinction. From the standpoint of a future music, and without de-expertizing education, the elec-tronics expert, the music expert, and any expert, is hopeless.

The age of specialization, rejecting both the variegated sounds of the vocal organ and the range of emotions they connote, and substituting therefore a single type refined to Mongoloid idiocy, has brought us the "musical tone." The age of specialization has given us an art of sound that denies sound, and a science of sound that denies art. The age of specialization has given us a music drama that denies drama, and a drama that—contrary to the practices of all other peoples of the world—denies music. Let this absurd age of specialization go into even slight eclipse, let there be even a slight abatement of what Henry Miller calls the "warfare between the col-lectivity and the individual,"[1] and as a minimal result the persons one meets in everyday living will be several degrees more interesting. And a world with a greater scope of common knowledge, and honestly admitted, validly and vividly ponderable common experience, will be an expertless world.

When the student finds that these things—the human ways he inherited and the usages of the subject closest to his heart—are alien to him, he has only one choice—to short-circuit as many of the obnoxious specialties as he possibly can in one lifetime, and entertain the hope that in so doing he has fatally electrocuted some vital organ of the interpretive age—if the euphemism can properly be applied to a devitalized culture. In the process he may succeed in designing a musical world that is not alien to him—a physical world, because music is a physical art. What he does to keep body and soul together meantime is another question—one that I ponder with the greatest sympathy, but without even a hint as to a possible solution.

No Barriers

1952

Once in a while it would seem desirable, between all the specialized stimuli—of music in concerts, of the verbal in plays, of the dynamically visual in ballet—to find all these apparent desires and responses in a single work of art in the theater. A work that would not exclude any area of response—visual, aural, verbal—in any combination, in order to engage the whole person, either as performer or as observer. Experience does not exclude, because the eye, the ear, the body, and the mind register, react, store away, and therefore evolve, consciously or otherwise. The mind does not put its reactions into little locked rooms to be opened laboriously, one at a time. Under appropriate stimulus they unlock without conscious effort, instantly and simultaneously.

If understanding is a valuable personal asset, it is desirable for each participant in such a work to be aware of the total potential of any human involvement. The musician as dancer, the dancer as ditchdigger, the ditchdigger as physicist, the physicist as hobo, the hobo as messiah, the messiah as criminal, or any other conceivable metamorphosis. Perhaps such a statement seems irrelevant to the idea of a work of art for the stage, yet I do not think so.

Without understanding of human experience there is nothing. No interpretation, therefore no communication. No at-oneness, therefore no universality. We may work, as artists and creators, toward originality and individuality. Yet we must know that this is not a goal, that it must simply be inevitable and incidental, because—in a true biologic sense—each of us is an original and individual being. Death alone, however we may interpret it, is evidence enough. For an artist to be different, with forethought, is to be as my playwright friend Wilford Leach has written, "just plain perverse (which is often the case), dealing in nonsense (which is often the case), either playing a big joke on his audiences or an even bigger joke on himself (which is generally the case)."[1]

The inspiring-exasperating and life-giving, life-destroying purpose of the creative artist or interpreter is the attainment of understanding that sires communication. Discovered books may help, and frequently do; teachers also, though seldom; the room crackling with witty conversation—however enjoyable—almost never. Experience, experience, experience, and after that some lonely walks along the railroad tracks or a thousand other places, to make experience meaningful— these are all-imparting.

Some philosophy, however personal, however put down, must— in my humble opinion—validate any statement regarding the actual mechanics of communication from the stage or any place else, but, here again, one can only point. The creator clears as he goes; he evolves his own techniques, devises his own tools, destroys where he must. If he wants a whole-experience reaction from his audience, he employs or stipulates every possible stimulus at his command, singly or simultaneously; including music of any imaginable bastardy; dance and drama in any historical or antihistorical form; noise, light, shadow, substance, or perhaps only the semblance of substance; and sounds from the mouth that communicate only as emotion.

The audience need not worry him too much. The separate ways in which people have been conditioned, with one attitude at a symphony, another at a play, still others—separate and distinct—at nightclubs and hash houses with jukeboxes, jam sessions, and community sings, are only skin-deep. Touch the total experience, which does have an underlying total affinity, and the conditioned attitude evaporates, though perhaps only for a moment.

That there is, in total experience, a deep and abiding tie with peoples removed both in time and space, seems to me beyond argument. In this regard music alone, of the elements that we ordinarily call culture, has all but been ignored by the Western world. Consider the ancient cultures of the Orient, where the synthesis mentioned is more or less constant practice. We specialize here, too; we study, separately, oriental languages, literature, art, even dance. We call in lecturers and teachers native to these subjects. Do we have them in music? We do not. We confine our instruments and our repertoire to a few hundred years of Western Europe, and when we do have an oriental instrument, it becomes an idly twanged "object of art," or when we are intrigued by an oriental melody, we bring it home to crucify it: "for violin and piano."

This is a small example, and says nothing of our European-conceived instruments, which we largely ignore. It becomes particularly evident when we peruse any student recital program—Suite for Violin and Piano, Sonata for Piano, Variations for Violin and Piano, Etude for Two Pianos—that there is a wealth of instruments of which audiences, teachers, and students are largely unaware.

To a disinterested observer we must seem to be on a conducted tour of a one-way street, anxiously picking up academic credits on the way, and coming finally to the end, signed DEGREE, after which there are only two choices (because the idea of imagination has already been pretty well squelched!): conduct others over the same route, or (God forbid!) stop.

I think of the little Negro boys of New Orleans street corners (their "instruments" might be frowned on by our serious musicians), who play washboards, tubs, tin cans, anything that intrigues their aural imaginations, and who dance and make sounds from their mouths and grimacing wrinkles on their faces. I feel we cannot ignore this basic impulse of the race.

The Ancient Magic

1959

Traditions in music do not begin with recent European centuries. They begin with the human race, in the deepest wells of wisdom. Knowing this, and knowing it deeply, I am incapable of discussing my particular direction in the arts as though it had a relationship only to the contemporary scene in music.

There are two essential ones: first, our world, this time and place, in every way that my experience has touched it; second, ancient usages and traditions as they concern my privilege as an individual.

After humanity's primary concern with food and self-protection comes an effort always to understand its experience. And as man's art life through both known and unknown millenniums lengthens, mere security carries ever less meaning in itself. The bringing into the world of babes, who in turn will stand for the perpetuation of the American way of life without thought of the singular perspectives that art alone can provide, is to compound human tragedy.

Ours is a time of scientific magic, and it would be great if one could say that insight is its invariable companion. But only in art— if it is truly art—is insight automatic. Art-magic is something that we desperately need to replumb. The people who first stretched a piece of gut over two bridges, or found tones in wood suspended at the nodes, discovered *magic,* just as certainly as the people who found tones in electronic tubes. Then, through art, they plunged intuitively toward an insight into the greater mysteries.

Ours has been called, among other things, the age of electronics, and a great deal has been said about the desirability of *expressing* one's own time.

The desideratum of a counterforce to the individual's diminishing significance in the face of an industrial machine is not to be disputed, but nothing could be more futile (or downright idiotic) than to *express* this age. The prime obligation of the artist is to transcend his age, therefore to show it in terms of the eternal mysteries. What this age needs more than anything else is an effective antidote.

The loss of values through the magic of science is at least lessened when we are aware of, and instinctively try to regain contact with, simpler ancient sources. The miracle button, the airplane, the automobile, have all taken their toll. I have walked through a section of country with a pack on my back, preoccupied constantly with all manner of petty personal problems, yet now and then I was aware of the magic of small growing things, the magic of a running stream where I threw down my pack, the magic of a fire by its side.

The pianist who has never studied the tuning of his instrument, and learned to achieve it, has never experienced the parallel of a fire of twigs by a running stream. He is already removed from that value by the analogy of a faucet in a sink and a button on a stove, because the miracle of tonal relationships comes to him already piped. And because of this failure, his education, which in its root word implies the opening of doors, is actually closing a door—the first door, I might add, to an insight into musical magic.

The monolithic nature of Western musical culture (which has an admittedly understandable historic basis) is symbolized by the rigid twelve-tone piano keyboard; while the potentiality of infinitely varied melodic and harmonic subtleties, the converse—which the piano and its forebears replaced in the West—is one of the ancient lost values.

This direction, toward greater melodic and harmonic subtleties, is one facet of my work—just one, although it is sometimes described, by people who ought to know better, as the only thing I stand for, aside from musical revolution, that is.

To assume that one who rebels against the king must want to overthrow him is characteristic of "king-thinking." I am not a king-thinker; I am supremely indifferent as to whether anyone chooses to follow in my footsteps, just as indifferent as an artist might feel if successive painters choose never to use his brushes, surfaces, paints, and techniques again. It is the artist's art that is at stake, not the followers he acquires. There is surely room in this great wide West for more than one philosophy of music, and room, surely, for any American who chooses—for good reasons—to reject the modern European musical hegemony.

Ever since the freshened vigor of the Renaissance began to dissipate, acoustical theories have largely been "proved" on paper. Thus critics and theorists, hardly one of whom has made an experiment on anything more acoustical than a typewriter, and all of whom function under a kind of semitone trance, expound, and quote each other on, the "limitations" of so-called microtones. The facts are demonstrably the reverse, as anyone who takes the question to the judgment of the ear—with the simple craftsman's integrity—knows full well.

The contemporary artist has a deep obligation; he is not obliged to confine himself to whatever he happened to find in his Christmas stocking. Percussion—the ancient rhythmic magic, so old that it might even antedate fire—is an example of an antidote that is virtually a specific for our age, and which is wide open to the construction of imaginative instruments, as anyone who contemplates the impoverished collection of percussive sounds from the modern symphony orchestra must realize.

It has been demonstrated successfully, to my mind, that sensitively tuned percussion with a wide variety of timbres and ranges can achieve an amazing eloquence, and even an amazing lyricism. To anyone familiar with the African music that has been available on records for at least twenty years, this is obvious. On the theater stage, as in primitive ritual, percussion becomes part of the "act."

My musical concepts are invariably involved with theater, or with dramatic ideas dramatically presented, and many years have been given to provoking musicians into becoming actors, and singers into making occasional ugly and frightening (but dramatic) sounds, appealing to them through heavy layers of Puritan inhibitions and academic intimidations. Once they are gotten out of the soul-destroying pit and the rut of *bel canto,* and shown that they are an absolutely necessary ingredient in latter-day rituals designed to castrate the machine age, their responses are positively electric.

In my version of Sophocles' *Oedipus the King,* I tried to rediscover some of the stature that the Western theater has lost in its long divorce from integrated music. More recently, in *The Bewitched,* I ventured into satire, in the feeling that a people dedicated to statistical scholarship and cause-and-effect rationality is hopeless only when it ceases to be able to laugh at itself intelligently. I wanted to prove that it could.

Satire need not be heavy-handed. It can descend lightly and with love, and imbue the listener and the viewer with a shaft of momentary recognition and delight. It can bring reevaluation and self-perception, and—without seeming labor—a spontaneous feeling for humanity through art, something that lies within our bones and is precedent to all recorded history.

It is one of the purposes of scholarship to discover ethical values and disciplines out of the past, verbally and visually stated, and to preserve them. I care a great deal about contemplating an age or ages that have been discovered through digging and presuming and learning. But I care even more for the divination of an ancient spirit of which I *know* nothing. It is this that I have tried to convey in *The Bewitched*.

A Somewhat Spoof

1960

I am a humbled traditionalist from ancient ages. In my previous life I stood for (alas!) *progress,* and this was too much, both for my ancient fellow man and the ancient gods. I was dispatched clandestinely, without even the honor of a public execution.

So—, numberless millennia later, I find that the kindly gods have relented. I am back in the world, simply because I have learned that man must also understand *regress.*

Let not one year pass—I now say to myself—when I do not step one significant century backward. And since there are so many full circles in a man's life, I am firmly convinced that when I have regressed as far as I can possibly go, I shall have actually arrived at a point some years in the wild future, and maybe it won't be so god-awful pure.

Ah, purity! The Shakespearean actor in a concert of pure readings (*Woe is me!*). Pure black-and-white tails, pure orchids on a pure bosom (*I love music!*). Pure, pure paintings (*We are in the presence of Ah——t!*). Pure moviemakers talking wistfully of sound track counterpoint (*Who wants to counter my point?*). Pure criticism in pure print (*Sunday circ., 1,367,455*). Massive lunges across the modern dance stage (*Puh-yure movement! Just puh-yure movement!*).

Ah, sweet purity!

> *Pure* dance, *pure* chance,
> *Pure* poetry to *pure* jazz,
> *Pure* music, *pure* drama,
> *Pure* telephones in the virgin grazz.

Relax!

Whistle softly, and as each loving muscle snuggles under, and each tiny cilia wiggles free, you will *see*—shimmering before you—the curves of *x* million perceptible changes in pitch, at least 127 varieties of female giggles, and no less than 17 kinds of falsetto wails, in each cubic foot of free vibrating air.

One does not find free vibrating air just anyplace, however. Let's not look for it in Town or Carnegie halls, or any other enclosure that has been dedicated to the services of Johann *Sempervirens* Bach. But— when you find it—you will see at once that it does not even faintly resemble a piano keyboard, the sweating brow of a laborer in the Columbia Concerts vineyard, or the stage set for *Lucia di Lamermoor.* Not one of its tones ever went through the dreadful ordeal of birth by logarithmic section, knifed by the twelfth power of two.[1] And not one of them ever got hung up in a clutch with Grandma Bel-Canto, or hung over with those fussy old twins, Uncle Faulty-Attack and Auntie Faulty-Release.

Observe the professors! There is excellent reason for believing that Giant Musicologists, in order to become Giants, must forever forswear the testimony of their ears and their eyes, and take the Oath of Total Anesthesia for the balance of their natural lives.

All wise men come out of the East

Because the litany of musical mythology is unexamined, the Giant Musicologist continues to entrench himself. Unchallenged, he accepts all new allegiances as a divine right, counts off another *Ave Mozart,* and bows ceremoniously in the direction of the Library of Congress.

So—, we have finally arrived at cultural "maturity"! Witness, along with European musicology, our addiction to the twelve-tone row and to electronic music, *after* these items became small fashions in Europe.

The young man in Los Angeles who makes music out of common sounds during the late thirties is ignored to extinction, but some young Europeans doing the same thing under the fancy title *musique concrète*—ten years later—are celebrated from New York to California. (The European composer sneezes—sotto voce—and the hairs in the ears of the American A&R man respond immediately with a tremolo.)

Now, with Europe sounding off in multitudinous electronic grunts, groans, and farts, the awakening is here again! The Europhiliacs of the American colleges and foundations go to work. Suddenly, it is not only respectable but even mandatory that Americans follow this lead. If Europe can fart, by golly we not only can, we *must!*

What was that again?

All wise farts come out of the East?

When things are hopping—definition: THE BIG WORLD, complex in excitement, simple in rules, no analysis.

When things are not hopping—definition: the little world, simple in excitement, complex in rules, *utter* analysis.

If things are hopping who cares how many tones you use? THE BIG WORLD has All Tones, All Ideas. The little world has twelve tones, one idea, and ten million libraries stacked with books and magazines and newspapers to glorify, to apologize for, and to analyze those twelve tones and that one idea.

How many millennia backward (or forward) must we go? to find art in a meaningful role? to find statesmen and artists in love with each other?

Live, die; then live and know.

The University and the
Creative Arts: Comment

1963

The various specialties of the various autonomous departments of the modern American university are taken for granted, and the system of education that is implied as a direct result is also taken for granted. It is my thesis that the state of the creative arts in universities springs largely from the interests of specialized men, who are determined at all costs to maintain their positions by keeping their specialties pure, undiluted, and therefore—as far as the world is concerned—sterile.

Purity is rampant. Given progressively antiseptic departments, there is no place else to go—pure music, pure dance, pure art, pure dialogue in the theater. Entirely apart from the obvious need for cross-fertilization among the creative arts, there are the same needs of invigoration beyond the arts. Music and physics are certainly related studies, yet aside from an occasional adventure into electronic music, there is little or no recognition of a cross-fertilization need, either by music professors or the what-was-good-enough-for-Bach-is-good-enough-for-me physics professors.

An insignificant work of art can be quickly forgotten, but we are forced to endure, over a period of decades, inacoustic theaters and auditoriums because of an earlier failure of cross-fertilization between the studies of acoustics and architecture.

Once the autonomous department is set up, we are at the mercy of that jealous specialist, the historical analyst. (He has quit—I thank heaven—the hypocrisy of paying lip service to "individualism.") And the time is past when it is profitable to say, "We need historical analysts, don't we?" Yes, we need them, but emphasizing that we need them when they are virtually all we have got is too easy. It would be more imaginative to create a situation in which people can function wholly and creatively in and because of this time and place.

The bright young musicologist or art historian and the individual with a strong creative drive are practically antithetical forces. The creative individual must decline to give assiduous years along the labyrinthine paths of historical technique and analysis. He has no other choice. He must create his techniques as they become relevant to his purpose, in much the way that the navigator of a ship plows through half-charted seas among half-known lands.

Dr. Lowry has said, "Under present conditions, the best service you can perform for the potential artist is to throw him out." If the creative student remains in a university only to face the economic future more securely, his drive cannot be very strong, and if his drive is strong he won't have to be thrown out because he won't be there.

This is fantastically sad. The university and the student with a creative potentiality need each other. Among many other values, the student needs the response of a widely read and intelligent community, and the facilities that the university plant offers.

Turning to the commercial art world, the adventurous person or group can find little to excite hope. Even if art commerce were not very nearly suffocated under production costs (of which those arising from labor union attitudes are very much a part), it is still dedicated to the same juiceless art form.

I include a quotation from myself, because it is appropriate: "The age of specialization has given us an art of sound that denies sound, and a science of sound that denies art . . . a music drama that denies drama, and a drama that—contrary to the practices of all other peoples of the world—denies music."[1]

The time must come when some sort of an institution is set up which will cut across departmental hierarchies, which will not only allow but encourage cross-fertilization, and which will establish creative vigor as a living tradition in the American university.

Monoliths in Music

1966

There has been, at least ever since Aristotle, a certain strong tendency in the West toward explanation—a kind of syndrome. The first and initial step is fairly innocent—to consider a verbal explanation of a creative art as necessary to an understanding of the art. The second step is less innocent. In this second step the explanation of the art becomes a substitute for the art. But the third step is really something. It is a sort of apotheosis, where the explanation actually becomes the art.

Words are not only surrogates for action but are just as good as action, and whole shelves of libraries are eloquent testimony to this tendency. Here is an example. We have preserved and preserved Aristotle and Plato, who explained everything in the then known world, including scales and modes. We have preserved Aristoxenus[1] and Euclid,[2] who also explained scales and modes. But the *enharmonic*, one of the most beautiful modes ever invented by man, was lost as an art and as an act long before.[3] Anyone who knows ancient literature knows the explanation of the enharmonic; yet, I seriously doubt whether anyone who knows all the explanations of the enharmonic has ever thought to consider it not as an explanation but as an act.

I have noticed that most interviewers for radio, TV, magazines, and newspapers are far less interested in hearing my music or seeing a show of mine, than they are in hearing me explain in words why I ever created this music. How does one explain his reason for existence? If I could come up with a version of "I'm Dreaming of a White Christmas" in unusual timbres, produced, for example, by using beer cans, the interest in my music might suddenly become enlivened. This was actually suggested to me in a phone call from New York by a TV producer. I do not, I hasten to emphasize, include all interviewers in these observations.

There are areas of human endeavor where words are inadequate (the enharmonic is a conspicuous example), where they should not be considered as vehicles of illumination, and where they might actually become inhibitory to insight, as they did in the case of the enharmonic. And if I seem to be suggesting something that might tend to undermine the whole university system of education, well I'm not really that radical. It has been said, in public print, that if my ideas were to become dominant in music schools it would be the end of music as we know it. May I say, first, that the danger is singularly slight. However, beyond this is the implication that music must be monolithic, that whatever is decided by the majority or the most powerful must be adhered to by everyone. This idea is totally outside the thrust of Western civilization, which has prided itself for over two thousand years, off and on, in the concept of allowing strong individualism without alienation. We have done no more than scratch the surface of possible harmonic music; we have certainly done no more than scratch the surface of possible rhythmic music.

One way in which musicians have endeavored to break out of the monolith is by so-called *improvisation.* There are some exceptions to what I am saying, but, generally, the improvisors use the same instruments that were developed by this monolithic culture—the same harps, celestes, pianos, vibraphones, woodwinds; they even use the same chord progressions we have been hearing for a hundred years! The only difference is that now these things are "improvised."

In this matter of breaking down the barriers to individualistic freedom in music, I suggest that the answer is not in improvisation, not in lighthearted chance, but in the contribution of several lifetimes of lonely dedication.

I use the word *ritual,* and I also use the word *corporeal,* to describe music that is neither on the concert stage nor relegated to a pit. In ritual the musicians are *seen;* their meaningful movements are part of the act, and collaboration is automatic with everything else that goes on. How could it be otherwise? Monoliths are just dandy—in stone. They do not belong in the world of ideas. To be sure, they have their advantages: because of the present musical monolith, it is possible for twenty or thirty musicians to get together in a recording studio and to create, practically on sight, a sound track for a film or a TV series. This is fine. Let the commercial people have their monolith. But in

schools of higher education, it is an obstacle to strong creative thinking, and I will prophesy that it will not be tolerated forever.

Underlying the various musical systems and philosophies in our
libraries is a common, basic assumption: twelve tones, equal temperament—the piano scale. But when we force acoustic intervals into
the octave, or x octaves, we falsify every interval involved, we effectively close all doors to any further adventures of consonance, and
also, amazingly, we close all doors to any meaningful adventures in
dissonance.

A great deal has been said about quarter tones, about cutting
each semitone exactly in half and creating twenty-four tones to the
octave. This would not give us acoustic intervals; on the contrary, as
far as I can see, it would simply provide material for a twenty-four
tone row.

It is not necessary to assume antimusic or nonmusic attitudes. It
is not necessary to resort to noise or nonrhythmic music, or even
excessive dissonance to achieve dynamism in creative art. The various
specialists do not come from sealed spheres of purity—pure art, pure
music, pure theater, pure dance, pure film. As far as large involvements
of music in this modern world are concerned, we have really only
two choices: we have the pit, or we have the excessive formality of
the concert stage.

On the theater stage, with Bertolt Brecht, and occasionally with
others, there is something like a ritualistic approach—a corporeal
approach to music as an integrated part of theater. But the degradation
of either the actual pit or the mental pit is the fate of nearly all other
music. If this ritual or corporeal approach accomplishes nothing else,
it frees the beautiful rhythmic movements of musicians from the
inhibitory incubus of tight coat and tight shoes.

A Quarter-Saw Section of
Motivations and Intonations

1967

The direction in which I have been going the last forty-four years has much in common with the activities and actions of primitive man as I imagine him. Primitive man found magical sounds in the materials around him — in a reed, a piece of bamboo, a particular piece of wood held in a certain way, or a skin stretched over a gourd or tortoise shell (some resonating body). He then proceeded to make the object, the vehicle, the instrument, as visually beautiful as he could. His last step was almost automatic: the metamorphosis of the magical sounds and visual beauty into something spiritual. They become fused with his everyday words and experiences — his ritual, drama, religion — thus lending greater meaning to his life. These acts of primitive man become the trinity of this work: magical sounds, visual form and beauty, experience-ritual.

Meaningfulness must have roots. It is not enough to feel that one's roots extend back only a decade or a century. It is my strong belief that the human race has known and abandoned magical sounds, visual beauty, and experience-ritual more meaningful than those now current. I must therefore decline to limit the dimensions of my rather intense beliefs by the modernly specialized word *music*. I believe devoutly that this specialty must become less specialized for the sake of its own survival. The experiential-ritualistic-dramatic area has constituted a very large part of my belief and work. And as for imaginative and sculptural forms of instruments, I have easily given as much time to this endeavor as to intonation.

Almost every one of my many instruments has been built and rebuilt (up to as many as nine times) for all or even just one of the following reasons: (*a*) good aesthetic form, (*b*) acoustical validity, (*c*) musical practicality. However, I shall pass over—with compelling sadness and with no further comment—easily two-thirds of my life's work to discuss and demonstrate intonation. And I shall narrow this down to a particular kind of intonation—just—and narrow it even further to the kind of just intonation that I call Monophonic, that is, the genesis of One.

News stories, and even reviews, have almost consistently latched onto the number forty-three, as though this were somehow the touchstone of my life. It is not. It is in fact about the one-half truth of the one-fourth factor. It is totally misleading. Even on instruments of fixed pitch, I do not necessarily limit myself to forty-three just monophonic tones. To explain further would consume too much time.

One further word of introduction about the language of intonational theory. The only clear, logical, rational terms are numbers, the relationships of numbers—that is, frequency ratios, or the ratios of parts of sounding bodies.

Ancient peoples in many parts of the world knew musical numbers. Modern man, including modern American music schools, persist in not knowing musical numbers. On the contrary, through my lifetime, I have seen how they jealously guard their precious misconception. And this, ironically, in a so-called scientific age.

It is either very difficult or very easy to recline alongside dogma with serenity. I have seen, through most of my life, how lonely and contemplative investigation of musical-human materials is discouraged by dogma. The doors that are closed *because* of education are the saddest doors that humanity never walked through. And there is at least the question whether the world has already known, and long ago abandoned, both habits of education and usages superior to those we currently adhere to.

Now that we have suffered the present dogmas in the West—for about 300 years—who would want to exchange them for a different set of rigid stipulations? I wouldn't. Responsible freedom, it seems to me, is the desideratum. The widely revered master-disciple concept represents, on both sides, too easy an escape into the limbo of *no* responsibility. I have said that if anyone calls himself a pupil of mine, I will happily strangle him. But this is simply the expression of an attitude. And amazingly—in the deeper meaning—it is an expression of hope.

PART 3

INTRODUCTIONS AND PREFACES

Barstow

1941

It's January 26. I'm freezing.
Ed Fitzgerald. Age 19. Five feet, ten inches.
Black hair, brown eyes.
Going home to Boston, Massachusetts.
It's 4:00, and I'm hungry and broke.
I wish I was dead.
But today I am a man.

The scribbling is in pencil. It is on one of the white highway railings just outside the Mojave Desert junction of Barstow, California. I am walking along the highway and sit down on the railing to rest.

Idly I notice the scratches where I happen to drop. I have seen many hitchhikers' writings. They are usually just names and addresses—there are literally millions of them, or little meaningless obscenities, on highway signs, railings, walls.

But this—why, it's music. It's both weak and strong, like unedited human expressions always are. It's eloquent in what it fails to express in words. And it's epic. Definitely, it is music.

Intrigued, I look further along the same rail, and immediately see another inscription:

> *Gentlemen: Go to 530 East Lemon Avenue, Monrovia,*
> *California, for an easy handout.*

Though we may be hungry, we are still presumed to be "Gentlemen." A third inscription is right beside it:

Marie Blackwell, age 19.
Brown eyes, brown hair.
Considered Pretty.
118 East Ventura Street,
Las Vegas, Nevada.
Object: Matrimony.

And at this "Lonely Hearts Club" of U.S. 66, Marie gets a bite:

Dear Marie: A very good idea you have there. . . .

The message doesn't end. Why? There is only one thing that would distract a hitchhiker from romance on such desert wastes. Yes, a ride. And one potential husband is snatched right out of Marie's grasp.

It takes a little pondering to understand the next inscription. It is legible enough, but what do all those marks mean? There are five successive dates, and figure ones in groups of five crossed off after each date, as though someone were keeping score.

Suddenly it dawns. This one has waited five days for a ride out of Barstow, and he scores each refusing car on the rail as it passes. But it is finally too much, and the hitcher ends his tally with:

To h—— with it. I'm going to walk.

I look off to the northeast. Yes, it's a mighty long stretch from here to Needles, or to Las Vegas, and nothing more than a few filling stations to break it. Barstow from the west is easy. But east it turns into a hitchhikers' bottleneck.

Which in itself explains the strange inscriptions. What better to do than sit here, as the cars pass you by, telling the world your story, your desires, letting your unconscious flow?

Thoroughly aroused by this sudden fountainhead of Americana, I look further. The next one is:

Jesus was God in the Flesh.

Everywhere itinerants stop, in huge red-painted or tiny penciled letters, under bridges, on walls, this sort of evangelism is seen. And even though it is neither creative nor original, it helps paint the complete picture of this Barstow railing.

Here is another:

All you have to do is find me, you lucky woman. Name's George.

Finally, an eighth inscription—a rambling story scribbled in a frightfully bad hand over a six-foot length of railing. It wanders, both actually and in thought—as though the hitcher were daydreaming, without awareness. Occasionally, however, there are good sequences:

> D—— it anyhow, here I am stuck in the cold. I've come 2700 miles from Chi, Illinois. Slept along the highway. Slept in open box car without top. Went hungry for two days (Raining, too). But they say there's a he——, What the he—— do they think this is? . . .

And a running description:

> Car just passed by—make that two more—three more. Do not think they'll let me finish my story. . . .

But they did. And he ends it on a query addressed to all hitchers, melancholy, but practical:

> Why did you come, anyway?[1]

Breathes there a hitcher who, on getting stuck in Barstow, never to himself hath said, "Why did I come, anyway?"

U.S. Highball
A Musical Account of Slim's
Transcontinental Hobo Trip

1943

Generally speaking, American hobos number five: Blackie, Whitey, Red, Heavy, and Slim. The last of these, Slim, is the protagonist of *U.S. Highball.*

U.S. Highball is no saga. It is common experience, the account of Slim's hobo trip from Carmel, California, to Chicago, Illinois. In the usual "word" sense it is not even a story. It has no introductory words for characters or speeches, nor connecting phrases for the speeches, and the protagonist himself utters no word whatever. Just occasionally, he thinks—and, in the musical account, out loud. These thoughts are the only words without quotation marks.

In effect, the text of *U.S. Highball* consists of *some* of the words that assailed Slim's consciousness on this trip, in exactly the order they assailed, and not a single word is introduced which did not actually assail. A true record of *all* the words that assailed Slim's consciousness would become an anthology of hobo lore, and so, the text is confined to those remarks, signs, and inscriptions which made him laugh, think, or merely startled him. The action and words have no integration but geography and the implied fortunes of the protagonist, the composition as a whole no integration but music.

Certainly the story of *U.S. Highball* could be told in words alone. But in the story with music a type has evolved. Possibly a new type, or one intuitively rescued from neglected centuries. It tells a different side of the same story. It gives aspects which it is not in the purpose or capacity of words to give—a peculiar introspective intensity, a peculiar humor, a peculiar drama, and a peculiar urgency—an illusion or a hallucination that the things of the story situation are being said and are happening here and now—which only this music can convey.

It integrates and intensifies the fragments of word thoughts, remarks, and signs into an account. Hence, "A Musical Account. . . ."

Perhaps the essence of almost any momentous trip, hobo or otherwise, is constituted of these things: (1) the exhilaration of moving; (2) relief at leaving the scenes of experience for a new life—a renascence; (3) a succession of geographical place-names; (4) the persons one meets, their remarks, and stories; (5) wondering what will happen next.

In *U.S. Highball* numbers 1, 2, and 5 are the province of music alone. Numbers 3 and 4 are the province of words, rationalized, intensified, dramatized, and integrated by music. Number 3, on the progress of the journey from place to place, is exuberantly represented in Slim's thoughts, "Leaving San Francisco," "Leaving Sacramento," et cetera.

Maybe it is symptomatic of Hobo Slim that the exhilaration of compassing each separate milestone is nothing compared to the exhilaration of having compassed and *left* each milestone. Consequently, he wouldn't think, "Arriving paradise at long last!" but, with jubilation, "Leaving paradise, thank God!" Into eternity the hobo mind seeks something different, something better, something beyond. By all means beyond—even beyond paradise.

The composition falls roughly into two parts: the first, in which speech-music, or musicalized words, is generally dominant, and the second, after leaving Little America, Wyoming, in which the music generally dominates the musicalized words. Slim's simple thoughts open the composition: departure from Carmel and the line from a letter which has galvanized his peregrinations in the direction of Chicago. With the first sense of exhilaration in moving, the music takes over completely, the voice singing meaningless "Nahs" or "Lahs." This particular move is an atop-a-boxcar exit from California through the Sierras, and comes to a nonexhilarating end at the division yards of Sparks, Nevada.

Days and nights of hobo confabulation atop or in boxcars, "gon-*do*-las," tank cars, and around fires in the yards end at Green River, Wyoming, where Slim jumps off an oil tank to find a dirty, broke, and stranded hobo, balked both by the highway and the railroad police. He is looking at himself.

To this point all three instruments have been used liberally, but with no regular structure of composition, since the music is sensitive to every word uttered, every idea, every act. Salvation for Slim's Green River predicament appears in the form of a dishwashing job at Little America, Wyoming, and here the Chromelodeon carries on alone, supporting the spoken word of waiters and hobo reminiscences, and so through the week-long pot-walloping interlude.

All three instruments again sound off with the departure from Little America. In a sense, this is starting the trip anew, after rest, food, and economic refurbishing. Thus, it becomes a logical recapitulation, with repetition, in the same key, of the departure from Carmel, and with reemphasis of the motivating lines from the letter.

A successful effort to get a ride on the clean, noiseless, jerkless highway introduces the second part of the composition, bringing a sudden change of feeling: strong rhythms, rather than subtle spoken rhythms, and—perhaps in keeping with success-induced conservatism—an almost traditional musical structure. Exceptions to traditional structure are in harmony and device. In device, the voice descends from its former dominant role into a continuous rhythmic undercurrent, on syllabic variations of the word *Chicago,* thus vitalizing the thematic material with urgency, prodding the movement forward, and never for a moment allowing a forgetfulness of the destination. This represents, of course, exactly what one feels on a trip beset with travel and economic difficulties, a half-exuberance–half-anxiety that keeps the name of his destination always on his lips. There is a constant stimulus in the fact of the ever-nearing destination, and jubilation increases as the distance lessens. This jubilation has its high point in the final enunciation of the line from the letter which started the jaunt in the first place: "May God's richest blessings be upon you."

For those who might wonder at a gullibility which would expect to find God's richest blessings in Chicago, or in any other given spot on the strength of one line in a letter, let it be remarked that from Slim's standpoint there was nothing to lose but California, and anyway, the mere suggestion of God's blessings somewhere else was no mean avenue of investigation.

After its exultant high point in the Illinois plains, the music peters off into a miserable anticlimactic end with actual arrival in the city. This is the way it happened; the music simply carries the happening out. And the anticlimax is the more miserable because, through music, the climax was more grand.

But the end of the trip is also the beginning of something more complex than the comparatively simple business of getting from one place to another as quickly as possible. It brings Slim face to face with a gulf of new problems, a new set of dismal difficulties—in a word, Chicago.

This somewhat confused and querulous feeling I have tried to put into the single and final line of music which follows the unaccompanied spoken word, "Chicago."

Finally, I am Slim. It would almost have to be so, and I may as well confess it.

U.S. Highball
A Musical Account of a
Transcontinental Hobo Trip

1957

U.S. Highball—Its History

Its history is very personal. The opening of World War II, in September 1939, doubtless marks the end of the Great Depression for historians, but my own personal Great Depression rolled along oblivious to world events, in its merrily confusing and gruelling way, for three and a half years more. For many reasons, all bound up in the personality makeup of a rebelliously creative art-worker, I found it easy during those particular years to get just one kind of job: dishwasher and flunky.

For me, this was just as true in 1942 as in 1937. If my personal history during the eight years 1935–43 could be frozen in space, it would become a finely detailed mosaic of federal works jobs and transient shelters mingled with hordes of wandering Okies in the fruit harvests and an incredible number of dirty dishes.

In the summer of 1941 I was working at small odd jobs, living in a cabin in Carmel, California. There—casually, without introduction—I met a young tourist, a divinity student. The acquaintanceship was of less than one full day, but during that time the man showed much interest in my musical ideas and my instruments, and in me. I was sick to death of the long years of the Great Depression in various parts of California, and granted—I said—that my personal depression is inevitable, I need desperately to see it from another perspective.

I have forgotten the man's name, even what he looked like, but he must have acted, because about two weeks later I received a letter from an acquaintance of his in Chicago, a musician and obviously a very religious man.

If I could somehow get to Chicago, he wrote, I could temporarily live in his house, and he ended his message: "May God's richest blessings be upon you."

Immediately, I got galvanized. On the evening of September 17, 1941, I left San Francisco with $3.50 or thereabouts in my pocket — $3.29 after paying the $.21 ferry and train fare across the bay to Berkeley. Getting around the country during the Great Depression was generally no large problem (though very often you were left with an experience to remember). One had his thumb, and when that failed there was always the last resort — the drag, the slow freight.

I had ridden freights occasionally, when hitchhiking failed, but I always tried the highway first. For one thing, trains are dirty, and the weary traveler who has just bounced off a soot-laden freight must be both ingenious and lucky in finding ways to clean up. A grimy hobo is conspicuous to everyone, including the police — and this is seldom a tasty prospect. Further, it is difficult to shift to the highway, once you have the color and smell of a freight train on and in your being.

On this particular trip, my success on the highway was not auspicious, and many times I headed back toward the freight yards muttering: "Back to the freights for you, boy."

I arrived in Chicago in the dull, dirty light of early dawn, on October 1, 1941, with one dime in my pocket. I had felt hopeful, throughout, that this would be the last ordeal of my personal Great Depression. I couldn't know that it would not be, that another year and a half of dirty dishes, in Chicago hash houses, in a Michigan lumber camp, and in a New York evacuation center, were still ahead of me. (I had other small jobs, too, but — for some reason — washing dirty dishes is all that I can remember.)

The musical concept that grew out of this trip and became *U.S. Highball* had much more experience in its background than I have recounted. In 1931 I had shuffled forward along some sidewalk near Howard Street in San Francisco with other derelicts — four abreast and sometimes several blocks long — in the "breadline." No music came out of this, but in 1935, as the result of experiences in federal camps and transient shelters, I had set hobo speech to music — "Bitter Music." Then, in 1940, I copied some inscriptions written by hitchhikers on a highway railing, and set these to music — *Barstow*.

On the trip to Chicago I carried a small notebook, as I had been in the habit of doing for several years, and I still have this particular one.[1] I used it for various purposes: to write letters, to remind myself of something, to put down addresses. It was the second day out of San Francisco that I began jotting down words in this notebook: fragments of conversations, remarks, writings on the sides of boxcars, signs in havens for derelicts, hitchhikers' inscriptions, names of sta-tions, thoughts. I really didn't do any editing, as such. I simply got weary of the constantly repetitive obscenities and left them out.

These fragments ARE the text of *U.S. Highball.* I did not know, when I wrote them down, that this is what they would become. But during the next year and a half, I would run across the little notebook and wonder exactly why I had gone to all this trouble.

On April 4, 1943, in Ithaca, New York, I knew. This day marked the end of my own personal Great Depression, because on this day I received notice of a Guggenheim Fellowship, and beginning on this day, my credit was okay. Since April 4, 1943, I have not experienced hunger in my belly, and in a world replete with hungers in myriad variety, that is something.[2]

The fulfilling of the concept of *U.S. Highball* became my first order of business under the Guggenheim grant, almost automatically, and I was so grateful for the opportunity that on the first page of my manuscript I inscribed: "To the John Simon Guggenheim Memorial Foundation and Henry Allen Moe."[3]

In the following winter I performed a guitar version of the work—doing all the voice parts myself—at the New England Conservatory, and for the executive committee of the League of Composers. A public performance, with an ensemble of three, under the sponsorship of this group, was given at Carnegie Chamber Music Hall, New York, in the spring of 1944, and shortly thereafter it was repeated at Brander Matthews Theatre, Columbia University.[4] It was also done twice, with an ensemble of four, in the spring of 1945, in the staid old music hall at the University of Wisconsin, which had experienced decades of sympathetic vibrations to the old masters. The shock must have been profound (I decline to speak for the ghosts of the old masters), because it took the university's radio station more than a decade to react. In 1956, eleven years after those performances, the station broadcast a satire on *U.S. Highball.*

The work was recorded, and pressed, by Dr. W. E. Gilson, in Madison, on three 12-inch records at 78 r.p.m. (six sides). The en-semble was now five. I realized, almost immediately upon hearing this recording, that I did not possess the instruments that the work really needed, and the most urgent need was percussion—percussion built for my system of music, my theories.

Nine years later, by the summer of 1955, my percussion section was more than adequate, and I rewrote the work. The new—and I believe revitalized—work is still (July 1957) just so many cryptic notes on so many pages of music manuscript paper.[5]

U.S. Highball—the Music

It is not epic, in either an ancient or a modern sense. Its protagonist is the exact opposite of a hero, as the word is used in either literature or folklore. He does not, at any time, yank himself by his own bootstraps out of the jaws of death. He resists no predatory sirens. He isn't suffering for the sake of his country, his mother, or the mother of his children, if any. And yet, in the *aloneness* of his experience, and in the psychological reaching for success, toward an achievement beset with petty difficulties—more or less constant hunger, lack of sleep, filth, and a good deal of petty apprehension and danger (the police and freight train)—he is the focus of a work that suggests epic feelings. And as a piece of music the concept has some slight affinity with the idea of epic chant.

It is not the value of an object gained that creates excitement. It is the intensity of the effort generated, and if the intensity is meaningful, the value of the goal judged by popular standards is of no consequence.

U.S. Highball is not essentially a piece of Americana, a documentary. If it were only this I would not minimize it. But it rises, in fact, beyond the documentary, to several levels of consciousness and communication. It is art, in an art form, but it is an art that surges up out of the strictly literal, the experienced narrative, even out of the abysmal. And, because it is art, the strictly literal time and place of its concept becomes merely the flight deck for what follows.

Certain extremes of feeling in those times were peculiarly characteristic, in part due to the continuing endeavors of many of us to be something that was virtually impossible. I, to be a composer, even as a hobo—thinking always of my philosophies in musical terms. The experience was a climax to years of similar experiences, and although I am hardly a typical American of my generation, my nonheroic and nonepic experiences were very typical of those times (the overcrowded transient shelters were eloquent evidence), and this fact endows the concept with a tie to other men.

I have called *U.S. Highball* the most creative piece of music I ever wrote, and in the sense that it is less influenced by the forms and attitudes that I had grown up with as a child and experienced later in adult life, there can be no doubt of it. The intensity of the experience, and all that preceded, and the intensity of my feelings at the time, generated over many years, forced me into a different welter of thought—one that I had to mold in a new way, and for this one work alone.

It is scored for seven instrumentalists (who also *speak on tones,* in turn) and one solo voice. This, the Subjective Voice, is that of the protagonist, and he is more or less constantly present. The protagonist does not speak, he thinks, and because this is music he thinks in tone! (As for his quality, he should be far more of a natural folksinger than a music school-trained vocalist.)

Because he thinks, without speaking, the names of stations go through his head. And as thoughts: "Winnemucca, Nevaducca," and "North Platte, Nebras-ass-katte," are not so ludicrous. The childish fantasy amuses him, and helps to pass the long hours.

Not all the protagonist's subjective words come from his own throat, in this music. A few of them, such as: "Back to the freights for you, boy," are spoken on tones by one of the instrumentalists, as though the phrases were coming from some unseen, supernatural commentator, as though the protagonist were projecting himself as that commentator.

The lines of what I call the Objective Voice are fairly constant also. These are remarks mostly, and they are taken, in turn, by the instrumentalists. For this reason, at least five of the seven should be men (this would almost inevitably be the case, anyway). The Objective Voice, though it must have the quality and speed of speech, is integrated with the musical complement, harmonically and rhythmically. The instruments always support it.

Of the seven instrumentalists, three are on percussion: the Bass Marimba, the Diamond Marimba and Spoils of War (played by one person), and the Boo; three are on plucked strings: the Kithara, Castor and Pollux (played by one person), and the Surrogate Kithara (played percussively much of the time); and one player is on the adapted reed organ: the Chromelodeon.

The work falls naturally into three parts: first, a long and jerky passage by drags to Little America, Wyoming; second, a slow dishwashing movement at Little America; third, a rhythmic allegro by highway to Chicago. The one word—*Chicago*—is the end of the text. Instrumentally, what follows implies a tremendous letdown from the obstinately compulsive exhilaration of *getting* to Chicago. It implies bewilderment, and that essentially dominant question in the life of the wanderer—*what next?*

King Oedipus

1952

Statement of Intention

I became interested in the Yeats version of the Sophocles *Oedipus* in 1933, and immediately produced a rough musical plan for the work. This I took to Yeats in Dublin, in 1934, between research on unusual instruments in England. Yeats's interest was easily won. In numerous writings over a period of years, he had expounded, and hoped for, a union of words and music in which "no word shall have an intonation or an accentuation it could not have in passionate speech."[1] Lack of the tonal means that seemed to be necessary to the mood, character, and length of the Sophocles tragedy caused seemingly endless postponements in the fulfilling of the rough dynamic sketch. The day came in the spring of 1951—seventeen years after my consultations with Yeats and twelve years after the poet's death.

The composition of the music for *King Oedipus* was begun in March and finished in July. In July, also, I moved my instruments into Lisser Hall. Arch Lauterer, professor of speech and drama at Mills College, had agreed to include this production in the year's program. Soon after the opening of the fall semester, I began training Mills students to play the instruments and to read my musical notation. Others, outside the college, volunteered to play their own instruments in unusual ways, and professional singers undertook to adapt their talents to a new manner of word delivery. Rehearsals for *King Oedipus* started in October.

I have not consciously linked the ancient Greece of Sophocles and this conception of his drama—twenty-four hundred years later.

The work is presented as a human value, necessarily pinned to a time and place, necessarily involving the oracular gods and Greek proper and place-names, but, nevertheless, not necessarily Greek. So viewed, the question as to whether the present work is consonant with what is generally taken to be the "Greek spirit" is somewhat irrelevant. Yet, from the standpoint of dramatic technique, it is a historical fact that the Greeks used some kind of "tone declamation" in their dramatic works, and that it was common practice among them to present language, music, and dance as a dramatic unity. In this conception of *King Oedipus,* I am striving for such a synthesis, not because it might lead me to the "Greek spirit," but because I believe in it.

The music is conceived as [the] emotional saturation, or transcendence, that it is the particular province of dramatic music to achieve. My idea has been to present the drama expressed by language, not to obscure it, either by operatic aria or symphonic instrumentation. Hence, in critical dialogue, music enters almost insidiously, as tensions enter. The words of the players continue as before, spoken, not sung, but are a *harmonic part* of the music. In these settings the inflected words are little or no different from ordinary speech, except as emotional tensions make them different. Assertive words and assertive music do not collide. Tone of spoken word and tone of instrument are intended to combine in a compact emotional or dramatic expression, each providing its singular ingredient. My intention is to bring human drama, made of words, movement, and music, to a level that a mind with average capacity for sensitivity and logic can understand and therefore evaluate.

Antecedent to the Drama

The time is the legendary period some generations prior to the Trojan War. Laius, father of Oedipus, is directly descended from Cadmus, founder of Thebes and giver of the Greek alphabet. Laius's queen is Jocasta, and her brother is Creon, who retains especial respect if not actual power through the still lingering institution of matriarchy. The birth of a son to Laius and Jocasta causes Laius to seek out the oracle at Delphi—a materialization of his unconscious fear of his son (that the son will take his place). He is told by the oracle that this son is destined to murder his father and marry his mother. The horrified parents, determining to thwart prophecy, bind the infant's feet and give the child to a herdsman to be left on a mountainside (Cythaeron) to die of exposure. But the pitying herdsman, without revealing the boy's identity, gives him to another herdsman (the Messenger in the Yeats drama).

Adopted by the childless king of Corinth and given the name Oedipus—"swollen feet," from the effects of the binding inflicted by his parents—the child grows to manhood. Hearing that he is really only an adopted son, he himself goes to the oracle—the unconscious wish for his father's removal—and receives the same dreadful answer that his parents had received. Like his parents, Oedipus seeks to avert fate, determining never to return to Corinth and the man and woman he still believes to be his true parents. At a crossroads he encounters Laius, his true father, not recognizable as a king. Laius attacks him (the second assault of father upon son) in a quarrel over right-of-way, and is killed by him.

Proceeding to Thebes, Oedipus finds the city plagued by the Sphinx, a half-lion–half-woman monster who exacts death from any passerby who fails to guess her riddle: "What is it that walks on all fours in the morning, on two legs at noon, and on three at night?" Oedipus answers, "Man." The Sphinx throws herself to death from a cliff in mortification. Laius having been presumed killed by robbers, the citizens of Thebes proclaim Oedipus king. The final fulfillment of prophecy comes when Oedipus takes Jocasta, his true mother, as his queen. This union results in four children, sons Eteocles and Polynices, and daughters Antigone and Ismene (subjects of continuing legend and other lyric tragedies).

As the play opens, another famine and plague has descended on Thebes. Seeking some relief, the populace first turns to Oedipus, who had shown his power effectively against the Sphinx-made blight, and later to the blind seer Tiresias, last of the Sophocles characters to be introduced here. Tiresias, in legend, was blinded by the goddess Athena for having chanced upon her naked, bathing in a stream. As compensation, she endowed him with "second sight." In the psychic realm, Tiresias is a projected part of Oedipus himself, his own internal necessity. The harsh, brutal words between them are an exhibition of self against self. The prophetic self, blind only to the outward world, is actually the force and determining voice of the unconscious desire. The Sophocles play revolves around Oedipus's relentless questioning into his identity—the supreme irony. Seeking to prove to himself and to others that he is not what and who he is, he succeeds only in demonstrating the irrevocable facts. The Sphinx, half-lion (or man), half-woman, represents the mystery of the child's creation. For the child to solve the riddle of the Sphinx is to regress, to go back into the womb, or darkness. The result of Oedipus's solving of the

riddle, figuratively—with the Sphinx—and actually—with Jocasta—
is his own blindness, self-inflicted, by means of his mother's brooch.
Blindness—part of the unconscious wish—completes the oracular
fulfillment.

There have been many psychoanalytic interpretations of the Oedipus myth, and the one presented here may differ from the reader's
own interpretation. Although it is impossible to discuss the Sophocles
drama without some awareness of the Freudian concept based upon
the Oedipus myth, this production concerns itself more with the
psychological content of the tragedy—the motivation and emotions
of the individual characters.

Musical Synopsis of the Drama

The story of *King Oedipus* and the musical form are one. Briefly, it is
as follows: *The Introduction;* singing of chorus (not on words), accompanied by most of the instruments, expresses the desperation of Thebes,
in famine and plague. The recurrent theme of the Harmonic Canon
introduces *The Opening Scene* in which Oedipus, distressed and anxious
for his people, cries, "Why have you come before me?" *The First
Chorus* completes the story of the affliction of Thebes, where "death
is all the fashion now." In all the choruses, the Spokesman intones on
various planes of the prevailing harmony, complemented by voices,
combinations of cello or guitar, clarinet, Chromelodeon, and the Marimbas. Cello (instrument of portent), Bass Marimba, and the seer-
priest begin dramatic action in *The Tiresias Scene,* telling Oedipus that
he is himself the "defiling thing" that must be purged before the
misfortune of Thebes ends, and prophesying of Oedipus's fall and
self-inflicted blindness, to an insistent Marimba Eroica beat.

The Second Chorus praises the oracular powers, and an angry,
arrogant Oedipus and bass viol accuse Creon of conspiracy with Tiresias in *The Creon Scene.* In *The Jocasta Scene,* the queen, clarinet,
guitar, and Chromelodeon calm ruffled tempers, but Oedipus's per-
sistent questioning (bass viol and Marimbas) as to his origin, goaded
by Tiresias's prophecies and Jocasta's answers, brings him to mental
"tumult." This questioning continues, and for the first time, Oedipus
tells the story of his early life and misgivings in *Incidental Music* (Kithara, Harmonic Canon, and Bowls), and leads to *The Third Chorus,* with
a melodically bizarre waltz theme (clarinet, voices, cello, and Marimbas).

Pursuing the question of his birth, Oedipus, with Jocasta and the
same instruments as in the previous scene, reaches a heartbreak climax

in *The Messenger Scene,* when Jocasta guesses Oedipus's real identity; again, the insistent Marimba Eroica beat. *The Fourth Chorus* repeats the single tonality theme of the second. *The Herdsman Scene,* with cello (instrument of portent) and Harmonic Canon and voices underlining the Herdsman's answers to Oedipus's questions, brings the climax, *The Oedipus Scene,* and full realization (all instruments) to Oedipus that he has murdered his father, Laius, and married his mother, Jocasta.

The Fifth Chorus commiserates with Oedipus on this denouement, and is interrupted by the Second Messenger, who announces that Jocasta has hanged herself. Immediately, in *Instrumental Commentary,* the various instruments become dominant, replacing word, and conversing. The vigorous scherzo-like section which ensues suddenly is, in a sense, a re-creation of the palace madness and is probably the most violent music of the work. This dissolves with the reentrance of Oedipus. Blind, he introduces *The Antiphony,* in which the voices echo his personal agony.

Music and dance take complete command in *Exit Oedipus: Dance-Pantomime,* which contains a coexistent contradiction — exultation because power has been broken and destiny fulfilled, and inconsolable guilt because of the fallen individual. The prelude to *The Opening Scene* is reintroduced — the desperation of Thebes is now transferred to a single victim — and, with the dance, renders what is left for dramatic completion. In the pantomime Oedipus asks the Spokesman to touch him, "Condescend to lay your hands upon a wretched man"; Creon, now king, enters, and tells Oedipus that he has ordered Oedipus's daughters, Ismene and Antigone, to appear. They enter haltingly and briefly take the center of attention. When emotions are exhausted Creon exercises his authority and orders Oedipus into the palace. Solo Kithara, then clarinet melody, accomplish the exit of the procession: Creon, Oedipus, his daughters, and attendants. *The Final Chorus* — "Call no man fortunate that is not dead" — repeats the three-quarter theme of *The Third Chorus,* more slowly, and the drama ends with a brief coda of resolution.

Oedipus

1954

The theater has many separate and specialized forms in our contemporary world, but they were not always separate and specialized. The central idea of *Oedipus* is to bring together more of the elements that belong to theater with the purpose of increasing its power—its power of communication, its power to give meaning to our existence. The germ of theater had its beginnings in prehistoric festivals and rituals. And if festivals among comparatively primitive people of the present day show anything, they show that no artifice or talent or formalized device or abstraction of some facet of life is excluded that contributes to the power of the performance. At present and in general, we see nothing like this. If we go to the ballet, we get ballet—and music incidentally. But we do not go to the ballet with any idea of concentrating on the music. If we go to the opera, we do go with this idea— and incidentally we are likely to get a spectacle. In all probability, we do not get drama. If we go to see a play, ninety-nine times out of a hundred we get just that—a play.

This specialized trend toward a specialized product involving specialized talents is, in my opinion, a form of unconscious starvation. The theater is starved for music and doesn't know it. The opera is starved for drama, even though drama is right in front of them. And ballet all too often is starved for both, not because both are not present, but because they must be subordinated to incidental roles.

We hear people say the important thing is the dance, or the important thing is the music, or the important thing is the play. In the kind of art I am talking about, they are important all at once. And at the top of the list, among those who prevent them being important all at once, are those purists who insist that the best music is pure music. Among all the trying attitudes of purists, this is undoubtedly the most trying. The purists are momentarily in the saddle. There can be no doubt of that. And I probably use the word "momentarily" in terms of centuries: one needs to look no farther than the prevailing fashions in avant-garde art. But the history of man shows us that purity also holds the seeds of its own rebirth; and a leavening with soil, with people, it has to find a rebirth in broader values if it is not to remain precious and esoteric and rarefying beyond any but the most intensely specialized perceptions.

Station KPFA, at least once in a while, seems to have a talent for a kind of reckless courage in running contrary to prevailing currents. It has proved this by sponsoring my music now and then for a period of about five years. *Oedipus*, the music drama or dance drama, is *not* in the pure tradition. It is exactly contrary to that tradition because it is not just music or dance or drama or music drama. And it is certainly not opera. It cannot be pigeonholed, unless terms are denied their present meanings.

To say that it goes back to a much more ancient tradition of the human race and of Western civilization is to be academic. And I mention this fact only because I wonder whether we can capture emotionally that ancient tradition. If we can't capture it emotionally, then the statement will be forgotten in five seconds; and such miserably little efforts as this *Oedipus* will be irrelevant and immaterial and, in fact, obnoxious.

There have been many attempts in the Western world to bring drama into music. They started with Monteverdi and Caccini in the Renaissance and continued with Gluck, Mussorgsky, Wagner, and Debussy, among others. Because his music was so widely heard and his influence so widely felt, Wagner is the composer we are most likely to think about in this connection. And he should be mentioned because, despite his frequently voiced theories about music drama, it never had a fighting chance with Wagner. In the wrestling match between Wagner's music drama and his symphony orchestra, Wagner's symphony orchestra (with yeoman help from his arias) gets both shoulders of Wagner's music drama on the floor within five minutes after the curtain rises and for the following two or three hours jumps up and down on the unconscious form. Which is to say, perhaps, that our climate is a purist's climate. It is also the climate of technicians in the various forms of purity and the climate of those who commercially exploit the techniques of purity. If this is so, it is futile to

talk about the precise elements that go to make up the music drama
Oedipus.

I can talk about them in the broad way in which I have, but the
details would constitute, in effect, a foreign language with no ear to
understand. I can only hope that my listeners will relax into a tolerant
and receptive state, like a patient under hypnosis. It might be interesting to relax and see what happens. If you begin to get angry over
what happens, you are undoubtedly a gentleman and a scholar and
a purist. If you succumb to the hypnosis, you are probably a lot more
primitive than you realize; and perhaps you may not have been born
in the right age either. If nothing happens, well, any comment on my
part would be gratuitous.

My music has been rather widely described as springing from a
forty-three-tone-to-the-octave scale. That "forty-three" is a convenient peg, an easy and slightly sensational label; and it is all right if
it isn't taken too seriously. If I have ever emphasized the number, I
certainly have not done so for a long, long time. It isn't even a half-
truth. It is about a one-tenth-truth, perhaps. I have adapted two organs
to multitoned scales, one to forty-three tones and the other to somewhat more. And others of my instruments contain the implications
of that many tones and sometimes more. Whatever total number of
tones that are available to me, they are simply a *source scale,* just as
they are with any composer. I have used forty-three tones, and more,
and a lot less.

It has been said, by rather prominent people in the music profession, both in the press and the academic world, people who are
themselves guiltless of any experimentation, that my music sounds
the way it does because I use a multitone scale. I must say that I am
mystified by the powers of observation in such people. In *Castor and
Pollux* I used exactly nineteen tones to the octave; two of the choruses
in *Oedipus* employ exactly eight tones to the octave (this was also true
two years ago). A simple examination of the score would show this.
And I have used at various times only five tones; yes, even only four
tones. And before I die, I have the firm intention of writing some
music in one tone to the octave. Then those who say that this music
sounds as it does because it has one tone to the octave will be approaching the truth. My only point in talking this way is that whatever
happens *I* am the guilty party, not forty-three tones. I am sure that
without any great exercise of ingenuity forty-three tones to the octave
could be made to take on the superficial character of Stravinsky,
Debussy, Wagner, Mozart, Johann Sebastian Bach, or Glenn Miller.

The Rhythmic Motivations
of *Castor and Pollux* and
Even Wild Horses

1952

"Do you write classical or popular?" This is a frequent question when I say I am a composer. We can be amused by the oversimplification, yet it indicates—among simple people—a profound feeling of a basic difference. Yes, a dichotomy—and in my opinion an annoyingly unhealthy one, too. The generally unspoken contempt of the one for the other is palpable, even though one may hear: "Some of my best friends are jazz musicians," or "Ditto-ditto-ditto—play in the symphony."

When I answer the simple question with a stumbling, "Neither, I write my *own* music," I directly convey my status as a rebel, but also indirectly admit that I am groping around for something *human* to hang on to. I don't *like* to be alone either. Spiritually—that is, by the standard of serious probing into the history and aesthetics of music, and also by the standard of belief which goes its way with little hope or expectation of financial reward—I belong to the "classicals." Yet by the touchstone of human needs of this age, I find myself looking upon the "populars" across the gully with frank admiration. Oh, I am *critical*—of technique of composition, performance, *and* concept. I can single out, almost never, a single composition or performance that I would want to hold on to for the rest of my life, in the way that I like to hold on to a certain Brahms trio. Nevertheless, the essence of the sum total adds up to *strength*.

What is the difference? The "classicals" carry on the tradition— if not the spirit—of musical insight, of a profound and subtle nature. The moods, the messages, run the various gamuts of intellect and emotion. The trouble with this is that the whole profession tends to become rarefied, to become something only for those *in the know*. And when the cognoscenti constitute the general staff of a culture, as they do in serious music in this country, it is time for those who think for themselves to start a revolution, or get out.

Let's talk about the disease itself. The disease is a loss of contact with this time and this place. The preoccupation with musical Europe of preceding ages by the "classicals" effectively blinds them to anything so mundane as this time and place. And in describing the situation in these terms, it becomes fairly easy to highlight the differences between the two cultures, coexisting on two sides of a chasm.

By my own definition of the "classical" attitude, it would seem that this side of the chasm has everything, yet there is at least one quality that is singularly lacking—a quality which spontaneously gains acceptance because it fills a need of this time and place, and it will be profitable to leave the subject of the degradation of values by the industrial era to the political economists and the social scientists, at least for the present. Let us be realists, yes, even optimists, in that we must and will proceed with what we have—a situation that exists—rather than lapse into an enchanted dream about a world where music critics get salaries paid to them for writing sense.

I spoke of one singular quality the "populars" have (if I seem to confound "popular," "Dixieland," "jazz," "progressive jazz," it is because of the recognition—in my simple mind—of the fact that they are all on the same side of the gully). I do not refer to the limited harmonies they use, which are infinitely boring; nor to the average subject matter—God forbid!—nor to the delivery of word, which is often fresh, often natural, often *human*, even in moans; nor even to the instrumentation and individual performance on instruments, which is frequently exciting. For the particular purpose of the point I am making, and of the motivations behind *Castor and Pollux* and *Even Wild Horses*, I refer to the potentialities of its rhythms, and its only half-conscious attitude toward its rhythms.

One is attracted to what stimulates his imagination, his spirit of adventure, his inherent creative desire—something we *all* have in common. As I have said—the harmonies suggest no possibility for development, the themes seldom, and the factor of the delivery of words in *Even Wild Horses* (*Castor and Pollux* involves no text) is a minor one. The rhythmic practices of the "populars" are the crux. After I have sat through a couple of hours with a good band in a nightclub, these are a source of both fascination and annoyance. Fascination because the music tends to fulfill a basic need—of both the naive and the sophisticated; annoyance because it goes endlessly on its way, with a strict, limited bong-bong-bong, almost always without retard or acceleration, almost always without subtle nuance or elaboration (except within the framework of that steady bong-bong), and almost always *with* the tawdriest kind of melodic utterance, however intriguing the instrumentation and delivery may be.

We can analyze these factors further. The steady, undeviating beat is a feature of all or nearly all primitive musical cultures. It sometimes proceeds for hours, to the point of stupid hypnosis—and *stupid* is to my mind *the* adjective. Yet within the frame of a limited objective, perhaps *even this*—this that annoys my susceptibilities so greatly—is one of the sources of the strength I seek! I am at least willing, in *Castor and Pollux,* so to postulate. Further, with "classical" music in mind, the matter of accents within the timed bong-bong is a *different* factor. In a sense, the flinging of every tone into the air in a time relation to another tone flung into the air is an accent. Some are stronger than others, and, when the percussive department is considered, the comparison between the strong and the weak (not called accents at all) is very striking.

A percussive sound is one in which the tonal envelope is initially wide, a sudden impact, which quickly—or slowly—diminishes, and, obviously, the rhythmic character of popular music is primarily determined by its percussion—only secondarily by its various winds (unless they are used in a percussive manner).

The expectation of a regular (or implied) beat in nearly all "classical" music, old or contemporary, frequently becomes, in "popular" music, an expectation of an *accent* only *halfway* through the beat, or *one-third* or *two-thirds* through the beat, or *one-fourth* or *three-fourths,* or even *two-fifths* or *three-fifths* through the beat—this last not notated but strongly felt. Much of the time these fractional "accents" are part of a running pattern—not always accented. This essay is no primer of the African musical influence, but it must contain a simple statement of African musical character, and at least mention in passing that of the "inferior" peoples of Europe, particularly the gypsies. That the African sense of rhythmic subtlety has degenerated, in the course of its evolution from tribal ceremony to Cuban ritual to Hollywood nightclub, requires no laboring, it seems to me. Its history is of little present concern to me, because I see in its developed forms—rumba, conga, samba—seeds for stimulating expansion and *strength.* And I like to build at least somewhat on the cognition of those around me. Even those who don't like rumbas, congas, sambas, have this cognition; they can't avoid it. This, then, becomes the rhythmic motivation behind *Even Wild Horses.* I will *put back,* if I can, the nuance and subtlety that the transatlantic crossing and two or three centuries have dissipated. Yes, and more, too—the insight and profundity of our European tradition in "classical" music.

I realize that I am not the first to undertake this kind of hybrid realization—or revitalization. Again, I am uninterested in history. Right here I am only concerned with this effort, to bring the attitudes I admire—the serious "classical" attitudes, both in music and dance (I call both *Castor and Pollux* and *Even Wild Horses* dance music)— into some rapport with an obvious need of this time and place, with what is to my mind admirable and strong. Yes, it has been done before, but it has never been done in a scale *different* from that used in popular music, nor with a strong and varied percussion department of *new* instruments, not one of which is to be found in a nightclub, and— frankly—more like those on the banks of the Congo (or in a Balinese temple) than on the Harlem River.

Because I use a forty-three-tone-to-the-octave scale, and because I use new instruments, which I myself have built, the sounds and harmonies of the two dance compositions under discussion are—I think—uniquely my own. Only the rhythms suggest—I repeat, *suggest*—some recognition of present-day musical experience. I imagine that any dogmatic drummer who is a technical master of rumba, conga, and samba would like to make me the central figure of an auto-da-fé, with my own Bass Marimba supplying the faggots, for my effrontery in using these names for this music.

So be it. Having efficiently antagonized "classical" musicians for thirty years, why should I leave undemolished the other possible bridges leading out of my lonely isolation? Still, I really do not expect this result: I wish that most "seriously" trained musicians had the open-mindedness toward new techniques that I have frequently found in jazz musicians.

But to get back to the first of the rhythmic elements, the one I questioningly admire, the steady—or steadily implied—bong-bong-bong. In *Castor and Pollux*, I preserved this steady beat for sixteen minutes with the intention of making it sufficiently varied and interesting in subsidiary rhythm and beat (it is in alternate measures of four and five beats, and three and four beats), and by melodic and harmonic elaboration and contrapuntal accumulation, that it would not only be bearable but—if my postulate is correct—give it a *strength* it would not otherwise possess. *Castor and Pollux* is entirely percussive—even plucked strings are essentially so, although the Kithara tone dies slowly—and *Even Wild Horses* is mostly percussive; the only singing tones are by Adapted Viola and Chromelodeon. Even the voice in musical speech should be mostly percussive.

In order to effect the kind of sum total of the parts—rhythmic and tonal—that I envisioned—*enauralized*—for *Castor and Pollux*, it was necessary to repeat phrases frequently, which in the playing of the pairs of instruments may seem musically pointless. Yet this helps in gaining familiarity with the themes, and on each second hearing—in the sum total—the juxtapositions cause each single repetition to be heard under entirely different musical conditions (the steady beat excepted). The work is constituted, in a sense, of a series of coincidences, of carefully calculated, musical "double exposures," as climaxes to series of "single exposures."

My elaborations upon the basic samba, rumba, conga, ñañiga percussive patterns in *Even Wild Horses* are mostly too complex for interesting, or even bearable, verbalization, and—of course—words give no idea of the emotional effect. Something besides the brain of a good musician has to vibrate in order to provide this. I have carried the samba through on the straight, traditional 4/4, but here and there it is interspersed with a few measures of fast 13/16 time—that is, three-sixteenths of the 4/4 beat are left out, in continuous passages. The rumba is kept on the traditional 4/4 only when the viola is silent. With the viola singing—obviously a solo—the measure pattern is alternate 3/4 [and] 4/4, which gives a somewhat Hindu *seven* character to the Cuban dance form.

The ñañiga I have notated as 2/4, rather than 6/8, because it is conceived as a straight two against three throughout the first fast section—Bass Marimba against the ñañiga Wood Block and Cymbal. The conga has a deleted beat in the second and fourth measures, but these two missed beats are added to the sixth measure, making it five. Thus, the measure beat pattern is 4–3–4–3–4–5, but the strongly characteristic conga beat is always present, as traditionally, in alternate measures. The scenes that I call Afro-Chinese Minuet and Tahitian Dance possess the implied elements; it would be futile to try to pin these down to experiences that the average American knows as well as rumba, conga.

These are dance forms—of a folk nature—yet this music is not folk music, it is art music written for interpretive dance techniques. I have written no choreography, but I feel sure that this music *can* be danced, and I would like nothing better than to inspire some inquisitive dancer, who feels that this exposition makes a little sense here and there, to undertake it. Does an interpretive dance *have* to have a story? It *does* have to have some implied dramatic dynamic sequence; it *does* have to grow and develop from related tensions, and these, I think, the music supplies, without story, although I am sure a story that fits it could be invented. The modern folk spectacle of a ballroom full of people doing a samba is quite an experience— without inherent dynamic sequence. Here again, there is the strength of this time and place, the immediacy, the rhythmic actuality.

Also (in the compositions under discussion), the dance forms are not maintained (the rumba excepted) throughout, but are metamorphosed, developed, into something very different from their starting moods—the minuet and the ñañiga become radically different. Thus, too, the dance should develop and evolve, assuming dramatic and dynamic significance in the process.

Fragments of voice are written into the five final scenes of *Even Wild Horses*—extracted from Rimbaud's *A Season in Hell*. Where do these fit into the rhythmic motivations? There is a reason deeper than the sheer animalistic exhilaration of well-exploded and explosive words. It is to be found in the poet's life and character and in the composer's feeling of affinity.

Rimbaud abandoned literature at an age—nineteen—that has nothing to do with insight, and not so terribly much to do with maturity. The insight of his poetry is essentially the attraction, of course, without which the subsequent abandonment would be meaningless. In a few almost-frenzied phrases, he explored most of the avenues of spirit attainment, contemplation, escape, conjecture, of most of the poets before him, and since. He poured out innocence, he dwelt on the primitive, the humanness (and doom) of those who transgressed. He "sought out" the rooming houses that the "intractable convict" might have "*consecrated* [italics mine] by his passing." Louise Varèse, one of his translators, speaks of his "mysterious honesty." There is also an expression of insufficiency, of nothingness, ". . . a face so dead, that perhaps those whom I met *did not see me*."

To imply that he abandoned literature because of some mystical search for the "meaning of life," in which literature seemed impotent, and not because his greatest effort was ignored by those who alone had the power to perceive, is to imply that he was less than human. If anything, Rimbaud was more than human. When he speaks of the already "intractable" boy poet "locking himself within the coolness of latrines," he suggests an honest humanness, and acceptance of his humanness, which we of the Anglo-Saxon milieu would deny even under extreme torture. Primitive innocence—the child—primitive man. A value lost? Not wholly. Never, so long as man is mortal. This, then, suggests a motivation for a musical wedding of Rimbaud with an elaboration of African and other rhythms.

In reading and rereading *A Season in Hell,* certain phrases came out of the book and hit me with a musical sock on the pancreas. So, I have taken these out of context, rearranged, juxtaposed them, in a pancreatically musical way. I doubt if the Rimbaud exegetes will forgive me, but I comfort myself with the belief that Rimbaud the Irreverent would.

To end, a slight digression. The titles, both of compositions and of their sections, were affixed spontaneously and lightheartedly—even whimsically. They seemed fitting at the moment of birth, but I feel sure that others, equally or more fitting, could be substituted with very minor if any effect on the total reaction, especially since this is *movement* music by concept. *Even Wild Horses* what? At one time I knew the answer. Perhaps I still do, but I cannot articulate it.

Plectra and Percussion Dances

1953

The music that we are playing tonight was conceived for dance theater, though much of the visual element of this conception will not be possible here tonight, of course. Only the visual element of seeing the instruments played is present, and I wouldn't minimize that. But this conception depends very much on a synthesis of music with other arts: with dramatic dancing, with lights, with costumes, with stage sculpture.

If we take the sonata idea, where music is utterly independent and doesn't want any association with other arts, and put it at a point on a globe or a point on a circle, then the idea that I am trying to describe is at the exact polar extreme, or is exactly diametric. This doesn't mean that it is passive music or that it is simply incidental music. This music very, very aggressively demands cooperation with other arts in order to achieve fulfillment — very aggressively.

I conceived *Plectra and Percussion Dances* as a unity, and it is in three parts: *Castor and Pollux, Ring around the Moon, Even Wild Horses.* And it is subtitled *Satyr-Play Music for Dance Theater.* I think this requires a word of explanation. I wrote it following the writing, or the setting to music, of the Sophocles tragedy *Oedipus* and after rehearsing this over a long period. Those who think that hearing or seeing this tragedy produces a catharsis might like to contemplate the kind of catharsis that is produced by setting it to music and rehearsing it for six months. At any rate, I understood the attitude of the ancient Greeks in producing a satyr play after a presentation of tragedy. In my case it was almost a necessity to give vent to feelings and ideas, whims and caprices, even nonsense that seems to have no place in tragedy. Also, philosophically, this first section, *Castor and Pollux,* is exactly diametric. Far from treating with the story of a man who is destroyed simply because he is who he is, it treats with a story where good luck is mandatory—in the story of Castor and Pollux, the twin stars of good luck.

The instrumentation begins with three pairs of instruments heard consecutively, and these represent the various paired creative processes. We're only concerned with the beginnings of Castor and Pollux: the beautiful, mortal woman Leda and the rampantly fertilizing and immortal Zeus in the form of a swan. The first pair is Insemination, the second pair Conception, and the third pair Gestation. And then all these pairs, all these six instruments, combine, playing exactly the music they played before in a kind of a triumphant "Chorus of Delivery from the Egg." "Pollux" follows the same plan.

The second section of *Plectra and Percussion Dances* is *Ring around the Moon.* And I'm always a little hard-pressed to find words to give any verbal validity to this piece of music. On the jacket of the record that the Gate 5 Ensemble made of the music, I call it a satire on concerts, on the world in general, and on people who write music in forty-three tones to the octave, among a lot of other things. I like the story I saw in a newspaper about the man who was brought into court and heard the clerk get his tongue twisted and say, "You're charged with being guilty. Are you drunk or not drunk?" I'm sure a great many people are going to consider this music guilty—drunk or not. But I do want to say that it is a serious expression of a philosophy unfamiliar to most lovers of classical music.

The third section, *Even Wild Horses,* has a dramatic plan. It is based on scenes and acts. The five final scenes have titles taken from Rimbaud's *A Season in Hell,* and fragments of the text appear toward the ends of those scenes—in French. The mood of each scene is created long before the voice enters, and the words are done in a semispoken, semichanted, intoned, and highly dramatic manner. Rhythmically, the eight scenes are based on well-known primitive and dance music rhythms. It's an amazing fact that the world of dance music, and of Latin American dance music particularly, has produced an army of purists that is the equal of anything that serious classic music can offer.

I say this in order to advise you that the first scene, for example, "A Decent and Honorable Mistake," may not be recognizable to you as a samba. The second scene, "Rhythm of the Womb, Melody of the Grave," is based on a rhythmically contrapuntal heartbeat. The third scene, "Happy Birthday to You!" begins with an African-sounding marimba and somehow gets involved with a Chinese-sounding guitar in a pentatonic melody, and so I call it an Afro-Chinese minuet. The fourth scene, "Nor These Lips upon Your Eyes," is perhaps recognizable as a rumba. The fifth scene, "Hunger, Thirst, Shouts, Dance," I have called a Cuban fandango with a bit of poetic license perhaps, or, perhaps more accurately, historic and geographic license. The sixth scene, "Land of Darkness and Whirlwinds," begins with a dark adagio, and this very, very slowly develops into a whirlwind allegro. The seventh scene, "Had I Not Once a Lovely Youth?" contains the characteristic and compulsive accent of the conga. But aside from this, any similarity to the conga is purely coincidental. The eighth and last scene, "Let Us Contemplate Undazed the Endless Reaches of My Innocence," I have called, perhaps whimsically, a Tahitian dance.

Philosophically, *Even Wild Horses* might be considered autobiographical by almost anyone in relation to himself, in certain moments of his life at least, perhaps in dark and humorous moments. It begins with his coming into the world as a decent and honorable mistake, and long before his life has run its course, he begins to be aware of the endless reaches of his innocence.

Some New and Old Thoughts after and before *The Bewitched*
(A Latter-Day Ritual Designed to Defertilize the Machine Age for a Period of Seventy-five Minutes)

1955

Even through a life given to at least occasional pursuit of them, the qualities of intuition and imagination are capricious and elusive. But they are the natural confines of a vision in art, and to the lonely, contemplative artist they hold the enduring rewards.

Traditions are found within this compass, indeed, but they lie far beyond the usual schoolroom concepts. To consider some period briefly preceding the present as the only valid tradition is to cultivate myopia. To encompass—at least intuitively and unconsciously—thousands of years of man's sensitivity to his world is to rise above triviality, and above the noncompulsive inventions mothered by scholarship. The scholarly inherence of "good usage" in the organization of art represents nothing so much as well-jelled tastelessness.

Always, after humanity's concern with sufficient food and sufficient protection, comes an effort to understand its experience. And as man's art life through both known and unknown millenniums lengthens, mere security carries ever less meaning in itself. The bringing into the world of babes, who in turn will beget more babes, who will stand for nothing more than the perpetuation of the American standard of living, is to compound human tragedy. Another tastelessness.

The modes and variable directions that the interpretation of experience takes have endured, and profited from, many shocks, not the least of which is man's own ingenuity. In a bare and microscopic few decades, the evolution of electronics has brought one to music.

Because of its innate conservatism, the words *in time* must be doubly underlined, in the case of music, when mentioning the incorporation of man's ingenuity into his art. Simply a servant at first to the already existing instruments, electronic sound is now emitting painful birth sounds as an art, or an element in an art.

The people who first stretched a piece of gut over two bridges, or who sounded tones on a reed from the marsh, or found tones in wood suspended at the nodes, discovered magic, just as definitely as the people who found tones in electronic tubes, and they went on from this to the infinitely greater magic of art. The magic of ingenuity was the springboard from which to plunge, through intuition and imagination, into an insight into greater mysteries.

Some part of the old and the new will—they must—be amalgamated. And by *old* one does not have to imply something as recent as harpsichords and clavichords. When getting caught up in resources resulting from new ingenuity, it is so easy to forget and dismiss the truly older values, some of which may be specific for this age, and are crying to be resurrected, as though from the dead.

The Japanese *koto* and the Chinese *kin* represent unspoken philosophies in the cultures in which they grew, and in the headlong plunge of the Orient to "catch up" with the West, these old instruments and the values behind them are being threatened. But this is not an imperative in a culture in flux. What is an imperative, if it is not to be lost, is that the old be encompassed by a new vision and a new imagination.

The symphony orchestra has a range of resources, in timbres and qualities, beyond those which come today from assembled speakers, and strengthened by ancient or imagined instruments, it can have a far greater one still. The formality-riddled and education-bogged symphony is anachronistic, yes indeed, but it contains values which should not be lost.

Electronics can reproduce any sound of any instrument so closely that no one knows the difference, according to various statements by engineers, but—even if true—it does not follow that direct man-on-instrument music is no longer desirable. Electronics for its *own* sounds' sake is a resource that one would be stupid to dismiss, but the implication is irrelevant, even misleading.

It says that music is a pure art of sound, for people with ears, but with little else—no eyes, no nerve endings anywhere but the ears, no interrelated functions. And as a matter of fact much electronic music leaves the impression that this *is* the attitude in which the sounds are composed.

It says that the functional shape of an instrument is not important as a sculptural object, and that the techniques developed on it, because of its particular virtues and its particular defects, are obsolescent. That the physical, sensual vision of the playing of it is no longer required.

This age has been called, among other things, the electronic, and a great deal has been said about the necessity of *expressing* one's own time. And this has led to the use of airplane sounds in music, of chaotic street sounds, sounds of machinery in operation, and sounds of plumbing in the modern home.

To be aware of this time and place, and the desideratum of the individual's significance in the face of the machine, is one thing. But nothing could be more futile or downright idiotic than to *express* this age. Or any other age. The prime obligation of the artist is to transcend his age, therefore to see it in terms of the eternal mysteries, to use its materials at the same time that he transforms them into magic. What this age needs more than anything else is an effective antidote. And if the contemporary artist could actually be present in any other age, it is probable that he would feel the same way about it.

The new art materials of a new age — concrete sounds, electronic sounds, what have you — are most certainly to be accepted, but with a reexamined philosophy of use, that they may be carried on the wings of a vision, to the limits of intuition and imagination.

Of the several areas of contemporary life urgently crying for antidotes, at least two or three are terribly relevant to music. Is there a despairing soul who, after some forty years of it, has not consciously yearned for some counter-irritant to so-called popular music?

A more appropriate term might be comic book music, because in the area of verbal communication comic books are roughly parallel. Both comic book music and comic books are produced commercially for very young, immature minds, and it is pertinent to observe that a large percentage of Americans have their musical and literary tastes frozen at this point, for the balance of their lives.

Those in the comic book music industry have frankly stated that their product is designed for girls and boys of high school age. Now everyone is aware that such adolescents are, of all people, the most maudlin conformists, excepting always a very few that could be numbered on one hand at the end of a lifetime. Yet this highly polished commercial product, tailored to the tastes of adolescents, assails our ears almost throughout our waking hours, through jukeboxes, through virtually every radio and TV station.

We do not let the adolescent drive a car until he is at least sixteen. We consider that he or she has insufficient self-control to sit at a bar over a glass of beer until he or she has reached a point several years past high school age. We believe that he or she is too immature to possess judgment as a citizen until he or she is that same age. Yet we accept the musical judgments of these same people until we are ninety years old.

What the adolescent needs, of course, is understanding and leadership, and he or she will never get leadership from the commercial musical world, which — despite its occasionally charming tunes — contains the seeds of ever-more imaginative orchestrations for consistently trivial concepts.

That this has all come about through a conspiracy of machines is obvious. But it is too easy to talk about *kitsch,* the substitute "culture" of the unrooted masses, because it is all too likely that the person with literary discretion — who wouldn't be caught dead buying a comic book — will stand in line to buy tickets for some publicized "hit," in order to make an offering in mass tribute to comic book music. Another evil by-product of Western "purity" and specialization: categorical discriminations are not automatically transferred.

What is the antidote? Can music be an antidote for music? Personally, I feel that it is the only effective one, since human beings carry within themselves at all times, in any art area, the potentialities of revolution and rebirth, and a very small fillip of fertilization is sometimes enough. One can have faith that the majority of Americans, who as a fact are not adolescent, will finally have received all that they can take.

Another element of contemporary life which cries for an antidote is the labor-saver, the miracle button, which does virtually everything, increasingly and progressively, the miracle dial of electronics. And in this category should be included services which the artist has forgotten how to do for himself. Labor is saved, and a value is lost in the process.

We automatically lose a value when cars speed us over the highway, although the loss is lessened when we realize it, and instinctively try to find it again. I have walked through a section of country with a pack on my back, preoccupied constantly with all manner of petty personal problems, yet now and then, as the result of the experience, I was aware of the magic of small growing things, the magic of a running stream where I threw down my pack, the magic of a fire by its side.

In musical magic, the roots can be seen with greater clarity in the simpler instruments, from simpler ages. Already, in the nineteenth century, when the freshened visions of the Renaissance had dissipated, the profession of music was removed some few degrees from the magic of nature. The pianist who has never studied the tuning of his piano, and learned how to do it, has never experienced the parallel of a fire of twigs by a running stream. He is already removed from that value by the analogy of a faucet in a sink and a button on a stove, because the miracle of tonal relationships comes to him already piped. And unfortunately his education, which in its root word implies that doors are being opened to him, is actually closing a door—the first door, I might add, to an insight into musical magic.

The discovering of this initial magic calls for a certain amount of dedication, but unlike electronics, it does not call for either huge sums of money or great technical know-how. Strings over bridges, blocks of vibrating wood, drums, are economical things, evolving under one's own hands, through imagination and a minimal ingenuity. And they bring the musician and composer into direct contact with miracles.

The forms that imagination may devise transform the primitive sound-generation ideas into vehicles for new and exciting adventures, and the act of transforming, in itself, like a fire by a stream, is an antidote to this age, a transcendence of its materials. And it is a small reaching back, through many thousands of years, to the first men who wished to find meaning for their lives through art.

Both to the player and his audience, the act of playing, especially on new instruments, can be galvanizing. The emerging popularity of percussion instruments, both in solo and ensemble work, might indeed be credited to an unconscious desire for this particular antidote. For nothing could be more human and therefore less expressive of a tyrant army of machines. Percussion as a human art goes back, at least— one would imagine—to the Old Stone Age. So well ensconced is it in the genes of some races that it might well antedate fire.

I have noted audience reactions to my own work in percussion, and have pondered it as profoundly as I am able. Until 1946 I had no percussion instruments whatever, although I sometimes used my guitar belly for finger percussion. But by 1952, when I had several, and all my music became characterized by percussive rhythms, there was an immediate change. This manifested itself in more intense listening, more excitement, and at least some eagerness to repeat the experience. And, best of all, in a general feeling that doors were being opened. My pre-percussion audiences never showed the same here-and-now excitement. Again I emphasize the unconscious response to a longed-for antidote, a small and sudden relief because—in the face of wizardous dials and jukebox comic books—there is still such a thing as ancient rhythmic magic.

This approach to the musical art certainly does not preclude the new materials of this age, neither electronic music nor common sounds. Its virtues are its humanness, its simplicity, its directness, its built-in momentum. And one needs neither a Ford grant nor a dying rich uncle to contemplate it. Only direction and dedication.

So far, I have talked about vehicles for sound generation. What of music itself? The purists' approach to music is bound up in the word *concert*, and calls for a very special antidote. Regardless of the composer's individual thinking about his work generally, the fact that he envisions his final product in concert terms reveals his academically conditioned attitude as to the place of "serious" music in our life. And the same attitude can be discerned in electronic music and/or *musique concrète*, even though more "organized sound" is heard on records than in staged performances. It is intended to carry communication without reliance on nonmusical arts.

This is the recent historical attitude, in Europe and—automatically—here. (And every Ivy League journalist and Ivy League A&R man who flies eastward across the ocean whenever a European idea sneezes politely, but is honor-bound to dismiss a veritable whirlwind of wheezing when it comes from west of the Hudson River, is eloquent testimony in behalf of the American automism.) The world outside the West, and indeed the West itself in more ancient times, is quite another dish of tapioca.

The value that we have lost—temporarily, I hope—is evident when we see a performance of the Japanese kabuki. It is not to be explained merely as a difference between widely separated cultures. The Japanese theater, which at the time of its revolutionary advent included all the skills of popular entertainment, such as juggling and tumbling, represents a quality in an integrated art, and however we may use music in conjunction with drama and dance, our value lies in "purity."

Thus, opera tends to be music only, drama tends to be drama only, and film art tends to be film art only. And *ballet* and *modern dance* are limited to exactly those terms. And the "incidental" designation that is applied to music in conjunction with these arts is a perfectly logical "purist" adjective. Integration as a dramatic or ritualistic imperative is neither desired consciously nor understood. We are too far removed in centuries of *pure* "progress." Yet it is a fact that we *do* respond, and magnificently—as in the case of kabuki— when we are somehow exposed to an ancient art that takes integration for granted.

In ancient Greece, and to some extent in medieval Europe, the value *was* taken for granted. To rediscover it calls for a fusing of many disciplines, or at least a willingness to use and understand many. It demands that the musician remain undismayed when he is asked to act, sing, dance, tumble, even to help design and light a stage. Or, begin with the term *actor*, or *dancer*, and let the other designations follow, being sure that *musician* is one of them. Herein lies the chief barrier to such a philosophy, since our tendency toward a precious "purity" in the arts has created departmentalized schools in everything. And the ancient value is buried under hegemonies and hierarchies and bureaucratic administerings.

Some thirty years of my life have seen how individuals can respond to such a philosophy, and do, because some part of them has been given to provoking musicians and singers into becoming actors—appealing, perhaps, to the ham in them, through heavy layers of Puritan inhibitions and academic intimidations. Once they are gotten out of the soul-destroying pit, and shown that they are an absolutely necessary ingredient in latter-day rituals designed to castrate the machine age, and to transcend the pit-cursed lives they have led, their responses are positively electric.

The human voice is another ingredient of our art that hasn't even begun to fulfill its potentialities, because the conventions of "art" singing have buried them in limbo. Both in the matter of spoken (or intoned) and sung words, and in the matter of pure emotional sounds—ugly, frightening sounds if called for—the possibilities of voice usage are vast. Here, the composer must struggle against a pervasive inertia, to achieve an integrated art in which he has the obligation to delineate dramatic as well as musical disciplines.

Too often, in peoples' minds, *discipline* means *convention*. This was clearly evident some years ago in the baroque art of ballet, and, as a direct result of the equating of discipline with convention in the minds of ballet masters, we now have the spectacle of boys and girls throwing their arms and their eyes to heaven in gestures of anguish and despair, in the women's gyms of colleges all over the country.

Through modern dance the inevitable revolt, the demonstration, came, several decades ago, showing that disciplines outside the purview of ballet could also constitute a dance art. Alas, like the Puritans, who—when they moved across the ocean and became masters—fathered a philosophy just as intolerant as that of their earlier tormentors, modern dance proceeded to consecrate the dogmas of its saints, and to put one of its disciples in every women's gym. The doors that close *because* of education are the saddest doors that humanity never walked through.

Obviously, any fine art involves a discipline, but it must be a force that cuts its own way, through a veritable jungle of possibilities. It may have only the most tenuous connection with momentary convention. When a concept is a so-called pioneering effort especially, it must create its own disciplines, in an inspired determination to administer a meaningful antidote to this age.

It has been said frequently, but I will say it again: art—concepts expressed through art—is an incalculable influence on the direction of our civilization, simply because it influences the children who become the men who find themselves in positions of world leadership. Its influence may be minute, or it may carry a force beyond that of armies. It need have no limitations of concept; it need be no less effective or significant, for example, if its vehicle is satire rather than tragedy.

More than one thoughtful person has stated that response to tragedy in the Aristotelian sense is not possible with modern American audiences. And it is certainly not to be expected, for one reason because its habiliments so constantly clothe the screaming violence that issues from picture tubes through so many hours of each twenty-four. One might be justified in saying that, in such a time as this, satire is in fact exactly what the doctor ordered. It is a specific.

Further, a people dedicated as we are to statistical scholarship and cause-and-effect rationality becomes hopeless only when it ceases to be able to laugh at itself intelligently. I think that it is important for this ability to be proved, not once but constantly. If we do retain it, one of the most effective ways of demonstrating that fact is through our response to satire, and satire communicated in theatrical form, where there can be a contagious audience response.

Satire need not be heavy-handed. It can descend lightly and with love, and imbue the listener and the viewer with a shaft of momentary recognition and delight. It can bring reevaluation and self-perception, because it precipitates momentary people and momentary scenes in a fresh-angle vision. And without seeming labor, finally, it can bring a spontaneous feeling for humanity through art, a feeling that lies within our bones and is precedent to all recorded history, and invokes the oldest of traditions.

It is one of the purposes of scholarship to discover ethical values and disciplines out of the past, verbally and visually stated, and to preserve them. I care a great deal about contemplating an age or ages that have been discovered through digging and presuming and learning. But I care even more for the divination of an ancient spirit of which I *know* nothing.

A Soul Tormented by Contemporary Music Looks for a Humanizing Alchemy: *The Bewitched*

1957

Communication, if it functions at all, comes in many disguises: in plain words, or in artfully inflected words, or perhaps no words at all; perhaps telepathically or, according to some, as the result of transmigratory souls recognizing each other from former lives. In any case, there *is* such a thing as extraverbal magic. And extraverbal magic is something I now wish to invoke.

Among a certain segment of our population, such a sentence as, "That cat's way out," carries a superficial communication—perhaps a key to the kind of person the "cat" is. But it also communicates the sense of a locked door, because it also seems to say that unless *you* are also "way out" you won't understand him or communicate with him. It is my purpose tonight to try to communicate, to try to unlock the door to something that is generally considered to be "way out." And with the help of a little extraverbal magic, I hope to succeed.

One fairly sure way to gain sympathy and understanding, and therefore to achieve communication, is to confess one's sins. But this involves a risk: because, although you may consider that you have sinned, both magnificently and deeply, there is always the possibility that your listeners won't have the foggiest idea what you're talking about. However, this little talk might be titled "The Musical Confessions of a Cat about Thirty-five Years 'Way Out,' " because it was just about thirty-five years ago—and you have only to look around me here to see substantial proof—that I abandoned the path of musical rectitude. To bridge a chasm of thirty-five years, I am going to *need* extraverbal magic. And a confession is meaningless, unless it is submitted—prayerfully—on the right altar.

During the past nine years in California, my work has been sponsored through the energies of a microwave laboratory; and lectures and performances of my music have been programmed through the energies of a department of speech and drama, a department of philosophy, and a heterogeneous group of painters; and at other times through the energies of a department of sociology and anthropology and a department even of zoology. Now it would seem pointless to confess musical sins before microwavists, dramatists, philosophers, painters, sociologists, anthropologists, and zoologists. The occasion on Tuesday evening I may say is a most auspicious one in my life — because a large performance of my music is being brought off through the energies of a school of music. This is the right altar, and if my confession on this singular occasion seems to take a whimsical or an inexplicable turn, or even a slightly belligerent one, please remember that I am trying to cross a gap of thirty-five years of comparative isolation from my own profession.

The official title of my talk tonight is "A Soul Tormented by Contemporary Music Looks for a Humanizing Alchemy." Let me clear the air immediately by starting off with a confession that, for the purposes of this talk, *I* am the soul tormented by contemporary music and that, needless to say, the music causing the torment does not exclude my own.

There was a time in the history of so-called Western man when music was so vital a part of ritual and ceremony as to have no pure and separate function. The integration of music with every important ceremonial in ancient Greece was so complete that, for example, the sounds of spoken words used in ceremonies were a basis for creating the sounds of music. But we do not have to theorize about ancient Greece. We can see contemporary cultures of our own world where the same kind of integration is taken for granted. The kabuki theater of Japan is an example. And here we have fact — not merely theory.

In the modern Western world, we do not have this kind of integrated experience. In the modern Western world, we have specialization and art segregation. We have specialization at the same time that all of us, no matter what our particular specialty, are assailed with music through much of our waking hours from phonograph records, radios, TV sets, jukeboxes. These sounds assail us regardless of our occupations at the moment. We are bathed in music, submerged in music up to — but not necessarily including — our ears. And still, we do not have integration. We don't have even integrated background.

I think it is possible to give our music a new and modern lease on life through integration with some of the more directly human elements still remaining in a machine age culture. In the more primitive cultures, they have puberty rites and mating ceremonies as outlets for creative music. Now it seems hopeless to imagine *our* puberty rites, if any, being integrated with music. And our marriage ceremonies seem to get integrated in a kind of incidental way only with Wagner, Mendelssohn, "I Love You Truly," or nothing. But we still have live theater, which I could call a directly human element; and we especially have live theater on college campuses and in the many little theaters in metropolitan areas. And it is the relation of music to theater that is uppermost in my mind right now.

Realization of the problem of live music in live theater includes facing up to this ingrained philosophy of specialization, facing up to the conspicuous failure of both drama and music to understand each other in this modern world, and facing up to the fact of separate schools of theater and music, and the fact of dancers—whether male or female—being not in theater or music but in the women's gymnasium. The symbol of a large part of this problem, so far as theater is concerned, can be found in one idea: the orchestra pit. To me the orchestra pit is a symbol of shame, the shame of both music and the theater. Each has gone its own way: music to the specialization of the symphony, drama to the specialization of the Broadway success.

I, for one, do not believe that these specializations automatically exclude the capacity to integrate. Each needs the other; and the need is historical and constant. They need each other so badly that they run to the edges of their specialties and shout to each other for help. They are both ambivalent up to the hilt. The theater gets its help from music—and then demonstrates its ambivalence by inventing the orchestra pit with the musicians operating in solitary confinement, excommunicated, stealing away through hidden secret passages to play cards or to shoot craps at every opportunity because they have no integrated part in the drama and are frankly bored. To show their ambivalence in turn, the musicians frequently drown out and render much onstage unintelligible.

Music, in its cry for help from drama, has gotten opera; and music dearly loves this help from drama. In fact it loves this help so much that it virtually loves it to death. In its grander forms, opera floods its drama in caresses—the caresses of massed strings and brasses, symphony orchestras, arias, and recitatives. I must not allow myself the liberty of elaboration that the word *opera* opens up. I want to get back to the theater, which, despite its orchestra pit, I honestly believe has the greater freedom from precise traditional limitations.

Someone recently asked me if there is any kind of tradition behind my work. I replied that this depends: first, on what particular piece of geography you have in mind; and second, on whether you mean A.D. or B.C. If traditions are considered to be only European and to date from A.D. 1700, I have few. However, if traditions are considered to be worldwide and to date, say, from 500 or 1000 B.C., the spirit of my work might even be called reactionary. It is curious that despite our retention of so much from ancient Greek civilization—musical words, for example, *melos* (melody), *harmonia* (harmony), *symphonia* (symphony), *antiphonia* (antiphony), and the word *chorus*, which I understand still preserves much of its ancient spoken sound—yet the spirit of integration of music and the important things in life, which was so significant a factor in Greek civilization, we have lost.

Forgetting all about 2,000 years of Christian civilization for a moment, I would call my music Dionysian and dithyrambic, even though what might be considered the opposite character is also present at times. But I believe spiritually and materially in ranging over the whole history and prehistory of man through work and divination. In the rest of my talk, I warn you, I am going to be fluctuating constantly between an ancient time in the millenniums around the dawn of history and the immediate American present—the immediate present of undergrads, basketball teams, adolescent lovers, detectives chasing culprits, and politicians—just as though all the intervening centuries never existed. I hope you will stay with me.

The musicians you see here are *not* in an orchestra pit. They are onstage. They are neolithic primitives in their acceptance of magic as real. They are at once both ancient and modern. They don't have time to get bored, to go offstage to play cards, because they are part of the cast of characters. They are part of the act: they sing, whistle, say *Woof* and *Bah,* and stamp their feet.

One always wonders just how a dramatic idea happened to develop. To me the germination of *The Bewitched* was one of the most natural things in my life. The germ of the idea was the fact of The Lost Musicians. In 1952 my music drama *Oedipus* was performed at Mills College in Oakland, California, through the interest of a man in theater, Arch Lauterer. It attracted a good deal of publicity simply because of the unusual nature of my instruments. Therefore, the musicians in the San Francisco Bay area were somewhat aware of my ideas. And after leaving Mills College, I found a studio in Sausalito, just across the Golden Gate Bridge from San Francisco. During the four years I was there, young musicians came in to see me now and then; and I would say that easily 90 percent of them fell into a certain category. They grew up, musically, in dance bands, became bored and dissatisfied, and so went to music schools looking for different and broader perspectives. Here they found what they wanted, for a time, but eventually realized that their music professors, generally speaking, simply marked certain areas *terra incognita* like the ancient geographers—and the less said about them the better because they weren't worth exploring. These musicians did not feel really at home in either musical world, either the serious or the not-so-serious. In my studio they generally played music I had written, although now and then they had jam sessions, one of which started at 9 P.M. and ended only at 4 A.M.; but they occasionally achieved a kind of magic perception through their music. Thus was created the Chorus of Lost Musicians, which is the basis for the dance-satire *The Bewitched*.

The titles of the scenes of this work take me again to Mills College. Shortly after the *Oedipus* performances, a man from a broadcasting organization visited me and suggested that, if I would put out a record of various strange sounds that radio and TV could use as background music wherever they wanted it, I might make a lot of money. There was something fascinatingly repulsive (or repulsively fascinating) about this suggestion, and I began to work on it. But I'm afraid I got carried away with the idea because my satiric sense gained the upper hand in no time at all, and I ended up with such impractical and visionary little items as "Background Music for Filibusters in the United States Senate." But some of this background music and the dramatic situations that I worked out then are actually a part of *The Bewitched*. It seems thoroughly right to me now that the Chorus of Lost Musicians should become the instrument for inducing perception.

Revelation in the Courthouse Park

1969

In endeavoring to attain the heights of Olympus, according to the old Greek myth, it is futile to pile Pelion on Ossa, as the Giants had sought to do.[1] Long before Shakespeare, the drama of Western Europe (and therefore America) took its present form as a specialized theater of dialogue. It is futile, in my view, to pile device upon device in this specialized theater and still expect to attain anything remotely resembling the heights of Greek drama. Yet both the professional companies and college groups that I have heard are guilty of doing so. The present practice of choruses reciting in unison (choral speech) in every variety of range and intonation—from low bass to high soprano— is non-Greek in spirit and also absurd beyond belief. Greek drama was far more than a theater of dialogue, although how much more we cannot know. Music, which was so essential, is a fragile art, and perhaps we will never know the full impact of its use in their drama.

I had tried a much different approach in using the Sophocles *Oedipus*, and however well the audiences responded who had actually *seen* one of the productions, as opposed to those who know only the record, the results somehow troubled me. It seemed that the drama of Oedipus, however compelling, was deposited by the mind in an ancient category called *classical*—that it was not brought home to the audience as a here-and-now work. Because of this insight, I first decided that I would bodily transfer Euripides' *The Bacchae* to an American setting. But in the end, the better solution seemed to be to alternate scenes between an American courthouse park and the area before the palace of ancient Thebes; and the physical courthouse itself (see below) reinforced this decision. I was determined to make this an American here-and-now drama, which, tragically, it truly is. Consequently, there are four alternations between the Courthouse Park and the area before the Theban palace. The Coda, which, in effect, is the ninth scene, brings the work to a close.

Many years ago I was struck by a strong and strange similarity between the basic situation in the Euripides play and at least two phenomena of present-day America. Religious rituals with a strong sexual element are not unknown to our culture, nor are sex rituals with a strong religious element. (I assume that the mobbing of young male singers by semihysterical women is recognizable as a sex ritual for a godhead.) And these separate phenomena, after years of observing them, have become synthesized as a single kind of ritual, with religion and sex in equal parts, and with deep roots in an earlier period of human evolution—all of which sounds delightfully innocent.

However, a menace may easily be hidden within them. The frenzied women in the Euripides play threaten both degradation and annihilation for anyone unwilling to praise or at least respect their particular pattern of mediocrity and conformity, and it is apparent that similar pressures toward the same end are implicit in this country. With this in mind, I have treated the Greek Choruses (much shortened and otherwise altered) as American revival meetings, even though the words I have chosen were suggested by Euripides and of course reinforced by my own experiences.

The Euripidean scenes are my version of *The Bacchae,* so abbreviated as to leave only the skeleton of the story. The rituals of the American Choruses, in theatrical detail and music, are entirely my own conception. In *The Bacchae,* revels are described but are *not* seen or heard. In the First and Third American Choruses, they *are* seen and heard, with the use of nonsense phrases, clichés, gibberish—the cult of Ishbu Kubu, "Deep inside, 'way 'way down, I am!" for example.[2] In *The Bacchae,* physical doom is implied, but it is *never* foretold, as it *was* foretold by the prophet Tiresias in a powerful scene with Oedipus. In the Second and Fourth American Choruses, a particular variety of psychological doom *is* foretold, in nighttime, sleepwalking, dream-nightmare sequences—the first with Sonny, the second with Mom. Both play their roles before a mocking offstage chorus, and both sequences end with a high male voice offstage: "Mother! Mother! No! No!"

There is thus a Greek influence operating in the American Choruses, and an American influence operating in the Greek Scenes (the revival meetings). The American Choruses are symbolic and psychological, the Euripidean Scenes mythological and realistic. Dion, the Hollywood idol, is a symbol of dominant mediocrity, Mom is a symbol of blind matriarchal power, and Sonny is a symbol of nothing so much as a lost soul, one who does not or cannot conform to the world he was born to. The fact that *mother* is a belonger and doer, and *son* is a non-belonger and voyeur, involves a bitter irony—one that is not only appropriate, but also necessary dramatically, in either the ancient or the modern sense.

As in the case of *Oedipus*, the anguished analyses and explanations at the end of the work are omitted, beginning with the mother's realization of what she has done, because they seem unnecessary, even tedious. This involves about an eighth of the total dialogue. I sometimes feel that Sophocles in *Oedipus the King*, Euripides in *The Bacchae*, and Aeschylus in *The Furies* all were fearful of a grand aposiopesis. But this may be a superficial judgment. It may be that the Greek audience, the Greek mind, demanded that every last drop of meaning be wrung from every action and reaction of both men and gods. (These Greek theater epilogues remind me of a time many years ago when I was reading the dialogues of Plato and came across the line, "I do not quite understand you, Socrates." I laughed and threw the book down. "That ought to be the title," I mused. Very frequently, I do not quite understand you either, Socrates!)

At any rate, the end of the Recognition Scene in this work is very quiet. Cadmus, the father, is gently persuading his daughter, Agave, to look at what she is carrying—her son's heroic mask, which represents his head. The music is exiguous and soft—a slow, steady Eroica beat and a muted cello. With complete realization she emits a low, whispered "No!" and drops the mask to the ground. A tremendous crash of percussion comes simultaneously, and as it diminishes, the mother removes her own mask and drops it on top of the first, with another crash of percussion. She then moves slowly backward (back to audience), downstage, and remains motionless until the Coda has run its inevitably structured course.

I feel impelled to say that whatever perception may emerge in a creative art form based on this idea must be a highly individual one. It is revealable more effectively through the abstractions of music and staging, in this case, than through verbal explanations.

Observations on *Water! Water!*

1962

It is not only difficult to define my theater concepts as a whole—it is impossible. Even if one of them is adequately pinned down for the moment, the next will very likely fail to fit into the prescribed mold.

Singing is always involved in these works, recitatives and choruses frequently, yet they are never *opera*. Dance is involved, yet they are as remote from the *dance concert* as can possibly be imagined. Dialogue is often used, but they do not emerge as *plays*, in any modern sense. Music is seen and heard, but the ideas call forth instruments that— in philosophy, design, and usage—obviously come from the other side of the world.

These concepts may involve songs of a quasi-popular nature, as in the present work, but they nevertheless differ from the Broadway "musical" as radically as John Henry differs from the concert folksinger who invokes his name. Finally, they are not, and never can be, concert music.

When one describes the person who is the father of the concept, he uses such words as *composer, playwright, author,* because he has no others. Each suggests an inherent specialty, in activity and creative interest. I object to all of them as misleading, when applied to myself, and I offer no substitute.

The creative man is not specialized by inclination, but by the autocracy of modern education. He is by nature a conglomerate, with infinite variables, and capable of numerous self-imposed disciplines. Ordinarily, however, he is so closely intimidated by his specialty that if he decides to make some slight deviation from the norm, in some creative work, it will seem like a "revolution," both to him and to others, and he can easily become the progenitor of a "new" movement. But the deviation must be slight, because a large deviation is not only incredible, it isn't even recognizable.

Finally, it is just ridiculous.

There is much talk, and vast activity, in the arts of music and theater, all aimed at avoiding the clichés of previous decades. Thus, in music, the clichés of the nineteenth century are sidestepped through adventures in dissonance, and in new sound-generation processes, which are not necessarily bad. In theater, the clichés of plot and naturalism are avoided through a flight to the "unorganized," to "unreality," to "nothingness," which — I suppose — is not intrinsically bad either.

What is *bad* is that the *forms* are unchanging, are never even spoken of, and are obviously so sacred as to be considered inviolable. The specialty of music in concert form, and the specialty of theater in dialogue form (with occasional incidental music) remain rigid and unalterable concepts, apparently, even to the "new" movements.

Unthinking devotion in high places stifles dynamism. The above-described habit patterns, and the endless parade of groups organized to perform them — glee clubs, orchestras, little theaters, opera work-shops, for example, all shining like the latest cars from the assembly line — constitute the status quo. And the various foundations, the commercial theater, and the thoroughly self-sufficient departments of the modern American university have seemingly undertaken to en-shrine them forever.

To the same degree that these forces continue to be successful, the whole, the variable, the conglomerate soul, will continue to dally in limbo.

There is at least one factor which my various theater concepts have in common; they tend to *include,* not exclude, and therefore to encompass a fairly wide latitude of human experience. They do not exclude — for example — "bad" material, simply because it is thought to be "bad." Gymnastics are not excluded from dance; the half-con-scious rituals of experience — an exhibition of gymnasts, or an insane basketball game — are not excluded from musical concepts. The key of C and the dominant seventh chord are not excluded, nor old jokes, nor nonsense, nor hoboes, nor commonplace tunes, if the overall dynamic, dramatic, or satiric purpose demands them. And as for the nineteenth-century cliché — well, he frequently fills the role of a long-lost friend, a consoler, a beloved and trusted comforter.

Beginning with a kind of musical story-poem, which I wrote when I was fourteen, variableness has been a fairly consistent factor throughout my work. My first long dramatic piece was *U.S. Highball,* a musical account of a transcontinental hobo trip. I was entitled to write it because I had made the trip. This was not a stunt; I was already two decades past the age. The work was performed at Carnegie Chamber Music Hall, and at Columbia University, in New York, in 1944, and in 1945 at the University of Wisconsin. *U.S. Highball* represented a very large deviation—not a small one—and it was obviously ridiculous.

My first large theater work, based on Sophocles' *Oedipus the King,* called for intoning voices, dancing and singing choruses, and instruments onstage. It was performed in California, at Mills College and at the Sausalito Arts Fair, in 1952 and 1954. My collaborator, Sophocles, gave the work respectability.

The second was a three-act work for dancers, with three loosely connected ideas, called *Plectra and Percussion Dances.* This was also performed in California, at the International House, Berkeley, in 1953. It had a kind of offbeat respectability because, in the last act, I used quotations from Rimbaud, in French.

The third was a dance-satire, *The Bewitched,* first performed here [at the University of Illinois], at the Auditorium, during the festival in 1957. It was also performed at Washington University, St. Louis, that same year, and in 1959 under the sponsorship of Columbia University, New York, and again in the Auditorium. This was entirely my own concept, and—like *U.S. Highball*—it had to grub for its respectability.

The fourth was *Revelation in the Courthouse Park,* after *The Bacchae* of Euripides, performed here last year, in April. As a direct result of my work with tumblers in *Revelation,* an exhibition of music and gymnastics was staged at the NCAA meet, also in April.[1] A film of this was produced by Madeline Tourtelot, and shown at the Edinburgh Film Festival.[2]

The present work, *Water! Water!,* the fifth in the series, was intended to have a farcical quality, but this in itself tells very little. Perhaps it is fundamentally a tragic farce, or simply a bizarre farce, or perhaps no farce at all. Again, definite words are elusive, and when I find them they do not fly straight. Momentarily appropriating the oriental philosophy of acquiescence, I will stipulate that it is anything that anyone cares to say it is, at any time.

Delusion of the Fury

1965

Act I. Pray for Me

Act II. In the Advent of Justice

At the end of Act I the stage darkens, but there is no inter-mission; music is continuous.

Act I treats with death, and with life despite death.

Act II treats with life, and with life despite life.

They have this in common: both convey the mood that reality is in no way real, despite the very different locales, subject matter, and the very different paths toward the awareness of unreality.

Both, essentially, are happy in their focus; the reconciliation with some kind of unreal death makes the one with some kind of unreal life possible.

Act I, on the recurrent theme of Japanese Noh plays, is a music-theater portrayal of release from the wheel of life and death. In simplest terms it is a final enlightenment, a reconciliation with total departure from the area of mortal cravings and passions.

It is based on the legend of a princely warrior who falls in battle at the hands of a young rival.[1] The act begins with the slayer's re-morseful pilgrimage to the scene, and to the shrine. The murdered man appears as a spirit, and his son, born after death, then enters, seeking the same shrine in the belief that he may see his father's face, as though in a dream. Spurred to resentment by the presence of his son, he lives again through the ordeal of battle.

Thus, the three principals:

> The slayer
> The slain (as a ghost)
> Son of the slain

Program:

> Chorus of shadows
> The pilgrimage
> Emergence of the spirit
> A son in search of his father's face
> Resentment beyond death
> Cry from another darkness
> Pray for me again

Act II, based on an Ethiopian folktale,[2] is a reconciliation with life, not as a separate mental act from that with death, but as a necessary concomitant, an accommodation toward a healthy—or at least a possible—existence. Its essence is a tongue-in-cheek understanding, attained through irony, even through farce.

A young vagabond is cooking a meal over rocks when an old woman who tends a goat herd approaches, searching for a lost kid. Later, she finds the kid, but—due to a misunderstanding caused by the hobo's deafness—a dispute ensues. Villagers gather, and after a violent dance force the quarrelling couple to appear before the justice of the peace, who is both deaf and nearsighted.

Thus the three principals:

> Young vagabond
> Old goat woman
> Justice of the peace

Program:

> Chorus of villagers
> The quiet hobo meal
> The lost kid
> The misunderstanding
> Arrest by the dervish dancers
> The trial and judgment
> How did we ever manage without justice?

In Act I, I am not trying to write a Noh play. Noh is already a fine art, one of the most sophisticated that the world has known, and it would be senseless for me to follow a path of superficial duplication.

The instrumental sounds (excepting my *koto*) are not Japanese, the scales I use are not Japanese, the voice usage is different, costumes are different. Act I is actually a development of my own style in dramatic music, particularly as evidenced in *Oedipus* and *Revelation*. If for no other reason than the music, its daimon is American.

I am using the basic motivations of Noh as a springboard for my style. The story elements are from *Atsumori,* by Seami, and *Ikuta,* by Zembō Motoyasu.

There is probably no art form in Ethiopia comparable to Noh in Japan, but—generally—I am not trying to depict African ritual, although African ritual, as I have heard it on records, has obviously influenced my writing, in this and several other works. The story line is from the book *African Voices.* No author is indicated, and I therefore call it a folktale. I have made both changes in the story and additions to it. Again, and despite the use of much percussion, the tone is American. The furious irony is deeply and certainly American.

Dialogue as such is never present. I feel that the mysterious, perverse qualities of these story ideas can be conveyed through music, mime, lights, with more sureness of impact than with spoken or sung lines, and spoken or sung lines in reply.

There are exactly ten recognizable English words, spoken or intoned, in Act I, not counting repetitions by principals and Chorus, and exactly forty-four in Act II, not counting repetitions by the Chorus.

Set

The instruments must be onstage, and they must not be pushed back into corners. They *are* the set, with only a cyclorama—a good sound-reflecting surface—behind. The movements required of principals and Chorus do not call for excessive stage space. In Act I they are generally slow and intense; in Act II vigorous and intense. The clichés of modern dance must be avoided, and I believe that the impedimenta of instruments will prove an effective deterrent. The vigorous movers of Act II will simply learn to avoid instruments, and—as a matter of fact—it is quite possible to execute a vigorous dance with feet firmly limited to a couple of squares.

Principals

The three principals in each act must certainly be trained in music. They must be singers in a strange sense. Strange, because it is difficult to find theater arts comparable to what is called for, outside the Orient.

The quality of the trained opera singer, and the quality of the prominent singer of "contemporary" music, are not right. The principals must be actors, mimes, and—in another strange sense—dancers. They must be able to move with firm dramatic or theatrical purpose, as cynosures.

I should like the principals to be the same three persons in each act: two men, one woman. (The woman takes the part of the young son in Act I.)

Singing

There is much singing, or—to be more general—sounds from the throat, meaningless in English verbal communication, but not meaningless in this music: for example, the "Ho——," in Act II, executed by the Chorus without using vocal chords, but—nevertheless—human vibrations from assembled throats.

There is nowhere, from the beginning of Act I to the end of Act II, a complete cessation of music, although at times it should be so soft as to invoke the imagined stillness at the center of the earth.

Chorus

The approximate twenty musicians (with conductor) *are* the Chorus, in both acts. This was true in *The Bewitched* also, and to my mind the arrangement was effective. The choral voice sounds were not coming from an uncomfortable body of people appearing just occasionally, but from among the instruments, from musicians who were deeply involved *throughout*.

In the present work I wish to progress beyond this concept. There are twenty-one instruments onstage (not counting small hand instruments), but never do the twenty-one play simultaneously. There are many fairly long periods where a small ensemble is employed, and duets and trios are frequent. The tacit musicians may thus become actors and dancers, moving from instruments to acting areas as the impetus of the drama requires: for example, as court attendants in Act II, bearers of the palanquin.

Where necessary, instrumentalists must memorize parts, or know them so well that faint light is enough. The effect of stand lights on white music paper—*onstage*—tends to destroy even the most elementary lighting concept. Actors and singers have always memorized parts, and it is irrational to exempt instrumentalists, especially when they are cast in such a way as to be indispensable to the action.

If it seems necessary to use a few extra persons as Chorus, the total company could still be kept to under thirty: one conductor, three principals, five or six chorus, nineteen instrumentalists.

Costumes

The musicians must of course be in costume, and I have a singularly clear idea as to what the costumes should be like, both as to detail and as to what they should convey: a sense of magic, of an olden time, but never of a precise olden time. They should certainly not suggest anything that is either Japanese or Ethiopian.

The basic garment of the musicians is a huge pair of pantaloons, wrapping around the waist in East-Indian fashion. In Act I they also wear a poncholike garment—a single, full piece of cloth with a neck hole. It must be completely unadorned, without collages or beads or anything that twinkles in the light. The poncho is discarded at the end of Act I. During Act II the musicians are naked from the waist up.

To compensate for this very simple costume, each musician will wear a fantastic headpiece. Each will be different, or frequently different.

In contrast, the three principals would wear more imaginative costumes, and imaginative makeup. Wigs, certainly, but no headpieces.

Curtain Calls

In abjuring curtain calls I am following the Japanese custom of leaving the audience with the most pleasing (or sensational) arrangement of people, set, and lighting that can be concocted.

However, I am eternally grateful to audiences. They endure hardship to appear, to see what you have to offer, and they put up their money as evidence of the aggressive curiosity.

What I suggest here is not an American custom, and I leave the question open.

In Retrospect

I have been pondering this idea for some five years, and during the past two years I have filled a considerable number of pages with notes, both verbal and musical, and I have built a few new instruments, and made experiments with older ones—all looking toward an eventual production.

This would not be a concert, in the usual sense. Thought channels in the creative arts tend to follow the immediate well-traveled paths, and it is not unnatural that people, seeing—or hearing about—my instruments, should immediately react through the words *concert* or *symphony.*

I do not disdain the idea of concert music, but theater work is the compulsive direction of my mind; it is what I want to do; it is the vehicle for whatever vision I possess. I could no more become a writer of acceptable concert music than I could become an acceptable kangaroo, simply by saying to myself that I must become a kangaroo because that is what I am expected to be. In my opinion, there are quite enough composers already producing concert music. But whether there are or not, I cannot be one of them.

This is indeed an adventurous concept. However, looking back on my thirteen or fourteen years' involvement with full theater production, I say flatly that it is not experimental. It is a logical development, beyond *The Bewitched,* and beyond *Revelation in the Courthouse Park.* In the case of *The Bewitched* alone, I remember clearly the reactions of six different audiences in three different places: the University of Illinois, St. Louis, New York. I feel sure—in this unreal world—that I know what I am doing.

PART 4

LIBRETTOS AND SCENARIOS

U.S. Highball

*A Musical Account of a Transcontinental
Hobo Trip*

⟨*Leaving Carmel, Californi-el—*⟩

Leaving San Francisco, Californi-o—

I got a letter and the letter said: "May God's richest blessings be upon you." Dtuh dtuh dtuh duh duh duh duh duh duh duh Dtuh dtuh dtuh duh blessings be upon you. And that's why I'm going to Chicago.

Leaving Sacramento, Californigh-o—

Going east, mister? Going east, mister? Going east, mister? It's the freights for you, boy.

Leaving Colfax, Californi-ax!

"Let 'er highball, engineer!"

Na na Na na Na na na na na na Na Leaving Emigrant Gap, Californi-ap!

"If you wanta stay in one piece sleep on the back end of the oil tank, buddy. She's tough goin' down the other side o' the Sierras."

Na na Na na Na na na na na na na na Leaving Truckee, Californigh-ee-ee—

Leaving Reno, Neva-a-a-a-a-a-a-do-o-o-o-o-o-o-O-o-o-o- La la La la la la la la la la Lo La la la la la la la la Lo lo lo lo Lo lo lo lo

"Hey, Mac, you'll get killed on that oil tank. There's a empty back here!"

Leaving Sparks, Neva-darks!

"I ain't got no matches, ain't got no tobacco, ain't got no chow, ain't got no money. Hey, Mac, is that blanket big enough for two?"

⟨"If you wanta eat today, boys, better get it here. The next division is just a little hole in the desert—not even a store."⟩

A glossary is given in "Sources and Notes."

⟨*Leaving Ocala, Nevada*—⟩

"Hey, ⟨Slim,⟩ don't sleep with your head against the end of the car. You'll get your neck broke when she jerks. ⟨How're the bulls down where you come from, Slim?⟩"

Leaving Lovelock, Neva-dock!

"She's gonna hole in to let a coupla passengers by!"
"There she jerks again! That engineer don't know how to drive this train."

Leaving Imlay, Neva-day—

"Freeze another night tonight, goin' over the hump. That's another bad hump this side o' Cheyenne. 'Tsa bitch! That Cheyenne, huh. That used to be a bad town, but not any more, so much. They used to have a school there for railroad bulls. ⟨They taught the rookie bulls the easiest way to beat up on poor helpless bums.⟩ But the school's moved to Denver ⟨now⟩. It moves back and forth, from Cheyenne to Denver. Stay out o' Denver, Mac!"

Leaving Winnemucca, Neva-ducca—

⟨"We'll highball it down to Omaha—then head for the carnival in Alabama. How 'bout it, Slim?"⟩

⟨*Valmy, Neva-dy*—⟩

⟨"No water here in these corrals. They only turn it on once a year—roundup time. No water for us today."⟩

⟨*Leaving Carlin, Neva-din*—⟩

"They've gone and sealed up our empty! And all the rest are sealed refrigerators. Sh——! Not even a gon-*do*-la!"

Moleen, Neva-deen—

"Wait for the next drag—there'll be lots a empties on it. Too cold to ride outside this weather. Look at them northern lights! See them long streaks up in the sky? You can't ride outside in weather like this. We'll build a fire so when the next drag stops all the 'bos 'll come runnin' over to get warm. Then we'll know where there's a empty."

Leaving Elko, Neva-do—

"There she jerks again! I can stand everything but them jerks. They make me nervous. And the dirt, too. Yesterday I washed all my clothes in the Roseville Jungle, and I looked so good when I put 'em on that I took a walk, up into town. Now look at me! Look at all the guys on this drag—not only dirty but they're old before their time. Ridin' freights 'll make an old man out of ya, Mac. Still, I can stand that, and the dirt. Can stand everything but the jerks."

Crossing Great Salt Lake, U-take!

⟨*Ogden, Uten—*⟩

⟨"No food when you're hungry, no water when you're thirsty. Burn up in the daytime, freeze at night. Nothing but dirt, noise, and jerks. Can stand everything but the jerks."⟩

⟨*Uintah, Utah—*⟩

⟨Going east, mister? Going east, mister? Going east, mister? Back to the freights for you, boy.⟩

⟨*Leaving Ogden, U-ten—*⟩

"Any thirty-nine hundred engine is going east ⟨Slim⟩. That oil tank's a tough one to ride, though ⟨but I guess there's nothin' else. Well, it's your funeral⟩."

Leaving Evansting, Wyo-ming!

"Watch out for those jerks the next fifteen miles, Mac. You've got to hang on every second, or you'll go under when she jerks. He really balls the jack goin' down the grade."

Green River, Wyo-mer—

"⟨No food when you're hungry, no water when you're thirsty. Burn up in the day time, freeze at night. Nothing but dirt, noise, and jerks.⟩ Can stand everything but the jerks."

Rock Springs, Wyo-mings—

Going east, mister? Going east, mister? Going east, mister? "There are lots of rides, but they don't stop much, do they, *pal?*" Back to the freights for you, boy. And—since the drags don't stop at Rock Springs—back to Green River, Wyo-mer!

There are rides on the highway at Green River, but they go right on by. There are rides on the freights at Green River, too, but the Green River bull says:

"You exclamation mark bum! Get your semicolon asterisk out o' these yards, and *don't* let me catch you down here again, or you'll get thirty days in the jailhouse!''

Green River, Wyo-mer! S-s-s-s-stuck! in Green River!

*   *   *   *

⟨"Want a job pot-wallopin'? Okay, get in!"⟩

Little America, Wyo-ma!

⟨"Short stack, fry 'em on the side, over easy. Coupla babies and a chicken in spuds. Say, boy, hurry up with them bread n' butter plates."⟩

{"Did I ever ride freights? Huh! You ask about the bulls in Cheyenne. Yeh, you have to get off this side of the yards, then catch it again on the other side of town. There was a pretty bad bull down at Yermo, too. They called him Yermo Red. Then there was another at Gila Bend. The 'bos called him the Gila Monster."

"With bums they's two kinds of horrors—the Chuck Horrors and the Bull Horrors. They only have the Chuck Horrors when they can't get enough to eat, but they have the Bull Horrors all the time."}

"Did I ever ride freights? Huh! ⟨That reminds me.⟩ One time I was in the yards in Pueblo, sitting with some other 'bos around a fire, waiting for the hotshot on the D. and R.G. Pretty soon an old man with a long white beard come out of a piano box on the edge of the yards, and come over to warm his hands by our fire. He didn't say anything until some of the boys left to catch a drag that was just beginning to move out. Then the old man, who just come out of the piano box, says: 'It's purty tough to be ridin' the drags on a night like this. I know. I was a bum once myself.' "

*   *   *   *

Leaving Little America, Wyo-ma!

"I have a letter and the letter says: "May God's richest blessings be upon you." Dtuh dtuh dtuh duh duh du duh du duh duh Dtuh dtuh dtuh duh blessings be upon you. And that's why I'm thinking Chicago.

Going east, mister? Going east, mister? ⟨Going east, mister? Whoopiday! I got one!⟩

Chicago, Chicago, Chicago, Chicago

Leaving Laramie, Wyo-mie—Yih! hoo—

Chicago, Chicago, Chicago, [etc.]

Leaving Cheyenne, Wyo-manne!

Chi-cago, cago. Chi-cago, cago [etc.]

Leaving Pine Bluffs, Wyo-o-o-o-o-o-o-o-o-o-o-o-o-o-muffs!

Chicago, Chicago, Chicago, [etc.] go Chicago, cago go Chicago [etc.]

Leaving Kimball, Nebras-kall—

⟨La la La la La la la la la la [etc.]⟩

North Platte, Nebras-katte!

"⟨The Salvation Army.⟩ Notice to transients: This town allows you two meals and bed for one night only. Do not leave this place after 6 P.M. By order of the chief of *po*-lice."

Praise the Lord, *O praise the Lord,* O praise the Lord, *O praise the Lord,* O praise the Lord, *O praise the Lord,* O praise the Lord—⟨(for coffee and sinkers).⟩

Leaving North Platte, Nebras-ass-katte!

"⟨Such damn people!⟩ I can't get a ride! To hell with Nebraska! Also to hell with Idaho, Wyoming, Colorado, California, Nevada, and Utah!"

Chicago, go Chicago, cago go Chicago [etc.]

Leaving York, Nebras-kork!

Chicago ogo ogo aga ogo, Chicago aga aga ogo aga [etc.]

Leaving Lincoln, Nebras-kon!

⟨Chicago, Chicago, Chicago, [etc.]⟩
Na na na na na Na na na na na [etc.]

⟨*Leaving Omaha, Nebras-kaw—*⟩

⟨Chicago go, Chicago go, Chicago going, Chicago going, Chicago gone! dah dah dah dah Shicka-go gaga Shicko-ga go go [etc.]⟩

{*Leaving Council Bluffs, Io-wuffs!*}

{Chicago, gahgo, gahgo, [etc.]}

Leaving Iowa City, Io-wuffs!

"Jack Parkin, 111 West William St., Champaign, Illinois. Telephone 8426 if hungry when there."

⟨Shi shi shi shi [etc.] gah go!⟩ *Yih! hoo —*

{*Leaving Atlantic, Io-wic —*}

{Chi-coga, coga, coga, [etc.]}

{*Leaving Des Moines, Io-woines —*}

{Chicago, cogo, cogo, [etc.]}

{*Leaving Iowa City, Io-wity!*}

{Shi-gahgo—! Yih! hoo—}

Leaving Davenport, I-ee-o-u-wort! Dah dah dah blessings be upon you.
Dah dah dah dah.

{"May God's richest blessings be upon you — May God's richest
blessings be upon you — May God's richest blessings be upon you —
May God's richest blessings be upon you."}
{Chicago, cago go go go gah gah gah [etc.]}
Chicago.

Oedipus

Dance-Drama

Place
Ancient Thebes

Cast
Intoners: *
SPOKESMAN
OEDIPUS
TIRESIAS ⎫ same person
HERDSMAN ⎭
JOCASTA

Singing voices:
CHORUS Complement, six women (individual Female Voices
are designated FIRST, SECOND, THIRD, etc.)
SOLO SOPRANO (from Chorus Complement)

Speaking parts:
PRIEST
CREON
MESSENGER
SECOND MESSENGER

Instruments

Clarinet in B-flat	Chromelodeon I
Bass Clarinet in B-flat	Chromelodeon I Sub-Bass
Adapted Viola	Chromelodeon II
Adapted Cello	Cloud-Chamber Bowls
Guitars I and II	Gourd Tree and Cone Gongs
String bass	Diamond Marimba
Kithara	Bass Marimba
Harmonic Canon II	Marimba Eroica
(Castor and Pollux)	

* In addition to intoning on specified pitches (with or without prescribed rhythm),
these characters also speak (indeterminate pitch and rhythm) in a performance style
Partch describes as "free."

Intoned Dialogue

The written notes [in the score] are not to be adhered to religiously. They are not sung, and generally speaking only accents need to be intoned accurately, in order to integrate the voices with prevailing harmony and rhythm. These accents are points in time, and of virtually no duration. The parts *do* allow a margin for individual interpretation and delivery. In performance it is better to hit any tone than to wait until the right tone asserts itself in the brain, since any delay arrests the dramatic continuity. Sustained tones are generally not required of the intoners at the low ranges indicated. These are simply the ends of the downward inflections, or glides. In the case of the Chorus the lowest tones are generally intended as a low murmur.

1. Introduction

{*Curtain down and total darkness as music begins. Lights and curtain as indicated.*}

{*Voices offstage or half-hidden as curtain goes up. Singers in two groups.*}

CHORUS: Oh— Oh— Oh—Ah— Ah— Ah—Oh—
SPOKESMAN [*sung*]: Oh—   Oh—   Ah—   Oh—

Ah— O—Ah Ah O— O— O— ü— ü— ü— ü— ü— ü—
Ah—   O— O— O—

[Chorus:] ü— ü—

{*Curtain begins to go up, lights come on.*}

2. Opening Scene

{*Oedipus advances, and singers enter.*}

OEDIPUS [*intone*]: My children, why do you sit before me with suppliants' branches? The city rings with prayers, and cries of sorrow, and is heavy with incense. I would not hear of your troubles from the mouths of messengers; so I, the renowned Oedipus, ask you myself. Old man, will you speak for these? What dread, what desire, brings you? For I would give all aid. *No* hardness of heart could fail in pity for such entreaty.

PRIEST [*free*]: Oedipus, king, you see here before you all ages: children, others bowed with age; priests—I of Zeus; and the chosen youth. The rest of our people sit and wail in the marketplaces. For our city, as you can see, no longer holds its head above the waves of death. The god has ravaged us with plague, and made black Hades rich in tears. With divine aid, it is said, you freed us from the Sphinx. Again we implore you to help us! Deliver our State! Guard your fame! May our memories never recall that you first saved us, then—afterwards—cast us down!

OEDIPUS (free): O my piteous children, your longings are not unknown to me. Yet, suffer though you do, there is not one of you who is so stricken as I am. Your suffering is for yourselves alone; mine is for the city, and myself, and you. You do not awake a sleeping man! Be assured that I have wept bitterly for you, through labyrinths of care. And—I have acted. I have sent Creon, my wife's brother, to the oracle, to learn by what act we may yet be delivered. Many days have passed, and this troubles me, for he should have returned. But when he comes, then call me false if I fail to act in every way that the god makes clear.

PRIEST: Your words fit the moment, for I see the signal that Creon is here.

OEDIPUS: O Lord Apollo! May he bring deliverance as radiant as his look seems to promise.

PRIEST: His news is good, or he would not be crowned with laurel.

OEDIPUS: Prince, my kinsman, what message do you bring?

(*Enter Creon.*)

CREON: Good news! For even the worst news is good, if it leads to good end.

OEDIPUS: But what is the oracle?

CREON: Will you hear it in public?

OEDIPUS: Speak before all! My burden of sorrow is more for these than for myself.

CREON: The oracle tells us to cast out a defiling thing which we cherish among us; to drive it out, lest it become incurable.

OEDIPUS: What defiling thing? How drive it out?

CREON: Once, my king, before you came to us, Laius was our leader. He was murdered. And the oracle now plainly tells us to revenge him—*whoever* the guilty may be.

OEDIPUS: And where find a clue to the riddle of this ancient guilt?

CREON: "In this land," the god said. We seek and we find.

OEDIPUS: And where was Laius killed?

CREON: He left the city on a mission to Delphi. He never returned.

OEDIPUS: And was there no witness?

CREON: All died *with* Laius—*except one.* This man said that robbers attacked them—not man for man, but in overpowering numbers.

OEDIPUS: Robbers? What robbers would dare attack a king—unless bribed from here?

CREON: So we thought too. But Laius's death came at the time of another trouble. *The riddling Sphinx.*

OEDIPUS: So, it is up to me. I will begin again and once more make the dark things clear. I shall serve myself as well as my country, for whoever murdered Laius might also wish to murder me. Quickly, my children, leave the altar steps, and take your olive boughs. Then call to the people of Thebes! Tell them that I have sworn an oath to leave nothing untried! Please heaven, we will be delivered, or—we are ruined.

PRIEST: Come, my children! We have heard what we came to hear. And now, may he who sent the oracle be our saviour, and deliver us!

3. First Chorus

⟨*Three-part movement counterpoint in this Chorus: (1) the Spokesman who has the stage, (2) Singing Chorus, (3) Dancing Chorus.*⟩

CHORUS: ü— Oh—
SPOKESMAN [*intone*]: Thebes, O Thebes!   What is the mean-

                    Oh—
ing of the Delphian Voice? What whisper of disaster, or word of

                                        Oh— ü—
terror that man has never seen before?   Hear us O

                              Ah—   Oh—
Healer! I shout, I tremble, and I wait. Hear!   and send us

                          ü—
help like the bright morning.   Wives and mothers mourn at

      Lo ah—   Oh—   ü—
every altar,   as one by one,   ghost follows ghost,

  ü—
to that god-haunted unknown western shore, like frightened

    Oh—
birds.   Gods of the earth, drive this god of death away!

ü— Oh—   Ah—   Ah—
    Wind, blow him out to the homeless sea, then thunder,

         ü—
lightning, blast him on the head! And let him taste the death he

                    O O O O O O O O O Oh—ü—
deals, till death himself is dead.

      Ah—   Ah—
I call against you, pale god, gods from above and below.

        Ah— Ah—
Apollo destroy you!   Apollo, with your golden bow

Ah—   ü—   ü—
    your stretched golden string, your golden arrow.

4. Tiresias Scene

(Oedipus's lines are free throughout this long scene. Tiresias intones throughout.)

OEDIPUS [*free*]: You are praying, and if you listen to me you may hope to find relief from your troubles. Whoever among you knows what Theban killed Laius, I demand that he come to me and tell all. If he is himself the guilty one, I command him to reveal himself, for he shall suffer nothing but exile. Or, if anyone knows that the assassin was from a foreign land, let him say so, and he will gain a reward and my thanks.

    Ha! But if you still keep silent—if anyone, through fear, shall try to shield a friend, or himself, listen to what I will do. I order that no one of this land is to give him shelter, or speak to him, or join him in prayer or ceremonies. In this I become the ally of the god and of the murdered man. And for myself, I pray that, should the slayer be a member of my own household, I may suffer the same curse that I have called down upon others. And I charge you to make all these words good, for my sake, for the god's sake, and for the sake of our land.

For even if the oracle had not provoked us to it, it would be wrong to leave this crime unpurged, when one so noble was murdered. And now, since it is I who hold the power he held once, and lie in his bed, with his wife for my wife — I will prosecute his cause as if for my own father. And for those who do not obey me, I pray that they have no harvest, either of the earth or of the womb, but that they waste away in the extremity of their grief, or in one more dreadful still.

But to you who hear my words as good words: righteousness and blessedness dwell with you forever, in doing my will.

SPOKESMAN [*free*]: As you have sworn me, so will I speak. I am not the murderer, nor can I point him out. Tiresias, the old seer, is the man most likely to understand the meaning of the oracle.

OEDIPUS: On the advice of Creon I have twice sent for him, and it is strange that he is so long coming.

SPOKESMAN: Unless he can help us, we have nothing but rumors, old and senseless.

OEDIPUS: What rumors?

SPOKESMAN: Wanderers were said to have murdered our king.

OEDIPUS: Oh, I have heard *that*, but where is the witness?

SPOKESMAN: If he knows what fear is, he will not remain silent when he learns of your curse.

OEDIPUS: The man who does not shrink from murder will hardly shrink from a speech.

SPOKESMAN: But there is *one* who will expose him! For here at last is the godlike prophet, who — alone among men — has the power of truth.

{*Enter Tiresias, led by a boy.*}

OEDIPUS: Tiresias, you whose soul divines all, both the heard and the unspeakable, the low things of earth and the secrets of heaven, you must know of the plague that reduces our State, for all your blindness, and in this extremity, great prophet, we see no help except from you. To our question, god's oracle has answered that rescue from our grief will come when we have singled out the murderers of Laius, and killed them, or driven them into exile. (*Intone.*) Oh, grudge us nothing! (*Free.*) Neglect no secret art, but save your own greatness, save me, save all that stand defiled because of a wrong against our old king! For we are in your hands; and man's noblest purpose is to help other men to the limit of his power.

TIRESIAS: Yes, and how terrible a thing it is to know, when knowing brings no good. This, in an evil moment I forgot, or I would not be here.

OEDIPUS: Your words are strange, *and* unkindly, to the State that bred you!

TIRESIAS: No, I see that you, for your part, know how to keep silent *opportunely!* So therefore do I.

OEDIPUS: For the love of heaven, do not refuse us! If you have knowledge do not turn away. All of us beg you, on our knees!

TIRESIAS: Ha! You are ignorant. *What* knowledge?

OEDIPUS: What! You know the secret and will not tell it! You would betray us, and destroy the State!

TIRESIAS: I will bring remorse upon neither of us. You will not learn it from me!

OEDIPUS: Basest of men! A stone would come to life in anger against you! Can nothing move you?

TIRESIAS: *You* blame me—and see nothing of what lies so close to you?

OEDIPUS: Who, pray, would not be enraged by your slighting words?

TIRESIAS: The future *will come,* though I shroud it in silence.

OEDIPUS: Very well—it will come. So *out* with it!

TIRESIAS: I will *not* speak. Rage your fill—bring out all the fiercest wrath within your heart.

OEDIPUS: I will contain myself no longer! It seems to me that you have conspired in the deed. Had you eyes that see, I would accuse you *alone* of doing it!

TIRESIAS: So it has come to this! I charge you to stand convicted by your own decree. *You* are the *accursed!* the defiler of this land.

OEDIPUS: Such shameless words! After this, how do you expect to go free?

TIRESIAS: I *am* free. My truth is the strength that makes me free.

OEDIPUS: Is this a sample of your famous art? Who taught you this?

TIRESIAS: You: for you badgered me to speech against my will.

OEDIPUS: Speech? What speech? Speak it again, that I may understand it better.

TIRESIAS: You are tempting me. Was I not clear before?

OEDIPUS: No. Not in the full meaning. Repeat it.

TIRESIAS: I say that *you* are the murderer—the murderer that you seek!

OEDIPUS: You will regret it for having spoken twice such words!

TIRESIAS: Would you have me continue, that you may become still angrier?

OEDIPUS: What you will! It will do you no good!

TIRESIAS: I say that you are living with your nearest kin in unguessed shame.

OEDIPUS: Do you think you can revel in such slanders without cost to you?

TIRESIAS: Yes, if there is any force in truth.

OEDIPUS: There is—but not for you. Not for you, maimed in ear *and* in eye.

TIRESIAS: Fool! you are but a poor wretch, throwing taunts that every man here will fling at you— (*deliberately*) soon! Soon! Soon!

OEDIPUS: Night, spawn of the night! Endless night is holding you fast, so that you can hurt neither me nor any other man who looks up to the sun.

TIRESIAS: Fate's decree stands fixed. Your doom is not to fall by me. It is the business of the gods to take the high and make them low.

OEDIPUS: Ha! Creon! Is it his, or yours, this plot?

TIRESIAS: No, it is not Creon. You are your own enemy.

OEDIPUS: O wealth and kingly power, that art of all arts excellent in this honored life, how great the envy you provoke, if for the sake of the power which this city has put into my hands unsought, my old friend Creon has stealthily crept upon me to oust me from it, and has suborned this scheming quack, this crafty beggar, who has eyes only for his gains, and blackness in his art!

Come now, tell me, where have you proved yourself a seer? Why, when that she-dog songstress was here, did you say nothing to end her spell of riddling death? Yet the secret was not for the common man to guess; it required the art of a seer, and you had none. No, I came, I, Oedipus the ignorant: I muted her, with only my wit for weapon. And it is I you are trying to lay low, thinking to stand close to Creon when he is in my place. But you and the instigator of this treachery will regret your zeal to purge the land. Ha! Were you not an old man, you'd have learned through suffering how brazen you are, and learned it well.

(*The Eroica beat should begin so softly that one is hardly aware of it, then increase. Tiresias's voice, in the prophecy, hovers around unison with the Cello.*)

SPOKESMAN: Both the prophet's words and yours, Oedipus, have been said in anger. We have no need for angry words—only those that best fulfill the oracle of the god.

TIRESIAS (*hover around unison with Cello; keep it rhythmic*): I tell you— since you have taunted me even with blindness, that though your eyes are light, yet you cannot see the misery of your lot, nor in what home you are living, nor with whom. You are the unwitting enemy of your own kin, in the regions below, and on the earth above; and the double pain of a mother's curse and a father's curse alike—shall drive you from this land in dreadful haste, with darkness then—on those eyes that now see light. What harbor of the sea, what place will not hear your cry, what in all Kithaeron shall not ring with it, soon! Soon! Therefore, heap your scorn on Creon and on my lips, for no one among men shall be crushed more utterly than you shall be crushed.

OEDIPUS: This I can bear no longer! Away! Away! Back from these walls!

TIRESIAS: I would never have come, not I, had you not called me.

OEDIPUS: And I would not have called, had I known you were mad!

TIRESIAS: Mad to you, yes, but not mad to your parents.

OEDIPUS: My parents? Stop! Who are they?

TIRESIAS: This day shall give you birth—and blot you out.

OEDIPUS: Riddles! Dark words! No *end* of dark words!

TIRESIAS: But are you not skilled in the probing of dark words?

OEDIPUS: Cast this in my teeth! Scoff! You shall *still* find me so!

TIRESIAS: This fortune is your pride—and your calamity.

OEDIPUS: I delivered this land, and I am not afraid to die.

TIRESIAS: Then I will go: boy!

OEDIPUS: Yes, let him take you. You will not be missed.

TIRESIAS: I go, but having spoken, I must speak to the end. And I
tell you—the man you have been seeking, that man is here.
(*Gradually slower.*) A blind man, who now has sight, a beggar, who
now is rich; he shall wander in a strange land, feeling the ground
before him with his staff, while children's voices murmur: (*sing*)
"See, there goes our brother-father,"—the seed, the sower, and
the sown. So you go in and think on this, and if you find I am
in fault, from here on out, (*strong retard*) say that I have no art
of prophecy.

{*Tiresias is led out by the boy. Oedipus enters the palace.*}

5. Second Chorus

CHORUS: Mo ho Ho ho mo ho Ho ho *ha* ho ho ho Ho
SPOKESMAN [*intone*]:

ho ho *ha* ho ho ho ho ü—   Oh— Ah— Woo— Woh—
          Yea   Yea   Yea— Yea—

Woo—   Woh—
Who is it that the Voice of Doom has singled out? Whose

          Woo—   Woh—
deeds of wrong? Whose bloody hands? He wanders now

                              Woo—
with dreary feet in dreary loneliness. Flying from the Fates

                              Woh —
that hover about him, living, incessant. Yet I am shaken

                    Woo —
with foreboding.   The dreaded things are still untold, and I

      Woh —   ü —
will pass no word on Oedipus, who is loved by all the land.

6. Creon Scene

{*Creon enters from the house.*}

CREON: Fellow citizens, having learned that Oedipus charges me with
   a criminal conspiracy against him, I have come to face him, and
   I am indignant. If he dreams, amid all this doom, that he has
   suffered wrong from me, in word or act, to tell the truth, life is
   not so precious. The wound of this accusation is too great to
   endure, if I am to be called traitor, by my friends, by the whole
   city.

SPOKESMAN [*free*]: If such words were spoken, it was not the heart
   that spoke them, but a burst of anger.

CREON: He said that I bribed the seer to speak lying words?

SPOKESMAN: Such things were said.

CREON: And while he was making this frantic charge, did he seem
   like a sane man?

SPOKESMAN: I do not know. I cannot say what my masters do. Here —
   he will speak for himself.

(*Enter Oedipus.*)

OEDIPUS [*intone*]: Ho! You come to *this* house? You! (*Free.*) What
   insolence! [*Intone.*] You, (*free*) the proved assassin of its former
   master; you, the designing, would-be king! [*Intone.*] God help you!
   Come, (*free*) tell me, in the name of heaven, [*intone*] did (*free*) you
   see cowardice in me, or stupidity, that you dared plot this thing?
   [*Intone.*] Did (*free*) you think that I would not see your sly moves,
   or seeing them, would not counter them? (*Intone.*) How (*free*)
   foolish can you be, to seek — without friends or followers — a prize
   like this?

CREON: Listen to me—to a fair reply—and then—*on knowledge*—judge for yourself.

OEDIPUS [*intone*]: Your speech is clever, but you will find me a poor listener, because I know your purpose.

CREON: Now hear me—on this very point.

OEDIPUS: Yes, the point. You are a traitor!

CREON: If you think you gain by being stubborn, you do not think straight.

OEDIPUS [*free*]: And if you think you can wrong a friend and go unpunished, *you* do not think straight.

CREON: Justly said, but what is this wrong? Speak!

OEDIPUS: Did you urge, or not, that I should send for the seer?

CREON: My mind has not changed.

OEDIPUS: How long has it been, then, since Laius—

CREON: Laius? What has he to do with this?

OEDIPUS: Died, disappeared—

CREON: It was many years ago.

OEDIPUS: And was this seer practicing his art then?

CREON: Skilled, and honored, as he is now.

OEDIPUS: And why did not this sanctimonious sage tell his story then?

CREON: I do not know. Where I lack light I am inclined to be silent.

OEDIPUS: This much, at least, you know—that if he had not first secretly seen you, he would never have pointed to me as the murderer of Laius.

CREON: You know what he said. I was not present. But now, I have a right to hear a few answers from you.

OEDIPUS: Hear your fill.

CREON: Good. You are married to my sister.

OEDIPUS: Certainly.

CREON: And you rule the country equally with her?

OEDIPUS: Again, certainly.

CREON: And am I not the peer of you both?

OEDIPUS [*intone*]: Exactly! See why, therefore, you are so false a friend!

CREON: Not if you will be persuaded by reason. Send to the oracle and inquire whether I delivered the message truly.

But do not pronounce my guilt in a corner, on one man's guess. It is hardly right to judge bad men good at random, or good men bad. And it is equally wrong to cast a true friend out of your heart. No, in good time you will learn these things with surety, for time alone reveals the true man — while only one day exposes the false.

SPOKESMAN: Well spoken, my king! These are words of deliberation: quick tongues are not safe tongues.

OEDIPUS: The wily plotter is moving in! and I must hurry in my part, or his ends will be gained, and mine gone foul.

CREON: What will you do then? Expel me from the city?

OEDIPUS: Expel you? No! As the price of your kind of envy, I demand your death!

CREON: Will you never soften, never believe?

OEDIPUS: Yes, after I have seen how traitors die!

CREON: You are mad!

OEDIPUS: I am sane enough in my own interest.

CREON: Then be sane in mine, too.

OEDIPUS: No! You are false!

CREON: But when you comprehend nothing?

OEDIPUS: Still, I must rule.

CREON: Not when you turn tyrant!

OEDIPUS: Hear him, O Thebes!

CREON (*speaks rhythmically*): Thebes is mine also — not for you alone.

(*Enter Jocasta.*)

SPOKESMAN: Stop princes! Jocasta is here, and she comes just in time.

7. Jocasta Scene

JOCASTA [*intone*]: Foolish men, why are you quarrelling? Aren't you ashamed of this private squabble when the whole land is sick? Go back into the house, Oedipus, and you, Creon, go to yours. Enough of this petty grief.

CREON: Jocasta, your husband has threatened me with exile, or worse—death.

OEDIPUS [*free*]: I have, for I have caught him in the act of treachery.

CREON: Now may I perish, and perish accursed, if I am guilty of your charges! There is my oath.

JOCASTA: Oh, for god's sake believe it, Oedipus—first because of his oath, then for my sake, and for the sake of the stricken people standing here before you.

SPOKESMAN [*free*]: Yield, king! we pray you.

OEDIPUS [*intone*]: Do you wish me to yield?

SPOKESMAN: Grant him the benefit of a doubt. He was not disloyal before, and he is now strong in his oath.

OEDIPUS [*free*]: Say exactly what you mean.

SPOKESMAN: I mean that you should forbear to use an unproved rumor to make a dishonoring charge against a man, the more so when he is a friend who has bound himself with an oath of fidelity.

OEDIPUS [*intone*]: So! then be aware, when you ask this, that you are also asking for my exile, or my death.

SPOKESMAN [*intone*]: No! (*free*) by him at the gates of heaven! Very simply, my soul is sick, with old sorrows now being crowned by new ones.

OEDIPUS [*free*]: Oh, let him go, even though I make a fatal mistake thereby. Wherever he goes, my hatred will follow him.

CREON: You are as slow in yielding as you were senseless in wrath, but such natures are their own bitter burden.

OEDIPUS: Then will you give me some peace and get out!

CREON: I will go my way. What do I care for *your* opinion? In the sight of all here I am an honest man. (*Exit.*)

JOCASTA [*free*]: In the names of the gods, Oedipus, tell me! Why do you hold onto this rage?

OEDIPUS: I will tell you, for I honor you. The cause is your brother, and the plots he has hatched. He says that I am Laius's murderer.

JOCASTA: On his own knowledge?

OEDIPUS: He has spoken through the lips of his bribed perjurer. [*Intone.*] Trust him to keep his *own* lips pure!

JOCASTA [*intone*]: The seer? Huh. Drop these worries. Listen to me, and learn to your comfort that no one of mortal birth can share in knowledge of the future. Let me give you proof. An oracle came to Laius once, not from the god himself but from the priests and seers of his sanctuary, saying that he would die by the hand of his own son, whom he should have by me.

Now, as the story goes, Laius was murdered one day by foreign robbers, at a place where three roads meet. Yet our babe was but three days old, god's mercy! when Laius drove a blade of iron through his feet, and had a servant throw him out on the rocks of a desert mountain, on the slope of Kithaeron.

So—as you see—we cheated the seer of his prophecy that Laius should die—the thing he so feared—by his own son's hand. Behold the prophecies that come to nothing! so forget them all. Whatever the god may seek, he needs no help from prophets, when he makes the dark things clear.

OEDIPUS [*intone*]: What a turmoil of the soul, lady, what a tumult of the mind, comes upon me while you speak!

JOCASTA [*free*]: What *is* this anxiety? Why do you turn your face?

OEDIPUS [*free*]: Did I hear you say—that Laius was killed where three roads meet?

JOCASTA: That is the story that is still being told.

OEDIPUS: And where is this place?

JOCASTA: It is a narrow pass with crowding woods, a secluded glen where three roads branch, the one going off to Delphi.

OEDIPUS: When? How long has it been?

JOCASTA: The news of it came shortly before you were first seen in our city.

OEDIPUS [*intone*]: O Zeus! What are you trying to *do* to me?

JOCASTA: Oedipus, tell me, what is it that troubles you?

OEDIPUS: Do not ask, but answer me. Laius—his build, his age—

JOCASTA [*intone*]: He was tall—the silver had just lightly streaked his hair, and in form he was very much like you.

OEDIPUS: Unhappy that I am! It seems that I have brought a dreadful curse upon myself, (*slow*) without my knowing.

JOCASTA (*fast*): What are you saying? O my king, I shudder when I look at you.

OEDIPUS: And I have a terrible misgiving that the blind can see indeed! (*Faster.*) Will you answer one thing more?

JOCASTA: But ask it. Though I tremble I will answer everything.

OEDIPUS (*free*): Did he command a small force, or travel like a chief, with many armed followers?

JOCASTA [*free*]: There were only five all told. One was a herald, and there was one carriage drawn by colts, for Laius.

OEDIPUS [*intone*]: Aye! It is now clear indeed! Who (*free*) was it brought back the news, lady?

JOCASTA: A servant, the only one who escaped with his life.

OEDIPUS [*intone*]: The only one? (*Free.*) Is he in the house now?

JOCASTA: Why no, for when he found you—

8. Incidental Music

[*The dialogue of this scene is spoken above a fourteen-measure passage of incidental music that is repeated as often as necessary.*]

(*Jocasta continues*): reigning in Laius's place he begged me, with hand on mine, to send him with the sheep in the mountains, that he might be far from the sight or call of this town. And there I sent him. He was a worthy slave, and could have asked much more.

OEDIPUS [*free*]: Can you find him? I want him to return to us immediately.

JOCASTA: That is easy, but why do you ask this?

OEDIPUS: I fear my own voice, lady. I must know what this man knows.

JOCASTA: He shall come. But I feel that I have a right to know this burden that lies so heavy upon you.

OEDIPUS: You do, and I shall not keep it from you, with dark forebodings storming in my head.

Here is my whole story: my father was Polybius of Corinth—my mother Merope of Doris; and I was the proudest man in all Corinthia. Then I heard a chance remark—at a banquet, where wine flowed more freely than wisdom. A man declared that I was not my father's son. I restrained myself at the time, but at dawn I went to my mother and father and questioned them. They were angry over the man's loose talk and comforted me. Still, this charge rankled, for it was being noised about. And, unknown to my parents, I went to Delphi. There I got no answer to my pleading, but the oracle set forth other things—of dread and terror; even that I was fated to share my mother's bed; and that I would bring among men a brood of incestuous children; and that I should kill my father.

Upon hearing this I fled. Measuring by the stars where Corinth lay, I turned in a direction where for a certainty I should never see the fulfillment of these infamies. And on the way, I came to the place where, you say, Laius perished. Now, I will tell you everything. In that narrow pass with crowding woods, at the crossing of those three roads, I met a herald, and a man seated in a carriage drawn by colts, as you described; and the one in front, and the old man himself, tried to jostle me out of the path. Angered, I struck the first. Then, as I passed his carriage, the old man came down full upon my head with his iron-studded goad. But I gave him more than equal payment; with one swift blow of my staff, I rolled him right out of the carriage, on his back; and I killed every man of them.

But if this stranger was truly Laius, what man can be more wretched than the man before you? What man could prove more hated of heaven? A man no citizen may greet; whom all must drive away! And this curse was laid on me by no mouth but my own. And I hold the dead man's wife in the same arms that committed murder! Am I not wantonly pursued by the gods?—seeing that I must be banished, but in banishment I cannot return to my own land and people, lest I be joined in marriage with my mother, and kill my father?

If one should say that something greater than mortal power brought all this upon me, who could deny him? [*Intone.*] Forbid, forbid, pure and awful gods! that I should see that day! May I be swept from among mankind into darkness before I have suffered a doom like that!

SPOKESMAN [*free*]: These things, my king, are fraught with terror; yet, at least, until you hear the man who saw the deed, do not lose hope.

OEDIPUS [*free*]: Hope, now is *all* I have. I await the man being called from the pastures.

JOCASTA: And when he appears? What then?

OEDIPUS: You said that this man spoke of robbers. If, then, he repeats that story, I am not the slayer. But if he names one lonely wanderer, then beyond a doubt god's finger points to me.

JOCASTA: Be assured that when the story was first told it was of robbers; he cannot revoke that, for the city heard it, and not I alone. But even if he should now change his story, never, king, can it be shown that this deed squares with prophecy, since the god said plainly that Laius must die by the hand of *my* child. That poor innocent did not kill him, or anyone, but died before him. [*Intone.*] So henceforth I would not for all divination turn my eyes to my right hand or to my left hand, or fear for the future at all.

OEDIPUS: You advise well. Nevertheless, send someone to bring the Herdsman.

JOCASTA [*free*]: I will send immediately. But let us go inside.

{*They go into the house.*}

9. Third Chorus

CHORUS: Ngo—
SPOKESMAN [*intone*]:   At life's very end, may I still be guided by

                    Ngo—
those timeless laws, straight from Olympian Zeus, and beyond

                    Ngah oh—ngü Oh—
the making of men.   Insolence begets the

Ah—ü—
tyrant. Fed by vanity, he rises to the summit,   and is then

ü— Ngo—
struck down to the abyss.   But if a man can scorn the

Ngo—
righteous ways, and never be despised, and even prosper for it,

Ngah oh   ngü—
how can we esteem the gods, or dance the sacred   dance?

10. Messenger Scene

{*Jocasta enters from the palace.*}

JOCASTA [*intone*]: Citizens, I have decided that I must go to the shrines of the land with flowers and incense. For Oedipus excites himself with all kinds of alarms, nor does he, like a man of sense, judge today's problem by yesterday's experience; no, he is at the mercy of every new word of terror.

Since my counsel is doing no good, I come to you who are nearest, God of the Sun, with offerings of prayer, to beg that you will bring us out of torment. Oh, help us now, for we are all afraid, just as men on a storm-tossed ship when they see their captain afraid.

(*Enter Messenger.*)

MESSENGER: May I learn from you, sir, where the house of King Oedipus is? Or, better still, where he himself is?

SPOKESMAN [*free*]: This is his house, and this lady is his queen, the mother of his children.

MESSENGER: Being wife to such a man, a blessing upon her!

JOCASTA [*free*]: My blessing upon you also, stranger, but why do you come?

MESSENGER: Good news, lady, for your house and your husband.

JOCASTA: News? Where are you from?

MESSENGER: Corinth. And you will find joy in my message, though perhaps it may grieve you somewhat.

Scene from 1952 Mills College production of *King Oedipus.* Scene 10: Jocasta and the Messenger. Photograph by Carl Mydans. LIFE MAGAZINE © Time Inc.

JOCASTA: What is it? How can it have such opposite effects?

MESSENGER: The people of Corinth will make Oedipus their king.

JOCASTA: How? Is Polybius no longer king?

MESSENGER: No. He is dead.

JOCASTA: What Polybius—gone?

MESSENGER: Strike me dead if this is not the truth.

JOCASTA [*intone*]: Hurry, girl! Get to your master with this news! O prophecies of the gods, where in heaven are you now? *My* Oedipus, this is the man you feared and shunned in dread of killing him, (*strict—fast*) and now he has died in the natural course of his destiny, and *not* by *your* hand!

(*Enter Oedipus.*)

OEDIPUS [*free*]: Jocasta! Why did you call me?

JOCASTA: Listen to this man, and judge for yourself my warning, *and* the depths of nothingness to which the oracles of the gods have come!

OEDIPUS: And he—who is he? Where from?

JOCASTA [*free*]: From Corinth, to tell you that your father is dead.

OEDIPUS: How! Tell me yourself, stranger!

MESSENGER: If I am to speak: indeed, he is dead and gone.

OEDIPUS: By treachery? Or of disease?

MESSENGER: The smallest weight may tip the scale and bring the aged to their rest.

OEDIPUS: Father! Of sickness, then.

MESSENGER: Yes, and of age.

OEDIPUS: Aye, aye! Why, indeed, my wife, should one look to the oracles, or to the birds screaming overhead, who had me murdering my father? For he *is* dead, and here am I, innocent— unless, perhaps, he died of longing for me. But by his death Polybius has swept the oracles down with him into the grave: they are nothing.

JOCASTA: Certainly. I told you this quite a long time ago.

OEDIPUS: But it is not over yet. Must I not still fear my mother's bed?

JOCASTA: O Oedipus! Must man live in constant fear when he has clear foresight of nothing? We live by chance, at random, as we may. The circumstances of your father's death are a good sign.

OEDIPUS: Yes, yet while *she* lives I *must* avoid her!

MESSENGER: And why do you think of the wife of Polybius with fear?

OEDIPUS: The oracle said that I was doomed to kill my father, and to marry my mother. And this is why I have never returned to Corinth.

MESSENGER: Have I not freed you from such care?

OEDIPUS: Indeed! And you will be rewarded.

MESSENGER: I came here, to tell the truth, to bring you home, with even greater reward in prospect.

OEDIPUS: No! I will never go!

MESSENGER: Ah, my son, it is plain that you do not realize . . .

OEDIPUS: What? For the love of heaven tell me!

MESSENGER: Your fear is for nothing.

OEDIPUS: How? If I was born . . .

MESSENGER: Because Polybius was *nothing* to you in blood.

OEDIPUS: What? Polybius not my father?

MESSENGER: No more than I.

OEDIPUS: You are *nothing* to me, but he fathered me!

MESSENGER: He did not father you any more than I.

OEDIPUS: No? Did he not call me *son?*

MESSENGER: You were his son as a gift, from these hands of mine, long ago.

OEDIPUS: Yet he loved me so dearly — I, who came from a stranger's hands?

MESSENGER: He had been childless, and therefore loved you the more.

OEDIPUS: And you! Where did you get me? buy me? find me?

MESSENGER: I found you—in a wooded glen on Kithaeron.

(*Jocasta starts.*)

OEDIPUS: And why were you there?

MESSENGER: I was tending my flocks.

OEDIPUS: A shepherd—a hired wanderer?

MESSENGER: Yes, my son, but one who saved you, and just in time.

OEDIPUS: Why, *in time?* Was I in peril?

MESSENGER: Do not your feet bear witness?

OEDIPUS: Yes—an old trouble, that wakes an old pain!

MESSENGER: It was I who took the spike from them.

OEDIPUS: These brands that I have carried as long as I can remember!

MESSENGER: Indeed, and from this misfortune you received your name.

OEDIPUS [*intone*]: Oh, for the love of heaven, was this deed my mother's or my father's? Speak!

MESSENGER: I do not know; he who gave you to me must answer that.

OEDIPUS: What? You yourself didn't find me? You got me from another?

MESSENGER: Another shepherd gave you to me—to carry far away.

OEDIPUS [*free*]: Who? Tell me plainly who he was.

MESSENGER: He was said to be from Laius's household. As I recall—

OEDIPUS: The king who ruled here before me?

MESSENGER: The same: the man was in his service.

OEDIPUS: Is he still alive—that I might see him?

MESSENGER: I cannot say. But you people here should—

OEDIPUS: Is there anyone here who knows the man? who has seen him in the town, or in the pastures? Answer! [*intone*] for the hour has come at last when all is to be revealed!

SPOKESMAN: I believe he is the Herdsman you have already summoned, but your lady here, Jocasta, can answer best.

OEDIPUS [*free*]: Is this true?

JOCASTA [*intone*]: Why ask about him? Why think about him at all? What can he possibly say that will not be vain? What he may say is of no importance!

OEDIPUS [*intone*]: What! With the secret of my birth all but revealed, and pass up a clue like this!

JOCASTA: For the god's love, Oedipus, no! If you cherish your life, give up this search! Let my anguish end!

OEDIPUS: Though I be shown as the child of slaves—yes, of slaves from great-grandmother down—you cannot be proved base-born.

JOCASTA: Yet hear me, I implore you: stop this search!

OEDIPUS: Stop at half a truth? I will *not* stop until I have learned the *whole* truth!

JOCASTA: I tell you for your own good—stop this search! My advice is for the best!

OEDIPUS: Your opinion of the best has nearly exhausted my patience!

JOCASTA: (*Long glide.*) Aye— Miserable man! May you never come to know who you are!

OEDIPUS: Go, someone! Bring that Herdsman, and leave this woman to glory in her princely blood.

JOCASTA: Aye— Aye— Miserable man! Miserable! This one word can I say to you, from here on—and forever!

{*She rushes out.*}

SPOKESMAN [*intone*]: Why has the lady gone, Oedipus, as one in a transport of wild grief? Is this silence to burst with another storm of sorrows?

OEDIPUS [*free*]: Let burst what will! I shall learn my origin, however lowly. That woman, proud with even more than a woman's pride, is disgraced by my base birth. But I will not be dishonored, for I am the son of Fortune. She is my mother, and my brothers are the changing months. Sometimes they have set me high, and sometimes flung me low. Such as I am I am. I must not be false; then how can I fear this search?

11. Fourth Chorus

CHORUS: Mo ho ho ho mo ho— ho ho *ha* ho ho ho Ho
SPOKESMAN [*intone*]:

    ho ho *ha* ho ho ho ho ü— Oh— Oh— Moo— Moh—
        Yea   Yea   Yea Yea—

Moo—   Moh—
O Kithaeron by tomorrow's full moon,   you will resound

               Moo—
with the voices of festivity.   For we honor you, in dance

        Moh—   Moo—
and song, as the nurse and mother of Oedipus.   What

                    Moh—
mountain-roaming lord conceived you, Oedipus?   In what

    Moo—   Moh—
wild glen?   Who was it, my son, that bore you, one of the

        ü—
nymphs of Helicon?

12. Herdsman Scene

OEDIPUS [*free*]: I would guess—that the man we have long been
seeking is finally here. His venerable age matches with our Corinthian messenger's, and I recognize my servants, who are bringing him. But perhaps you, friend, will know better than I. Have
you seen this herdsman before?

SPOKESMAN [*free*]: Yes, to be sure; I knew him well. He was once a
shepherd in the service of Laius—the most trusted of all.

(*Herdsman is brought in.*)

OEDIPUS: I ask you first, Corinthian stranger, is this the man?

MESSENGER: He is the very man.

OEDIPUS: Ho there, old man! Look up, and answer my questions.
Were you once in Laius's service?

HERDSMAN [*free*]: I was—born in his house, but not a bought slave.

OEDIPUS: What was your work?

HERDSMAN: I have tended flocks for the best part of my life.

OEDIPUS: In what region?

HERDSMAN: In Kithaeron; sometimes the mountains nearby.

OEDIPUS: Did you know this man, then? Did you ever see him there?

HERDSMAN: I do not recall him to mind, right off.

MESSENGER: And it's no wonder, sir. But I will bring back his memory. For I am sure that he well remembers the three half-years, from spring to autumn, when we tended our sheep in Kithaeron, he with two flocks, I with one. At wintertime we drove them home, mine to my fold, and his to the fold of Laius. Do you now recall, or not?

HERDSMAN: Yes, I now recall, though it was long ago.

MESSENGER: Come, tell me—do you remember giving me a boy in those days, to rear as my own son?

HERDSMAN: What do you mean? Why do you ask this?

MESSENGER: This man, my friend, *was* that boy.

HERDSMAN: A curse on you, fool! Will you hold your tongue?

OEDIPUS: Ha! Don't rebuke him, old man. Your own words are the more offensive.

HERDSMAN [intone]: And how do I offend, master?

OEDIPUS: The child he asks about—where did it come from?

HERDSMAN: He is meddlesome! He speaks folly!

OEDIPUS: So you refuse to speak with a good grace! *But you will on pain!*

HERDSMAN: No! for the love of heaven—do not misuse an old man!

OEDIPUS: Ho, someone! Twist his arms behind him!

HERDSMAN: Aye! Why! What more would you know?

OEDIPUS: Did you give the boy to this man, as he says?

HERDSMAN: I did—I wish to God I had died that day!

OEDIPUS: Well, you shall still come to that unless you tell me the honest truth.

HERDSMAN: Much more am I lost, if I tell it.

Scene from 1952 Mills College production of *King Oedipus.* Scene 12: Oedipus uses force to make the Herdsman reveal the truth of his birth. Photograph by Carl Mydans. LIFE MAGAZINE © Time Inc.

OEDIPUS: How? Is the fellow determined on more delay?

HERDSMAN: No, no! I said before that I gave it to him.

OEDIPUS: Where did you get it? From your own house, or from another?

HERDSMAN: No, not mine. I had it from another.

OEDIPUS: Look around! From anyone here? *What* house?

(Beginning here both voices and instruments get progressively softer — yet more intense — until the line "you were born for misery" is barely audible.)

HERDSMAN: Stop, master, for the god's love! Do not ask any more!

OEDIPUS: You are lost if I have to ask you again.

HERDSMAN: It was a child — then — from the house of Laius.

OEDIPUS: A slave? Or one of his own blood?

HERDSMAN: Oh! I am on the brink of dreadful words!

OEDIPUS: And I of hearing: yet *heard they must be.*

HERDSMAN: Know, then, that it was said to have been his own son — but your lady within can tell you best, how this all was.

OEDIPUS: How? She gave it to you?

HERDSMAN: Yes, my king.

OEDIPUS: And ordered you — ?

HERDSMAN: To make away with it.

OEDIPUS: With — her own child?

HERDSMAN: Aye! in wild fear of dreadful oracles.

OEDIPUS: Saying — ?

HERDSMAN: That he must kill his father.

OEDIPUS: Why, then, did you give him away?

HERDSMAN: From pity, master, thinking that he would take him away to a distant land, where he himself came from; but he saved him for dreadful doom, for if you are what this man says, you were born for misery.

{Everyone onstage except Oedipus must be as still as statues from this point to the opening of the next scene.}

13. Oedipus Scene

OEDIPUS [*intone*]: Oh—! Oh—! All— brought to pass—! All—
true—! Here— O light! na—ked before— men—, I shall look
my last— upon you! For I am accursed in marriage, accursed in
blood, and in my coming into the world I— am— ac—cur—
sed!

{*Oedipus takes his first step offstage. He must be completely off in
eight beats.*}
⟨*First slight movement of dancers begins here.*⟩

CHORUS: Oh— Oh— Oh—ü—

14. Fifth Chorus

CHORUS: Oh   Oh Lo   Oh   Lo
SPOKESMAN [*intone*]: Generations of men,   your life is but a

Oh—
shadow. After the semblance, it falls to nothing. See thus your

Oh   Oh Lo Oh   Lo—   Oh   Oh
fate,   unhappy Oedipus! You were first among men,

Lo Oh Lo Oh—
                you killed the wildly singing Sphinx, and then

                    Oh   Oh Lo Oh   Lo—
became the king of ancient Thebes,   Glorious Oedipus!

        Oh Oh   Lo   Oh   Lo Oh—
But then,   you entered where   you had once come

                                Oh   Oh   Lo
wailing forth. How could the soil your father had sowed have

Oh   Lo—   Oh Oh Lo Oh
suffered you so long in silence, Bold Oedipus?

        Lo   Oh—   Oh   Oh
With eagle eye, time found you out. For every act of man is

Lo   Oh—   Oh   Oh
known, and all who doubt are lost. Oh, that you had never

Lo   Oh Lo   Oh—

guessed the dark riddle of the woman-breasted Fate, nor come

Oh—

to Thebes at all, nor saved us then! Oh, that I had never sung

[Spokesman:] this song—Broken Oedipus!

15. Instrumental Commentary

SECOND MESSENGER: Thebans! Townsmen and friends of this house!

SPOKESMAN [*free*]: You bring us another tale?

SECOND MESSENGER: The shortest tale to tell and to hear. Our lady, Jocasta, is dead.

SPOKESMAN: Aye! Crushed with sorrows. How did she die?

SECOND MESSENGER: By her own hand.

CHORUS: Oh— Oh—

> {*In the dance, beginning here, each individual has a characteristic movement—not continuous; one movement of figure to correspond to each instrumental comment, after which the individual is still. This is a dance of indecision.*}

CHORUS: Oh— Oh— ü— mu mu mu mu mu mu Oh Oh

> {*Sharp, furious, scherzo dance begins here, the dancers correlating their movements into something resembling unity. This is a violent kind of resolution.*}

CHORUS: Oh—
SPOKESMAN (*intone*):   Oh Oh Oh Oh Oh Oh Oh Oh Oh Oh—

16. Antiphony

> {*The curtain is parting.*}

SECOND MESSENGER: The bars of the gate have fallen. You are going to look upon a sight which even those who abhor it must pity.

> {*Oedipus enters, blind, and led by a boy. In the course of the Antiphony, Oedipus crosses the stage slowly, aimlessly, perhaps twice, and is followed by attendants (dancers) who—in measured but quick movements—register shock and mortification. The singers stand stock still.*}

SPOKESMAN (*free*): Dreadful to the eye!

OEDIPUS (*intone*): Where, where am I?

CHORUS: Where,   where am I?
SPOKESMAN: Dreadful to the ear!

OEDIPUS: Miserable, miserable that I am!

CHORUS: Miserable, miserable that I am!

OEDIPUS: Where shall I turn?

CHORUS: Where shall I turn?

OEDIPUS: Where am I wandering?

CHORUS: Where am I wandering?

OEDIPUS: O— wild Kithaeron!

CHORUS: O— wild Kithaeron!

OEDIPUS: Who hears my voice?

CHORUS: Who hears my voice? Who hears my voice?

OEDIPUS (*free*): Why was I given sight when sight could show me
    nothing sweet? How unkind the cursed pity of the man who took
    the shackle from my feet. If I had only died then!

SPOKESMAN: This is truly as you say. I, too, would have had it so.

CHORUS: Who hears my voice?

OEDIPUS (*intone*): O three roads!

CHORUS: O three roads!

OEDIPUS: O secret glen!

CHORUS: O secret glen!

OEDIPUS: O crowding woods and narrow pass where three roads
    meet!

CHORUS: O crowding woods and narrow pass where three roads
    meet! O crowding woods and narrow pass where three roads meet!

OEDIPUS: Hide me   somewhere
CHORUS: O crowding woods and narrow pass   where three roads

    far from this land,   or   cast me adrift upon the sea,
    meet!   O three roads!

where no one shall see me again.

O secret glen!   O crowding

[Chorus:] woods and narrow pass where three roads meet!

17. Exit Oedipus — Dance-Pantomime

{*From this point whatever action is necessary is done in pantomime. More vigorous dancing begins here, the dancers of the Commentary joining with Oedipus's attendants.*}

⟨*Voices progressively softer, instruments progressively louder.*⟩

CHORUS and SPOKESMAN (*intone*): Hide me! Hide me! Hide me! Hide me! Hide me!

{*Oedipus talks with the Spokesman, asking that the Spokesman touch him—"Come near, condescend to lay your hands upon a wretched man. . . ."*}

{*The Spokesman responds.*}

{*Creon, now king, enters with attendants, in movements which are integrated with the music. This is no triumphal entry—but one of confusion and tragedy. Having taken his place near Oedipus, Creon stands still and talks to Oedipus, while the dancers—who have taken no notice of Creon—continue. Creon's attendants join in the dance. Oedipus asks Creon for his daughters, Ismene and Antigone, and Creon tells Oedipus that he has ordered them to appear.*}

{*Ismene and Antigone enter at this point, and advance slowly toward Oedipus.*}

{*In pantomime, Oedipus begs Antigone and Ismene to come to him, and asks Creon to show, by touching him, that he (Creon) will care for them.*}

SOLO SOPRANO: Oh— Oh—   Oh— Oh—
SPOKESMAN: Oh—   Oh— Oh—

{*Creon responds.*}

SOLO SOPRANO and SPOKESMAN: Oh— Oh—

{*At this point Ismene and Antigone join in the dance and become the central figures.*}

{*At this point the sisters are prostrate.*}

Scene from 1952 Mills College production of *King Oedipus*. Scene 17: Blinded Oedipus begs Creon for his daughters. Photograph by Carl Mydans. LIFE MAGAZINE © Time Inc.

SOLO SOPRANO: ü—

⟨*The sisters rise and dance.*⟩

SOLO SOPRANO: ü— ü—

{*The sisters are again prostrate.*}

SOLO SOPRANO: ü—

{*Again, rise and dance.*}

SOLO SOPRANO: ü—

{*Prostrate again.*}

SPOKESMAN: ü— Oh—

{*Rise and dance again.*}
{*The dancers begin to resolve into something resembling unity here.*
Ismene and Antigone becoming anonymous.}
{*Singers in two groups. Unity in the dance is achieved at this point.*
The dance now revolves around Oedipus. Creon stands at the side
with attendants and takes no part. Dance is slow and dignified.}

CHORUS: Oh—   Oh— Oh— Oh—
SPOKESMAN: Oh— Oh— Oh—

{*Violent, chaotic movement begins again here, suggesting the furious*
dance of the Instrumental Commentary.}

CHORUS and SPOKESMAN: No no no no no no no no no no no
no No

{*Here the violence quickly resolves into a vigorous yet dignified dance*
of the whole company.}

CHORUS: Oh—Ah— Ah— Ah—   Oh— Oh— Oh—
SPOKESMAN: Oh—Ah—   Ah— Ah— Oh— Oh— Oh—

{*Sudden shift of emphasis here.*}
{*Another shift of emphasis: gentle, dolorous movement.*}

CHORUS: ü— ü— ü— ü— ü— ü— ü—

FIRST FEMALE VOICE: Ksee—
SECOND FEMALE VOICE: Ksee—
THIRD FEMALE VOICE: Ksee—
FOURTH FEMALE VOICE: Ksee—
FIFTH FEMALE VOICE: Ksee—

Ksee—   Ksee—   Ksee—
   Ksee—   Ksee—   Ksee—
        Ksee—   Ksee—   Ksee—
            Ksee—   Ksee—   Ksee—
                    Ksee—   Ksee—

{*Creon finally moves forward and orders Oedipus into the palace, and Oedipus—led by Creon and the boy—slowly begins to respond.*}

{*The procession forms, and begins its exit here, in this order: Creon, the boy, Oedipus, Ismene, Antigone, and attendants (most of the dancers).*}

CHORUS: Oh— Oh—

18. Final Chorus

{*The procession must be completely offstage.*}
{*Only three or four dancers are left. These repeat the waltz dance of the Third Chorus, more slowly.*}

CHORUS: Ngo—
SPOKESMAN [*intone*]:   Let Oedipus pass, for he has met

[Spokesman:] his fate head-on— Now do we know the deceit of

Ngo—
Fortune. One moment of greatness— Then storms of sorrow.

Ngah-oh—
        Call no man fortunate until his life has run to its

[Spokesman:] appointed end, free from pain.

Coda

{*All dance movement ends here. All those onstage must be stock still through these final measures.*}

The Bewitched

A Dance Satire

Introduction

The idea contains three human elements: the Witch, the Witch's Chorus (the orchestra), the Bewitched (the dancers).

The Witch belongs to the ancient, pre-Christian school. She is an omniscient soul, all-perceptive, with that wonderful power to make other people see also, when she feels so inclined. And she is always willing to wait for the right psychological moment to strike, which she can of course predict.

The Witch is a different Greek oracle, and the Chorus — like the choruses of ancient tragedy — is her instrument, always under the oracular power of suggestion. The Chorus is a corporeal part of the drama — more directly than it would be as mere instrumentalists. It both sings and plays; it stamps its feet, it whistles, it says *Woof!* and *Bah!* in low and aspirate exclamations. More, it is a child of magic.

The bewitched dancers become the players on the stage, the principals, in this analogy with lyric tragedy. The work is completely nonverbal, and the occasional dialogue of this outline is merely intended to give verbal animation to the idea; it is most inadequate if considered as a substitute for theater. In a performance, the possessed dancers would speak with their bodies.

Dominating and tying the ten psychological scenes together is the Witch. When she is not singing, shouting, murmuring, or trumpeting, she dominates merely by her presence, because her vocal entrance into each situation is always imminent.

The music runs to about seventy-five minutes, one scene leading into the next without, or with very slight, musical pause, and each new beginning is aided by comparative darkness. Each new day, as it were, brings a new situation to test the Witch's power to reveal, and it is always uncertain how she will exercise her power, if at all.

These are stories of release — through salutary and whimsical witchery — from prejudice; from individual limitation; even from the accident of physical form; of sex that creates mental obstacles to vision; and the release is the climax. In its characteristic way, each one is a theatrical unfolding of nakedness, a psychological striptease, or a diametric reversal, with the effect of underlining the complementary character and the strange affinity of seeming opposites.

The instruments dominate the set. They are on risers of different heights, the risers being connected by a stairway, or a nexus of stairways, which mature into an ascent without evident end, at one of the far corners of the rear. Some of the instruments may be only partially visible.

The stairways are seldom used in a respectable manner, and the dancers constantly show their contempt for the symbol by jumping straight from the stage to platform or platform to stage, with feet together, on beats of the music.

Generally, the Witch is on a throne near the front of the stage, facing the opposite entrance, draped in robes which assume different colors with the changing lights. To the audience, she is more frequently a dark silhouette, creating the illusion of a *presence*, one which is invisible to the dancers, who hear but cannot see. She sits immobile, she stands, she moves rhythmically on the throne, and occasionally assumes command of her Chorus as ostensible conductor.

In writing this outline, I have let my mind wander with little hindrance. My suggestions regarding stage set, lights, costumes, and movements about the stage go into highly technical areas, and I would like to invoke experience and attitudes beyond my own. My statements are really questions: is this particular idea a good idea? in costume? in set? in lighting? in movement? is what I am asking, throughout. The important thing is an agreed-on basis for performance, so that a true collaboration and integration results. And *if* it results, a major step may have been taken in rediscovering—in Western terms—an ancient value.

On the Dancing

There are at least three customs or conventions of various oriental dancing—negative or positive—that I find attractive, for dramatic reasons. (In the case of satire, exceptions must be made.)

1. Arms and eyes never go to heaven together. Separately perhaps, but never together. Together, the effect is a cliché, on a par with *Woe is me!* spoken on the stage, and might be desirable only as a bit of obvious satire.
2. The occasional statuelike immobility of the dancers. This has the effect of making movement more vital, more uncertain, therefore

more tensive to the viewer, when it does occur. There should be no innate compulsion to move constantly, simply because one is on a stage.

3. In a serious love duet or a fight duet, a dancer never touches another dancer, in a gesture of endearment or anger. I noted, long before I ever saw oriental dancing, how tension was likely to drop the moment two such characters became physically embroiled. In dance terms, either a love-brawl or a fight-brawl is the end of art, however pleasurable in reality. Tension can be maintained indefinitely if the clinch is avoided; after the clinch there is nothing worth saying. In dance aesthetics, the human body has a sacred, mysterious identity which can be easily and shockingly damaged, and the body's preserved sacredness tends to illumine the terrible fact of every person's aloneness.

In general, I have conceived the characters [and scenes] of *The Bewitched* in the following types or manners of dancing:

The Witch: Kabuki—slow, dignified movements with rigid trunk, and occasional quick, furious movements.

Scene 1: Imitations of the Cantonese music hall.

2: Eighteenth-century formality, with satiric twentieth-century expressionism, in part.

3: East Indian, with—I hope—some tumbling.

4: A formal solo, with modern dance farce at the end.

5: Slightly satiric expressionism at first.

6: Satiric ballet, almost throughout.

7: Modern-dance comedy throughout.

8: Kabuki throughout.

9: Near East throughout.

10: I leave this open.

Where oriental styles are stated, the dancing would only *suggest*. The result would *not* be oriental, of course, any more than my music is oriental, even though most Americans hearing it for the first time say so.

It is to be hoped that the lost musicians and the dancers, as opposing forces, will be mingled in the staging; that entrances and exits be made through the musicians or down the musicians' stairways occasionally; that close involvement of *a* dancer and *a* musician be planned occasionally, so that the work will come off as a bold and forthright venture into integrated art. The differences of dress and occupation in the performance are quite enough to prevent confusion.

Scenario

From the center of the idea, three shafts are projected: (1) titles and verbal notes, (2) music, (3) dance. None of the three competes with the others, or offers contradiction, since no two paths cross. And none presumes to "interpret" the others. Each radiates through the energy of the faculties peculiar to itself. The shafts begin to revolve around the center, they whirl, become interwoven, and finally resolve into an entity, solitary and seemingly stationary.

Argument

We are all bewitched, and mostly by accident: the accident of form, color, and sex; of prejudices conditioned from the cradle on up; of the particular ruts we have found ourselves in or have dug for ourselves because of our individual needs. Those in a long-tenanted rut enjoy larger comforts of mind and body, and as compensation it is given to others who are not so easily domesticated to become mediums for the transmissions of perception, more frequently. Among these are the lost musicians. The present-day musician grows up in a half-world between "good" music and "not-so-good" music. Even when he has definitely made his choice between the two, he is still affected by the other, and to that extent he is dichotomous and disoriented. His head is bathed in an ancient light through a Gothic window while his other end swings like a miniature suspension bridge in a cool right-angle gale. The perception of displaced musicians may germinate, evolve, and mature in concert, through a developing at-one-ness, through their beat.

Prologue—The Lost Musicians Mix Magic

The forms of strange instruments are seen onstage. How did they get here? They came on in a dark celestial silence, doing tumbles and handsprings, and for no other purpose than to be discovered by *these* musicians in *this* theater before *this* audience.

One of the musicians gives a low beat, and others swing in, one at a time. They are neolithic primitives in their unspoken acceptance of magic as real, unconsciously reclaiming an all-but-lost value for the exploitation of their perception in an age of scientific hierarchs—a value lost only about a minute ago in relation to that ancient time when the first single cell moved itself in such autoerotic agitation that it split in two. The first animate magic.

In the enveloping ensemble the lost musicians have momentarily found a direction, a long-arm extension of first magic. Their direction becomes a power, and their power a vision: an ancient Witch, a prehistoric seer untouched by either gossip or popular malevolence, and with that wonderful power to make others see also. The perceptive Witch corresponds to the Greek oracle, while the Chorus (the orchestra) — like the choruses of ancient tragedy — is a moral instrument under the power of perceptive suggestion.

The lost musicians are quite without malice. On wings of love they demolish three undergraduate egos temporarily away from their jukeboxes. It is the kind thing to do. On wings of love they turn an incorrigibly pursuing young wooer into a retreating misogynist. It is the kind thing to do. On wings of love they catapult the cultural know-it-alls into limbo, because limbo will be so congenial. It is certainly the kind thing to do.

The Witch surveys the world and immediately becomes sad and moody, then takes command: "Everybody wants background music!" the Witch-like sounds seem to murmur, and the conspiratorial tone is clear even in gibberish. Let us dance.

Scene 1 — Three Undergrads Become Transfigured in a Hong Kong Music Hall

The bewitched enter, and the analogy with lyric tragedy is complete: the Chorus, the Perceptive Voice, the Actors. These actors dance their parts, and they unconsciously seek perceptive guidance. Although they seem always to ignore the person of the Witch, the voice is heard distinctly. Like the bewitched everywhere, they also seem to ignore the Chorus of the displaced, while at the same time revealing that they are terribly aware of that displaced presence.

If this painting tends to portray the bewitched as unattractive, it is not intended. These undergrads particularly are charming and exuberant children, with plump bodies, shining teeth and eyes — exuding from a thousand pores a soap-scrubbed pinkish gleam.

The job taken on by the Chorus of displaced musicians is — briefly — to divest the undergrads of the confirmed xenophobia that once blanketed them so lovingly in their cradles. That in this instance the conditioned rejection, dislike, and even ridicule of anything strange is tied to exotic music is incidental. The comeuppance is a broad one, and for one moment the undergrads become aware, far beyond their young years and experience. The exotic — East or West — does not hold more mystery than it ought.

Alwin Nikolais Dancers in a pose from the 1957 production of *The Bewitched*. Photograph courtesy of The Alwin Nikolais Dance Theatre.

Scene 2—Exercises in Harmony and Counterpoint Are Tried in a Court of Ancient Ritual

Like the Mindanao Deep of the Pacific, the bewitchment in musical conditioning is profound and mysterious. It is indeed so deep that a term such as *the scale* is accorded a silent and mysterious Mindanaon acceptance as obvious as *the robin* in spring.

One can conjure up, long before this particular deep, a whole series of deeps, some perhaps even vaster and deeper. In the interests of perspective let us plumb some of these others, long since lost sight of by everyone except the Witch and Chorus. For there is probably nothing so disorienting to modern man as suddenly to have to consider how many other deeps he may have occupied—that is, how appallingly ancient he is.

The bewitched exercises in harmony and counterpoint are cast into a sea of ancient rules and ritual. Now the immediate colors are strong and violent, and rich with symbolism, while the distant pastels of the eighteenth century are barely perceptible in the dim, dim future. Instead of an ignominious drowning, the unwitched exercises suddenly look to an inspired new day—parthenogenetic and apocalyptic.

Scene 3—The Romancing of a Pathological Liar Comes to an Inspired End

The scene focuses on the sad life story of a boy and a man. He is a pathological liar for one reason: he is pursued by the magic of his fancy just as relentlessly and in the same way that he pursues the object of his fancy. Driven in a less than conscious way to avoid the final catastrophe of his seduction, he must himself seduce. By every conceivable physical means—rhythmic, eurhythmic, cryptorhythmic, catarhythmic, anarhythmic—he must transform the mortal danger at his back to a threat of his own, in front. His fancies are his weapon, and he proliferates them before him only to die many little deaths as they breathe down his neck from behind.

In the pedestrian life of the day-to-day world, this spinning triangle must finally end in tragedy—one big death as the correct sum of many little deaths. But in the jet stream magic of this night, the Chorus of displaced musicians and their Witch find a poetic way out. In a flash the boy's driving bewitchment abandons him to light momentarily in the temple of his ladylove. Too late, the boy sees himself. But too late, too late! for out of the corner of his vision, he sees a woman with lust in the shaft of her eye. A dull thud.

Scene 4—A Soul Tormented by Contemporary Music Finds a Humanizing Alchemy

Of all the sad tales sung by the poets of old, some are sadder than this, some more poignant, many more tragic, but none more pathetic, for this is a scene of inner conflict—a conflict arising out of an absorbing regret over the passage of time.

The story of this soul began with the injustice of having been born at such a miserable time in history as the present. But as the years passed, the regret became equivocal, because—except for such modern trivia as the current price of baby-sitters—it became so immersed in the bewitchment of some preceding century as in fact to function only in that century. Even the growing child falls somewhat behind the surge of the modern world, because of the shelter of his home, and during a year or so out on his own, he must catch up. Imagine, then, the degree of nervous tension that is generated in the excruciating ordeal of being forced to catch up through a couple of centuries!

The Chorus whistles dolefully, while the slow beats toll off the neuroses—one by one. The amplitude of the shocks increases. Now utter silence. Breathing loudly in a crescendo of emotion, the Chorus of displaced musicians brings the climax. The other-century soul has returned to the world of living people through a whole-souled abandonment to modern slapstick comedy!

Scene 5—Visions Fill the Eyes of a Defeated Basketball Team in the Shower Room

It seems perversely characteristic of the human male to think of his moments of weakness and failure in a female context. He may say: "Today I'm a sick woman," but he does not intend his words to mean that he has just undergone a sex-changing operation. For the sake of a moment of magic perception, let us impose this idea on the defeated side after a game of basketball.

The potentialities are tremendous, because the bewitchment is profound. Now, with women as subjects, an area of group behavior is open to the adventurous watcher that he could never observe in a group of men under similar conditions. With the incorrigible optimism of healthy young women, for example, these very quickly conclude that one defeat in a basketball game (played by themselves as women) is of exceedingly trivial consequence, and immediately thereafter, with a capricious Witch and a conniving Chorus in the background, fling themselves into something really important—a wild dance that makes the shower room ring with adulation for the nude god Hermes (or his clothed TV equivalent), knaviest among the Olympian knaves. The dance becomes more abandoned with each passing moment, until it can end only with a catapulting of the women down into darkness.

The basketball team—now unwitched—has fallen completely under the charming belief that reality contains a compound of both experience and imagination.

Scene 6—Euphoria Descends a Sausalito Stairway

The scene is one of the landings of a stairway on the steep hills that rise from San Francisco Bay at Sausalito. Adolescent love can make do with whatever scene it's got, of course, but there is something of poetic justice in placing the scene among conservative suburban homes where, at the same time, baroque leaps, baroque swoons, pirouettes, trunks revolving around necks, and the various other devices of adolescent love in ballet form might attract hardly even second notice.

Magic is a wonderful thing, and although Pythagoras is reputed to have arrested a man in motion with a single chord—to release him with a second chord—it has remained for the young man of Sausalito to accomplish this feat with his dancing partner for the purposes of undisturbed examination. From this point on, adolescent love becomes so athletic as to be intolerable.

Anyone can *dream* of bringing control to a Sausalito love affair, but the Witch actually accomplishes it. Facing each other, the boy and girl now move backward and forward on the stairway—with quiet dignity and tenderness—in a way that suggests eternity.

Scene 7—Two Detectives on the Tail of a Tricky Culprit Turn in Their Badges

Obsession makes this a melancholy scene, and notwithstanding the bloody ghosts in its background, obsession also makes it a slapstick love affair. Let cities decay, let armies of souls ascend on high, but never, never allow even one minor culprit to believe that he does not need those conspicuous gentlemen whose lives are dedicated to the single purpose of complementing his ego!

Perhaps he is aware that he wants his ego complemented in exactly this way. Perhaps, on the other hand, he needs convincing. Now the form of this convincing may vary widely, but probably never before this night of magic have two detectives applied their persuasion in the guise of toothsome chorus girls.

This culprit is a recidivist. His automatic *who, me?* response to interrogation leads to a third degree, a fourth degree, and even a fifth degree, each progressively more delightful. With a whistle and a stamp, he takes off on a spontaneous angle of his own, and is only temporarily stopped when the detectives plead with him to honor the memory of his dead mother—hoping that she will rub off.

This is too much for the Witch and Chorus, who waste no time precipitating a crisis. At the scene's end, the unwitched trio tenderly pledge eternal cooperation, to the end that each may achieve the ultimate fulfillment.

Scene 8—A Court in Its Own Contempt Rises to a Motherly Apotheosis

The scene's gist: The heroes of a matriarchy are the sons who gain public attention in futile rebellion against it, thus making their mothers proud. It begins as a double exposure: underneath is the quality of the very ancient matriarchy, on top the personalities of a modern trial—judge, attorneys, witness (the accused in absentia). The tension in the court arises not so much from the overriding necessity everyone feels for posing with his revolving head's most handsome face, as from the fact that the human male is himself on trial.

The lady witness tells a lilting sad story, and the stern decorum of the court is unruffled. But as things proceed lady witness becomes flippant, even indignant, and tempers begin to flare. She is obviously in contempt, and suddenly the Witch wonders about the court itself: hasn't even one court ever become so disgusted with *itself* as to be in its *own* contempt? Flip its calendar, so to speak?

Well, it's high time, says the Chorus of the displaced, for some judicious unwitching, and from the single stroke of a double-bladed axe, two events transpire. First, the court—unwitched—exclaims: "Why, this *is* a matriarchy!" and by the old standards is immediately in contempt. Secondly, the lady witness—unwitched—exclaims: "Why, this *is* a matriarchy!" and by the new standards administers the citation. His Former-Honor moves alone now, with shining eyes, to his lonely apotheosis. Her Honor gazes down proudly.

Scene 9—A Lost Political Soul Finds Himself among the Voteless Women of Paradise

The mood in paradise is static, suspended somewhere between exquisite joy and exquisite melancholy. Gyrating fitfully between the layers of his conscious and unconscious, the lost political soul dreams. Ideas such as these have not come into his head since adolescence! (He sees the dreadful vision of a confession forced under torture before the League of Women Voters.) Conscious and unconscious are not mutually exclusive, and the resulting ambivalence is straight anguish. Gone is the matriarchy, and in vast relief he clutches at this paradise—final refuge of patriarchal entrenchment! And yet—at the same time—how melancholy that there is no electorate to sway, no supporter to allay, and—most distressing of all—no security to administer.

This terrible conflict gives the lost political soul the countenance of Death. The beautiful houris of paradise are only an inanimate stage set, but even now, although he is quite unaware of it, Transfiguration is moving beside him.

The Chorus of lost musicians begins to rip away the sources of conflict. Dig! say the two kitharists, as they tear the last layer off, and the houris, who have very slowly emerged from paradisian refrigeration, have by now fallen into the houriest of all houri dances. Finally purged, the lost political soul dreams his dream peacefully, and finds himself functioning contentedly among constituents who played no part in his election.

Scene 10—The Cognoscenti Are Plunged into a Demonic Descent While at Cocktails

It is soon evident that cognoscenti as subjects for unwitching are by all odds the most difficult. Their armor, for all practical purposes, is untouchable, and they are to that extent the rarest of mortal creatures—not a heel of Achilles in a drawing room load. Probe them mentally where you will—there is not an unfilled crevice. Or, if you suddenly discern one, like lightning they find a filling for the crack, wise or otherwise, even before you have time to open your mouth to remark on the phenomenon.

Now the power of magic seems an unfair advantage in anybody's game, but we must remember that the displaced musicians have had encounters with the cognoscenti before, and on those humiliating occasions their retreating feet invariably got tripped on their own vocal chords. Not so tonight. The power they have generated is both fierce and controlled, and a bit frightening even to the cognoscenti.

"Bah!" says the Chorus, and that one word makes up in violent delivery what it lacks in intellectual sparkle. "How extraordinary!"

say the cognoscenti, propelled by a chorus of dragons in backward somersaults into the middle of limbo.

Not a bad night's work. "Rrrrrrr-ee—eh!" says the Witch, and as everyone knows this may be rendered: "I really don't give a raspberry about all this nonsense. Furthermore, it's time you children were in bed."

Epilogue

"Later!" says the Witch, and vanishes. But the lost musicians cannot unwind so fast, and a few of them linger with their beat, as a kind of final refuge. Then, one by one, they wander away, and finally the last hurries after them.

Like their Witch, the musicians vanish, again to become almost— if not wholly—as bewitched as everyone else. The moment is gone, because perception is a sand flea. It can light only for a moment. Another moment must provide its own sand flea.

Revelation in the Courthouse Park

After The Bacchae *of Euripides*

Time
    Choruses: present
    Scenes: ancient

Place
    Choruses: an American Courthouse Park
    Scenes: before the Palace in ancient Thebes

Cast
    MOM, devotee of Ishbu Kubu and mother
        of Sonny
    AGAVE, leader of the Theban Bacchae and } same person
        mother of Pentheus

    DION, Hollywood king of Ishbu Kubu } same person
    DIONYSUS, ancient god of the Bacchae

    SONNY, young man in the Courthouse Park } same person
    PENTHEUS, young king of ancient Thebes

    TIRESIAS, blind prophet
    CADMUS, founder of Thebes and grandfather of Pentheus
    GUARD
    KORYPHEUS, leader of the Chorus of Eight Women
    HERDSMAN

    CHORUS OF EIGHT Women (including Korypheus), who follow
        Dion and Dionysus (individual members are designated as
        LEADER, SOLO, ONE, TWO, THREE, etc.)
    CHORUS OF FOUR Men, in the American Choruses (individual
        members are designated as LEADER, SOLO, PAIR, TWO, THREE,
        etc.)
    ENTERTAINERS
        Band: 2 piccolos, 3 trumpets, 2 trombones, tuba, snare drum,
            bass drum
        Guitarists (2)
        Drum majorettes (4)
        Clog dancers (4 women, 4 men)
        Tumblers (4)

OTHER INSTRUMENTAL PARTS

Kithara II	Chromelodeon II
Kithara I	Chromelodeon I
Harmonic Canon II (Castor	Blo-boy
and Pollux)	Spoils of War
Harmonic Canon I	Diamond Marimba
String bass	Bamboo Marimba (2 players)
Crychord	Marimba Eroica (2 players)
Adapted Guitar II	Drone Devils (jaw harps)
Adapted Guitar I	Bass Marimba (2 players)
Spanish Guitars	Bowls, Gongs (2 players)
Adapted Viola (or Cello)	Prerecorded tape

The Stage

Alternately, it is designed to be the park in front of the Courthouse of a medium-small American county seat, and the area before the Palace of Thebes.

These are the same set, with one slight alteration involving scrim (or something else that achieves the same purpose). Silhouettes of large, dark trees are at each side. A rocky crag, which serves as a park bench in the Choruses, is right. A portico, which is either the entrance to the Courthouse or to the Palace, is far left. Two steps, long and broad, lead to it. Here the band stands, on the two levels, during parts of Choruses One and Three.

Backstage — slightly right — is a small and charming fountain, reminiscent of the nineteenth century. A higher circled pool is within a lower circled pool. In the middle of the higher pool are two figures, a small boy and a small girl (about life-size or perhaps slightly less than life-size), the boy holding a small, black umbrella over their heads, and with simulated water shooting gently up from the umbrella's apex and falling down over its edges.

The boy's jacket is a bright blue, his long trousers and cap are black. The girl's skirt and her bonnet are bright red, her blouse white. There is a narrow passage between fountain and cyclorama, so that park strollers can exit downstage left, appear behind the fountain, and exit right. Or, vice versa.

The fountain represents stability, respectability, tenderness, gentleness within the human community, protection from an unpredictable Mother Nature, the national red-white-and-blue.

Lights play on the fountain throughout the Choruses, but at the end of each Chorus the backstage area is dark, and scrim descends or travels in front, so that it is blocked out completely. This change creates the area before the Palace, in which the Euripidean Scenes take place.

A stairway leads from the far left aisle onto the stage. This is used for the initial entrance of the majorettes, the band, Dion, and his revelers.

The instruments are all onstage, and are placed in two groups, downstage, far right and far left. The strings and Chromelodeons are right, percussion instruments left.

⟨It is essential that the musicians appearing prominently onstage *memorize their parts*. The convention that calls for lighted music in front of musicians is not valid in a production such as this. Small bright lights on white music sheets tend to raise havoc with general lighting, specific lighting, and to diminish the impact of both moods and ideas.⟩

Chorus–Scene Changes

The spotting of masks high above the stage (please see below) denotes the end of an American Chorus and the beginning of a Euripidean Scene. Scrim removed from before the fountain and slow lighting of the fountain denote the end of a Euripidean Scene and the beginning of an American Chorus.

Kitheron, or the Great World, is presumed to be right. The Palace of Thebes, or the County Courthouse, is left.

Costumes

Dionysus, Pentheus, Agave, Cadmus, Tiresias, Guard, Herdsman, the Chorus of Eight, and possibly also the instrumentalists who appear onstage, wear a basic costume. This is a starkly simple poncholike garment—a single piece of cloth with a round neck hole in its approximate center, and with bracing across the shoulders, so that the shoulder line is a right angle to the neck. This, or something similar, avoids the dreadful spectacle of ancient Greek characters being buried under mounting folds of bedclothes. No one deserves such fate.

The women's ponchos fall to the ankles, the men's barely below the hips. In the Choruses the men also wear slacks, with the ponchos falling outside. The slacks are peeled off for each Euripidean Scene, put on again for each American Chorus. These on-and-off pants are regrettable, but pants on the American male in situations where he normally wears them are a necessity. He may wear stylized pants, transparent pants, or pants made out of daisies, but recognizable pants he must wear. All who participate in the Scenes wear sandals—no headpieces.

The drum majorettes wear the traditional costumes, the tumblers sports clothes (shirts, and slacks or skirts). The clog dancers: boys — dark slacks and white pleated shirts, with black string bow ties; girls — colored blouses and full peasant skirts. The ten-piece band wears gorgeous costumes.

Stark contrasts are intended: the dazzling and superficial show of Choruses One and Three (with profound implications) against the melancholy simplicity of Choruses Two and Four.

Masks

All characters in Scenes who intone or speak (eight) wear heroic masks, or partial masks, in about the ratio 1½ to 1, or possibly 2 to 1. Where appropriate — that is, where a character is already onstage in a Chorus, as in the case of Dion from Chorus One to Scene One — the mask he will assume will be spotted high above the stage, toward the end of the Chorus, and will slowly descend. He will release it, attach it, and proceed with the Scene.

The mask of Dionysus will be fitted with removable bull horns. This will not descend. The horns will be attached before Dionysus reenters toward the end of Scene Three.

CHORUS ONE.   Late afternoon in
the Courthouse Park. Ritual of Welcome for
Dion, Hollywood king of Ishbu Kubu.

⟨*Although [the numbered sections of this Chorus] may be considered
as "numbers," each one merges into the next without pause, the
merges being designed to avoid audience applause. There are no
grand flourishes. When a logical end seems to be arriving, the
music is interrupted in some way, or it simply fades away to nothing,
as at the Chorus end. Those onstage in Chorus One frequently
applaud, themselves and each other, but these moments are also
interrupted. Applause from the audience, anywhere in the work,
would tend to reduce dramatic continuity and momentum.*⟩

1. Park Prologue

(*House lights dim. Dark stage for twenty-five bars.*)

(*Stage lights come up. Sonny is upstage left. He advances slowly,
hesitatingly.*)

(*The theme of Chorus Two—the sacrificial dream—is heard briefly.*)

(*Prerecorded tape of Diamond Marimba and Bamboo Marimba
suggests high female chatter. Sonny looks toward right wing, then
hurries downstage.*)

(*Sonny steps to the side of a tree, as though hiding.*)

(*Mom enters, right. The four female cloggers flutter around her.
Everything about Mom—voice, manner, gesture—must suggest
a strong and dominant woman, gently and insidiously aggressive.*)

MOM ⟨*singing*⟩: Ah—! An intuition! Just! Just! Right or wrong! No!
No! (*Half laugh.*) No—! Don't tell me! I am—! I am—! Like—
I am—!

(*Nearly everyone onstage speaks or sings, "I am!" before Sonny/
Pentheus does so. Yet it is Sonny/Pentheus, finally, who sings these
words—recounted by another—desperately, in the effort to imbue
a life-death significance into them.*)

(*Sonny is startled by percussion; looks nervously.*)

2. Fanfare and March

(*Band is far back in the auditorium, left aisle. Thirteen bars of the
Fanfare are played before the procession begins to move. Percussion
onstage ends completely with the first brass.*)

(*Sonny turns his head quickly in the brass direction, and Mom and the cloggers move downstage. Mom stands on the proscenium, or its equivalent, and vigorously beats time, but she is soon too overwhelmed by excitement to continue.*)

(*The four majorettes, swinging sticks, begin the March, preceding the eight brass pieces (and piccolos) and drums. Dion follows the band, and the Chorus of Eight follows Dion, all in single file.*)

(*Those onstage move about excitedly, anticipating the greatest day in the history of the Courthouse Park. The two guitarists with instruments, and the male cloggers, enter, but stay near the right wing.*)

⟨*At the end of a particularly vicious blast of the trumpets, Sonny swings into the lower branches of the tree, and watches through the leaves. The stage lighting is such that the audience virtually forgets his presence* until—*lights dim at the end of the Ritual of Welcome.*⟩

(*As the procession nears, stage percussion begins to join in.*)

(*The band must be wholly onstage at this point. Majorettes and bandmen do a simple geometrical figure on the stage, then move to the Courthouse steps, where they stand, left.*)

(*Dion does not mount the stage, but stands on the steps to stage, with the Chorus of Eight behind him.*)

MOM and CHORUS OF EIGHT (*throaty percussion; this must be a nasty belligerent sound; no* bel canto): Ah Ah Ah Ah Ah Ah! Ah Ah Ah Ah Ah Ah!

(*The band should be standing in place on the Courthouse steps when the trumpets again take up the Fanfare theme.*)

(*As the Fanfare and March ends, Dion moves onstage, and Mom, cloggers, and majorettes come forward to acclaim him.*)

MOM: Dion! Dion!

MOM and ALL FEMALES (*shouting*): Di—on! Yah—! (*Claps.*)

(*Those women who do not sing, take* any *tone. Shout, but observe time values exactly.*)

3. Forever Ummorra—To the Happy Way, Right or Wrong, Dead or Alive, for Evermore. First Ritual

⟨*Chorus of Four enters.*⟩

LEADER (*shouting rhythmically—progressively higher—with great vigor*): Right or wrong! Right or wrong! The Happy Way!

CHORUS OF EIGHT/TWO (*singing*): Heavenly daze—!

CHORUS OF EIGHT/THREE (*singing*): Forever ummorra!

> (*The audience will consider several of these "numbers" as parodies of popular or religious singing styles and lyrics if it chooses to. But it must never be led to feel that the actors are thinking of them as parodies. They must be performed straight, with great will and enthusiasm. The audience should be kept guessing; there must be no break in momentum. The actors applaud and shout for themselves as though the audience did not exist, in calculated measures and beat values.*
>
> *In order to bring this off with conviction, Dion, Mom, and the two choruses face upstage—backs to the audience—just as frequently as they face front. Movement and pseudo-dance must be constant.*)

CHORUS OF FOUR/PAIR: Right or wrong—
CHORUS OF FOUR/PAIR   Heavenly daze—

for a million years—   Dead or
                    from shore to shore—

alive—
          for evermore—

MOM and DION ⟨*singing*⟩: Heavenly daze—!

> (*Crack the hev wide open. Rape all the consonants. The vowels are impervious—they've had it for 300 years.*)

CHORUSES OF EIGHT and FOUR ⟨*singing*⟩: Forever *um*morra! *um*-morra, *um*morra, *um*morra, [etc.]

> (*At this point Mom and Dion head up a snake dance. They simply march, arm in arm, but the two choruses, majorettes, and cloggers go single file, in the traditional manner. However, this dance is somewhat different. Steps are taken on* one *and* three, *and the pelvis is snapped forward on each* um. *Those dancers who prefer not to demonstrate their pelvic aptitudes before an audience may simply bend their knees on* um.)

MOM: Heavenly daze—   Heavenly daze—
DION: Heavenly daze—   Heavenly daze—
CHORUSES: morra, *um*morra, *um*morra, *um*morra, *um*morra, *um*morra,

Heavenly daze —   Heavenly daze —   Heavenly
            Heavenly daze —   Heavenly da —
ummorra, ummorra, ummorra, [etc.]

dazuh! Heavenly daze —!
zuh! Heavenly daze —!
   Mora.

CHORUSES: Fo eh eh eh eh eh ver ummorra, ummorra, [etc.]

(*The cloggers 〈though taking part in the dance〉, begin to draw
apart, and clap and stamp to the rhythm. The cloggers, impatient
to show their stuff, force the choruses off with insistent applause.*)
(*The choruses shout and applaud themselves and everybody else,
wildly.*)

CHORUSES: Yah —!

〈*Trumpets end the First Ritual with three bars from the Fanfare.*〉

4. Save My Soul and Bless My Heart — Ritual for Strings and Clogs (in Four Sections)

– Section One –

(*The two guitarists sit on the Courthouse steps, or half-sit on a tree
stump, or railing.*)

DION 〈*singing*〉: Break my heart but bless my soul —

MOM 〈*singing*〉: Deep inside, way way down —

LEADER (*shouting*): I am!

MOM and DION: Blow —   Blow —
LEADER: I am!   (and CHORUS) I am!

Blow —   Blow —
   I am!

(*Cloggers get ready — walk in rhythm to places.*)
(*Clog dance begins.*)

CHORUS OF FOUR (*falsetto*):
                Ho de ho de ho ho
                Oh ho ho ho de ho de ho ho
                Ho de ho de ho ho
                Oh ho Oh Ho de ho de ho ho

(*As Dion begins to sing, the cloggers dance on tiptoe, softly. They
back upstage.*)

DION ⟨*singing*⟩: Soul— Blow—low—

LEADER ⟨*speak*⟩: Blow high!

MOM (*singing*): Blow low—

– Section Two –

⟨*The cloggers stop dancing, and make a semicircle about the guitarists, who both play and sing.*⟩

VOICES: Deep inside, way way down I am—
Deep inside, way way down I am— I am—

CHORUS OF FOUR: Blow— blow—

VOICES: Deep inside, way way down,
Way way up and away way down,
So high— so high— so low— so—

CHORUS OF FOUR: Low— low—

GUITARISTS: So high, so low—
Well, break my heart but bless my soul
Oh, break my heart but bless my soul
Well, bless my

CHORUS OF FOUR: Soul— Soul—

– Section Three –

(*Those who play Drone Devils hover about a stage mike. The cloggers move immediately, on the first beat, into a soft-shoe routine.*)

CHORUS OF EIGHT/TWO: Ah hah—!

CHORUS OF EIGHT/THREE: Hey hey—!

CHORUS OF EIGHT/FOUR: Hoo hoo—!

(*Dion makes with Mom. He smiles. She too.*)

MOM ⟨*singing*⟩: You're teasing! Oh— you're— teazzzzzz—ing—!

(*Dion smiles again, and turns toward choruses.*)

DION ⟨*singing*⟩: Blow— blow— and bless their hearts!

MOM and DION: Blow—   Blow—
LEADER: I am!
CHORUS: I am!

Scene from 1961 University of Illinois production of *Revelation in the Courthouse Park*. Chorus One: Dion, Hollywood king of Ishbu Kubu, and Mom, devotee of Ishbu Kubu. University of Illinois Archive.

– Section Four –

(Drone devilers return to their place, and the cloggers move suddenly into another dance, this time fortissimo.)

CHORUS OF EIGHT/TWO: Hey hey—!

CHORUS OF EIGHT/THREE: Hoo hoo—!

MOM and DION ⟨*singing*⟩:
> Deep inside, way way down I am—
> Deep inside, way way down I am I am—

CHORUSES: Blow— blow—

MOM and DION:
> Deep inside, way way down
> Way way up and away way down
> So high— so high— so low— so—

CHORUSES: Low— low—

MOM and DION:
> So high— so low—
> Well save my soul and bless my heart—
> Oh, save my soul and bless my heart—

CHORUSES ⟨*fortissimo*; bash *it on the head*⟩: Well— bless his heart—

(Cloggers make a final stamp on the word heart, *stand rigid, and break on the first beat of the next bar.)*

5. Wunnantu Anda—Primitive Percussion Ritual

CHORUS OF EIGHT/TWO ⟨*screaming*⟩: He's— for me—

CHORUS OF EIGHT/THREE ⟨*screaming like a raid siren*⟩: Ee—

CHORUS OF EIGHT/FOUR ⟨*screaming*⟩: I— want ro—mance—!

(Tumbler, without mat, tumbles in from right—fills two bars—right to left, exits left.)

CHORUS OF EIGHT/FIVE ⟨*screaming ever higher*⟩: Ee—

(Second tumbler enters from right—fills two bars—exits left.)

CHORUS OF EIGHT/THREE: Hoo hoo—

DION ⟨*shouting*⟩: Wunnantu Anda!

CHORUSES: Yea-ah Yea-ah Yea-ah

(*Dance begins. Everyone onstage—except Sonny in the tree and possibly the band—must take part in this simple dance. It is fairly static—no mad rushing about the stage, but very intense. Trunks should be straight up and down—no leaning forward. Elbows and hands horizontal—arms free at shoulders.*

Left foot thuds down on one *of 4/4 bar, but does not advance. Right takes one step forward on* three. *Left steps beside it on* one *of the 2½/4 bar. On the* two *of* two-and *hips snap to right—* on exactly that beat.

Thus, in the entire 6½ beats only one advance step has been taken, although the body should be moving to the beat constantly. Repeat this for the next three patterns of 4/4–2½/4.

On one *of the 5/4 bar, which ends the percussive phrase, left foot takes a wide step forward, and arms arch to about head level. This position is held—with swaying to beat—through* two-three-four. *On* five *right foot steps beside left, and elbows go back to horizontal position at sides.*

On the second 4–2½–4–2½–4–2½–4–2½–5 sequence, the above pattern is exactly reversed in direction. Thud the left foot without moving, step back with right, etc., etc.

On the third sequence move forward again, but with arms arched above head. The dance must become progressively more intense and frenzied, without *the multiplying of steps.*

On the fourth and fifth sequences, the formal rigidity of the pattern dissipates. Men and women pair up, whirl, and indulge in a spontaneous whoop-de-do, provided *that the* hip snap *to right on the* two *of* two-and *of the 2½/4 bar is always executed.*

The music was conceived and written for this dance—nothing else. It is rhythmic but uncomplicated, and possible for singers who are not trained dancers.

Throughout, where general choral voices are called for, it is desirable for the musicians to join in—those who are not too preoccupied with their instrumental parts. And in any general dance, it is absolutely essential that the musicians sway their bodies and snap their hips as indicated.)

CHORUS OF FOUR: Tumble on—

CHORUS OF EIGHT: Wunnantu Anda

(*Speak* Wunnantu Anda *under the breath at first—then progressively stronger.*)

MOM, DION, and CHORUS OF FOUR: Tumble on—

CHORUS OF EIGHT: Wunnantu Anda

MOM, DION, and CHORUS OF FOUR: Tumble on—

CHORUS OF EIGHT: Wunnantu Anda

MOM, DION, and CHORUS OF FOUR: Tumble on—

CHORUS OF EIGHT: Wunnantu Anda

MOM, DION, and CHORUSES ⟨*speaking*⟩: Wuannantu *An*da, Wunnantu
   *An*da, [etc.] ⟨*Singing.*⟩ Wuannantu *An*du, Wunnantu *An*da, [etc.]

   ⟨*With the beginning of the 3/4, the coupled dancers whirl in a fast
   waltz. Brass becomes prominent.*⟩
   (*Dancers stop momentarily to sing, then recall briefly the* Ummora
   snake dance of Ritual No. 3.)

MOM, DION, and CHORUSES: Wo—uh!

MOM and DION: Forever *Um*morra, *Um*morra, *Um*morra,
CHORUSES: *Um*morra, *Um*morra, *Um*morra,

   *Um*morra, Um*mor*—ra!
   *Um*morra, Um*mor*—ra!

6. Heavenly Daze and a Million
Years—Climax of Welcome

CHORUSES: Yea-ah—!

MOM and DION: Heavenly da—zuh!

CHORUSES ⟨*on offbeats*⟩: Hey Hey Hey Hey

MOM, DION, and CHORUSES (*bash it on the* Hev!): Heavenly daze—,
LEADER (*shout*):

   and a million year—   zuh! Heavenly daze— from
               Right or wrong!

   shore to shore—   Heavenly
               From north to south and east to west!

   daze—   Dead or alive!
          The happy way!   Right or wrong!

MOM and DION: Heavenly daze—
CHORUSES: Heavenly daze— forever, ever, ever, ever, ever, for

   ⟨*All singers breathe in through nose on rest; the result should be
   an audible beat.*⟩

MOM and DION: for ev—er—
CHORUSES: eh— eh eh ver maw aw ore—

more—
Heavenly daze— (*crack it open!*) forever ever ever [etc.]

(*A spot picks up the heroic mask of Dionysus, high above the stage. Scrim travels before fountain. Stage lights begin to fade. Mask slowly descends.*)

CHORUSES: ever ever ever ever [etc.]

(*Voices and percussion should diminish to virtual inaudibility, without retard. They should fade out with the lights, in the same way that a film shot fades.*)

(*All onstage—except Sonny and musicians—melt into the wings as quickly as possible.*)

(*Immediately after the voices have finally faded, Sonny is seen slipping down from the tree. He quickly moves upstage and exits right.*)

(*The final four bars may be repeated until Scene One is ready for presentation.*)

(*Dion removes his pants in the right wings, and reappears in the half-light, meeting the mask as it descends to head level. He attaches it.*)

SCENE ONE. Late afternoon
at the entrance to the Palace of Thebes.
King Pentheus denounces the Bacchae.

(*A spot lights Dionysus. In the course of his monologue of self-glorification, which he intones throughout, he executes a pose dance—in line with his character as the god of ritualistic and flamboyant mediocrity. The spot follows his movements, and is the beginning of a cycle. The cycle ends when the tragedy has run its course, and another spot, the final one, fades on his American counterpart, Dion.*)

(*The pose dance consists of a series of narcissistic postures, all indicated, including at least one profile. The music allows beats in which each new pose is assumed. Once it is taken, there should be no movement until the next. Eyes should be directed straight ahead, on a horizontal level, and this applies to all dancers. The only exception is the Not-So-Young sequence in Chorus Three, where the suggested movements are a caricature of female modern dancers.*)

(Lights come up on the first pose.)

DIONYSUS:

      I am Dionysus—god, son of Zeus. *(Pose.)*
      Here I stand, in Thebes, home to my mother,
      And close beside her tomb;
      Beside her house, burning still, in Zeus's
         flames. *(Pose.)*

      Behind me are the triumphs of other lands,
         Phrygia and Lydia. *(Pose.)*
      Arabia too.
      On Asia's coasts my initiates dance.
      Praise me in the way they have learned
         to praise.
      Behold me as I am, *(profile pose)* a god. *(Pose.)*

      But Oh, in Thebes, with slanders in the air,
      I come, in mortal form,
      To damn the lies—the lies that say *(pose)*
      "He is his mother's shame—no son of
         Zeus! *(Pose.)*

      And now I pay them for that lie!
      For I have laid a craze upon the women
         of Thebes. *(Pose.)*
      Pentheus, alone among my enemies, remains
         untouched.
      Pentheus—his mother leads my revelers. *(Pose.)*

      Young Pentheus! New King Pentheus! *(Pose.)*
      Me he outlaws!
      My name he omits from his prayers!
      My singers, who chant my deity, he wars
         upon! *(Pose.)*
      And I shall teach him. *(Move freely.)*

      (Free, except rhythmically.) Come, my Bacchae!
         Pound the palace doors!
      While I observe this strange new madness—
      (Under the breath—not too corny.) Heh heh
         heh heh—
      In the valley of Kitheron!

(Exits quickly, right.)

Hymn to Dionysus: Holy Joy and Get Religion

CHORUS OF EIGHT ⟨*intoning, chanting, singing, dancing*⟩/ONE: Come, Bacchae!

CHORUS OF EIGHT/TWO: To the mountains, Dionysus!

CHORUS OF EIGHT: Dionysus! Dion-y-y-sus!

CHORUS OF EIGHT/THREE: Sweet leader! Sweet leader of the revel band

CHORUS OF EIGHT/FOUR: To the mountains, Dionysus! Where all are possessed with holy joy—

CHORUS OF EIGHT: Holy joy! Holy joy!

CHORUS OF EIGHT/FIVE (*sing staccato*): In holy joy, blessed by the gods, to get ruhligion in holy joy!

CHORUS OF EIGHT: Holy joy! Diony—sus!

CHORUS OF EIGHT/SIX: To the mountains, Dionysus!

CHORUS OF EIGHT: Holy joy and get ruhligion, Diony—sus!

CHORUS OF EIGHT/SEVEN: To the mountains, in racing frenzy, trance of rapture!

CHORUS OF EIGHT: Holy joy and get ruhligion, Diony—sus!

CHORUS OF EIGHT/EIGHT: Leap, Bacchae! Leap like colts in holy joy!

> (*Each woman leaps as she sings* joy. *The last four all leap together, omitting* holy *but positively screaming* joy.)

CHORUS OF EIGHT/ONE: Holy joy!

CHORUS OF EIGHT/TWO: Holy joy!

CHORUS OF EIGHT/THREE: Holy joy!

CHORUS OF EIGHT/FOUR: Holy joy!

CHORUS OF EIGHT/REMAINING FOUR: Joy—!

> (*Tiresias and Cadmus enter together, left.*)
> (*Seeing the two ancient men, the Chorus of Eight draws back startled.*)

TIRESIAS: It is not becoming to question the traditions of our fathers, to try to be logical about gods, and this god requires that we dance. What people say, that I have no *shame*, at my age, to deck myself out and join the dance of revel for the god, is so much gabble. I ask you, has the god decreed: "Only *youth* may dance for me?" Certainly not.

CADMUS: My feelings exactly. (*He lowers his voice.*) And I must further do honor to this god because there is a good possibility that he is my daughter's son. (*Normal voice.*) What was the name again? Dionysus, I believe. And his revels always take place in the mountains. Ah! I am blessedly forgetful of my age. (*He does a sprightly little dance, then obviously creaks, bends over and punches his back.*) Oh, I say, perhaps we should go by chariot.

TIRESIAS: No, I feel quite young enough both to dance *and* to walk. Anyway, walking honors the god.

CADMUS: So be it then. I shall lead you, age guiding age.

TIRESIAS: The god will guide us; we need make no effort.

CADMUS: Are there no others? No Theban men other than ourselves to honor Dionysus in the dance?

TIRESIAS: They are blind. We *see*.

CADMUS: Ah, yes. But since you do not see with your eyes, Tiresias, I must tell you that my young grandson is coming. And he looks *furious*, in a young and kingly way. (*He laughs.*)

(*Pentheus enters right, with Guard.*)

PENTHEUS (*speaking to Guard*): I leave town, and what happens? *Everything!* Reports of misdeeds begin to come in immediately: that our women traipse over the mountains, in burlesque ecstasies, pursuing the latest fashion in *gods*—some Dionysus, whoever he is.

(*The entrapment theme, in incidental music, is here heard for the first time. It ceases to be incidental and is precisely with Pentheus on the word* hair, *and on the words* cheeks *and* love.)

PENTHEUS (*continues, without pause*): That the wine flows freely— too freely; that the women then steal away, and service their lovers in rocky nooks. That my own mother is one of the leaders in this obscene madness.

I am told about some foreign magician also, some quack with perfumed hair— and rosy cheeks— and love— in his eyes. They say he teaches *mysteries*, and under the pretext of *teaching* he sleeps with young girls night and day. Mysteries indeed!

This mysterious stranger, who repeats the claim that Dionysus is the son of Zeus, delivered from Zeus's thigh, and thereby adds new outrage to the original outrage. If I could catch him in some act! Convict him!

GUARD: He prefers the mountains, as I understand it! Maybe we could go up there, climb a tree, and *spy* on him.

PENTHEUS: Climb a tree and spy on him! Yes—!

⟨*Music ends.*⟩
(*He is suddenly aware of Tiresias.*)

Oh, no—! The ancient seer! (*He arches an arm and drapes a hand over his head in an effeminate gesture.*) Tiresias, entwined for the dance! (*He now faces Cadmus.*)

    And my own grandfather! My mother's father! I shrink to find you as the aging fool. Shake off that ivy. Drop your wand! (*He turns furiously on Tiresias.*)

    You! You bird-watcher!

    You made him do this. You exploit *any* device—such as a *new* god. *New* fees for *new* rites, eh, Tiresias? I tell you, when women get groggy on grape juice, something rotten always happens.

KORYPHEUS (*calmly, but with measured indignation, in sharp contrast to Pentheus's explosive manner*): Irreverent stranger, you honor neither heaven nor your own family.

TIRESIAS: Given an honest theme, the honest man speaks easily, strongly. But you! The strength of *your* tongue lies in its impudence. And when a man's rashness is armed with power, he is the more dangerous.

    I will tell you this: the god whom you scorn will rise to mighty heights in this land. Already, his mad ecstasies have dispersed whole armies, with never a spear thrown. He is, indeed, one of our two supreme blessings.

    For first there is Demeter, the earth, who gives us dry grain for our nourishment; then Dionysus, who ministers with flowing wine to wash it down, and to bring us mortals blessed sleep, surcease from grief. A god's libation, it leads to god's blessings, seals our peace.

    And you mock him? You sneer at the womb in Zeus's thigh?

    This god is a prophet, and the ecstasies of his votaries are fulfilled in prophecy.

    Listen, Pentheus. Do not believe that naked force has power over men, nor consider yourself wise if you think so. Welcome Dionysus to the city, and remember also that he cannot compel a woman to be chaste. In the matter of love, one must ponder the nature of the woman. And in his rites the virtuous remain virtuous.

Think on this also. Dionysus finds joy in homage from the multitude, even as you and I, Pentheus. So—Cadmus and I— we offer it. We shall dance in his honor, however ridiculous we seem in your eyes. You cannot persuade us to war with the gods.

KORYPHEUS: You are most wise, sir, in offering words of homage to the mighty Dionysus.

CHORUS OF EIGHT: Dionysus! Aye—!

CADMUS: Son, the counsel of Tiresias is good counsel. Stay *with* us, not *against* us. And just suppose, for the sake of argument, that the god *is* a fraud, as you say. Think of the honor that falls on our family, your mother's sister the mother of a god! What a glorious fraud! ⟨*He removes his own wreath.*⟩ Come, let me crown your head with ivy.

PENTHEUS: Don't touch me! Go to your Dionysus, but keep your stain away from me! (*Under his breath.*) This seer, who has misled you—he'll pay for this. (*He turns to Guard.*) Go. Find the girl-faced villain, defile his place, provoke him. Then tie him up and bring him to me.

(*Guard exits right.*)

(*Again under his breath.*) He shall regret his visit to Thebes.

TIRESIAS: You do not know what you say. Before, you spoke nonsense. Now, insanity. ⟨*To Cadmus.*⟩ Come, we must not fail the god. However disgraceful we may look, we must pray, and ask for intercession, for the city of Thebes, and for this rash man who is now its king. (*Sings.*) Pentheus— Pentheus— Beware, Cadmus, the echo of that name. Pentheus— Beware, Pentheus, the echo of that name— Sor—row—

(*On Tiresias's last word,* sorrow, *Pentheus moves backward suddenly, as though struck, moving in the direction of the area behind the fountain. He then moves backward on each of the Herdsman's* sorrows, *and on the final one before disappearing—next to last— he shields his face. Scrim is removed from fountain as Pentheus nears it.*)
(*Tiresias and Cadmus exit right. The Chorus of Eight exits left, to be ready for Chorus Two. The Chorus of Four is offstage right.*)

HERDSMAN (*offstage*): Pentheus— Sor—row— Pentheus— Sor— row— Sor—row— Sor—row— Sor—row—.

(Lights fade.)
⟨*Pentheus exits in the dark area behind the fountain, removes his mask, and dons slacks as quickly as possible, then reenters, slowly, standing behind the fountain.*⟩

CHORUS TWO.   Early evening of the same day in the Courthouse Park. Sonny, ghost walking, sees himself in a dream vision, offered up as a sacrificial victim.

(Chorus of Four and Chorus of Eight are both offstage.)

CHORUS OF FOUR: Oo—

CHORUS OF EIGHT: *(Female giggles offstage.)*

(Lights come partially on. The park is dim, shadowy.)
(The Chorus of Four enters right. They walk in, leisurely, in pairs, stroll in front of the fountain. The Chorus of Eight enters from left—first a trio, then a pair, then a trio. They move in a direction contrary to the men, in the Mexican Plaza tradition. They do not remain together, as do the men. As they pass the pairs of oo-ers, they steal glances, and the men stare back. The strolling must be so planned that the gigglers are always behind the oo-ers, so that the giggles are never emitted face to face.)

CHORUS OF FOUR: Oo—

CHORUS OF EIGHT: *(Giggles.)*

(Sonny enters as soon as possible, after removing mask and donning pants, and stands motionless in the dark area behind fountain.)
(The men turn, still walking, stare at the gigglers.)

CHORUS OF FOUR: Oo—

CHORUS OF EIGHT: *(Giggles.)*

(This time the men do not bother to turn.)
(This Chorus is centered around a personal and intimate dilemma, as dreams almost invariably are. Sonny's basic dilemma is the feeling of being lost—alone.)

SONNY *(singing slowly)*: As— if— I— had— nowhere—

CHORUS OF FOUR: Oo—

CHORUS OF EIGHT: ⟨*Louder giggles, as though to force the men's attention.*⟩

(*All voices, throughout the rest of the Chorus, that seem to speak directly to—or taunt—Sonny, must be offstage. Those onstage pay not the slightest attention to him. There must be an impression of constant strolling.*)

(*Sonny steps out from behind the fountain on the first beat. He is spotted, perhaps bluishly, in order to separate him completely from the strollers. As he moves downstage, the strollers should be far right or left.*)

CHORUS OF EIGHT/SOLO ⟨*softly*⟩: Drift away— oo— ee— uh, O— drift away—

CHORUS OF FOUR/SOLO ⟨*softly*⟩: Go away—!

SONNY: O— where—! O— where—? O— where—?

CHORUS OF FOUR (*soft, breathy sound, as though in a whisper*): Where—? Where—? Where—? Where—? Where—? Where—?

CHORUS OF EIGHT/SOLO: Oo— Oo—

(*At this point Sonny reaches the downstage area where he remains for the balance of the Chorus, slightly right, near the string instruments.*)

SONNY: as— if— I— had—

CHORUS OF FOUR/PAIR (*soft, breathy*): Nowhere! Nowhere! (*Nasal or falsetto.*) No—where—

SONNY: Where—! Where—! Where—! Where—!

SONNY:		Where—?
CHORUS OF EIGHT/SOLO:	O— oo—	ah,
CHORUS OF FOUR/PAIR:	Your mother's arms—!	Your Mother's

Where—?
O— oo— ah, Oo—
arms—! Your mother's ah ha ha ha ha ha harms—!

CHORUS OF EIGHT/SOLO: (*Shrieks of laughter.*)

SONNY ⟨singing slowly⟩: I— see— two— moons— above me—

SONNY: I— see— two— arms— around— me—
CHORUSES: O— O— O—   O—

(Sonny stands rigid during this and the following line.)

SONNY and CHORUS OF EIGHT: O O
CHORUS OF FOUR: O— Why—?   Why—?

O O   O O O O O O O
Why— dream—?   Why—

SONNY and CHORUS OF EIGHT: O
CHORUS OF FOUR/SOLO: trouble yourself uselessly?

O O O O O O
                Stop and reflect. Rest. There is nothing but

[Chorus of Four/Solo:] Eter—nity— In—fin—ity—

⟨Bowls continue the rhythmic pattern of eternity-infinity.⟩

————————

⟨The basic music—enunciated first by Harmonic Canon—has a
hymnal-folk quality. The voices—supported by about half the
instruments—are completely different in character, but obscure
the hymnal-folk quality only occasionally.⟩
(With the first beat of Canon, Sonny begins to walk to the rhythm,
in a very limited area.)

CHORUS OF EIGHT: Oh— oo— ee—

SONNY: Oh— oo— ah— ee—

CHORUS OF FOUR: Wo wo wo wo wo uh! Wo uh!

SONNY: Ho dah dee duh   dah dee duh
CHORUSES: Wu wu wu wu ah   wu wu

                    Oh—oh—
wu wu ah   wu wu wu wu ah   wuh wuh wuh whuh whuh

[CHORUSES:] whuh whuh,

SONNY: O oo— oh— no— wee, duh
CHORUS OF FOUR: Yanh—! Yanh—! Yanh—!
CHORUS OF EIGHT:

du du   duh—ha—oo—   N na— d da— Ho ho ah
Yanh—!   Yanh—!
                    O o o o o o   d da—   ah

Ee—oh— ah— Oh— ah—O—ah—
                    Yanh—!   Yanh—! Yanh—!
ee—

[Chorus of Four:] Eeyanh—! Yanh—! Yanh—! Yanh—!

(*The groups of men and women have broken up. At this point a couple sits on the park bench and begins to neck.*)

SONNY (*fortissimo*): The wind—!   The wind—! Wind—!
CHORUSES: Carried about, Carried about,

Wind—! Wind—!
Carried about   Wind—! Wind—! Oo— Oo—

(*At this point another couple moves to the side of the fountain and begins to neck.*)

SONNY: Drifting—, drifting— about—

CHORUSES: as on the sea— uh See— uh See— uh See—!

(*Spot fades on Sonny.*)
(*The two guitarists enter. They walk in a leisurely way past the bench neckers, and stare back—then past the fountain neckers, and stare back.*)
(*The pairs of neckers reach the height of their necking spree— embrace passionately. Sonny cowers.*)

HERDSMAN (*offstage; gasping*): Mother! Mother! No no! No no! I— I— I am!

(*The two starers exit.*)

(*This section must be presented with great dignity. It represents a psychological reconciliation, following upon virtual hysteria. With the crash of Bowls and Gongs the bench neckers get up, straighten their clothes, and stroll offstage.*)
(*The fountain neckers stroll off, arm in arm.*)
(*Stage lights begin to fade.*)
(*Spot returns on Sonny.*)
(*Sonny sings quietly, softly, almost casually, with mouth half-closed, and accompanied by a Bowls theme—the suggestion of eternity— that will be heard again in Chorus Four, and again in the Coda.*)

SONNY (*very soft* d's): Duh duh duh duh— du duh— duh duh duh
    duh— duh du duh du du du duh—

(*Sonny walks slowly off, left. Spot fades.*)
(*The Chorus of Eight enters in the darkness. The mask of Pentheus
    is spotted high. It slowly descends.*)

SCENE TWO.   Early evening of
the same ancient day, at the entrance to
the Palace of Thebes. Dionysus
goes to jail, then escapes.

(*In the brief darkness between Chorus Two and Scene Two, the Chorus
of Eight enters, and begins to sing in the dark. Each one sings a
different snatch of melody, but all sing virtually the same words.
Each dances as she sings. The last line is in unison, and without
movement. Pentheus walks to his mask and attaches it. Lights come
up slowly.*)

Hymn to Dionysus—What the Majority Believes

CHORUS OF EIGHT/ONE: What the majority believes and does—

CHORUS OF EIGHT/TWO: De doh de doh de doh de doh de duz—

CHORUS OF EIGHT/THREE: What the simple folk believe and do—

CHORUS OF EIGHT/FOUR: De doh de doh de doh de doh de doo—

CHORUS OF EIGHT/FIVE: What the humble crowd believes and
    does—

CHORUS OF EIGHT/SIX: What the people of the street believe and
    do—

ALL: What we   believe—
CHORUS OF EIGHT/SEVEN: What the honest throng

        and   do—
    believes and does—

CHORUS OF EIGHT/EIGHT: De doh de doh de doh de doh de duz—

CHORUS OF EIGHT/SOLO: What the common people believe and
    do—

ALL (including MUSICIANS): What the common people believe and
    do—

CHORUS OF EIGHT/ONE (*spit out the syllables! sing brashly*): What the majority believes and does—

CHORUS OF EIGHT/TWO: What the simple folk believe and do—

CHORUS OF EIGHT/THREE: What the humble crowd believes and does—

CHORUS OF EIGHT/FOUR: What the people of the streets believe and do—

CHORUS OF EIGHT/FIVE: What the honest throng believes and does—

CHORUS OF EIGHT/SIX: What the common people believe and do—

ALL: We— believe— and— do—!

(*Pentheus moves center. Guard enters from right, ushering in Dionysus, whose hands are tied.*)

GUARD: Well, Pentheus, here he is, but I don't feel exactly proud. The way *you* talked, I thought it might be exciting, but it was all pretty tame.

He didn't try to run. He *smiled*, and even helped me bind him! He *waited* for me to do my duty! I was ashamed. "Look," I said, "I don't make the rules. I just follow the orders."

PENTHEUS: Untie him. He won't escape.

(*Entrapment theme is heard again. Guard unties Dionysus and retires upstage. Pentheus takes his time, surveying the captive.*)

PENTHEUS (*rhythmic, to a strict beat*): Well, you *are* pretty. Your curls are beautiful! (*Lower voice; free.*) I take it that you don't care much for athletics. (*Now normally mocking; free but rhythmic.*) Your complexion is ravishing! (*Free, except rhythmically.*) But you musn't let the harsh sun strike it. No. Preserve it for the special joys of night. (*Harshly.*) Where are you from?

⟨*In the following dialogue, the lines of Dionysus are intoned; those of Pentheus are free.*⟩

DIONYSUS: Lydia.

PENTHEUS: Lydia. And why did you come to Thebes?

DIONYSUS: Dionysus, the son of Zeus, sent me.

PENTHEUS: In Lydia, you have a Zeus who begets new gods?

DIONYSUS: He is no different than yours. I saw him.

PENTHEUS: You dreamt that you saw him!

DIONYSUS: I saw him. He made me the keeper of his sacred rites.

PENTHEUS: What are they like—these rites?

DIONYSUS: They are secret, except to those who are allowed to know them.

PENTHEUS: What good is it, then, in knowing them?

DIONYSUS: I may not tell you. But they are worth knowing.

PENTHEUS: You calculate your words—to make me the more curious.

DIONYSUS: No, I do not. Our rites abhor the unbeliever.

PENTHEUS: You said that you saw Zeus. How did he look?

DIONYSUS: As he chose to look.

PENTHEUS: Another evasion!

DIONYSUS: Wisdom is always folly to fools.

> (*Pentheus draws back in anger, but quickly decides to get on, to the subject that interests him most.*)

PENTHEUS: These rites—are they performed by day or by night.

DIONYSUS: Night, mostly. Darkness befits solemnity.

PENTHEUS: And befits fornication even better.

DIONYSUS (*bored*): It happens in the daytime.

PENTHEUS: You will be punished the more for your agile answers!

DIONYSUS: And you the more, for your irreverence.

PENTHEUS: In wrestling with words you are quite athletic!

DIONYSUS: Tell me, this interest in fornication: is it based wholly on moral grounds?

PENTHEUS: You shall regret that!

DIONYSUS: And how do you propose to make me regret it?

PENTHEUS: You shall be imprisoned.

Scene from 1961 University of Illinois production of *Revelation in the Courthouse Park*. Scene Two: At the entrance to the Palace of Thebes, Pentheus prepares to imprison Dionysus (Bacchae [behind], Korypheus, Dionysus, Pentheus, and Guard). Harry Partch Estate Archive, San Diego.

DIONYSUS: And the god will free me when I ask. For he is with us now, witnessing the abuse that I endure.

PENTHEUS: I see no god. (*To Guard.*) He mocks me! Bind him!

DIONYSUS: I warn you—do not!

PENTHEUS: And I say—bind him!

(*The Guard binds him.*)

DIONYSUS: You do not know what you do. You do not know your desires. How would you like, for example, to be seen here, disguised as a woman?

PENTHEUS: What!

DIONYSUS: Do you even know who you are?

PENTHEUS: I am Pentheus, son of Echion and Agave.

DIONYSUS: Pentheus! Unlucky Pentheus! Unlucky in that name, Pentheus!

PENTHEUS (*to Guard*): Take him. And since he prefers darkness, jail him in the darkest stable. There let him dance!

Hymn to Dionysus—Glory to the Male Womb

(*The Chorus of Eight sings in distress and horror. Pentheus merely looks at them, then exits left. The Guard, conducting Dionysus, follows left.*)

CHORUS OF EIGHT/FIRST HALF: Oh— Oh— Oh— Oh—

CHORUS OF EIGHT/SECOND HALF: Oh— Oh— Oh— Oh—

CHORUS OF EIGHT/ONE: When Zeus had snatched him from the lightning—

CHORUS OF EIGHT: Dionysus!

CHORUS OF EIGHT/ONE: He found a womb in his father's thigh—

CHORUS OF EIGHT: Found a womb in his father's thigh. Glory! Glory! Gloree— to the male womb!

CHORUS OF EIGHT/TWO: The monster, Pentheus, seed of the dragon, chains our sweet leader.

CHORUS OF EIGHT: Dionysus!

CHORUS OF EIGHT/TWO: Zeus, do you see? O Zeus, do you see?

CHORUS OF EIGHT: Found a womb in his father's thigh. Glory! Glory! Gloree— to the male womb!

CHORUS OF EIGHT/THREE: Our bodies are bound to the god— with passion to the god.

CHORUS OF EIGHT: Passion! Passion! Dionysus!

CHORUS OF EIGHT/THREE: Zeus, do you see? O Zeus, do you see?

CHORUS OF EIGHT: Found a womb in his father's thigh. Glory! Glory! Gloree— to the male womb!

CHORUS OF EIGHT/FOUR: Passion! Passion! Dionysus! Gloree— to the male womb!

CHORUS OF EIGHT: Passion! Passion! Dionysus!

(*Stage darkens.*)
⟨*Lightning flashes offstage left, and rumbling percussion continues through this next dialogue.*⟩
(*From here to the end of the Scene, Chorus of Eight and Dionysus— offstage left—shout—no precise tones but a very strict beat.*)

CHORUS OF EIGHT: Zeus! (*Lightning.*) Zeus! (*Lightning.*) Zeus! (*Lightning.*)

DIONYSUS (*offstage*): Ho! Bacchae! Ho!

CHORUS OF EIGHT: Yes, Dionysus! (*Lightning.*)

DIONYSUS: Ho again!

CHORUS OF EIGHT: Yes again! Dionysus! (*Lightning.*)

DIONYSUS: And ho again!

CHORUS OF EIGHT: Yes again! Yes again! Yes again! Yes again! Dionysus! (*Lightning.*)

DIONYSUS: Shatter! Shatter! Shatter the pillars! Crumble! Crumble!

(*Big lightning.*)

CHORUS OF EIGHT ⟨*hung up with excitement over the miraculous happenings offstage; long downward glide*⟩: Ah—!

⟨*Scrim is removed from before the fountain. General lights fade. Lights come up on the fountain, dimly. Chorus Three follows immediately.*⟩

CHORUS THREE.   Later that night in
the Courthouse Park. In celebration of Dion,
Hollywood king of Ishbu Kubu.

1. These Good Old-Fashioned
Thrills—Fireworks Ritual

(*Part of the crowd witnessing the fireworks is offstage right. Those who are visible face the display, having their back to the audience. The music and staging are in* Two Coincident Parts. *The literal interpretation of the fireworks display—principally by Harmonic Canon and the exclamatory "ah—s" of the crowd—constitute one part. The other part concerns, at first, only the conductor and musicians onstage. They ignore the film, in any rhythmic sense, the Canons, the "ah—s."*

The Harmonic Canon sounds are recorded and synchronized onto the optical tape, and are heard through a speaker.

Stage lights come on partially, simulating a dimly lit park. Soft, low percussion begins, and immediately thereafter the first fireworks are seen. The first "ah—," from those on- and offstage, follows.

The film is a one-minute loop, which will run three times. The end is characterized by three successive "ah—s," heard for the third time.

Words, in Chorus One, *through the mouths of singers, had a large responsibility in implying moods and enthusiasms. Here, there is greater dependence on sounds and rhythms. Also, unlike* Chorus One, *there is little applause, there are no exclamations. Now, everyone is deeply involved in the more formal ritual. Each knows the part he must play, and fulfills it abundantly.*)

Fireworks Ritual—Second Coincident Part

(*The Chorus of Eight enters right. They hold their arms in graceful feminine poses—make slow, generously full turns. They are enchanted.*)

CHORUS OF EIGHT/LEADER (*spoken*): These good old-fashioned thrills—!

CHORUS OF EIGHT/TWO ⟨*singing*⟩: This spell—!

CHORUS OF EIGHT/THREE ⟨*singing*⟩: This— lucky— day—!

2. Not So Young—Ritual for Adolescent Girls
and Brass—in Two Sections

– Section One –

(The twenty-two bars of 7/8 are a young girls' dance. Only three of the eight take part in the initial phase. The other five move in a limited area; mostly, they sway to the beat. The three main dancers whirl slowly, moving forward and backward constantly, except for an exaggeratedly feminine pose for the duration of one bar, every third bar. Each begins on a different bar, so that there is only one *girl posing in any* one *bar. They use all the available stage—moving to the far corners, center, and back area. In the final six bars, the five join the three in whirling slowly about the stage.*

The dance is a literal interpretation *of the music. Any so-called counterpoint lies in the fact of human bodies related to the music. It must not be intellectual. It must be convincing as the way simple girls would spontaneously move because their mood and the music move them.*

It should not be a skilled or "finished" dance. It is valid only as amateur ecstasy, and it would be as inappropriate to use the studied movements of highly trained dancers here as to use operatic bel canto *voices in the chorus of* The Bewitched.*)*

CHORUS OF EIGHT/TWO: This spell—! This spell—! This spell—! This spell—!

CHORUS OF EIGHT/THREE: Lucky day!

CHORUS OF EIGHT/TWO: This spell—!

(Posing ends. The remaining five join in a general whirl.)
(Solo trumpet and solo trombone enter left, and walk leisurely together while playing their muted instruments, moving on every other beat, to about center stage.)

CHORUS OF EIGHT/LEADER *(speaking intensely—not too loudly)*: We want to be young—young forever!

CHORUS OF EIGHT/TWO ⟨*singing*⟩: But not too young!

CHORUS OF EIGHT/THREE ⟨*singing*⟩: Not so— young that our youngness will be frightening!

(This is also a dance, with occasional singing. The basic movement: step on one *of 7/8 bar; the other foot steps beside it on* three *of the same bar. No forward movement on first 3/4 bar. Step on* one

of second 3/4 bar; again on one *of the 7/8 bar. Repeat the pattern.*

Trumpet and trombone simply walk, and the eight girls follow them, dancing, and with an enchanted sway. They won't have gotten very far before they are interrupted by the three final rockets.)

CHORUS OF EIGHT/TWO *(singing to trumpeter)*: Not— so young, Hey hey!

CHORUS OF EIGHT/THREE *(singing to trombonist)*: Not— so young, Hoo hoo!

CHORUS OF EIGHT/FOUR *(singing to heaven)*: Not— so young!

CHORUS OF EIGHT *(just singing)*: Not— so young, Hey hey!

(The two brass players exit right, circle behind cyclorama, and rejoin band.)

(This is about the point where the three final rockets, in close succession, will be seen for the third time, and the tempo should be such that the music reaches at least this point—it would be better a little too slow than too fast. In order that the Chorus of Eight does not miss the final rockets, they should be dancing so that they can see the cyclorama at their last song snatch. The Chorus of Eight stops singing and dancing in order to admire the rockets, and adds its "ah—s" to those of the people back- and offstage, loudly.

The three bars at the end of this section may be repeated in whole or in part, or omitted, in order to end the music with the film. As the last "ah—" trails off, the conductor gives the cue for fireworks applause, *by all, on- and offstage, and for the opening beat of Diamond Marimba and other percussion, which prepares for the second entrance of majorettes and band. This is the same cue. Music must not cease. It starts immediately on the next section.)*

– Section Two –

(Cloggers, guitarists, and Chorus of Four enter from right. There is some milling about the stage—all awaiting the anticipated entrance of Dion.)

(Majorettes enter from right, swinging sticks, single file. Band follows, single file. It marches to Courthouse steps and stands.)

(Majorettes stand at attention during the two bars of Fanfare theme.)

(The majorettes here do their fanciest figures and tricks.)

CHORUSES *(nasty!)*: Yang yang yang yang yang yang yang yang yang yang yang yang!

(This must be a positively nasty sound. It must have a mob-power sound, impossible to achieve through beautiful tones.)

CHORUSES: Yang yang yang yang yang yang yang yang Yooong—Yooong—

(Majorettes come to a standstill here.)
(Stage lights begin to dim.)

3. Ishbu Kubu—Revelation of the Mystic Power—Theme Ritual. In Three Sections

– Section One –

(All singers have had, by now, the opportunity to display athletic, versatile, and powerful vocal abilities. In this section of Ishbu Kubu, *the reverse of power is called for—infinite subtleties of voice sounds, even mouth sounds—vibrations in which vocal chords take no part whatever.*

The rhythmic variations must be soft and precise. The first section should never rise above mf, *and* p *should be normal. However, this is a* p *of great rhythmic intensity.*

The sh's and k's frequently indicated for the Chorus of Eight are mouth sounds entirely. They are of course vibrations, or they would not be heard at all, but of very high frequencies. It seems pointless to try to give them precise pitches. The sh is a front mouth sound, the k a back mouth sound. Glides for both are indicated in the score. These are accomplished by a lessening of breath forced through the mouth, which tends to cause the pitch frequency to glide downward, and also by controlling the size of the mouth opening: large mouth—high; small mouth—low.)
(Dion enters, right. He is silhouetted in the color sequences—a dark, faceless, swaying figure. He moves sinuously, not disgustingly, with the intensity of an exotic priest at an altar. His revolving ass is not a lustful and transitory whim, but a divine right, and perfectly normal to Dion.)
(The a's are in parentheses to indicate that this is an under-the-breath sound. Mom enters, right, as Dion finishes his first mutterings, and moves quickly to lead the Chorus of Eight. She is also a dark silhouette.)

DION: Ish (a) bu (a) Ku (a) bu (a)

MOM and CHORUS OF EIGHT: Ya ya ya ya ya ya ya yah— Ya ya ya ya ya yah— Sh sh Sh— Sh—

DION: bu Ku bu (a)

MOM and CHORUS OF EIGHT: K k k k k k k k k
DION: u bu (a) u bu

          b   b   Sh— (down-
(a) Ku— (a)   Ku— (a)   b bu bu bu bu bu (a)

ward glide)   K   K   K
            b bu (a)   b bu (a)   b bu (a)   b bu bu bu bu bu

       K   K   b bu—ah—eewuh!
bu bu bu bu   b bu (a)   bu bu bu b bu—ah—eewuh!

(*The Chorus of Eight occasionally circles Mom and Dion, while singing.
Chorus vibrates hands upward on each* b bu a bu a.)

MOM:
DION:
CHORUS OF EIGHT/LEADER:
CHORUS OF EIGHT: K k k k sh sh sh sh sh sh sh

     Ya uh— Ya uh—   Ya uh—oo—
Ya uh—   Ya uh—oo—
                     Ish ku bu,
sh—   b bu a bu a

    oo   hoo—   oo hoo—   oo
oo—hoo—   Ya uh— hoo—   Ya uh—
    Ish   ku bu,   Ish ku bu,   Ish
         b bu a bu a,   b bu a bu a,

hoo—
hoo—   Kuh m   m m m m m m m m   Ee—
ku bu   Ish   ku   bu   Ish   ku bu,
     b bu a bu a,   b bu a bu a,

Ku bu a   Ya uh—
Ku bu a   Ya uh—
          Ish   ku bu,   Ish ku bu,
b   bu a bu a,   b bu a bu a,   b bu a bu a

(*Each woman moves trunk of body suddenly—to right or left—at
the beginning of each* k *or* sh *sound. On* k, *clap hands to the basic
rhythm but make no sounds of clapping. On* sh, *clap hands over
left breast, over the heart, to the basic* sh *rhythm.*)

MOM and DION: O oo—   Ya uh—   Ya
CHORUS OF EIGHT: K k k k k k k k   k k k k k k k k

oo —   Ya oo —   Ya uh —
Sh sh sh sh sh sh sh sh   Sh sh sh sh sh sh sh sh   K k k k

      Ya oo —
k k k k   K k k k k k k   K k k k k k k k k k k k

Sh —   Sh —
      Sh sh sh sh sh sh sh sh sh sh sh sh sh

                    Sh sh sh sh Ya uh — Ya uh — Ya oo —
K k k k k k k k k k k k   K —

Sh sh sh sh Ya oo   Ya oo — Ya oo —
            K —   Sh —

MOM and DION: b bu a
CHORUS OF EIGHT/LEADER: Ish ku bu   Ish ku bu
CHORUS OF EIGHT: b bu a bu a   b bu a

bu ah oo —   b bu a bu ah — oo —
      Ish ku bu,   Ish ku bu,   Ish ku
bu ah   b bu a bu a   b bu a bu a

                              Ya uh —   Ya uh —
bu,   Ish ku bu,
      b bu a bu a   b bu a bu a   K k k k k k k k   Sh sh

[Chorus of Eight:] sh sh sh sh sh Ku — bu — (*long glide; raise hands*)

– Section Two –

DION: Ish (a) bu (a) Ku (a) bu (a)

MOM and CHORUSES: Ish a ba Ish a ba Ku a Yangde yangde yang

(*Choruses circle Dion as they sing.*)
(*I can hope that the music and rhythms will prove so exciting to the
players and singers that the volume will simply* have *to rise. However,
this rise will be more effective, when it comes, if it is restrained as
long as possible.*)

DION: Ish (a) bu (a) Ku (a) bu (a)

MOM and CHORUSES: Ish a ba Ish a ba Ku a Yangde yangde yang

DION: Ish a ba Ish a ba Ish a ba
MOM and CHORUSES: Ish a ba Ish — a ba Ku —

(*Color sequence fades and ends.*)

(*Mom, Dion, and the two Choruses here begin a second kind of snake dance. They sway constantly, move forward very little, stand upright on the* ha ha *bars, and squat low on the floor on the* hoo hoo *bars—still swaying.*)

MOM and DION: Ish bu ha ha   Ish bu hoo hoo
CHORUSES: ha ha ha

               Ish bu ha ha   Ish bu hoo hoo
hoo hoo hoo   ha ha ha

               Ish bu la la   Ish bu lu lu
hoo hoo hoo   la la la   lu lu lu

Ish bu la la   Ish bu lu lu   Ish bu lu—wuh!
       la la la   lu lu lu Ish bu lu—wuh!

(*The Choruses are here squatting on the floor, and as they hold their tone they slowly rise. Stage lights come up slowly at the same time.*)

– Section Three –

(*This is an almost exact repeat of the short section at the end of the* Wunnantu Anda, *in Chorus One, and is used here for transitional purposes, so that the cloggers can dance on with the tumblers' sixty-foot mat. They gather at the right wing, during the chorus singing above, and begin clogging across with the 3/4, while the mat is being unrolled, or pulled on.*)

MOM, DION, and CHORUSES ⟨*singing forte*⟩: Tumble Tumble Tumble Tum—ble on—

4. Tumble On—Climax of Welcome

– Section One –

(*All onstage begin to congregate right, downstage at the beginning.*)
(*The first tumbler starts running.*)

MOM, DION, and CHORUSES (*fortissimo*): Tum—ble oh tumble oh tumble tumble tumble on— (*Applause.*)

(*This is the same pattern, slightly altered melodically and rhythmically, as the* Ishaba Ishaba *response to Dion in Section Two of* Ishbu Kubu.)

MOM and DION: Round-off Flip-flop Somersault Tumble Round-off Flip-flop Somersault Tum—ble— on—

(*The second mat tumbler runs.*)

MOM, DION, and CHORUSES: Tum—ble oh tumble oh tumble tumble tumble on— (*Applause.*)

MOM and DION: Round-off Flip-flop Somersault Tumble Round-off Flip-flop Somersault Tum—ble— on—

(*Third mat tumbler enters.*)
(*Fourth tumbler enters.*)
(*Contrary tumbling begins.*)
(*Chase-off begins.*)

MOM, DION, and CHORUSES: Tum—ble oh Tumble oh tumble oh [etc.] tumble tumble on— (*Applause.*) Round-off Flip-flop Somersault Tumble Round-off Flip-flop Somersault Tum—ble— on— (*Applause.*)

– Section Two –

MOM, DION, and CHORUSES: Hey   Hey   Hey
LEADER (shout):   In a heavenly daze, tumble

    Hey
on!

MOM, DION, and CHORUS OF EIGHT: Heavenly daze— and
CHORUS OF FOUR:

    a million year—   zuh!   Heavenly daze— from
              tumble tumble tumble

    shore to shore—   Heavenly daze—
              tumble tumble tumble   tumble

     The happy way!
    tumble   tumble tumble

MOM and DION: Heavenly daze—
CHORUSES: Heavenly daze— forever ever ever ever ever,

                  forev—er— more—
    foreh— eh eh ver maw-aw ore—   Heavenly daze—

CHORUS OF EIGHT: forever, ever, ever, ever,
CHORUS OF FOUR: tumble on tumble

    tumble on tumble on   ever ever ever
on   ever ever ever ever

ever
    tumble on tumble on

(*After the final tumbler has exited right, and while choruses are diminishing and general stage lights fading, Mom and Dion step downstage. A spot picks them up immediately.*)

(*I am convinced that the tumbling, once it begins in earnest, must continue almost without letup. If it reappears, after a considerable nontumbling pause, it could only be an anticlimax—that is, in a dramatic, as opposed to a gymnastic, sense.*)

(*Another spot picks up the solitary figure of Sonny, at left wings. One could easily assume that he has stood there quite a long time already. He stares fixedly at Mom and Dion, who do not see him.*)

(*The choruses and chorus music have faded to virtual inaudibility, without retard. Chorus members melt into the wings. Sustained piccolos, Castor and Pollux increase as the final singing fades. With spot on Sonny, Castor and Pollux recall, in seven bars, the theme phrase of Chorus Two—sacrificial dream.*)

DION: (*intoning slowly*): Yours— is the power—

MOM (*intoning slowly, with extravagant ceremony*): And— yours— the glory!

⟨*Dissonant, high, prerecorded tape of Harmonic Canon I comes in on the word* glory.⟩

(*Dion takes Mom's hand, and they move slowly off in the half-light, exiting right. As they move off, Adapted Viola uses four slow bars anticipating the opening phrase of the Chorus Four theme— nightmare vision.*)

(*Immediately, when Mom finishes intoning, the two spots swing directly upward to the heroic masks of Dionysus and Pentheus, high above the stage. The masks begin to descend, and spots follow them.*)

(*Rebound rack and mat are removed in the darkness; scrim travels over fountain. Dion and Sonny remove trousers in respective wings, return, and meet the masks, which they attach.*)

SCENE THREE.   Later in the ancient night, at the entrance to the Palace of Thebes. Pentheus is tricked into transvestism.

(*The Chorus of Eight enters, crowds around Dionysus. Only this area—right—is lit. Pentheus remains in comparative darkness. Dionysus performs the same pose dance that accompanied his opening monologue.*)

DIONYSUS: (*Pose.*) Instead of me he found a bull. (*Pose.*) A Bull! (*Profile pose.*) Hm—! A man who dares to confront a god!

(*As lights come up on Pentheus, Dionysus moves freely—stops posing.*)

DIONYSUS: Here he is now. (*Almost under the breath.*) Let him storm!

PENTHEUS: Well! How did you escape? Answer!

DIONYSUS: Walk softly here. Your anger is out of place.

PENTHEUS: *How* did you escape?

DIONYSUS: Didn't you hear me before? I said that someone would free me, whenever I asked.

PENTHEUS: Clever! But not clever enough!

DIONYSUS: More than enough when I need to be.

⟨*Herdsman enters right.*⟩

DIONYSUS: Here, a herdsman from Kitheron! And I think he has a story to tell you.

HERDSMAN ⟨*intones*⟩: Pentheus, king! I come from the mountain of eternal snows—

PENTHEUS: Come! Tell your story!

HERDSMAN: I have seen wild bacchanals—the women of Thebes, stung with frenzy, strange and fearsome things. But, king, I fear your hasty moods, your royal and violent temper.

PENTHEUS: Speak! I absolve you. The greater the wickedness you describe, the greater the penance I shall exact.

(*During the long account that follows, the stage darkens, and on the cyclorama right of the scrim, the assumed direction of Kitheron, a film of strange and mysterious lights, color merging into color, is projected.*)

(*Agave's voice—vowels, all imprecise—is heard offstage right. Here, her sound is that of loving mother. She is coincident, as mother, with the description of her as savage leader of the Bacchae. This background provides a total picture, and is intended as ironic contrast. It is at once a projection into the past and into the future.*)

HERDSMAN (*free*): First, I saw three bands of bacchanals—your own mother, Agave, was among them. They were sleeping the sleep of exhaustion, wherever they happened to fall. Then your mother heard the lowing of our cattle, rose up, and cried: "Shake the sleep away!"

Suddenly the place was filled with women—matrons, maidens, young girls. Some cradled fawns, or wolf cubs, in their arms. Others—young mothers who had left their babes at home—suckled wild things at their swollen breasts. They fastened their skins about them with writhing snakes.

One struck a rock, and a fountain gushed forth. Another stabbed her wand into the ground—wine spurted up. Honey dripped from their ivy staves.

Several of us herdsmen were together, and we consulted. Shall we chase the mother of Pentheus out of this mad revel, we asked each other, and do our lord a favor?

Then, at a signal, the orgy began. They shouted: "Dionysus! Son of Zeus!" Even the wild animals joined in, and the whole mountain went crazy with religion. Agave leaped, and I sprang out to grab her. "What!" she shrieked, "Ambushed by men!"

I tell you, we barely got away with our lives. Missing us, they turned their fury upon the cattle. Calves were torn into crimson shreds. Charging bulls were tripped and hurled to the ground, dragged down by *girls'* hands.

Whatever they placed upon their shoulders stayed there, unfastened. They carried fire in their streaming hair, and it remained unburnt.

They plundered a village, and steel-tipped spears, thrown by the village men, did not hurt them, yet their own frail wands made wound upon wound. The men *ran*, routed utterly—routed by *women*.

⟨*Intones.*⟩ Exhausted finally, they retired to their fountains, where they washed, while serpents licked the blood from their cheeks.

(*Colors on cyclorama vanish.*)

HERDSMAN: O my king, welcome this god to the city. He is great in other ways also, for I am told that he is the divinity of wine. When wine is no more, love is no more, and that will be the end of joy in the world.

KORYPHEUS (*softly*): I know the risk of speaking out before the tyrant, yet I must. (*Shouting loudly.*) Sweet Dionysus! None is greater!

CHORUS OF EIGHT (*shouting*): None! None!

PENTHEUS: The fire spreads, and we must act at once, or we shall become the shame of Greece. ⟨*To Guard.*⟩ Go. Give the order, to the swiftest of the horsemen. Rouse the archers.

⟨*Guard exits left.*⟩

It passes all bounds! To endure from *women* what we now endure.

DIONYSUS: You will not hear me, Pentheus. You will do exactly what you wish, yet I must tell you: beware. Do not war against a god. It were more appropriate to offer him a sacrifice.

PENTHEUS: He will get his sacrifice, and the woods of Kitheron are full of the victims! (*Whispering to himself.*) I only wish that I could catch them in their *foul acts!*

DIONYSUS (*superciliously*): My friend! Let us discuss the situation.

PENTHEUS: Enough of this! Where is my armor?

(*He strides toward left exit, but Dionysus hastily interrupts.*)

DIONYSUS: Wait!

(*Pentheus stops but does not turn.*)

You say you would like to *catch*—them. How would you like to *see*—these revels. (*He pronounces the word* see *lecherously.*)

PENTHEUS (*turns, obviously deeply affected by an overwhelming desire to see*): *See* them? Yes, I would like to see them.

DIONYSUS: Why?

PENTHEUS: Well—it would pain me to see them drunk, but I—

DIONYSUS: But for all your pain you would like to *see* them.

PENTHEUS: Yes, I would. If— Perhaps I could hide among the trees!

DIONYSUS: I will guide you. Are you ready?

PENTHEUS: I am ready.

DIONYSUS (*hesitates*): I'm afraid I'll have to suggest that you wear women's clothes.

PENTHEUS: What—! But why?

DIONYSUS: If they saw you were a man— Well, you know what I mean!
       If you hadn't been *invited* there, and you were caught *spying* (*both* invited *and* spying *are spoken lecherously*), they would tear you apart, instantly. I will gladly help with your disguise.

PENTHEUS: *Me*—in a *dress!* Ridiculous!

DIONYSUS: Well—! You want to *see!* Unless you are *one* of them, you *can't* see.

PENTHEUS: But *me!* In a *dress!*

DIONYSUS: You would be safe only if you are *one* of them.

PENTHEUS: I would die of shame.

DIONYSUS: Very well, if you don't *wish* to *spy.*

PENTHEUS (*hesitates*): What must I wear?

DIONYSUS: First, a wig, with long and beautiful curls.

PENTHEUS: Yes?

DIONYSUS: You must have a wand for your hand.

PENTHEUS: Anything else?

DIONYSUS: A net for your hair, and a dress falling to your feet.

PENTHEUS: I can't do it! No—! No!

DIONYSUS: Then there is only one alternative. Bloodshed.

PENTHEUS: But I might be *seen! Me*, in a dress!

DIONYSUS: We can take devious byways. I will conduct you.

PENTHEUS: I can't bear to be ridiculed. (*He hesitates.*) Let me think about it.

> (*Entrapment theme again. Pentheus mutters to himself, moving slowly offstage left.*)

PENTHEUS (*free, except rhythmically*): —in a woman's dress—a net for my hair— (*Pentheus exits.*)

DIONYSUS: (*Pose.*) Our fish is ensnared!
            The revelers he shall see!
            For a price! (*Pose.*)

            Madden this man!
            Possess his soul!
            His threats so foul!

            Pay him back!
            Show him on the streets of Thebes,
            A woman!

Now I must go to assist with his toilet! (*Exits left.*)

Hymn to Dionysus—Oh, to Be Free
Where No Man Is

(The Chorus of Eight sings and dances.)

CHORUS OF EIGHT/HALF: O O O O O O O O

CHORUS OF EIGHT/HALF: O O O O O O O O

CHORUS OF EIGHT/ONE: Oh, to be free—

CHORUS OF EIGHT/TWO: Oh, to be free—

CHORUS OF EIGHT/THREE: Oh, to be free, to dance with joy—

CHORUS OF EIGHT/FOUR: Oh, to be free, leaping for joy—

CHORUS OF EIGHT: Where no man is— Oh, to be free where no man is—

CHORUS OF EIGHT/FIVE:
> The gods are cunning—
> They hide and wait.
> Long, long they wait, to— trap!
> the unbeliever—

CHORUS OF EIGHT: To— trap! the unbeliever. Oh, to be free where no man is—

CHORUS OF EIGHT/SIX:
> Whatever the olden times have done—
> This is the way of the gods—
> This is the way forever—

CHORUS OF EIGHT: This is the way forever— Oh, to be free where no man is—

CHORUS OF EIGHT/SEVEN: Whatever the ways of tradition are— These are the ways forever—

CHORUS OF EIGHT: These are the ways forever— Oh, to be free where no man is—

CHORUS OF EIGHT/EIGHT: Day by day, the happy life— This is the way forever—

CHORUS OF EIGHT:
> Whatever the olden times have done,
> Whatever the ways of tradition are—
> Day by day the happy life—

CHORUS OF EIGHT and MUSICIANS: This is the way forever—

CHORUS OF EIGHT: Oh, to be free where no man is—

CHORUS OF EIGHT/ONE: Oh, to be free—

CHORUS OF EIGHT/TWO: Oh, to be free—

CHORUS OF EIGHT/THREE: Oh, to be free, to dance with joy—

CHORUS OF EIGHT/FOUR: Oh, to be free, leaping for joy—

CHORUS OF EIGHT: Where no— man— is—

> (*Dionysus enters. Gestures for silence.*)
> (*Bull's horns have been attached to Dionysus's mask. He walks quickly, motions to the Chorus of Eight for silence, then walks back slowly toward the palace portico and gently beckons.*)
> (*The entrapment theme is heard for the final time.*)

DIONYSUS (*free*): Come, Pentheus. Let us have a look at you. Come!

> (*Dionysus advances downstage center.*)
> (*Pentheus enters from portico. He is wearing a wig, and a garment similar to Agave's. ⟨He is obviously dazed.⟩ He sways his head slowly from side to side on beats* one *and* three *of each bar.*)

DIONYSUS: Why, you are the *image* of your *dear* mother!

PENTHEUS ⟨*intones in deep and grotesque melancholy*⟩:
          I see two moons up in the sky—
          I see two cities—Thebes, both.
          And each of them has seven gates.

> (*Pentheus stops swaying.*)

          You—you are a bull, with horns on your head.
          You are most surely a bull.

DIONYSUS: It is the god himself who attends us. He is making peace with you.

> (*As Pentheus advances, the Chorus of Eight moves toward right, and during the next few lines exits.*)
> (*Excepting for his final line, Pentheus's words are all free. The Herdsman—as before—is heard offstage right.*)

HERDSMAN (*offstage*): Pentheus—

PENTHEUS: Do I really look like my mother?

HERDSMAN: Sor—row—

DIONYSUS: Were you together, I could not tell you apart. Wait— one of your curls needs tucking.

HERDSMAN: Pentheus—

PENTHEUS: It must have fallen out when I was dancing, I was trying to play the Bacchante.

HERDSMAN: Sor—row—

DIONYSUS: I am your maid; I'll fix it. Hold still.

PENTHEUS: Help me. You see how much I look to you.

DIONYSUS: Now your dress is crooked.

PENTHEUS: Only on the right, I think. The left hem seems straight. Should I hold the wand like this? Or like this?

DIONYSUS: No, with the right hand. And time the stroke with your right foot. (*Pentheus does so.*) That's better! I commend your spirit of cooperation.

HERDSMAN: Pentheus—

PENTHEUS: I shall hide among the pine trees!

HERDSMAN: Sor—row—

DIONYSUS: Yes, you shall find a nest for spying, the one that you have earned.

PENTHEUS: Imagine! Already I can see them there—mating *furiously*—caught in the throes of love.

DIONYSUS: That is your purpose—to watch. You may catch them by surprise, or—they may catch you.

PENTHEUS: I—alone among the people of Thebes—dare to do this.

DIONYSUS: You—and you alone—are doing this for Thebes. I will lead you there, but someone else will bring you back.

HERDSMAN: Pentheus—

PENTHEUS: My mother?

HERDSMAN: Sor—row—

DIONYSUS: She will carry you in her arms, for all to see.

HERDSMAN: Pentheus—

PENTHEUS: Such luxury! Nestled in my mother's arms.

HERDSMAN: Sor—row—

DIONYSUS: Gloriously! This is your destiny.

HERDSMAN: Sor—row—

PENTHEUS: You are too good to me.

HERDSMAN: Sor—row—

DIONYSUS: You are an unusual young man, and you go to a strange and unusual experience.

HERDSMAN: Sor—row—

PENTHEUS: It is my reward.

DIONYSUS: Yes, a fame ascending to the skies!

(*Dionysus looks up and gestures. Pentheus begins to move off, right, and Dionysus quickly goes downstage as far as possible, center, holding out his hands toward Kitheron.*)
(*Scrim is removed before the fountain, and lights come up gradually on it. The figure of Mom, immobile, is seen dimly behind it.*)

DIONYSUS: Agave! I bring you your son! Reach out your arms—!

PENTHEUS: Nestled in my mother's arms— Nestled in my mother's arms—

(*Pentheus exits right.*)
⟨*Dionysus—who till now has stood with arms outstretched toward Kitheron—races on tiptoes across the stage to follow him.*⟩
(*Lights dim.*)

CHORUS FOUR. Midnight of the same evening in the Courthouse Park. Mom, ghost walking, witnesses an attack upon her son.

(*The park is dim, shadowy, deserted, and remains deserted up to the nightmare vision. Mom is seen dimly behind the fountain. All voices—except Mom's—are offstage.*)

CHORUS OF EIGHT (*not vocal chord sounds*): Whoo—sh— (Z *plus indefinite vowel.*) Z—

CHORUS OF FOUR: Z—

CHORUSES: (*Whistle.*)

MOM ⟨*intoning softly*⟩: The night is still dark

CHORUSES (*a vocal chord sound—indefinite vowel*): Z z z z z z zoo—

MOM: O O O O O— O O O O O O O—

⟨*Mom takes her first step out from behind the fountain. She continues to move downstage, very slowly, reaching the area where—generally—she remains during the balance of the Chorus.*⟩

MOM: —and in the briefest moment they are away—

CHORUS OF EIGHT (*soft, breathy*): Away—! Away—! Away—! Away—! Sh—

MOM ⟨*loudly*⟩: Away—!

CHORUS OF FOUR (*soft, breathy*): Away—! Away—! Away—! Away—!

MOM: —hardly stop at all—

CHORUSES (*soft, breathy*): Not at all—! Not at all—! Not at all—!

MOM: At all—! At all—!

CHORUSES ⟨*very softly, in long glides*⟩: Fall— Fall— Sh—

MOM: as they fall—

CHORUSES ⟨*softly*⟩: Stop—! Stop—! Stop—! Stop—!

MOM: they hardly stop—

CHORUSES: at all—, at all—, at all—

MOM ⟨*loudly*⟩: Stop—!

CHORUSES ⟨*very softly*⟩: Softly, softly, softly

MOM ⟨*softly*⟩: ever so as they

CHORUSES ⟨*in a long soft glide*⟩: Fall—

MOM (*low, vibrant, gutteral*): No—! No—! No—!

CHORUSES (*softly*): Not at all— Not at all— Sh—

(*At this point Mom has reached the stage area where she remains.*)

MOM: and in the briefest moment they are

⟨*Now the Choruses sing loudly and in a strong rhythm, for the first time.*⟩

CHORUSES: Away—, away—, away—, away—, away—

MOM: How can I imagine that they are here
CHORUSES (*singing fortissimo*):

> when with these eyes   I have seen them taken before a
>   I   am—!
>
> hundred winds beyond my power to control—
>   I   am—!   I am—

⟨*The theme is the same hymnal-folk tune which preceded the dream
in Chorus Two. Here, it is given only three times, and it is roughly
two semitones higher.*⟩

MOM: a hundred
CHORUSES: b bu a, b bu— a, b bu a, b bu a, b bu a, bu —a,

> winds— Oh—   Oh— Oh— Oh—
>   b bu a, b bu a, b bu a   N no— n no—a
>
> Ah—   Oh—oo—oh—ah—
>   b bu a b bu—   oh—ah—

(*Mom begins to move to the beat, the triplet figure, in a very limited
area.*)
(*The same two neckers of Chorus Two enter, sit on the bench, and
embrace.*)
(*The second pair of neckers enters, stands beside the fountain, and
embraces.*)

MOM: the dawn the dawn the dawn the
CHORUSES ⟨*up and down glides*⟩:   oo—

> dawn the dawn the dawn the sun—   Nuh noh a
>   a hundred winds
>
>   Nuh noh a   Nuh noh a   Nuh noh a   Nuh noh a
>   O——a   O——a   O——a   O——a
>
>   Nuh noh a
>   O——a   O——ah—

(*Spot on Mom fades. The two guitarists enter, and repeat their Chorus
Two actions, passing, staring back. All of this suggests that Mom's
vision is the same as Sonny's.*)

CHORUSES ⟨*gliding, pianissimo*⟩: O—a o—a

(*The neckers embrace passionately.*)

HERDSMAN (*high, gasping, breathy*):
                    No no—! No no—!
                    I— I—
                    I am— I am—

(*The two starers exit.*)
(*The bench neckers get up and wander off.*)
⟨*Six bars of instrumental crescendo follow.*⟩
(*The fountain neckers wander off.*)
⟨*With a strong sforzando, stage lights begin to dim.*⟩
⟨*Spot returns to Mom. She begins singing the chorus theme, softly, almost casually. Mom and Viola take alternate phrases.*⟩

MOM (*soft* d's): Duh du du duh— du du du du duh duh— [etc.]

(*Mom walks slowly off, right.*)
⟨*Music ends completely.*⟩
(*She hesitates, then speaks very softly—not facing audience.*)

MOM: —ever so softly—

⟨*Bowls and Spoils of War strike. Spot fades on the strike, and coincident with strike and fade is a high wail.*⟩

CHORUS OF EIGHT/SOLO: Yai—!

CHORUS OF FOUR: Oo—

(*Mask of Herdsman descends.*)

SCENE FOUR.   Early dawn of the next ancient day, at the entrance to the Palace of Thebes. Agave comes out of the night with a trophy of her power.

Hymn to Dionysus—Hell-Hounds of Madness

(*The Chorus of Eight enters immediately, right, and very quickly reaches the left part of the stage. The Herdsman enters behind them, adjusts his mask, and stands watching. The Chorus of Eight spits fury and malice, and uses a movement that suggests more madness than dancing.*)
(*The beginning of the hymn is mezzo forte, fast, intense. It slowly increases, picks up speed very slightly, and ends fortissimo.*)
(*The stage is dark.*)

CHORUS OF EIGHT/ONE (spit out *the syllables!*): Hell-hounds of madness—

CHORUS OF EIGHT/TWO: Stung with fury—

CHORUS OF EIGHT/THREE: Justice draw close—

CHORUS OF EIGHT/FOUR: Slay the unrighteous—

(*Lights come on.*)

CHORUS OF EIGHT/ONE: Hell-hounds of madness—

CHORUS OF EIGHT/FIVE: Strike at the throat—

CHORUS OF EIGHT/SIX: The mad spectator—

CHORUS OF EIGHT/SEVEN: Girlish impersonator—

CHORUS OF EIGHT/ONE: Hell-hounds of madness—

CHORUS OF EIGHT/EIGHT: Bring him down—

CHORUS OF EIGHT/TWO: In toils of destruction—

CHORUS OF EIGHT/THREE: His mother shall scream—

CHORUS OF EIGHT/ONE: Hell-hounds of madness—

CHORUS OF EIGHT/FOUR: Who suckled this seed—?

CHORUS OF EIGHT/FIVE: Stung with fury—

CHORUS OF EIGHT/SIX: Justice draw close—

CHORUS OF EIGHT/ONE: Hell-hounds of madness—

CHORUS OF EIGHT/SEVEN: Slay the unrighteous—

CHORUS OF EIGHT/EIGHT: Strike at the throat—

CHORUS OF EIGHT/TWO: The mad spectator—

CHORUS OF EIGHT/ONE: Hell-hounds of madness—

CHORUS OF EIGHT/THREE: Girlish impersonator—

CHORUS OF EIGHT/FOUR: Bring him down—

CHORUS OF EIGHT/FIVE: In toils of destruction—

CHORUS OF EIGHT/ONE: Hell-hounds of madness—

CHORUS OF EIGHT/SIX: His mother shall scream—

CHORUS OF EIGHT/SEVEN: Who suckled this seed—?

CHORUS OF EIGHT/EIGHT: Stung with fury—

CHORUS OF EIGHT/ONE: Hell-hounds of madness—

CHORUS OF EIGHT: Jus—tice— draw— (*long gliding scream*) close—!

HERDSMAN (*shout*): Stop! Stop!

> (*He waits for the hubbub to subside.*)
> (*The lines of both the Herdsman and Korypheus are free, except rhythmically.*)

HERDSMAN: I am only a servant, yet I mourn the fate of this house.

KORYPHEUS: Fate? What fate?

HERDSMAN: Pentheus—is dead.

CHORUS OF EIGHT ⟨*shouting in joy*⟩: Dionysus! Dionysus!

KORYPHEUS: A god indeed!

HERDSMAN: It makes you *glad*—this calamity?

KORYPHEUS: Dionysus, not Thebes, holds my loyalty.

HERDSMAN: Nevertheless, it seems hardly fitting to exult in disaster.

KORYPHEUS: Tell us— Tell us— the death he died.

(*Agave is offstage right, as before* [Scene Three].)

HERDSMAN ⟨*intones slowly, carefully, and chants frequently*⟩: I was there with them—Pentheus, and this stranger who led him. We stopped in a grassy dell, silently, cautiously, so as not to be discovered. And Pentheus climbed into a tree, the better to witness the revels.

Suddenly a great voice came out of the darkness: "Bacchae! Bacchae! The mocker is here! Avenge yourselves!"

An unearthly light filled the sky as they rushed—with maddened feet—toward that voice. Seeing Pentheus, they showered him with stones, pulled him down from the tree, and stabbed him with sharpened spears of fir.

Like a priestess at the altar, his own mother, Agave, bent over him. Then Pentheus tore off his wig, his net, touched her on the cheek, and screamed: (*Here, the Herdsman sings in the high, gasping voice of Choruses Two and Four. This is the onstage reality, prophecied offstage before.*) "Mother! Mother! No no! No no! I— I am! Pentheus! Pentheus!"

But she was possessed, heard nothing—only the frenzy of the Bacchae. With bloody hands, when it was all over, they tossed parts of his body about, as they might play ball. ⟨*He hesitates.*⟩ She is coming now—holding high the head. A lion's head, she says. ⟨*Low and soft.*⟩ Mad—! ⟨*Higher and softer.*⟩ Mad—! ⟨*Very high and extremely soft.*⟩ Mad—! ⟨*He hesitates again.*⟩ I must go. I do not care to encounter her, or see any more. ⟨*Spoken while walking off, half to himself.*⟩ Humility before the gods— that is best, and wisest too.

Continuation of Hymn to Dionysus

(*This is a brief echo of the* Hell-Hounds of Madness *lines—same music, same character. The Herdsman takes one sad look, after the Chorus of Eight begins, and exits right.*)

CHORUS OF EIGHT/ONE: Dance to the death—

CHORUS OF EIGHT/TWO: Of the seed of the dragon—

CHORUS OF EIGHT/THREE: The mad spectator—

CHORUS OF EIGHT/FOUR: Girlish impersonator—

CHORUS OF EIGHT/ONE: Dance to the glory—

CHORUS OF EIGHT/FIVE: Of the bull! Of the bull!

CHORUS OF EIGHT/SIX: Of the bull who led him—

CHORUS OF EIGHT/SEVEN: Down to his fate—

CHORUS OF EIGHT/ONE: Dance to the glory—

CHORUS OF EIGHT/EIGHT: Of the god Dionysus—

CHORUS OF EIGHT/TWO: Of the women of Thebes—

CHORUS OF EIGHT: Of vic— to— (*long screaming glide*) ree—!

KORYPHEUS: Here she is!

(*Agave enters right, holding the mask of Pentheus in her arms.*)

AGAVE (*shout, triumphantly*): Bacchae! Bacchae! Oh ho ho ho— O— Oo— I come—! O—ah— A huntress with prey-ee— Ah ha ha ha—ugh!

(*Korypheus's voice here is in diametric contrast to that of Agave, which is high and lilting, as at the opening of Chorus One. She sings in a kind of* bel canto, *final proof of her absolute madness.*)

(*The attitude of the Chorus of Eight undergoes a strange change. Although they wished the death of Pentheus, and exulted in it, they turn chicken when faced by a woman who has murdered her son.*)

KORYPHEUS: From where?

AGAVE: From Kitheron!

KORYPHEUS: What Kitheron has brought forth!

AGAVE: And I struck first. Oh— O O O fortunate— fortunate hunting!

KORYPHEUS (*groan*): U— Fortunate!

(*Cadmus enters right, and stands listening, but Agave—her back to him—is unaware.*)

AGAVE: An extraordinary kill!

KORYPHEUS: Indeed! Extraordinary!

AGAVE: You *do*— praise me?

KORYPHEUS: How can I avoid it?

AGAVE: The men of Thebes will praise me.

KORYPHEUS: Your son Pentheus especially!

AGAVE (*free, delivered rather quickly*): Ah, Pentheus. He must come. And my father. Where is he? Where are they? The men of Thebes use nets and spears, boast of their prowess, but here is a quarry brought down by the bare hands of women, and a young lion—

CADMUS ⟨*interrupts*⟩: No— more—! No more—! No more—! No more—!

AGAVE ⟨*shocked and confused by his sound and manner*—bel canto *ends*— straight intoning⟩: Father!

⟨*Both Cadmus and Agave intone. This dialogue begins in voice of normal volume, but becomes progressively softer—yet more intense, so that, on Agave's final "No!" it is barely audible. The first music of the Coda then comes as a shattering blast.*⟩

CADMUS: If you are so fortunate as to abide in your present mind till the day you die—you will seem to be happy, even though *cursed!*

AGAVE: Father, what are you saying?

CADMUS: Daughter, look up to heaven.

AGAVE: Yes, I am looking.

CADMUS: Does it seem the same? Or does it seem different, *now*.

AGAVE: The sun is beginning to come up. It seems more bright, more clear, than before.

CADMUS: And is the sickness still tossing about in your head?

AGAVE: Sickness? Yes, I feel strange.

CADMUS: Yet you can hear, and answer me.

AGAVE: No, father. Yes, I hear, but — I forget.

CADMUS: Whose head — whose — do you hold — in your arms?

(*Agave neither moves nor speaks.*)
(*Cadmus changes position slightly.*)

CADMUS: Look at it. What do you see?

AGAVE: I see —

CADMUS: Tell me what you see.

AGAVE (*deep and soft*): No —! (*Barely audible.*) No!

⟨*Following this last whispered* No! *Agave must count exactly three seconds — there is no music, no more, no less. On what would be the fourth count she lets the mask drop. And the moment it touches the floor is the beginning of the Coda.*⟩

CODA.   Rays of the early morning sun strike horizontally across the Courthouse Park.

(*The moment Pentheus's mask hits the stage floor is the first beat of the first bar of the Coda. Scrim removed from fountain.*

By the first beat of the fourth bar, Agave has disengaged her own mask, and drops it so that it hits the stage floor on this beat. ⟨*The dropping of masks, in both cases, is musically characterized by a blast of brass, gongs, and other percussion.*⟩

On the sixth bar she takes her first backward step, downstage — her back is to audience.

On the seventeenth backward step — they need not be long ones — she is in the same stage position in which she received the fatal vision — Chorus Four. This direction is away from the charming fountain, symbol of love and security.

On the eighteenth bar ⟨to a brass crescendo⟩ stage lights begin to fade.

On the nineteenth bar, in the dim light, Dion—wearing pants, no mask—steps beside the fountain—to left of it.

On the twentieth bar two spots pick up the fallen masks and the figure of Dion.

⟨When brass reenters in the twenty-fifth bar, it is muted.⟩ On the twenty-ninth bar the spots begin to fade.

On the thirty-first bar the stage should be dark, and it should remain dark through bar thirty-four, the last.)

⟨*Stage lights come up partially for* Incidental Music for Applause.⟩

Water! Water!

An Intermission with Prologues and Epilogues

The social occasion known as the "intermission," in contemporary play and concert going, finds nearly all guests headed for the drinking fountains. Hence the title. Perhaps the length of lines at these fountains is in direct ratio to the degree of anguish generated by the piece presented, but aside from this question there can be little doubt as to the audience's feeling of eager anticipation and outright relief when the "intermission" finally arrives. I believe that it is worthy of a title.

—H. P.

Prologues and Epilogues

Time

About now. In a more constricted sense time is suspended. It is always immediately after sundown.

Place

Santa Mystiana, a medium-large American city.

Cast

WATER CRIERS, one male, one female
PHOEBUS the Disc Jockey
PRODUCER
CONDUCTOR
HER HONOR, mayor of Santa Mystiana
CLARENCE, president of the Board of Aldermen
AQUARIUS, supervisor of the Water Works
ARTHUR, leader of a jazz band; the God of Rain
WANDA, the Water Witch
Five INDIAN RUNNERS (individual runners are designated FIRST, SECOND, THIRD, FOURTH, FIFTH)
PURA, Clarence's bartender [barmaid]; secret leader of the Hysterical Ghosts

YOUNG BUSINESSMAN
YOUNG IDLER
COLLEGE GIRL
MIDDLE-AGED SECRETARY
ELDERLY MAN
SINGER, female
WIFE, HUSBAND, middle-aged couple
BEATNIK PAIR
VISITOR, teenage girl
VOICE FROM BLEACHERS
INDIAN WOMAN
CLERK
BAILIFF

VERY WHITE JAZZMAN
NEGRO JAZZMAN / NEGROES
MAN WITH LADIES' PARASOL

CHORUSES
Board of ALDERMEN (individual aldermen are designated FIRST,
    SECOND, THIRD, etc.); also MALE BLEACHERS CHORUS at
    baseball game
LADIES' AUXILIARY of the Junior Dragons of Mystery; also FE-
    MALE BLEACHERS CHORUS at baseball game
JAZZMEN (Jazz Band), accompanying the God of Rain (individual
    jazzmen are designated FIRST, SECOND, THIRD, etc; solos as
    FIRST, SECOND, THIRD, etc.; recitatives as FIRST, SECOND,
    THIRD, etc.)
Chorus of Passionate Ancient Water WITCHES (individual witches
    are designated FIRST, SECOND, THIRD, etc.); also Chorus of
    Hysterical American Indian GHOSTS (individual ghosts are des-
    ignated FIRST, SECOND, THIRD, etc.)
Mystic Order of Empirical RIFLEMEN

The Set

A medium-wide partition is in the exact center, upstage, leaving only
enough room for the mobile instruments to slip behind it. This is a
psychological barrier.

Right, the stage is bare, but in a partial semicircle a transcendent
horizon is seen. It is somewhat like a southern Arizona horizon immediately after sundown. Time is suspended; it is always immediately
after sundown. When the rains come the horizon is black, but the
luminous light emerges again through most of the Epilogues.

Left, the stage is also bare, except for a kind of throne, far left—
a seat for Her Honor. At the rear is a huge picture window, looking
out on modern skyscrapers, and a brilliantly lit neon street trailing
off in the distance. This scene is at dusk, and blocks of windows, or
isolated windows, are lit, except during those Epilogues where floods
have damaged the power plant.

To the audience, the half of the stage to the right represents a
world in which there is only a casual interest in what is called progress.
It is a world of intuition, spontaneity, of unspoken reconciliation with
the powers of a mysterious nature. The half of the stage to the
audience's left represents social order, duty, law, convention, and progress. It is a world which probes and analyzes and exploits nature to
the point that it has virtually lost reverence for the mysteries of nature.

Stage set for 1962 University of Illinois production of *Water! Water!* (left half of stage representing Santa Mystiana). Photograph by Danlee Mitchell.

Foreground, right or left, should be variably mysterious — never brilliant. This foreground, like Christianity, must suggest promise only in the rosy distance.

The characters belonging to their particular half of the stage generally do not move across the invisible center line. They move up, down. However, they cross freely after the exciting announcement that the rains have come. They also cross freely during the last large song and dance: *Gone, Man, Gone!*

Costumes

With a few exceptions, everyday American street clothes.

1. *Aldermen.* Aside from business suits, white shirts and ties, they wear masks on the *tops* of their heads. These are simple flattop haircut masks, made of painted cardboard. Each — whether red, blond, brown, black — shows a light stripe down the middle of the flat top of the head. In the Seventh Epilogue they enter naked, except for underpants and hanging strips of cloth which move freely in movement breezes. Flattop masks remain.
2. *The Ladies' Auxiliary.* They wear small, outlandish hats. In the Seventh Epilogue they also enter naked, or virtually naked.
3. *Chorus of Passionate Ancient Water Witches.* They wear only patches and strands of clothing that move freely in the breezes of movement, and show them to be absolutely lovely from the shoulders down. Above, the necks are made up to be scrawny, the faces hideous, and short, wispy strands of gray and white hair fall from their heads — less than shoulder length. They are barefoot, except in the burlesque routine, Sixth Prologue, where they wear high-heeled slippers. As the Hysterical Indian Ghosts they attach small feathers at the backs of heads, with headbands. This idea is a cliché, but I can think of no easier way, costume-wise, to suggest the American Indian.
4. *Indian Runners.* They wear loincloths and feathers at the backs of heads on headbands.

Caution: Tumblers must not wear gym clothes. They may wear outlandish costumes, or light sports clothes.

The Instruments

Six of my instruments (seven players) are onstage, on very low platforms with casters, so that they move freely in any direction they are pushed, either propelled by the player or by designated helpers. They are:

> Eroica (two high blocks only)
> Bass Marimba
> Diamond Marimba
> Surrogate Kithara
> Castor and Pollux (two players)
> Kithara II

Diamond Marimba, Surrogate Kithara, and Castor and Pollux are propelled by the respective players. The larger instruments are propelled by others.

Nine instruments are on the floor of the auditorium (substitute pit):

> Chromelodeon II
> Two violins
> Viola
> Cello
> Clarinet
> Bass clarinet
> String bass
> Spoils of War
> Jazz percussion

The Conductor and Water Criers are also on the floor (pit). The Water Criers will of course have no acting responsibilities, but will hold all Chorus parts and act as Chorus leaders.

Additional Notes

Jazz arrangements. There are indications for seven jazz numbers, which should be arrangements of songs or themes already present in the work. In addition, there are three numbers, indicated, in which jazz instrumentation may—or should—be added to the score. Piano must not be used. Entirely apart from the constitutional misery of its tuning, it would introduce a quality and timbre inimical to this dramatic concept.

Improvisation. Suggestions for instrumental improvisation are made here and there. The lines of Phoebus are open to alteration, improvisation, expansion.

Opening Prologue

⟨*House lights dim. Pit lights on. Stage remains dark.*⟩

MALE WATER CRIER ⟨*intoning very deliberately*⟩: The highest goodness is like water. It seeks the low place that all men dislike.

WATER CRIERS: Wa—ter! Wa—ter! Wa—ter! Wa—ter!

CHORUSES ⟨*from dark backstage*⟩: Wa—ter! Wa—ter! Wa— ter! Wa—ter!

Second Prologue

WATER CRIERS: Wa—ter! Wa—ter! Wa—ter! Wa—ter!

(*Spot picks up Phoebus the Disc Jockey. He is always far left, downstage.*)

PHOEBUS: I am Phoebus the Disc Jockey. I know all, see all, compute all, refute all, amuse all, confuse all! That's a joke. Heh-heh. (*Suddenly to himself.*) Or is it?

(*Spot picks up Producer, entering right.*)

PHOEBUS: Here's the Producer.

PRODUCER: Phoebus Apollo!

PHOEBUS: That's me.

PRODUCER: Phoebus, prophet of the record industry! And you get your name from the same Apollo who killed the python and set up housekeeping for oracles in a gaseous cave at Delphi?

PHOEBUS: The same.

PRODUCER: I'm curious. How do you tick? Do you have prophetic visions while gazing into a vortex of whirling platters? Or does the verbal gas you generate finally overwhelm you, and thus endow you with oracular judgment? Is that the idea?

PHOEBUS: More or less. I am so constituted that I take part in nothing, but I am impelled nevertheless to comment on everything, and to render snap judgments broadside, along with intimate and amusing chatter. Of course. As for being gassed—well, it sometimes helps.

CONDUCTOR: So—Phoebus Apollo—let's get on with the show. That is to say, Phoebus the Disc Jockey. (*He bows to Phoebus, and Phoebus bows back.*) As I understand it, you are the emcee.

PHOEBUS: Always, Mr. Conductor.

CONDUCTOR: Very well. Have you jockeyed yourself into a position where you can give us a few *disky* insights?

PHOEBUS: Disky insights! Heh-heh. You are taking *my* lines, Mr. Conductor. Am I ready? Yes. But (*he raises a hand*)—is my engineer ready? (*Lowers hand on next word.*) *Ready.* Carry on, Mr. Producer. *Water! Hm*—!

(*Spot on Phoebus fades.*)

PRODUCER: What a subject! Where is the drama, the violence, the mystery, where is the *sex!* in water? "The low place, that all men dislike." Hah! On Broadway it would cost three hundred thousand just to open the doors. Three hundred thousand, and no mystery, no murder, no sex!

⟨*He begins to intone, in the style of a Hebrew chant for the dead, with the usual vocal ornaments, and accompanied by plucked strings.*⟩

Three hundred thou—sand— dol—lars— (*speak*) and no sex! ⟨*Intone.*⟩ Three hundred thou—sand— doll—

(*As he sustains* doll— *the second time, spot fades on him and picks up a slow parade of dolls, the Water Witches. The spot shows them only from the shoulders down; it carefully leaves their heads in darkness. The spot does not move. Dolls enter and exit.*) ⟨*Spot fades.*⟩

PRODUCER (*speaking gleefully*): Three hundred thousand doll—

⟨*While he is speaking, Surrogate Kithara propels itself down from left, beats out a delicate rhythm with sticks.*⟩

PRODUCER (*free*): What are you doing here? Back to the pit!

(*Surrogate Kithara recedes. Liking the miraculous result of his chant, Producer decides to try again.*)

PRODUCER ⟨*chanting*⟩: Three hundred thou—sand— doll—

(*Diamond Marimba advances upon Producer from right. It plays without regard for tempo.*)

PRODUCER (*speak*): Say, what is this? Get back to the pit! Back to the pit where you belong!

(*Diamond Marimba recedes.*)

PRODUCER ⟨*chanting*⟩: Three hundred thou—sand— doll—

(*Again spot fades on Producer, and another picks up the same parade of dolls. This is interrupted by an advance, generally down center, of all mobile instruments. All are playing. Bass Marimba and Kithara II especially loom large and menacing. Spot on Producer.*)
(*Spot on parade fades.*)

PRODUCER ⟨*speaking*⟩: Come, come! Back to the pit! Down to the pit!

(*Instruments advance; begin to play furiously.*)

PRODUCER: You disrupt me! I'm the producer! Get away!

(*Instruments hem him in.*)

PRODUCER: Don't hem me in! Help! I'm getting attacked! Help! They're assaulting me!

CHORUSES (*in dark rear*): Help—! Help—! Help—!

PRODUCER (*scream*): HE-E-E-E-ELP!

CHORUSES ⟨*singing mournfully*⟩: Succor! Succor! Succor!

PRODUCER (*despairingly*): Succor? All I want is help—!

(*Instruments in a crescendo of fury.*)

PRODUCER (*a long, soft moan, as he collapses on the floor*): He-e-e-e-e-e-e-e-elp!

⟨*Instantaneous darkness. Instruments stop playing and recede.*⟩

Third Prologue

WATER CRIERS: Wa—ter! Wa-ter! Wa-ter! Wa—ter!

(*Spot on Phoebus.*)

PHOEBUS: Well, I guess that disposes of the Producer. He's always a troublesome character. Now let's interview, haphazardly, a rough cross section of the population of our beloved city, Santa Mystiana. What is it *you* need most, right at this moment?

CHORUSES ⟨*from dark backstage*⟩: Succor! Succor! We need succor!

(*Spot picks up [a] young businessman, down right.*)

YOUNG BUSINESSMAN: I make swimsuits. Yeh, suits for swimming. That means water. But there ain't none! (*He raises his hands to heaven, looks upward, and sings.*) Wa—ter! Wa—ter!

(*Spot picks up a parade of dolls passing through the light, dressed in swimsuits. Heads in darkness.*)

YOUNG BUSINESSMAN: Well, who needs water?

(*Spot fades on young businessman, but remains on parade. Another spot picks up a young idler, down left. Spot on parade fades.*)

YOUNG IDLER (*staring at the fading parade*): A vision like that does things to my adrenal glands. And my adrenal glands make my mouth dry. (*He raises his hands to heaven, looks upward, and sings.*) Wa—ter! Wa—ter!

(*Spot fades. Picks up a college girl, down right.*)

COLLEGE GIRL: He said he loved me—he couldn't live without me. And now he's gone! I could *drown* myself! But how can I drown without *wa*—ter? (*She raises her hands to heaven, looks upward, and sings.*) Wa—ter! Wa—ter!

(*Spot fades, picks up a stout middle-aged secretary, down left.*)

MIDDLE-AGED SECRETARY: My complexion needs a mud bath. My complexion is cry—ing for a mud bath! But there is no mud! (*She raises her hands to heaven, looks upward, and sings.*) Wa—ter! Wa—ter!

(*Spot fades, picks up an elderly man with white hair, meticulously dressed, down right.*)

ELDERLY MAN (*disgustedly*): Whiskey and soda! Whiskey and soda! (*Plaintively.*) All I want is whiskey and *wa*—ter! (*He raises his hands to heaven, looks upward, and sings.*) Wa—ter! Wa—ter!

CHORUSES ⟨*in dark background*⟩:
        Help—! Help—! We need help—!
        Wa—ter! Wa—ter! We need— wa—ter!

(*Left foreground area lights up dimly, and the view through the picture window lights up brilliantly. Her Honor and the Board of Aldermen are conferring. The Ladies' Auxiliary of the Junior Dragons of Mystery is listening.*)

PHOEBUS: So much for the cross section. Now to the beating heart of dear old Santa Mystiana, our *honored* and beloved mayor, Her *Honor*, in her seat of *honor*, in Her *Honor*'s most *honor*able chambers. What's your particular bitch this evening, Your Honor?

HER HONOR: With our great international exposition opening barely *one breath* away, we have nothing but drought!

PHOEBUS: Clarence, sir, I wonder whether you—as president of the Santa Mystiana Board of Aldermen—would care to give us a brief amplification of Her Honor's statement?

CLARENCE (*mournfully*): Drought indeed!

PHOEBUS: Ah, brevity, brevity! It's the soul of something or other, but try not to break down, old fellow. I have a feeling that you are slated to be the straight man for this whole gone evening.

HER HONOR: And our *dear* sponsors. How they have worked! The Santa Mystiana Chamber of Commerce, the Betterment Association of Santa Mystiana, the Ladies' Auxiliary of the Junior Dragons of Mystery—

(*Pause, while the Ladies' Auxiliary bows.*)

CLARENCE: The Sweet-Dreams-Come-True Club, the Big-Plans-Are-Big-Actions Club—

FIRST ALDERMAN: The Santa Mystiana Chapter of Juvenile Delinquents Anonymous, the We-Are-For-You Club—

HER HONOR: And the Committee Against Obscene Literature Through the Mails.

SECOND ALDERMAN (*caught by surprise*): The males!

CLARENCE: Ah, yes! The males! (*He conducts the Aldermen.*)

ALDERMEN (*in unison*): Of— course!

(*On* of *they put their right hands at their waists, and on* course *they bow low.*)
(*The Ladies' Auxiliary, feeling that it is being slighted, immediately lines up for its cheer song.*)

LADIES' AUXILIARY ⟨*singing*⟩:
　　　　　The Ladies' Auxiliary!
　　　　　Dragons of Mystery!
　　　　　Junior! Junior!
　　　　　Rah! Rah! *Roo*-ha!

HER HONOR: Drought! Drought!

CLARENCE: And with visitors coming from strange and foreign places!

THIRD ALDERMAN: What will they see? Brown, dead hills, crisp as toast!

FOURTH ALDERMAN: Burned lawns, withered flowers!

FIFTH ALDERMAN: Business is ba-a-ad!

HER HONOR: And how we tried—tried—*tried* to avoid this calamity!

CLARENCE: Tried, indeed!

HER HONOR: Through long and gruelling effort we built the great big dam.

CLARENCE: Let me put it this way: the great big *beautiful* dam.

ALDERMEN and LADIES' AUXILIARY (*choral speech*): The great big beautiful Santa Mystiana Dam!

HER HONOR (*free*): Thank you. How *could* I have omitted that *most important* adjective. (*She looks into the distance, out the picture window.*) See what the great big beautiful Santa Mystiana Dam has produced! Ah—! ⟨*She begins to sing.*⟩ Santa Mystiana the beau—tiful— Jewel— of mystery—!

⟨*The Ladies' Auxiliary hums an obbligato.*⟩

CLARENCE (*interrupting*): Hm—. Excuse me. But the *reason* that you have called us here, Your Honor—. We must find some way out of this calamity, some succor!

CHORUSES: Succor! Succor!

FIFTH ALDERMAN: Business is ba-a-d!

CLARENCE: Yes, we know.

HER HONOR: Well, as you are aware, I have sent for Arthur. He makes rain, of which you are also aware, because I informed you.

CLARENCE: But where is he?

HER HONOR: I do not know. I have been awaiting the mails.

CLARENCE: The mails?

SECOND ALDERMAN: The males!

CLARENCE: Of course!

(*He conducts the Aldermen, and they all bow low, from the waist, in unison.*)

ALDERMEN: Of— course!

(*Aquarius enters left.*)
(*The Ladies' Auxiliary attempts to repeat its previous performance; lines up for its cheer.*)

LADIES' AUXILIARY: The Ladies Auxiliary!
Dragons of Mystery!

HER HONOR (*slightly irritated*): Yes, Yes. Rah, rah, *roo*-ha. Let us get on.

AQUARIUS: Good evenin'.

HER HONOR: Aquarius, your mother misnamed you. Well, what new calamity have you to report? Water bearer indeed! Bearer-of-evil-tidings would have been more appropriate.

AQUARIUS: Yes, ma'am.

HER HONOR: Well, go ahead. As supervisor of the Water Works, make your report. What *is* the latest gauge reading on the lake at Santa Mystiana Dam?

AQUARIUS: Lake! Lake, she says. A crusty puddle! There ain't no gauge readin'! Unless you can find somewhere below zero.

HER HONOR: Remember your name, Aquarius. Your speech is hardly classic.

AQUARIUS: No, maybe it ain't classic. But it's the truth. How classic can ya get?

CLARENCE (*in despair*): A crusty puddle!

AQUARIUS: Even the pollywogs is gaspin' for breath.

SIXTH ALDERMAN: Pollywogs don't breathe.

AQUARIUS: Even the pollywogs is dyin' from lack of water.

(*He moves to left exit.*)

SIXTH ALDERMAN: That's better.

AQUARIUS (*speaking to audience*): Classic! She wants *me* to be *classic!*

(*He remains at left exit; joins in singing the final line.*)

HER HONOR: *What* are we to do? We need *rain*—!

FIFTH ALDERMAN: Business is ba-a-ad!

SEVENTH ALDERMAN: Succor! Succor!

(*All raise their hands to heaven, look upward, and sing.*)

ALL: Water—! Water—!

(*Lights fade foreground; remain brilliant through the picture window.*)

Fourth Prologue

WATER CRIERS: Wa—ter! Wa—ter! Wa—ter! Wa—ter!

(*Lights come up dimly stage right, and turn beautifully luminous behind the mountainous horizon. The Jazz Band begins to play, in the pit. This is the* First Jazz Number. *Arthur mounts the stage and is followed by band.*)
(*Spot on Phoebus.*)

PHOEBUS: Arthur and his combo! It looks like they have a new gig. King Arthur and his swingin' Roundheads! They remind me of a bunch of bums. Where've you been, Arthur, on the bum?

(*Bass Marimba moves down left, playing a strong rhythm. Jazzmen begin to sing.*)
(*The voices marked* solo *are extremely important as solos. Voices added to solo voice may increase vocal volume, but they do nothing whatever to promote the intelligibility of sung words. Generally, they tend to destroy intelligibility. Fragmentation of words by multiple voices may have a good effect on very simple, repetitive words, or where the audience is already prepared to understand because of previous dialogue.*)

JAZZMEN: Misty, Misty, here we come!
　　　　　Always, always, on the bum—
　　　　　Always, always, sinking down—
　　　　　Sinking bums in a stinking town!
　　　　　Whoo, Whoo, Whoo, Whoo,
　　　　　Whoo, Whoo, Whoo whoo Whoo, Misty, Misty!

FIRST SOLO: We dig your dumps, your dives, your screaming joints—

SECOND SOLO: We dig your dopes, your jerks, your crazy squares—

THIRD SOLO: We dig your sluts, your slums, your shattered souls—

JAZZMEN: We dig dig dickety dickety dig!
        Misty, Misty, here we come!
        Always, always, on the bum—
        Always, always, sinking down—
        Sinking bums in a stinking town!
        Whoo, Whoo, Whoo, Whoo,
        Whoo, Whoo, Whoo whoo Whoo, Misty! Misty!

FIRST RECITATIVE: Misty, Misty, Crossroads of the Mists, we come—

SECOND RECITATIVE: Always, always on the make—

THIRD RECITATIVE: Vagrants, like the vagrant mists—

FOURTH RECITATIVE: Dreaming, dreaming, that we are here?

    ⟨Song ends.⟩
    (*Bass Marimba retires.*)

ARTHUR (*holding hands toward Santa Mystiana*): Here!

FIRST JAZZMAN: Yeh, and like somebody said, it's probably a dream.

SECOND JAZZMAN: A dream roughly two weeks late. At least, that's
how long I've been hungry.

ARTHUR: *I* know. It's *my* fault. But what was I to do? I was on my
way to Misty when this weird chick stopped me.

THIRD JAZZMAN: You mean Wanda?

ARTHUR (*annoyed*): *Yes*, Wanda.

FOURTH JAZZMAN (*derisively*): A chick?

ARTHUR: It's just a term. Anyway, below the neck she really *is* a
chick.

JAZZMEN ⟨*singing*⟩:
        Wanda, Wanda! Woo woo woo woo
        Below the neck she really is a ⟨*long* a⟩ *chick.*
        M— delightful! Dee—lightful!

ARTHUR: Well, let me continue. She said she was looking for water.
Professionally, that is. And when she found out who *I* was, she
said, "Let's don't compete. Let's cooperate!" What could I do?
Except pick her up?

FIFTH JAZZMAN: And all her gang?

ARTHUR: We need help, don't we? Maybe she and her gang can help. Did you ever see a drier country than this? Did you ever see a place that calls for more heroic rainmaking?

SIXTH JAZZMAN: And what could help a hero more than a few loose heroines?

(*Diamond Marimba moves down.*)

SEVENTH JAZZMAN: Oh, what could help him more? (*To Diamond Marimba.*) What do you say?

⟨DIAMOND MARIMBA: (*Plays approvingly.*)

(*This is a Diamond Marimba solo. The instrument moves back and forth, to and fro, while being played, in a casual kind of dance.*)⟩

JAZZMEN ⟨*singing*⟩: Oh, what could he do— Oh, what could he do—? but pick her up?

SOLO: He met her— at the water— tank—
He met her— where the witches— meet—
He met her— at the witching hour—

JAZZMEN: Oh, what could he do— Oh, what could he do—? but pick her up?

(*The band improvises on this tune—Second Jazz Number. At the end it slowly exits, right.*)
(*Lights fade in foreground, remain brilliant beyond the horizon.*)

Fifth Prologue

WATER CRIERS: Wa—ter! Wa—ter! Wa—ter!

(*Lights come up dimly in Her Honor's chambers. She, the Aldermen, and the Ladies' Auxiliary are in the positions last seen. Spot on Phoebus.*)

PHOEBUS: Did anyone ever hear of Ruanda Urundi? I think it's down there in Africa somewhere. Where the gorillas live, maybe? Now, *why* did I mention Ruanda Urundi? (*He attempts to sing.*) Let's say nothing of Ruanda U-run-di!

HER HONOR: With people coming to our great international exposition from everywhere—from Cambodia, Estonia, Ethiopia, Nova Scotia, Algeria, Nigeria, Liberia, Rumania, Lithuania, Tasmania, Ukrainia, and Haiti, and Turkey, and Bali—

CLARENCE ⟨*interrupting*⟩: To say nothing of Ruanda Urun—di!

(*He conducts Choruses on the line below.*)

CHORUSES ⟨*singing*⟩: To say nothing of Ruanda Urun—di!

CLARENCE: And people from Pakistan, Turkestan, Baluchistan, Afghanistan, Champaignistan, Urbanistan—

FIRST ALDERMAN ⟨*interrupting*⟩: To say nothing of Ruanda Urun—di!

(*He conducts Choruses on the line below.*)

CHORUSES (*singing*): To say nothing of Ruanda Urun—di!

PHOEBUS: From strange and foreign places.

SECOND ALDERMAN (*to Phoebus*): From outer space?

THIRD ALDERMAN (*to Second Alderman*): Even from Alabama.

PHOEBUS: Strange and foreign.

HER HONOR: With all these strange and foreign people coming to our city from strange and foreign places, we cannot spare any effort to make the town and country beautiful. Nor can we let our sponsors down. Our wonderful sponsors! The Santa Mystiana Chamber of Commerce, the Betterment Association of Santa Mystiana, The Ladies' Auxiliary of the Junior Dragons of Mystery—

(*The Ladies' Auxiliary, instead of bowing, launches suddenly into its cheer.*)

LADIES' AUXILIARY: The Ladies' Auxiliary!
                   Dragons of Mystery!
                   Junior! Junior!
                   Rah! Rah! *Roo*-ha!

CLARENCE (*glaring balefully at the Ladies' Auxiliary*): And—the Sweet-Dreams-Come-True Club, the Big-Plans-Are-Big-Actions Club—

FIRST ALDERMAN: The Santa Mystiana Chapter of Juvenile Delinquents Anonymous, the We-Are-For-You Club—

HER HONOR: And the Committee Against Obscene Literature Through—*the*—*Mails.*

(*Her Honor spaces* the mails *very deliberately. On* the *right hands of Aldermen go to their waists, and on* mails, *they have reached the low point of their bow.*)

Scene from 1962 University of Illinois production of *Water! Water!* Fifth Prologue. Ladies' Auxiliary, Clarence, Her Honor, Aldermen. Photograph by Danlee Mitchell.

HER HONOR (*disgustedly*): Oh, knock it off!

(*Arthur is seen slinking across stage from right. He cups his ear at the partition.*)

HER HONOR: The man we have to find is Arthur. He has a tremendous reputation. Reportedly, he brought rain to a country so dry that the rabbits had forgotten how to drink.

CHORUSES (*choral speech*): Forgotten how to drink? Horrible!

HER HONOR: I am expecting him at any moment. I have learned that he is already on his way—with his jazz band.

CLARENCE: Jazz band!

HER HONOR: That's the way he makes rain. With jazz.

CLARENCE (*recoiling*): Jazz!

CHORUSES (*physically revolted, they move backward and shudder in unison*): Jazz!

HER HONOR: Oh, jazz schmazz! We want rain, don't we?

FIFTH ALDERMAN: Business is ba-a-ad!

CLARENCE: Oh, shut up! We know it's bad.

FIRST ALDERMAN: Furthermore, you sound like a sick sheep.

HER HONOR: Why do we care how he makes rain? The question is, what incentive do we offer? How much?

CLARENCE: We must demand a guarantee. Let me put it this way: no tickee, no laundly—no rainee, no monee.

HER HONOR: I suggest that we put a ceiling of ten thousand dollars per inch on his fee. Of course, I'll try to get him for less. (*She suddenly recoils.*) Jazz! Ugh—!

(*Arthur is seen slinking away. Exits right.*)

CHORUSES: Yes, get him for less! Yes, get him for less! Jazz! Ugh—!

HER HONOR: Do I hear the motion?

CLARENCE: I submit the motion.

FIRST ALDERMAN: Second.

HER HONOR: Carried. Meeting adjourned.

(*Lights dim in foreground.*)

PHOEBUS: Just like that! Meeting adjourned! (*Hums.*) La-dies' Aux-il-iar-y! Dragons of Mys-ter-y! (*Stops humming.*) The mystery seems to be, where *are* they? Them-there dragon husbands 've been draggin' their heels! Heh-heh. Or are these ladies the *widows* of dragons? Self-made widows, maybe? The Lady Dragon-Killers! Whew—!

Sixth Prologue

WATER CRIERS: Wa—ter! Wa—ter! Wa—ter! Wa—ter!

PHOEBUS (*singing*): Oh, what could he do? Oh, what could he do? but pick her up! (*Stops singing.*) Wanda, Wanda! Wait'll you see her! Wanda and all her gang. I think I'd pick them up too, as a public service. I'd pick them up and cart them off to the nearest Laughing Academy.

(*Lights up dimly stage right. Wanda and the Chorus of Passionate Ancient Water Witches enter immediately, and begin their water-witching dance. Each carries a forked stick, and as the tempo and excitement of their search for water increase, the forked sticks begin to tremble violently. The Witches sing—or shout—and dance.*)

WITCHES (*may be spoken or shouted rhythmically; it need not be sung*):
    Witch! Witch! Witch! Witch, Witch, Witch,
      Witch— for water
    Woo Woo woo woo woo woo
    Woo Woo woo woo woo woo
    Woo woo woo woo woo woo for water

    Witch— for water
    Woo Woo woo woo woo woo
    Woo Woo woo woo woo woo
    Woo woo woo woo woo woo for water

⟨*Each finds an exact spot on the stage where she stands, vibrating both her forked stick and her entire body. Near the end of the number the Witches turn their sticks toward heaven and shout gleefully. All mobile instruments participate.*⟩

WITCHES: Ee—ow— K-moo— K-ma—o— K-wee—ow!
          K-moo— K-ma—o— K-wee—ow!

⟨*Music subsides somewhat, but dancing and percussive beat continue—music is very soft. Lights come up partially stage right. Aldermen stick heads around the partition, one at a time. Lights remain constant stage right.*⟩

CLARENCE (*peering around partition*): Woo woo! (*To himself.*) Try to get hold of yourself boy! (*To Aldermen.*) I wouldn't call it particularly original.

FIRST ALDERMAN (*peering*): Woo woo! (*To himself.*) Watch it, watch it! (*To Aldermen.*) Plenty weird.

SECOND ALDERMAN (*peering*): Woo woo! (*To himself.*) Careful! An election's coming up. (*To Aldermen.*) Ha ha. Awful.

THIRD ALDERMAN (*peering*): Woo woo! (*To himself.*) Speak for the record! (*To Aldermen.*) Pretty primitive.

FOURTH ALDERMAN (*peering*): Woo woo! (*To himself.*) The Ladies' Auxiliary was never like this! (*To Aldermen.*) Bad taste.

FIFTH ALDERMAN (*peering*): Woo woo! (*To himself.*) Down, down, boy! (*To Aldermen.*) If you ask me, it's academic.

SIXTH ALDERMAN (*peering*): Woo woo! (*To Aldermen.*) It does *not* remind me of *Humoresque.*

(*Music ends. Aldermen retire from the partition. Witches stop dancing.*)

WANDA (*peering around partition*): You don't like our music?

CLARENCE (*rolling eyes toward Aldermen*): No!

FIRST WITCH (*peering*): Or our dancing?

FIRST ALDERMAN (*rolling eyes ditto*): No! No!

SECOND WITCH (*peering*): Or our costumes?

SECOND ALDERMAN (*rolling eyes*): No! No! No!

THIRD WITCH (*peering*): Or the way we vibrate our bodies?

THIRD ALDERMAN (*rolling eyes*): No! No! No! No!

FOURTH WITCH (*peering*): Well, then, do you *like* our profession?

FOURTH ALDERMAN (*rolling eyes*): Your profession? (*With horror.*) No! No! No! No! No!

(*Aldermen are now in a rough circle, facing each other.*)
⟨*Exit Witches left.*⟩

CLARENCE: *No* tax increase!

FIRST ALDERMAN: *No* zoning revisions!

SECOND ALDERMAN: *No* aspersions on motherhood!

THIRD ALDERMAN: *No* un-Santa Mystiana activities!

FOURTH ALDERMAN: *No* more than twelve tones to the octave!

FIFTH ALDERMAN: *No* nakedness!

SIXTH ALDERMAN: *No* indecency!

(*Percussive beat begins.*)

CLARENCE: *No*— sin!

⟨*The Aldermen begin a four-part fugue, sung entirely on the word*
no. *If four competent males cannot be found for this section, two
of the parts may be taken by members of the Ladies' Auxiliary.*⟩

ALDERMEN: No no no no no [etc.]

(*Mobile instruments move down and mimic—or tease—Aldermen.*)

ALDERMEN: No no no no no—

⟨INSTRUMENTS: (*Mimic Aldermen.*)⟩

ALDERMEN: No no!

⟨INSTRUMENTS: (*Mimic Aldermen.*)⟩

ALDERMEN: No!

⟨INSTRUMENTS: (*Mimic.*)⟩

ALDERMEN ⟨*bringing polyphony to a final cadence*⟩: No no no no no
[etc.] No— no!

(*Witches enter, now wearing high-heeled slippers.*)

CLARENCE (*speak*): No— striptease!

ALDERMEN (*speak*): No— striptease!

FIRST ALDERMAN: No— burlesque!

ALDERMEN: No— burlesque!

WITCHES: Boo!

(*Aldermen jump on* Boo!)
(*Lights dim left. Wanda starts off, right.*)

WANDA: Later! Date with Arthur! Eeeeeeeeeeeeeeee! (*She squeals, and exits right.*)

ARTHUR (*offstage*): Wanda!

(*The Chorus of Witches goes into a burlesque routine on the music that follows. Some of the Jazzmen play, but most of them sing in the Chorus. This is the first number in which jazz instrumentation may be added.*)

JAZZ SOLO:
    Oh, what could he do— Oh, what could be do—? but
       pick her up—?
    He met her at the water— tank—
    He met her where the witches— meet—
    He met her at the witching hour—
    Oh, what could he do— Oh, what could he do— but
       pick her up?

(*Wanda enters right.*)

JAZZMEN (*shout*):
    Wanda, the Water Witch! Wan—da Wanda!
    Woo woo woo woo Wanda!
    M— delightful! Dee—lightful!
    Wanda brings water— oceans of water—
    And beneath the waves— she really is a (*long* a) doll—
    Below the neck— she really is a chick.

JAZZ SOLO:
    Picture Wanda at the well—
    Wanda at the river—
    Wanda at the water works—
    Bring your wand, Wanda, and make the dry lands
       bloom—
    Here's the spot, Wanda! Vi—brate—!
    Vi—brate—!
    Here's the way, Wanda! Sha-ha-ha-hake! Sha-ha-ha-hake!

JAZZMEN (*shout*):
    Wanda, the Water Witch! Wan—da Wanda!
    Woo woo woo woo Wanda!
    M— delightful! Dee—lightful!

Wanda brings water— oceans of water—
And beneath the waves— she really is *a (long* a) doll—
Below the neck— she really is *a* chick.
Wan—da Wanda! Woo woo woo woo Wanda!
M— delightful! Dee—lightful! (*Suddenly soft and slow.*) Dee—
lightful!

(*Lights in foreground dim. Horizon and city lights remain brilliant.
Jazzmen and Witches exeunt.*)

Seventh Prologue

WATER CRIERS: Wa—ter! Wa—ter! Wa—ter! Wa—ter!

(*Spot on Phoebus.*)

PHOEBUS: Rain through jazz? I've heard a little poetry through jazz.
A little of that and you're *through* with both of 'em. Some swingin'
rain, man! That's what we need. Some swingin' rain! Now, *who—*
exactly—are *you?*

(*Lights come up dimly, both foregrounds. Arthur, carrying horn,
enters right, Her Honor left, simultaneously. They walk to the
invisible center line and stop. The Jazz Band enters right, behind
Arthur, but stays at right entrance. Aldermen and Ladies' Auxiliary enter left, behind Her Honor, but stay at left entrance.*)

HER HONOR: Who are you?

ARTHUR: Arthur.

HER HONOR: I thought so. But *who,* exactly?

ARTHUR: The God of Rain.

HER HONOR: Indeed! Where are you from?

ARTHUR: Up north. You know, the mountains. All gods come from
the mountains.

HER HONOR: Why, you look like a college boy!

ARTHUR: All gods are—. No, I take that back.

HER HONOR: You begin to sound like an idiot.

ARTHUR: All idiots are—

HER HONOR: If you're a rain god, why do you carry *that* thing? (*She
points to horn.*)

ARTHUR: How do you think the gods get— (*shakes a hip*) fertilized? Nothing can happen unless something gets— (*shakes a hip*) fertilized.

HER HONOR: And this— (*shakes a hip*) fertilizes you?

ARTHUR: Without this I am nothing. With it I am everything.

HER HONOR: Especially a rain god.

ARTHUR: Right.

HER HONOR: Very well, then. Go ahead. Make some rain.

ARTHUR: Look. Are we going to start *making* things right off? I haven't even had time to look over the burg.

HER HONOR: The *burg!* It's your own fault. I sent for you weeks ago. What took you so long?

ARTHUR: Well, Your Honor, it was this way. I was headed for Misty when I ran across this chick—

HER HONOR (*aghast*): *What* did you say?

ARTHUR: This chick. She was at the Water Works.

HER HONOR: *What* did you *say?*

ARTHUR: She's a witch. Water attracts her.

HER HONOR: I'm not talking about *her.* What *name* did you use for our beloved city?

ARTHUR: Oh. Misty.

HER HONOR: *Anyone* who uses *that name* in my presence is subject to a one hundred dollar fine! It shall be deducted from your fee.

(*Surrogate Kithara, later Diamond Marimba, move downstage, playing softly.*)

ARTHUR: My fee. Okay, at least we're getting some place. (*He looks at the audience.*) The *hazards* of rainmaking!

HER HONOR: What do you propose?

ARTHUR: Well, Wanda and I together—

HER HONOR: Wanda!

ARTHUR: Yes, Wanda.

HER HONOR: You called her a chick.

ARTHUR: Oh, it's just a *term*.

(*Wanda rushes onstage with her forked stick, right, and dances wildly.*)

JAZZMEN ⟨*singing*⟩:
Wan—da, Wanda! Woo woo woo woo
Below the neck—she really is *a*—

(*Music stops abruptly. Mobile instruments retire.*)

ARTHUR (*in a loud whisper, turning on Jazzmen*): Sh—! What're you trying to do, queer this gig?

(*He turns back. Wanda exits quickly.*)

JAZZMEN (*whispering, turning backs on Arthur, in admiration of Wanda*): Too— much!

ARTHUR: Excuse me, ma'am.

HER HONOR: We were discussing Wanda.

⟨*Mobile instruments begin incidental music, softly.*⟩

ARTHUR: Sure. She's my public relations counsellor. I just appointed her. As I said, she digs water, and she has a whole gang of witches with her. They shake down. We shake up. But we all shake-luck. Ha-ha. Get it?

CLARENCE: Shake-luck?

HER HONOR: You should try to be *au courant*, Clarence. He means shake-luck.

CLARENCE: Shake-luck. Thank you. It's *very* clear.

ARTHUR: We're crazy about water. It absolutely lootches us.

(*Her Honor looks at Clarence.*)

HER HONOR: I'll explain later, Clarence.

ARTHUR: Wanda's really a big help. She invokes spirits that haven't been around in at least a couple of centuries.

(*Irritated, Her Honor turns on Conductor. Incidental music ends with the next line.*)

HER HONOR: Stop that silly music! It doesn't do a *thing* for me. It fails to underline my thoughts.

CONDUCTOR: Sorry. Let's try again.

(*Music begins again, on the theme of* Santa Mystiana the Beautiful.)

HER HONOR: *Much* better. Thanks for your cooperation.

CONDUCTOR: Not at all.

⟨*Music continues.*⟩

HER HONOR: Isn't it beautiful? It's *my* melody.

⟨*She begins to sing* Santa Mystiana the Beautiful, *and the Conductor joins in, singing with her. Suddenly she stops, advances toward the Conductor. Music stops.*⟩

HER HONOR: Say, whose number is this, anyway?

(*Pause.*)

CONDUCTOR: I was only trying to help.

HER HONOR (*sweetly*): Oh, (*pause*) thank you!

(*Arthur begins to play his horn, the Conductor turns toward audience, and he and Her Honor sing the duet below.*)

HER HONOR and CONDUCTOR (*singing*):
Santa Mystiana, the beautiful— jewel of mystery—
We love thy light, so bright in beauteous night—
We love thine urns, thy turns, thy trail—ing ferns—
We thank— thee— Soul of mystery— for thy sign—
It tells us, won—drous sight, that we— are— thine—
Santa Mystiana, the beautiful—
Oh, Santa Mystia—na— mine—!

CLARENCE (*advancing from left to center*): All this is very touching, but *what* about the arrangements? (*Whispering.*) What about the ten thousand per inch?

ALDERMEN and LADIES' AUXILIARY: Get him for less! Jazz! Ugh—!

HER HONOR: Enough of this palaver! Let us get to the question at hand: *rain*.

ARTHUR: That suits me. But first of all, doesn't a god have to be propitiated?

HER HONOR: Propitiate you!

LEFT CHORUSES ⟨*choral speech*⟩: Propitiate him!

ARTHUR: That's the way it's always been.

JAZZMEN ⟨*choral speech*⟩: Don't give an inch! Make her propitiate!

ARTHUR: Well, go ahead. Propitiate me.

HER HONOR: How absurd can you get?

ARTHUR: Make a little sacrifice.

HER HONOR (*sarcastically*): Yes, of course! A sacrifice.

ARTHUR: Some bread. Just a little bread.

HER HONOR: How much *bread* do you want?

> (*At this point Arthur begins to play his horn, unaccompanied. This does not upset Her Honor in the least. Although she does not particularly care for the dialect, she understands it perfectly.*)

ARTHUR: (*Improvises.*)

HER HONOR: Ten thousand dollars per inch! Outrageous! (*She turns to Aldermen.*) How could *he* know? Maybe he *is* a god!

> (*Surrogate Kithara advances on Her Honor, playing.*)

HER HONOR: Now, what do *you* want?

SURROGATE KITHARA: (*Plays and stops.*)

HER HONOR: Oh, very well! Dig wherever you like.

ARTHUR and SURROGATE KITHARA: (*They improvise.*)

HER HONOR: Do you *all* have to use such bad English? Has eye-ther of you ever been—

ARTHUR: *Ee*-ther.

HER HONOR (*after hesitation*): *Eye*-ther.

ARTHUR: *Ee*-ther.

HER HONOR (*with a very superior air*): *Nye*-ther of you uses good English.

ARTHUR: *Nee*-ther.

HER HONOR: Nyether! Nyether! Nyether! Nyether! Nye—ther!

> ⟨*This leads into a rhythmic pattern, and a song—a duet—follows, by Her Honor and Arthur. Surrogate Kithara accompanies.*⟩

HER HONOR and ARTHUR [*alternating*]:
  Eether, Eyether, Neether, Nyether,
  Eether, Eyether, Neether, Nyether,
  Ee—ther—, Eye—ther—, Nee—ther—, Nye—ther—
  Ee—ther—, Eye—ther—, Nee—ther—, Nye—ther—

ARTHUR: *Ver-y* nice! You now have my permission to say *eye*-ther.

HER HONOR: Thank you. (*She ponders.*) Tell you what. I'll make you a geometrical proposition.

ARTHUR: Yes, please. *Do* propose.

HER HONOR (*to herself*): No, it's too complex. (*To Arthur.*) That is to say, an *arithmetical* proposition. (*She now speaks very slowly, deliberately.*) The city of Santa Mystiana will pay you ten thousand dollars per inch of rain, to be prorated for any fractional part thereof, registered at our weather bureau station within the next week, starting today. But—and listen closely—you may *not* earn *more* than one inch worth. That is, ten thousand dollars. And—one hundred dollars will be deducted. Of course.

ARTHUR: Withholding tax?

HER HONOR (*rising inflection*): Certainly not!

ARTHUR: Oh, I get it. Because I said *Misty*.

HER HONOR: *Two* hundred!

ARTHUR: Okay, okay!

  (*Arthur begins to play his horn, in long, sweet, sweeping phrases. He turns toward right exit.*)

JAZZMEN (*singing in wondrous whispers*): Ten thousand dollars per inch! (*Half whistle—down.*) Whoo—! But only one inch worth!

FIRST JAZZMAN: Cheats!

SECOND JAZZMAN: Tricksters!

THIRD JAZZMAN: We'll show 'em!

  (*Arthur and Jazzmen exeunt.*)

ALDERMEN and LADIES' AUXILIARY (*singing in whispers*): Bravo! Your Honor! Bravo! Your Honor! Jazz! Ugh—!

  (*Her Honor, Aldermen, and Ladies' Auxiliary exeunt. Lights dim in both foregrounds. Backgrounds remain luminous. Spot on Phoebus.*)

PHOEBUS (*contemptuously*): Bravo, bravo, bravo. Bravo to the rain-seekers, bravo to the rainmakers. (*He sings.*) Ee—ther—, eye—ther—. (*Speaks.*) Personally, I'll take (*sings*) nee—ther—, nye—ther—. What a drag! All this yakety-yak just to try and find a little recreation. Heh-heh. What is the purpose of life in this world? Why, *re*-creation, of course!

(*Spot fades. Phoebus exits, laughing hysterically.*)

Eighth Prologue

WATER CRIERS: Wa—ter! Wa—ter! Wa—ter! Wa—ter!

(*Spot on Phoebus.*)

PHOEBUS: From strange and foreign places.

(*He announces the* First Foreign Routine. *These all occur stage right. Comedy routines alternate, and occur stage left.*)

First Foreign Routine

(*Spot on a female singer, left, obviously a visitor to the exposition, and on Phoebus.*)

SINGER ⟨*singing in highly disjointed intervals and arbitrarily sustained syllables*⟩: Spo—le—to— ah!

PHOEBUS: From strange and foreign places! (*He throws up his hands in resignation.*) Now, where are you from?

SINGER ⟨*repeating exactly what she did before*⟩: Spo—le—to—!

PHOEBUS: Oh, you really mean it! *Yes!* Spoleto! Now I remember. Where they do that (*he sings*) ho-ho-he-he-ha-ha-opera, isn't it? *Ha-ha*-opera! Pretty good!

⟨*Kithara II moves downstage and accompanies Singer in the following passage.*⟩

SINGER (*speaking*): It is *not* ho-ho-he-he-ha-ha-opera. It is ⟨*she sings, in the same disjointed intervals*⟩ Ho—ho—hee—hee— ⟨*She is obviously taking two parts of a sung dialogue.*⟩ Do— you— love— me—? Love— you— How— can I not—? Then kiss— me—! Kiss— you—? ⟨*Now staccato.*⟩ Ha, ha, ha, Ha—! How— dare— you—! ⟨*Singer now speaks.*⟩ It is *that* kind of opera.

PHOEBUS: How stupid of me! You mean *con-TEMP-o-rar-y!*

SINGER (*to Phoebus*): You *are*— a doll! (*To Kithara*.) And *you*— *too*—!

KITHARA: ⟨*Long glide.*⟩

(*Kithara retires. Lights dim left, come up right.*)

PHOEBUS: From strange and foreign places.

(*He announces* Second Foreign Routine.)

Second Foreign Routine

(*Spot on Phoebus.*)

PHOEBUS: From strange and foreign places.

(*Spot on middle-aged couple, obviously man and wife, obviously American, obviously visitors to the exposition.*)

WIFE: Isn't it thrilling! Santa Mystiana, City of Mystery!

HUSBAND (*to Phoebus*): You know, we've never seen a beatnik. And we've been reading about them for so long.

PHOEBUS: Ah, yes. A great tourist attraction. Believe me, Santa Mystiana has its share.

HUSBAND: I hope you can point one out.

PHOEBUS: Ah, we're in luck! There's a female beatnik, right over there.

HUSBAND: What's she doing?

PHOEBUS: Beating, I think.

WIFE: Oh, do you think she'd *mind* if we watched her *beat*?

(*Spot shifts to stereotype female beatnik; black stockings, black sloppy sweater, long, stringy black hair. Surrogate Kithara is directly behind her, and seems to be motivating her gums, which beat in slow, precise rhythm. Spot back to couple and Phoebus.*)

WIFE: Isn't it thrilling! I understand that Santa Mystiana is *full* of painters. I wish we could *see* a painter!

PHOEBUS: Here's one, right here.

HUSBAND: What's he doing?

PHOEBUS: Eating, I think.

WIFE: Oh, do you think he'd *mind* if we watched him *eat?*

(*Spot shifts quickly to stereotype artist, also stage left, with easel and brush. Surrogate Kithara is directly behind him, and motivates his jaws, in slow, rhythmic jerks. Spot on Phoebus.*)

PHOEBUS: From strange and foreign places.

(*He announces* Third Foreign Routine.)

Third Foreign Routine

PHOEBUS: From strange and foreign places.

(*Spot is again on Phoebus, and on a visitor, a teenage girl with a lush southern accent.*)

VISITOR: Santa Mystiana, City of Mystery! Hi, everybody!

⟨*Clarinet plays the first bar of* Yankee Doodle, *quite fast, and repeats it ad infinitum.*⟩

PHOEBUS: Did you bring *that* (*points to clarinet*) with you?

VISITOR: Why, that's my mockingbird!

PHOEBUS: Your mockingbird?

VISITOR: Yes, honey, and doesn't he sound beautiful? He's from *my* home, Alabama.

PHOEBUS: But he's singing *Yankee Doodle!*

CHORUSES (*choral speech from dark background*): A mockingbird from Alabama singing *Yankee Doodle?*

VISITOR: Oh, sure, honey. But he only learned the *first measure.* He *rebelled* after the first measure. Therefore, he's a *rebel.* Don't you love him?

⟨*Violins take up the first measure of* Yankee Doodle, *in unison or octaves, and repeat it and repeat it. Visitor, Conductor, and Choruses sing* Alabama, Dear Old Alabama *above the fast repetitious figure. Phoebus dances in the spot.*⟩

VISITOR (*to Phoebus*): I think you're darling!

Ninth Prologue

WATER CRIERS: Wa—ter! Wa—ter! Wa—ter! Wa—ter!

(*Spot stage right. Arthur and Wanda are talking.*)

ARTHUR: Her Honor isn't so bad.

(*Wanda shrugs, says nothing.*)

ARTHUR: She's kind of a half-swinging square. But that Clarence! He louses me.

WANDA: Now, Arthur. I think Clarence is *real* lovable.

(*Spot moves suddenly stage left. Her Honor and Clarence are talking.*)

HER HONOR: Arthur intrigues me, in a vulgar sort of way, but *that woman*—I can speak of her only in jest!

CLARENCE: Now, Your Honor, Wanda isn't so bad. Why, below the neck she really *is*—

HER HONOR: Clar-ENCE!

CLARENCE: Well, let me put it this way—

HER HONOR: Oh, put it some other way!

(*Spot moves suddenly stage right.*)

ARTHUR: They're really laughable, when you come right down to it. And you've got to get your funny kicks somewhere.

WANDA: Yes, we need them, don't we. For comedy relief.

ARTHUR: They're squares, yokels, profiteers, exploiters. Still, we need them.

WANDA: For comedy relief.

ARTHUR: Right.

(*Arthur and Wanda exeunt. Spot moves stage left.*)

HER HONOR: How did we ever get mixed up with such trash? Oh, well. The tourists ogle them, seek out their bars, read feature-length articles about them in national magazines, and so on and so on. They are one of Santa Mystiana's main attractions. Amusing, isn't it, Clarence?

CLARENCE: Heh-heh. Indeed, Your Honor. Let me put it this way: they provide comedy relief.

HER HONOR: They're beats, loafers, barflies, parasites. Still, we need them.

CLARENCE: For comedy relief.

HER HONOR: Oh, have it your way.

(*Her Honor and Clarence exeunt. Foreground stage right brightens normally. Witches and Jazzmen are on. The following passages are shouted on beats and sung. Individuals are simply designated Right or Left, and when they are throwing epithets they direct them to the opposite part of the stage. In the refrains they sing and dance. Jazzmen sing but do not play.*)

RIGHT ONE (*speak*): They're squares, they're yokels!

RIGHT TWO: Hypocrites, exploiters!

RIGHT THREE: They're boors, they're grafters!

RIGHT FOUR: Tricksters, cheaters!

RIGHT CHORUSES:
> But we need them, and they need us,
> We really love— each other.

(*Foreground dims right, comes up left. Aldermen and Ladies' Auxiliary are on.*)

LEFT ONE (*speak*): They're beats, they're loafers!

LEFT TWO: Barflies, parasites!

LEFT THREE: They're bums, they're delinquents!

LEFT FOUR: Anarchists, scum!

LEFT CHORUSES:
> But we need them, and they need us,
> We really love— each other.

(*This Prologue is a good spot in which to introduce "battles," and at this point particularly a Chinese sham battle, spotted, center stage. Or—a farcical fencing duel.*)
(*Castor and Pollux are at the partition. In the following sequence, when it accompanies Left Whine it moves left; when it accompanies Right Whine it moves right.*)
(*Foreground comes up right.*)

RIGHT FIVE (*speak*): They get all the dolls, make all the rules.

RIGHT SIX: They get all the breaks, have all the bread.

(*Foreground comes up left. Both sides stay lit now, till end of Prologue.*)

LEFT CHORUSES:
            Whine, Whine, Whine, Whine, Whine,
            In forty-three whines— to the octave!

LEFT FIVE: They get all the attention, all the publicity.

LEFT SIX: They get all the freedom, have all the fun.

RIGHT CHORUSES:
            Yak, yak, yak, yak, yak,
            In forty-three yaks— to the octave.

RIGHT SEVEN (*speak*): They have the beautiful pads, all the country estates.

RIGHT EIGHT: They have the solvent mamas, all the big connections.

LEFT CHORUSES:
            Yak, yak, yak, yak, yak,
            In forty-three yaks— to the octave.

LEFT SEVEN: They have the willing women, all the wild parties.

LEFT EIGHT: They have the easy living, all the public glory.

BOTH CHORUSES:
            Whine, Whine, Whine, Whine, Whine,
            In forty-three whines— to the octave!

(*At this point one of the saxophone players and the Surrogate Kithara indulge in a sham battle, spotted, center stage. They try to outdo each other in virtuoso passages. Finally, there is a kind of explosive dialogue between them.*)
(*Surrogate Kithara pulls out a New Year's horn that makes a loud* TOOT *and explodes a snake in the face of the saxophone.*)

SAXOPHONE (*retiring*): Touché.

(*Surrogate Kithara also retires.*)
⟨*In the following passage Right and Left epithets are shouted simultaneously.*⟩

RIGHT ONE: They're squares, they're yokels!
LEFT ONE: They're beats,   they're loafers!

RIGHT TWO: Hypocrites, exploiters!

LEFT TWO: Barflies,   parasites!

RIGHT THREE: They're boors, they're grafters!

LEFT THREE: They're bums, they're anarchists!

RIGHT FOUR: Tricksters, cheaters!

LEFT FOUR: Anarchists, scum!

ALL CHORUSES: But we need them, and they need us,
            We really do— we really do—
            We really love— each other.

RIGHT FIVE (*speak*): I love you!

LEFT FIVE: And I love you too!

RIGHT SIX: And I love you too. No, not you, You!

LEFT SIX: And I— do— love— you!

(*Phoebus enters left.*)

PHOEBUS: Oh, cut it, cut it!

(*Sudden silence and blackout, both foregrounds.*)

This is getting too corny even for me. (*Exits.*)

Tenth Prologue

WATER CRIERS: Wa—ter! Wa—ter! Wa—ter! Wa—ter!

(*Lights come up foreground stage right. A terraced, round platform is in its exact center. Arthur is on the pinnacle, alone. Below him in a circle are three or four Jazzmen. Below them in a larger circle are other Jazzmen. Finally, there is a circle on the floor. Thus, we have a hillock of Jazzmen, which should create a semidark silhouette against the luminous sky.*)

FIRST JAZZMAN: Cheats!

SECOND JAZZMAN: Tricksters!

THIRD JAZZMAN: We'll show 'em!

(*Arthur holds up his hands to quiet the protests.*)

ARTHUR: Like—

FOURTH JAZZMAN: Like like—

FIFTH JAZZMAN: Like like like—

SIXTH JAZZMAN: Like golden!

SEVENTH JAZZMAN: Like golden golden golden golden—

ARTHUR: Rain—!

> (Third Jazz Number *begins on the word* Rain *or immediately after, but continues for only a few beats before Conductor waves his hands, then taps something with his baton.*)

CONDUCTOR: Wait a minute! *Just* a minute. If you'd stick to the beat we'd have a better chance of getting some *rain.* That's what we want, isn't it? That's what we're here for, isn't it? How can you get rain without rhythm?

JAZZMEN (*choral speech*): Rain without rhythm? Neh—*ver!*

CONDUCTOR: Very well. Now, once more. *From the top.*

> (*Lights fade. Water music begins again.*)

WATER CRIERS: Wa—ter! Wa—ter! Wa—ter! Wa—ter!

> (*Lights come up foreground left.*)

FIRST JAZZMAN: Cheats!

SECOND JAZZMAN: Tricksters!

THIRD JAZZMAN: We'll show 'em!

> (*Arthur holds up his hands to quiet the protest.*)

ARTHUR: Like—

FOURTH JAZZMAN: Like like—

FIFTH JAZZMAN: Like like like—

SIXTH JAZZMAN: Like golden!

SEVENTH JAZZMAN: Like golden golden golden golden—

ARTHUR: Rain—!

> (*In this second start on the* Third Jazz Number, *there is more percussion, so that it* seems *as though the beat is better. Jazz continues for as long as desirable, in view of the dramatic alternations with the baseball game. When the scene shifts to stage left,*

*the band continues to play, but very softly, or fades out entirely
except for percussion, so that Phoebus can be heard.)*

*(Shouts, murmurs, commotions of one kind or another come from the
darkness stage left, in anticipation of the day's baseball game,
which is about to start.)*

*(Lights come up in an announcer's booth down left. Phoebus is in
it. The Bleachers Choruses, male and female, are seen dimly in
the background.)*

*(Jazz percussion follows the beat of Bleachers shouts, wherever they
occur. It improvises softly through all of Phoebus's lines. Phoebus
improvises a rhythmic integration with it.)*

PRODUCER (*heard through a loudspeaker as* Third Jazz Number *fades*):
Ladies and gentlemen: it is my pleasure to give you that Man-
about-the-Studios and your favorite baseball announcer, (*shout*)
Phoebus the Disc Jockey!

VOICE FROM BLEACHERS: Kill 'im!

BLEACHERS CHORUSES: Kill 'im!

*(Phoebus's voice also comes through the speaker. He chatters easily,
smoothly, and rather fast. He speaks in a kind of double-talk. The
lines can be read — they need not be memorized, since Phoebus is
in the announcer's booth.)*

PHOEBUS: Ah, thank you, thank you, my friends. The Central City
Satyrs are playing our Mystiana Mockingbirds, or as they are
affectionately known to their many fans — the Mockers —

BLEACHERS CHORUSES: Boo —!

PHOEBUS: — in the final game of the series. Lineups are being handed
in. Wait a minute! A record has just been broken. With our national
anthem barely finished, an umpire has just greeted a pitcher!
Warmly! For the first time in the history of organized baseball.
First batter strikes out. Count one and two on the second. He
goes to first on the catcher's dropped ball. An error! An error!
A real Mocker! Heh-heh. Up to their old Mocking tricks. A record!
A record! The first third baseman who ever caught a pop fly with
his left hand while winking his right eye *on — Sunday —*, in the
history of organized baseball. It's never happened before *on Sun-
day.* That last was a screamin' meemie. Now we have two out.
And there's a foul ball. It hit the catcher in the leg. He's injured!
He's injured! I sure hope he can shake it off — not the leg but
the *in-ju-ry —*. Heh-heh.

BLEACHERS CHORUSES: Boo—!

(Lights dim in announcement booth, and come up dimly stage right. Witches have entered, and are now dancing around the jazz hillock. The Jazz Band plays strongly—Fourth Jazz Number, working up its rainmaking power. This continues to its own particular jazz climax. Occasional shouts or boos come from the Bleachers Choruses. Finally, after climax is achieved, lights dim somewhat, and come up again in the announcement booth, left.)

PHOEBUS: Here's the pitcher coming to bat. Listen to the hand he gets!

BLEACHERS CHORUSES: Boo—!

VOICE FROM BLEACHERS: Kill 'im!

PHOEBUS: Look at that catch! Ah, the judgment, speed, the sliding balance of such catching! A record! A record! Another record! An attempted steal at home plate, and he got thrown out. A conviction for trying to steal. Heh-heh. Let's see, now. What's the record? Oh, yes. The first time a left-handed second baseman has been thrown out on an attempted steal at home plate on July thirty-first. It's never happened before on *July thirty-first*. Now there's a long fly ball, a two-bagger, and there's the runner sliding into second. Watch that Mocker second baseman! I'm afraid he got spiked! Oh-oh. And the Satyr runner! *He* got spiked right back! *He* got spiked! The Satyr got spiked! That's the way. Turn the tables on 'em.

BLEACHERS CHORUSES: Boo—!

PHOEBUS: Heh-heh. Satyrs at bat. Count two and one. Now *there's* a wicked line drive. The pitcher is adjusting his britches. Adjusting his britches *after* that ball went screaming between his legs. Next batter, struck him out! *He* must be *mad*, and who can blame him? I guess he had premonitions of suddenly becoming a high tenor! Heh-heh.

BLEACHERS CHORUSES: Kill 'im! Kill 'im!

PHOEBUS: Pity a poor pitcher on a night like this. The fans are still on 'im.

VOICE FROM BLEACHERS: *Not* the pitcher! The announcer! Kill 'im!

BLEACHERS CHORUSES: Kill 'im!

Scene from 1962 University of Illinois production of *Water! Water!* Tenth Prologue: Phoebus announcing baseball game. Photograph by Danlee Mitchell.

PHOEBUS: Heh-heh. Oh-oh! There it goes!

BLEACHERS CHORUSES: (*Loud shouts.*)

PHOEBUS: Clear out of the apple orchard! He smacked it 'way out in Homerville. And another run is in. There he comes, dancing in from third. Look at his buddies grabbing his hand. He's a little fellow, and, you know, he reminds me of Narcissus, the Mocker batboy from a few years back — a great favorite with the fans. The last I heard, Narcissus joined a health club, and almost got crushed under two tons of mirrors. What a fate for Narcissus! Heh-heh. I understand he changed his name, so as to tempt the gods no further.

VOICE FROM BLEACHERS: It's a great idea! Tempt the gods no further!

BLEACHERS CHORUSES: Kill 'im!

PHOEBUS: Heh-heh. Top of the third. Here's the first pitch to the Satyr shortstop, and what a ballplayer! After six years as a professional he owns three banks, four restaurants, five bowling alleys, and when the son of a poor North Carolina sharecropper can do that! Huh! And you still hear foolish questions about what's wrong with America. A record! A record! Another record! *What — a — day* —!

(*Lights fade in announcement booth, come up dimly stage right. Solo dance by Wanda; the other Witches are fairly stationary. This is the final effort, the one in which rainmaking power is achieved. Shouts, murmurs, boos, continue to come from the Bleachers Choruses, occasionally. This is the* Fifth Jazz *Number.*)

(*Luminous light behind the horizon slowly fades. At the climax foreground lights fade right, and come up left.*)

(*In the announcement booth Phoebus is seen making exaggerated jaw and lip movements, but no sounds come from the speaker. This continues for about half a minute. Bleachers Choruses continue to make sounds; an occasional* Kill 'im! *Suddenly, the speaker is alive.*)

PHOEBUS: Incredible! Incredible! The game is called on account —

FIRST LEFT (*advances slowly, looks up, holds palms upwards*): Incredible!

PHOEBUS: The game is called — on account —

SECOND LEFT (*advances timidly, looks up, holds palms up*): Incredible! Incredible!

PHOEBUS: The game is called—

(*Third and Fourth advance, look up, hold palms upward.*)

THIRD LEFT: Incredible!

PHOEBUS: The game—

FOURTH LEFT: Incredible! Incredible!

PHOEBUS (*finally recovering power of speech*): The game is called on account of—

(*Lights do not dim.*)

Final Prologue

(*Bleachers Choruses are now downstage.*)

BLEACHERS CHORUSES (*shout*): Rain—!

WATER CRIERS ⟨*in lazy syncopation*⟩: Wa—ter! Wa—ter! Wa—ter! Wa—ter!

FIFTH LEFT (*shouts rhythmically*): To hell with the game! Rain! Rain!

BLEACHERS CHORUSES (*sing*):
>   To hell (*shout* hell) with the game! Rain—
>   Rain— Rai-rai-rai-rain—!
>   To hell with the game!
>   Rai-rai-rai-rai-rai-rain—!
>   Rai-ai-Rai-ai-Rai-ai-Rai-ai-Ra-ai-ai-
>   Rain—! Rain—! Rain—! Rain—!

(*Jazz may begin about here, in a small way.*)

BLEACHERS CHORUSES: Wa—ter! Wa—ter! Wa—ter! Wa—ter! O O O O O O O O O— Water! Water! Wa—ter!

(*Lights dim left, come up right. The luminous sky is gone. The band is improvising softly on the foregoing theme. The Witches move slowly to the music—their great effort is now over. This is the* Sixth Jazz Number *and should be fairly brief—long enough only for Indians to tumble on and speak their lines, for further*

*comic tumbling, for left lights to come on again, for Clarence to
scream his line, and for Her Honor to scream hers.)*
(An Indian runner tumbles wildly on, right.)

FIRST INDIAN RUNNER: Rain on the mountain! *(Exits quickly.)*

(Another tumbles on.)

SECOND INDIAN RUNNER: Rain on the foothill! *(Exits quickly.)*

(A third tumbles on.)

THIRD INDIAN RUNNER: Rain on the plain! *(Exits quickly.)*

(A fourth tumbles on.)

FOURTH INDIAN RUNNER: Rain on papa! *(He holds out his palms.
Exits quickly.)*

(An Indian woman tumbles on.)

INDIAN WOMAN: Rain on mama! *(She holds out her palms.)*

*(Lights fade right, come up left. The announcement booth is gone.
Her Honor, Clarence, the Aldermen, and the Ladies' Auxiliary
are all moving about excitedly. Umbrellas have appeared, and
are being swung rhythmically, to the soft jazz. One of the men
carries a bright ladies' parasol and swings a large ladies' handbag.
He appears with the same accessories in the Seventh Epilogue.)*

FIFTH ALDERMAN: I grossed only thirty-seven twenty-five yesterday,
and only forty-one fifty-six the day before that. But *now*—today,
tomorrow, and on, and on—I will gross, and gross, and gross!
(He improvises a melody and begins to sing and dance.) Oh, I could
gross— all night—! Oh, I could—

CLARENCE *(screaming with delight)*: The highest goodness is like water!
Indeed it is! *Indeed it is!* Money! Money! Money! Money! Ha ha ha
ha! Whoops!

*(Lights come up again stage right, and remain up left. This is the
climax of the Final Prologue, and there is general movement by
everyone, back and forth across the invisible line. A huge umbrella—large beach umbrella—now covers the Jazz Band, or
part of it, and it continues to play, on the same theme,* To hell
with the game. *Mobile instruments move about restlessly.)*
(Her Honor moves down center.)

HER HONOR *(screaming)*: The highest goodness is like water!

Scene from 1962 University of Illinois production of *Water! Water!* Final Prologue: Rain comes to Santa Mystiana. Harry Partch Estate Archive, San Diego.

(The Jazz Band takes up the new theme, and the entire ensemble sings. This is the second number in which jazz instrumentation is to be added.)

BLEACHERS CHORUSES:
> The highest goodness is like— water. Indeed it is! Indeed it is! Water! Water! Water! Water!
> The highest goodness is like— water. Indeed it is! Indeed it is! Water! Water! Water! Water!
> *(Maestoso—Swing it!—sustain* r, *not* uh.*)*
> Wa—ter— Wa—ter— Wa—ter— Wa—ter—
> *(Sudden piano; sustain* s, *not* eh.*)*
> The highest goodness is like— water. *(Fortissimo.)* Indeed it is! Indeed it is—!

⟨*All stage lights begin to fade. Conductor faces the audience, raises his hands to heaven, looks up, and sings.*⟩

CONDUCTOR: Wa—ter—! Wa—ter—!

(Water Crier hands Conductor a glass of water. This is a ceremonious action, not casual. Conductor bows to Water Crier, accepts water, drinks it, bows again to Water Crier, hands back the glass, turns to the audience and bows, then walks out.)
(Stage lights out. House lights on.)

INTERMISSION

Opening Epilogue

MALE WATER CRIER: The highest goodness is like water.

(Spot on Phoebus.)

PHOEBUS: Yes, we know. It seeks the low place, that all men dislike. The low place! Huh! Where did that ever get you?

(Spot fades.)

WATER CRIERS: Wa—ter! Wa—ter! Too— much— Wa—ter!

CHORUSES ⟨*mournfully, from dark backstage*⟩:
        Rain—! Rain—! Too— much rain—!
        Wa—ter! Wa—ter! Too— much wa—ter!
        Suc—cor! Suc—cor! We need— suc—cor!

PHOEBUS: I think the Producer wants to make an announcement. Here he is now.

PRODUCER (*through loudspeaker*): Hear ye! Hear ye! A proclamation by His Excellency, the governor, at the request of Her Honor, beloved mayor of Santa Mystiana, in the face of a threatened flood disaster! The Mystic Order of Empirical Riflemen is hereby mobilized, to preserve public peace and order, to maintain the sacred traditions of law, to guarantee the commonweal, and to prevent the delivery of obscene literature through the mails. Now let's all give them a great big hand. (*He shouts.*) The Mystic Order of Empirical Riflemen!

CHORUSES ⟨*from dark backstage*⟩: We need— suc—cor! Not— riflemen, but suc—cor!

(*Riflemen go through their comedy act. Lights come up only as necessary for their routine.*)

PHOEBUS (*as Riflemen depart*): *Empirical* Riflemen! Whatever that means. If they don't shoot you the first time, they'll be *empirical* about it, and gain a little *experience*, I guess. Try a second shot? Or judo? Or that art where they kill you with the thrust of *one thumb? Karate? Wow!*

Second Epilogue

WATER CRIERS: Wat—ter! Wa—ter! Too— much— wa—ter!

PHOEBUS: Demanding, demanding! They want water, but *just the right amount* of water. No more, no less. One inch too little and what happens? They get Wanda, Arthur, and all *that* jazz. One inch too much and what do they get? The Mystic Order of Empirical Riflemen. *Too—* much!

CHORUSES ⟨*from dark backstage area*⟩: Suc—cor! Suc—cor! We need— suc—cor!

(*Lights come up left. Lights in picture window also come up. Her Honor, in raincoat and hood, and Clarence, are on. Lines of empty whiskey bottles are on two shelves, against the wall.*)

HER HONOR (*pacing*): Three days of *rain*—!

CLARENCE: Oh, *what* have we come to? *What?*

HER HONOR (*pacing*): We are being *drowned*—!

CLARENCE: *What?* Because of Wanda, Arthur, and all *that* jazz. (*He suddenly recoils.*) Oh, *what* did I *say?* Jazz! Ugh—!

(*Aquarius enters.*)

AQUARIUS (*out of breath*): Get the announcements over the air! Boil yer water! But don't turn on the gas. Ya might explode. And don't try to go home. Y'll never make it. (*He rushes out.*)

HER HONOR: Well, do something!

CLARENCE (*weakly*): What?

HER HONOR: Serve a subpoena.

CLARENCE: Serve *me* a drink.

HER HONOR: You've had a drink.

CLARENCE: Very well, then. Serve a subpoena.

HER HONOR: And serve *me* a drink. (*Pause.*) No, never mind. *I* shall confront that god of rain!

(*She begins to see her vision again, and hums softly,* Santa Mystiana the Beautiful, *in any key, but without words—no accompaniment. She moves to exit, stands there. Now she speaks in the singing tones of prophecy.*)

HER HONOR: Other things will pass, other things will crumble, other things will fade into nothingness, but the great big beautiful Santa Mystiana Dam will stand forever!

PHOEBUS and CLARENCE (*in unison*): Ah—   For—
HER HONOR (*singing words*):   Jewel— of mystery—

ever!

(*Her Honor exits, as though in a trance.*)

Third Epilogue

WATER CRIERS: Wa—ter! Too— much— wa—ter!

PHOEBUS: Now, what's this? A refugee from a nudist camp?

FIRST INDIAN RUNNER: I'm a runner.

PHOEBUS: Runner? So you run. Where?

FIRST INDIAN RUNNER: Wherever it is necessary to report!

PHOEBUS: What's wrong with the telephone?

FIRST INDIAN RUNNER: Hah!

PHOEBUS: Well, then, how about the telegraph?

FIRST INDIAN RUNNER: Huh!

PHOEBUS: We'll stipulate that you run. Is that all you do?

FIRST INDIAN RUNNER: Sometimes I walk.

PHOEBUS: No kidding!

FIRST INDIAN RUNNER: No kidding.

PHOEBUS (*to audience*): Hey, look, guys! He *walks!* (*Pause.*) Where's your car? Why don't you drive?

FIRST INDIAN RUNNER: Without roads?

PHOEBUS: So it's *that* bad!

(*Second Indian Runner enters.*)

SECOND INDIAN RUNNER: Highway 2. Impassable.

(*Third Indian Runner enters.*)

THIRD INDIAN RUNNER: Highway 39. Bridge gone.

(*Fourth Indian Runner enters.*)

FOURTH INDIAN RUNNER: Highway 603. Mountain on top of it.

(*Fifth Indian Runner enters.*)

FIFTH INDIAN RUNNER: Rain is ended.

(*Spot fades right. Lights come up dimly left. Clarence is alone, looking out the picture window.*)

CLARENCE: Finally, finally! The rain is ended. Finally. I think this calls for a celebration. Oh, Pura! Pura!

PHOEBUS: Pura! What a name for a barmaid. A flesh-and-blood barmaid? I think she's a myth. Myth Barmaid of Nineteen Thicthty-Two. Heh-heh.

(Pura enters.)

Hey-hey! Flesh and Blood! Don't know about the blood, but the flesh isn't bad!

CLARENCE: What a day! What a night! And before that! And before that! Pura, get me a drink. The usual.

PURA: The usual?

CLARENCE: Certainly. Whiskey and water.

PURA: No water.

CLARENCE: Whaddaya mean? There's water everywhere!

PURA: *No* water.

CLARENCE (*weakly*): Yes, I see what you mean. Very well, whiskey on the rocks.

PURA: No rocks.

CLARENCE: No rocks?

PURA: *No* rocks.

CLARENCE: No— rocks—. The end— of the world!

> *(He moans, and sinks to the floor in a dead faint. Pura gestures wildly toward right, for the other Ghosts.)*
>
> *(During the music that follows, the first five Ghosts enter separately, as indicated in the score. The remaining Ghosts enter as a body, as indicated. They dance eagerly across the invisible line, arrange the empty liquor bottles in neat rows, and two of them play the bottles with metal drink mixers. They are accompanied by percussion mobile instruments. The other Ghosts dance wildly, over and around Clarence's prostrate body, as though it were a fallen enemy. This is virtually a dervish dance.)*

PURA: Ghosts! Ghosts! Undele! Undele! Oomph! Oomph!

⟨*Second Ghost rushes on, gestures to others.*⟩

SECOND GHOST: Ghosts! Undele! Oomph!

⟨*Third Ghost rushes on, gestures to others.*⟩

THIRD GHOST: Ghosts! Undele! Oomph!

⟨*Fourth Ghost rushes on, gestures to others.*⟩

FOURTH GHOST: Undele! Oomph!

⟨*Fifth Ghost rushes on, gestures to others.*⟩

FIFTH GHOST: Oomph!

⟨*Remaining Ghosts rush on.*⟩

REMAINING GHOSTS: Oomph!

GHOSTS ⟨*at height of dance*⟩: Oomph! Oomph! Oo— oo oo oomph!
White man! (*Shout.*) Ha! Ha! Ha!

(*Pura runs to left entrance, cups her ear.*)

PURA: She's coming!

PHOEBUS: Run, run, run away! Back to the Funny Farm! Ha—! Ha—!
Ha—!

(*Ghosts run across stage, exeunt right. Lights fade.*)

Fourth Epilogue

WATER CRIERS: Wa—ter! Wa—ter! Too— much— wa—ter!

(*The brilliant luminosity behind the horizon returns. The Jazz Band
is in the pit, but spills partially onto the stage. Foreground lights
do not come on.*) ⟨*This is the* Seventh Jazz Number.⟩
(*Her Honor enters almost immediately, in the comparative darkness
stage left, walking very, very slowly toward center. Violins strike
four-string chords, in the guitar manner.*)

JAZZ SOLO: Misty, Misty, here we are!
　　　　　Always, always, under par—
　　　　　Always, always, sinking down—
　　　　　Stinking bums in a sinking town—

(*The words "sinking town" provoke a few half-hearted and half-
contemptuous laughs. Following the laugh some desultory jazz
phrases are heard.*)
(*As Her Honor reaches the invisible line, a spot comes on, exact
center stage.*)

HER HONOR: So—!

(*Arthur moves toward left.*)

ARTHUR (*entering spot*): Hi.

HER HONOR: "Sinking town" indeed! And whose fault is it? Haven't you done enough damage? Jazz! Ugh—!

ARTHUR: Don't worry. This isn't for rain. Just kicks.

HER HONOR: Just kicks! And all these floods! Are these *kicks* too?

ARTHUR: Well, what can you expect? When you don't know how to propitiate.

JAZZMEN (*choral speech, from dark right area*): What can you expect? If you don't propitiate?

HER HONOR: We'll propitiate! We'll throw the book at you! In fact, we'll throw the whole damned library! And after that we'll sue! We'll sue you for a hundred thousand! No, we'll sue you for *five* hundred thousand! Even better, we'll sue you for— a— million!

JAZZMEN ⟨*beaming, in choral speech*⟩: A million dollars? Whew—! We must be pretty important people!

HER HONOR (*to Conductor*): *Please!* Let me sing it.

ARTHUR: Cool!

JAZZMEN (*choral speech*): A cool— million!

HER HONOR: It will be *much* more effective, and my high B is really not bad.

CONDUCTOR: As you wish.

ARTHUR: And we'll give you the good old harmonic support. Come on, fellas, swing it!

HER HONOR: That is so— good of you.

ARTHUR: *Our* pleasure!

JAZZMEN ⟨*choral speech*⟩: A million dollars worth of pleasure!

(*Mobile instruments make themselves conspicuous. Spot fades. Lights come up both foregrounds, dimly. Only part of the Jazzmen play; the others keep the beat with the words indicated. Wanda and Witches enter right.*)

HER HONOR: We'll sue, we'll sue, we'll sue, sue, sue! We'll sue you for *a*— (*long* a) million!

JAZZMEN and WITCHES (*speak*): Jazz, ugh!

HER HONOR: We'll break you, we'll blast   you, we'll
JAZZMEN and WITCHES: Jazz,   Ugh—!

bring the law   upon you!
Jazz,   ugh—!

(*The Witches deliver a wicked hip movement on each* Ugh! *and
grimace nastily.*)

HER HONOR: Law,   law, law, law, law   law,
JAZZMEN and WITCHES: Jazz, Ugh—!   Jazz,   Ugh—!

law—
Jazz, Ugh!

(*As the song develops, all begin to march. Surrogate Kithara leads
the parade. Diamond Marimba follows, and Her Honor follows
Diamond Marimba. The Jazz Band and Witches are a phalanx
behind Her Honor. Bass Marimba and Eroica bring up the rear.*)

HER HONOR: We'll wring, we'll wring, we'll
JAZZMEN and WITCHES: Jazz,   Ugh—!   Jazz,

wring, wring, wring! We'll wring   you through the statutes!
Ugh—!   Jazz,   Ugh—!   Jazz,   Ugh—!

(*Her Honor makes* wringing *gestures, so that the audience will not
think* ring.)

HER HONOR: We'll bring the law   upon you!
JAZZMEN and WITCHES: Jazz,   Ugh—! Jazz,   Ugh—!

(*First, they make a kind of circle, then walk directly stage left, which
is now a courtroom.*)

JAZZMEN: Misty, Misty, we are here!
         Always, always, year by year—
         Always, always, sinking down—
         Stinking bums in a sinking town!

HER HONOR: We'll sue,   sue, sue! We'll sue, sue,
JAZZMEN: Who, who, who, who, who, who,

sue!
who, who, who, Misty! Misty!

HER HONOR: We'll sue you for *a*— (*long* a) million! A
JAZZMEN and WITCHES:

mil—lion, million, million, million, million, million, mill—yun!
                                                        Jazz,
                We'll break   you, we'll blast you, we'll set—
Ugh—! Jazz,   Ugh—!   Jazz,   Ugh—!
you— back   a— mill—
Jazz,   Ugh—!   Who, who, who, who, who, who,

        yun!
who, who

(Her Honor walks to the little throne, where she finds the black robe and the powdered wig of an English judge. Arthur, the Jazz Band, and the Witches stand before her. Aldermen and the Ladies' Auxiliary enter left, and pack themselves closely around the bench. After Her Honor has assumed robe and wig, she sits. Lights do not dim.)

Fifth Epilogue

WATER CRIERS: Wa—ter! Wa—ter! Too— much— wa—ter!

CLERK: Join! Join! Join! *In the pres-ence of the law! The law!* (He bangs a gavel.)

JAZZMEN and WITCHES: Boo—!

PHOEBUS: They're still at the baseball game.

HER HONOR: Let the accused be named!

CLERK: Arthur, the God of Rain.

ALDERMEN and LADIES' AUXILIARY: Boo—!

PHOEBUS: They don't like that pitcher. Not at all!

HER HONOR: Let the accused stand forth! (*Arthur stands forth.*) Read the indictment.

(*Clerk has a scroll, which he swiftly rolls down as he reads.*)

CLERK: You are charged with making water—

HER HONOR: *Bringing* water!

CLERK: You are charged with *bringing* water—

HER HONOR: *Too much* water!

CLERK: You are charged with bringing *too much* water. You are further charged with producing, promoting, provoking, and inciting—

(*Clarence has a scroll, which he unrolls, down on Clerk's head as he reads.*)

CLARENCE: Delinquency, Vagrancy, Libel, Desertion, Fornication, Adultery, Bribery, Perjury—

(*Her Honor has a scroll, which she unrolls, down on Clerk's head as she reads.*)

HER HONOR: Mutiny, Barratry, Piracy, Arson, Mayhem, Rape, Riot—

(*Clerk now has scroll paper all over him.*)

CLERK: And the Delivery of Obscene Literature Through the Mails. (*Bangs gavel.*) How do you plead?

ARTHUR: (*Improvises on horn.*)

(*Bass Marimba pushes insistently downstage, playing.*)

⟨BASS MARIMBA: (*Big racket.*)⟩

(*Pause.*)

CLERK: Contempt of court!

(*Pause.*)

CLERK: Contempt of court! Contempt of court! Contempt of COURT—!

(*Bass Marimba virtually drowns out* court.)

HER HONOR (*shouting*): Bailiff, arrest the Bass Marimba!

BAILIFF: Now, Your Honor, let's be *rea*sonable!

LADIES' AUXILIARY ⟨*choral speech*⟩: Let the coconspirator be named!

(*Bass Marimba retires.*)

HER HONOR: Yes! Let the coconspirator be named! *This* is what *I'm* waiting for!

JAZZMEN and WITCHES: Boo—!

CLERK: You are in *the pres-ence of the law! The law!* (*Bangs gavel.*)

HER HONOR: Let the accused stand forth! (*Wanda stands forth.*) Read the indictment.

(*Clerk has another scroll, which he swiftly unrolls as he reads.*)

CLERK: You are charged with being an accessory—

(*Her Honor has another scroll, which she unrolls on Clerk's head.*)

HER HONOR: Before, About, Without, Within, and *After* the Fact!

CLERK: You are further charged with producing, promoting, provoking, and inciting—

(*Clarence has another scroll, which he unrolls on Clerk's head.*)

CLARENCE: Delinquency, Vagrancy, Libel, Desertion, Fornication, Adultery, Bribery, Perjury—

(*Scrolls continue to unwind.*)

HER HONOR: Mutiny, Barratry, Piracy, Arson, Mayhem, Rape, Riot—

(*Clerk is now buried under scroll paper.*)

CLERK (*from beneath paper*): And the Delivery of Obscene Literature Through the Mails. (*Bangs gavel.*)

HER HONOR: How do you plead? *Guilty! Take*—her away!

ALDERMEN and LADIES' AUXILIARY: (*They applaud and shout.*)

JAZZMEN and WITCHES: Boo—!

CLARENCE: Now, Your Honor—

HER HONOR: Well, *how* do you plead?

WANDA: (*She does a handspring, a back somersault, then crouches low on the floor and emits a blood-curdling growl.*) Bee—aw—au—!

JAZZMEN and WITCHES: (*They applaud and shout wildly.*)

HER HONOR: Silence! (*Pause.*) That's an equivocal plea if I ever heard one! But I take it that she also protests *innocence!* Hah! Let the trial proceed!

(*Harmonic Canon pushes insistently downstage, playing.*)

⟨HARMONIC CANON: (*Big racket.*)⟩

CLERK (*shouting from beneath paper*): Let the trial proceed!

(*Mobile instruments begin to hem in the courtroom.*)

ALDERMEN and LADIES' AUXILIARY ⟨*choral speech*⟩: Let the trial proceed!

HER HONOR: Si-   lence!   Si-   lence!
CLERK: Contempt of court! Contempt of court! Contempt of

SI—LENCE!
COURT—!

⟨*Racket suddenly ends on a strong beat.*⟩
(*An Indian Runner rushes in from right.*)

FIRST INDIAN RUNNER: Flood in the mountain!

(*Clerk gets one eye free under paper.*)

CLERK: What!

(*Second Indian Runner rushes in from right.*)

SECOND INDIAN RUNNER: Flood in the foothill!

CLERK: What *is* this? Sure, floods are *every*where!

(*Third Indian Runner rushes in.*)

THIRD INDIAN RUNNER: Flood in the plain!

CLERK: Contempt of court! (*He bangs gavel.*)

(*Fourth Indian Runner rushes in.*)

FOURTH INDIAN RUNNER: Flood in the *power plant!*

ALDERMEN and LADIES' AUXILIARY: Oh— no—!

(*Lights in the picture window and foreground begin to fade. Fifth Indian Runner rushes in.*)

FIFTH INDIAN RUNNER: Darkness is coming!

(*It comes. Lights go completely black in the picture window, and in both foregrounds. Luminous light behind the horizon, right, remains.*)

ALDERMEN and LADIES' AUXILIARY: Oh— no—!

HER HONOR: Grab a flashlight! Grab a candle! *Don't* let them get away!

ARTHUR: Split!

WANDA: Scram!

FIRST WITCH: Shake!

FIRST JAZZMAN: Shuck!

OTHER JAZZMEN and WITCHES:
> Split! Scram! Shake! Shuck!
> Split! Scram! Shake! Shuck!
> Split! Scram! Shake! Shuck!

> (*The above line begins slowly and increases in tempo, so that it sounds something like a steam engine getting up speed. The last two lines are repeated until the sounds die away into inaudibility, with the Witches and Jazzmen moving off, right.*)
> (*One of the ladies has found a torch, and enters with it.*)

HER HONOR: *Too*— late!

JAZZMEN (*at right exit*): Hey-hey! Torchlight! Ain't it fun? Just like the Middle Ages!

ALDERMEN and LADIES' AUXILIARY (*low moans, in almost total darkness*): Oh—! No—!

> (*Spot on Phoebus.*)

PHOEBUS: To split: to separate into parts, by force. To scram: colloquial; to run or climb in all directions. All directions *at once?* Hey, *there's* a trick! *Split* from the scene, *Scram* from the law, *Shake* that judge, and *Shuck* that clerk!

> (*Spot fades.*)

Sixth Epilogue

WATER CRIERS: Wa—ter! Wa—ter! Too— much— wa—ter!

> (*Lights come up dimly, both right and left. Picture window remains dark. The Chorus of Hysterical American Indian Ghosts is seated, cross-legged, on the floor, in a circle. A few of the Aldermen and Ladies' Auxiliary lounge dispiritedly, in a rough circle, on the floor stage left. Two or three of them have flashlights. The two sides of the stage do not hear each other. Remarks alternate, left and right. Those on left speak mournfully. The sequence is very deliberate.*)

FIRST LEFT: First time I've missed that program in two and a half years.

FIRST RIGHT: White man! Ha-ha. (*Low chuckle, or giggle.*)

PHOEBUS: Oh, well! It looks like we're all back at the Laughing Academy.

(*Pause.*)

SECOND LEFT: My basement is a swimming pool.

SECOND RIGHT: White man! Ha-ha. (*Louder chuckle.*)

(*Pause.*)

THIRD LEFT: Haven't seen my wife in three days.

THIRD RIGHT: White man! Ha-ha. (*Laughter.*)

(*Pause.*)

FOURTH LEFT: Bridges out all the way to my favorite golf course.

FOURTH RIGHT: White man! Ha-ha! (*Louder laughter.*)

(*Pause.*)

FIFTH LEFT: Make merry tonight? Huh!

FIFTH RIGHT: White man!

GHOSTS: (*Very loud laughter.*)

(*Pause.*)

SIXTH LEFT: For tomorrow we get washed down the drain like rats!

(*A Very White Jazzman, carrying his horn, enters right, goes to the middle of the circle of Ghosts, faces audience, and speaks innocently.*)

VERY WHITE JAZZMAN: White man!

(*The Ghosts eye him stonily. He pauses a moment, then throws his hands over his head and doubles up with hysterical laughter.*)

GHOSTS: (*Prolonged and convulsive and hysterical laughter.*)

(*As the laughter dies away the two circles get up and begin slow Indian dances, in contrary motion, in circles, moving down from center and out, to right and left. Ghosts move clockwise, others counterclockwise.*)

LEFT CHORUS: Do lo do— lo— doom!

RIGHT CHORUS: White man! Ha-ha. (*Low chuckle.*)

LEFT CHORUS: Do lo do— lo— doom!

RIGHT CHORUS: White man! Ha-ha.

LEFT CHORUS: Do lo do— lo— doom!

RIGHT CHORUS: White man! Ha-ha.

> (*Finally, they circle and exeunt—Ghosts right, others left. One Ghost stands at exit. Spot on Phoebus.*)

PHOEBUS: Other things will pass, other things will crumble, other things will fade into nothingness, but the great big beautiful Santa Mystiana Dam will stand forever.

GHOST (*at exit*): White man! Ha-ha. (*Low chuckle.*)

PHOEBUS: I think *that* was a *nasty* remark.

> (*Spot fades.*)

Seventh Epilogue

WATER CRIERS: Wa—ter! Wa—ter! Too— much wa—ter!

> (*Spot on Phoebus.*)

PHOEBUS: This is our last evening together, but let there be no gnashing of teeth, let there be no beating of breasts, let there be no wailing at the gates. Don't get out the handkerchiefs, because there'll be other times, there'll be other shows. I'll be around. I'll be with you in spirit, always—. Boo hoo hoo hoo hoo—.

> (*He walks away, wracked in convulsive sobs. Spot fades.*)
> (*Lights come up dimly stage left. Only Her Honor, Clarence, Aquarius, and Pura are on. Aldermen and the Ladies' Auxiliary are changing costumes, in preparation for the climactic end of this Epilogue.*)
> (*First Indian Runner rushes in, breathless.*)

FIRST INDIAN RUNNER: The dam is gone!

> (*Shocked silence follows.*)

HER HONOR (*soft and low*): No—!

CLARENCE (*soft and low*): No—!

FIRST INDIAN RUNNER: The crest of the flood is two feet high, and it will be here in thirty minutes! (*He exits.*)

CLARENCE: The end of the world as we know it!

AQUARIUS: I coulda told ya.

PURA (*smiling contemptuously*): Hah!

HER HONOR (*still in shock*): No—!

(*Second Indian Runner rushes in, breathless.*)

SECOND INDIAN RUNNER: The crest is four feet high, and it will be here in twenty minutes!

(*He exits. Third Indian Runner rushes in, breathless.*)

THIRD INDIAN RUNNER: The crest is eight feet high, and it will be here in *ten* minutes!

(*He exits. The next four words follow each other in quick succession.*)

HER HONOR: No—!

AQUARIUS: Hah!

CLARENCE: No—!

PURA and AQUARIUS: Hah!

(*Her Honor and Clarence launch into a kind of dirge, while Aquarius and Pura keep the beat with their contemptuous* Hah.)

HER HONOR: The end of the world   as we know it!
PURA and AQUARIUS: Hah!   Hah!

        The end of the world   as we know it!
Hah!   Hah!   Hah!   Hah!

(*Fourth Indian Runner rushes in, breathless.*)

FOURTH INDIAN RUNNER: Final flash! The crest is *sixteen* feet high, and it will be here in *five* minutes!

(*He rushes out. A tumbler comes in wildly and stops about center stage.*)

PHOEBUS: This is *too*— much! Now where are *you* going?

TUMBLER: Going? Who's going? Man— I'm *gone!*

(*He goes, tumbling off left. Other tumblers follow, right to left, in quick succession.*)
(*Jazzmen and Witches enter right. Music begins, on the melody* Santa

Mystiana the Beautiful. *Words are shouted or screamed on the beat. The Beatnik Pair of the Eighth Prologue come down center.*)

PHOEBUS: The end of the world as we know it!

BEATNIK PAIR: Gone, man, gone!

(*Aquarius and Pura march down; Pura is beaming.*)

AQUARIUS and PURA: The end of the world as we know it! Gone, man, gone!

(*Arthur and Her Honor march down, arm in arm. Her Honor is making a wry face.*)

HER HONOR and ARTHUR: The end of the world as we know it! Gone, man, gone!

(*Clarence and Wanda march down; Clarence is making a wry face.*)

CLARENCE and WANDA: The end of the world as we know it! Gone, man, gone!

(*A Negro Jazzman comes down, snaps his fingers, smiles broadly.*)

NEGRO JAZZMAN: The end of the world as we know it!

(*All other Negroes in the cast make themselves conspicuous.*)

ALL NEGROES: Gone, man, gone!

(*The man with ladies' parasol and large ladies' handbag of the Final Prologue comes down, screams at the top of his lungs.*)

MAN WITH LADIES' PARASOL: The end of the world as we know it! Gone, man, gone!

CONDUCTOR (*shouting*): This is ridiculous! Can't anybody scream? (*He screams.*) The END OF THE WORLD AS WE KNOW IT! GONE, MAN, GONE!

⟨*Crash of gongs and cymbals.*⟩
(*The Ladies' Auxiliary enters left, virtually naked, wearing patches of cloth similar to costumes of Witches; they continue to wear their small outlandish hats.*

CHORUSES ⟨*on- and offstage, singing fortissimo*⟩: The end of the world as we know it! Gone, man, gone!

⟨*The melody* Wanda, Wanda! Woo woo woo woo, Wanda! *is*

heard and is played jubilantly. The Ladies' Auxiliary sing-screams at Jazzmen.⟩

LADIES' AUXILIARY: The deluge is coming!

LADY (*solo*): Love me!

JAZZMAN (*solo; running with open arms toward Lady*): Just stab me with a fork!

(*They clinch.*)

(*Aldermen enter left, virtually naked, wearing patches of cloth similar to costumes of Witches. They continue to wear flattop haircuts masks. The change of costume of both Ladies' Auxiliary and Aldermen suggests a metamorphosis, not a physical experience. Their clothes have represented both status and security; both are now meaningless.*)

(*Aldermen and Witches rush together, and clinch, center. The final song and dance, by the entire ensemble, follows. This is the third number in which jazz instrumentation is to be added.*)

ALDERMEN: Disaster is upon us!

ALDERMAN (*solo*): Love me!

WITCH (*solo; running with open arms toward Alderman*): Just say the word!

(*They clinch.*)

CHORUSES:

> The world as we know it— Gone, man, gone!
> The end, the end! Here, man— here!
> The end, the end of the world as we know
> it. Gone, man, gone!
> The end, the end! It's here, man, here!
> Gone, man, gone—!

HER HONOR (*to Arthur*): Disaster is upon us!

(*They hold out arms toward each other.*)

HER HONOR and ARTHUR: Too— much! (*Clinch on* much.)

AQUARIUS (*to Pura*): Doom is a-comin'!

AQUARIUS and PURA: Too— much! (*Clinch on* much.)

CLARENCE (*to Wanda*): The deluge is approaching!

CLARENCE and WANDA: Too— much! (*Clinch on* much.)

(*Fifth Indian Runner rushes in, breathless.*)

NEGRO JAZZMAN (*screaming at Runner*): The deluge is coming!

(*Negro holds out arms, as though to add,* Too— much!)

FIFTH INDIAN RUNNER: Coming—? Like— man—! It's— here!

(*A siren begins to scream, and a sudden brilliance, throughout the stage, lasts for about two seconds. Instantaneous darkness follows, and the ensemble exits.*)

(*A spot picks up the figure of Phoebus the Disc Jockey high above the stage, in a contrivance such as a breeches buoy. His hands are in an attitude of prayer—his legs are spread and his knees bent; he is squatting, in midair.*)

(*The spot follows his fast descent, and fades as he falls into black nothingness through the trapdoor in the stage floor. This is the final vision. The final sound is the descending moan of the siren.*)

(*If this staging is impossible, Phoebus may face audience at the edge of the open trap, speak his line, then jump into the hole, onto a couple of mattresses.*)

(*If descent is slow Phoebus speaks in transit.*)

PHOEBUS: Too— much!

Eighth Epilogue

WATER CRIERS: Wa—ter! Wa—ter! Wa—ter! Wa—ter!

(*Spot picks up Producer, far right. Mobile instruments approach him, playing, coming out of the backstage murk.*)

PRODUCER: An end to this nonsense! Back to the pit!

(*Bass Marimba and Kithara recede.*)

PRODUCER: You've had your fun! Down to the pit!

(*Castor and Pollux and Eroica recede.*)

PRODUCER: The show's over! Back to the pit!

(*Diamond Marimba recedes.*)

PRODUCER: Down to the pit! Back to the pit! Down to the pit!

(*Surrogate Kithara recedes. Producer walks toward left exit, throws his hands above his head.*)

PRODUCER: What a rehearsal!

(*Spot fades.*)

Final Epilogue

MALE WATER CRIER: The highest goodness is like water. It seeks the low place that all men dislike.

WATER CRIERS: Wa—ter! Wa—ter! Wa—ter!

Delusion of the Fury

A Ritual of Dream and Delusion

Time

An olden time

Cast

Act I:

CHORUS
PILGRIM (the slayer)
GHOST (the slain)
SON of the slain

Act II:

Deaf HOBO
CHORUS
OLD GOAT WOMAN
VILLAGERS
Deaf and Nearsighted JUSTICE of the Peace
KID
MUSICIAN
VOICE

Words cannot proxy for the experience of knowing—of seeing and hearing. The concept of this work inheres in the *presence* of the instruments onstage, the *movements* of musicians and chorus, the *sounds* they produce, the *actuality* of actors, of singers, of mimes, of lights; in fine, the *actuality* of truly integrated theater. These introductory pages consist largely of technical data. They contain no argument, no exposition. I feel that the only investigation which has genuine integrity is the seen and heard performance.

Synopsis

It is an olden time, but neither a precise time nor a precise place. The Exordium is an overture, an invocation, the beginning of a ritualistic web. Act I, on the recurrent theme of Noh plays, is a music-theater portrayal of release from the wheel of life and death. It opens with a pilgrim in search of a particular shrine, where he may do penance for murder. The murdered man appears as a ghost, sees first the assassin, then his young son, looking for a vision of his father's face. Spurred to resentment by his son's presence, he lives again through the ordeal of death, but at the end—with the supplication, "Pray for me!"—he finds reconciliation.

There is nowhere, from the beginning of the Exordium to the end of Act II, a complete cessation of music. The Sanctus ties Acts I and II together; it is the epilogue to the one, the prologue to the other. Act II involves a reconciliation with life. A young vagabond is cooking a meal over a fire in rocks when an old [goat] woman approaches, searching for a lost kid. She eventually finds the kid, but— due to a misunderstanding caused by the hobo's deafness—a dispute ensues. Villagers gather, and during a violent dance force the quarrelling couple to appear before the justice of the peace, who is both deaf and nearsighted.

Following the judge's sentence, the Chorus sings in unison, "Oh, how did we ever get by without justice?" and a voice offstage reverts to the supplication at the end of Act I.

Set

The instruments *are* the set, with only a cyclorama—a good sound-reflecting surface—behind. They must not be pushed back into tight corners. The movements required of principals and Chorus do not call for excessive stage space. In Act I they are generally slow and intense; in Act II vigorous and intense. The vigorous movers of Act II will simply learn to avoid instruments.

Principals

The principals in each act must certainly be trained in music. It would be fine if they can be mimes, singers, dancers, simultaneously. However, the parts are essentially those of mimes and dancers, and it would be theatrically acceptable for a musician, or someone stationed among instruments, to assume the rather slight singing roles of each principal, becoming a somewhat disembodied voice.

Chorus

Singing—or, to be more general, sounds from the throat, meaningless in English verbal communication but not meaningless in this music—

is rather general. The eighteen or twenty musicians (with conductor) *are* the Chorus, in both acts. This was true in *The Bewitched* also, and to my mind the arrangement was effective. The choral voice sounds were not coming from a body of people appearing just occasionally, but from among the instruments, from musicians who were deeply involved throughout.

In the present work I wish to progress beyond this concept. There are twenty-five instruments onstage (not counting small hand instruments), but never do the twenty-five play simultaneously. In fairly long periods, only a small ensemble is employed. The tacit musicians may thus become actors and dancers, moving from instruments to acting areas as the impetus of the drama requires.

Where necessary, instrumentalists must memorize parts, or know them so well that faint stage light is enough. The effect of stand lights on white music paper—*onstage*—tends to destroy almost any lighting concept. Actors and singers have always memorized parts, and it is irrational to exempt instrumentalists when they are cast in such a way as to be indispensable to the action.

Costumes

The musicians must be in costume; they should convey a sense of magic, of an olden time, but never of a precise olden time.

The basic garment is a huge pair of pantaloons, wrapping around the waist in East Indian fashion. In Act I they also wear a poncholike garment—a single, full piece of cloth with a neckhole. It is completely unadorned, without collages or beads or anything that twinkles in the light. The poncho is discarded at the end of the Sanctus. During Act II the musicians are bare from the waist up.

To compensate for this very simple costume, each musician will wear a fantastic headpiece. Each will be different, or frequently different.

In contrast, the three principals will wear more imaginative costumes, and imaginative makeup. Wigs, perhaps, but not headpieces.

Instruments

Chorus hand instruments, used only occasionally, are at the top. The remaining order follows generally the placement of stationary instruments, stage left to stage right. Stage left and center hold instruments with a long ring-time, or sustained tones. Stage right holds percussion instruments with a short ring-time.

Small hand instruments
        Ugumbo, copy of a Zulu instrument
        Bolivian double flute
        Rotating drum
        Two waving drums
        Six bamboo claves
        Three bamboo ceremonial poles
        Four pairs of eucal claves
        Thumb piano
        Two belly drums
        Gourd drum
        Fiji rhythm boat
        Gubagubi
Stage left and center
    Plucked strings:
        Harmonic Canon I
        Adapted Guitars I and II
        Koto
        Kitharas I and II

    Sustained-tone instruments:
        Chromelodeons I and II
        Blo-boy
    Percussion instruments with a long ring-time (the first four, Castor
        and Pollux through Crychord, are string instruments that are
        generally played percussively, with sticks, but are occasionally
        played with picks and fingers):
        Castor and Pollux (Harmonic Canon II)
        Blue Rainbow (Harmonic Canon III)
        Surrogate Kithara
        Crychord
        Cloud-Chamber Bowls
        Spoils of War
        Gourd Tree and Cone Gongs, played by one musician
Stage right
    Percussion instruments with a short ring-time:
        Mazda Marimba
        Zymo-Xyl
        Diamond Marimba
        Quadrangularis Reversum
        Eucal Blossom
        Boo (Bamboo Marimba)
        Bass Marimba
        Marimba Eroica
        Bass drum

Scene from 1969 UCLA production of *Delusion of the Fury*. Exordium. Photograph by Cecil Charles Spiller.

Exordium—The Beginning of a Web

(Stage very dark. Only enough light to allow competent playing of instruments.)

Act I—On a Japanese Theme

1. Chorus of Shadows

(The Chorus is onstage as lights come up. About seven and at least two should be men. It is conceived as a constant part of Act I, periodically advancing into the light and then receding into comparative darkness.)

CHORUS (*piano*): Ee— (*Closed mouth.*) M— O—ee O—ee Mo— mo— O-ee— O-ee— O-ee— O-ee—

CHORUS/HALF: O la klu   Klu la o
CHORUS/HALF: Boo day tho   Tho day boo day—

   O la o   la o   O la o   la o
      Boo day boo   Boo day boo   boo day

        O la klu   Klu la o
   boo— day—   Boo day tho   Tho day boo day—

CHORUS: (*Whistle.*)

CHORUS: Ma Ma Ah M— Ah ee— Ah—o O—ee—

CHORUS/HALF: O—
CHORUS/HALF: Boo—day tho—day tho— Boo day tho—

CHORUS: M— (*Whistle.*)

2. The Pilgrimage

(Shadows exeunt. Spot right.)
(Pilgrim enters—moves slowly, solemnly, in contrast to music, which moves rather fast. He moves generally toward the shrine—blue light left of center—upstage.)

CHORUS: O-ee O-ee O—ee— O-ee O-ee O—ee— O-ee— O—ee— O— O-ah O-ah O-ah O-ah

PILGRIM: Ee—ah— O—ee—ah

CHORUS: Mo mo mo mo [etc].

PILGRIM: Ee-o-ah-o-ee-o— (*As Pilgrim approaches shrine, he is overcome by the anguish of remembering.*) O-ee—o-ee—ah-o— O-we-O-we-oo-we-ah! O-we-o-we O-ee— O O-ee—o—

(*At this point Pilgrim gently kneels—he does not fall—bows his head—far downstage, right of center. He will later become a dark silhouette.*)

PILGRIM: Moo moo moo moo moo moo
CHORUS: Oo— oo—

(*Spot fades. Pilgrim becomes a statuelike dark silhouette, remaining immobile for some ten minutes.*)
(*Preparation for the spirit.*)

CHORUS: Th lo th lay th lo   Th lo th lay th lo   Th lo th lo

3. Emergence of the Spirit

(*Spot. Ghost enters left.*)

CHORUS: Th lo th lay th lo—

GHOST: ü—yah ü—yah ü—
CHORUS: Ee-yoh ee-yoh ee-yoh Ee-yo ee-yo

Ee-yo Ee-yo ee yo ee yo ee yo ee yo ee yo ee yo ee yo Tho—
          Ee yo   Ee yo   Ee yo   Ee yo Tho—
tho— tho—   Tho th lo th lo th lo— Tho th lo th lo th
tho— tho— Tho—   Tho th lo th lo th

lo th lo—   Tho— tho—   Tho th lo th lo th lo—
lo th lo th lo— Tho— tho— Tho

Tho th lo th lo th lo th lo—   Tho lo tho lo tho—
Tho th lo th lo th lo th lo th lo— Tho lo tho lo tho lo tho—

(*Ghost begins exit left. He backs out—slowly—seeming to imply that he is not really leaving.*)

CHORUS: Th lo th lay th lo—

(*Exit Ghost.*)
(*Brief reappearance of Moving Chorus.*)

CHORUS: M— (*Whistle.*)

Scene from 1969 UCLA production of *Delusion of the Fury*. Act I, Scene 3: Emergence of the Spirit. Photograph by Cecil Charles Spiller.

4. A Son in Search of His Father's Face

(Son appears immediately, right center — right of shrine — emerging through instruments. Percussion must be soft. They would destroy the dream quality in excessive loudness.)
(Son begins his quest — dancing, miming.)

SON *(timidly)*:   O—O—
CHORUS: O—lo—   O— lo— o— lo— o

(The Son has a sense of expectation, foreseeing the vision of his father.)

SON: O O O O O O   O O O O
CHORUS: Lo—   O lo—   O lo th lo th lay th lo—

(Son withdraws, backing away far right.)

CHORUS: *(Whistle.)*

(Ghost father reappears left.)
(Moving Chorus here.)

CHORUS/HALF: Bo—
CHORUS/HALF: Boo—day tho—

(Ghost Father-Son dance begins. It is slow, tender, even though the tempo of the music is very fast. They must never touch. Their bodies must be inviolate.)

CHORUS: ü— *(Whistle.)* ü—yah!

(Ghost and Son begin to be aware of the kneeling figure of Pilgrim.)
(Pilgrim begins to rise, very slowly. He takes thirty-six beats to reach standing posture.)
(Pilgrim at full height. Lights begin to fade.)
(Moving area now dark.)
(Brief reappearance of Moving Chorus.)

5. Cry from Another Darkness

CHORUS *(throughout leaving an aperture appropriate only for a small tongue)*: ü— ü— ü— ü ü— ü—   ü— ü—

(Lights come on. Pilgrim and Ghost hold sticks or short poles — surrogate swords — and dance in confrontation and very gradually quicken tempo. Son remains upstage, watches with mounting apprehension.)

Scene from 1969 UCLA production of *Delusion of the Fury*. Act I, Scene 5: Cry from Another Darkness. Son watches as Pilgrim and Ghost reenact battle. Photograph by Cecil Charles Spiller.

Scene from 1969 UCLA production of *Delusion of the Fury.* Act I, Scene 6: Pray for Me (Chorus of Shadows, Pilgrim, and Ghost). Photograph by Cecil Charles Spiller.

(*Ghost is the aggressor.*)
(*Pilgrim the aggressor.*)
(*Ghost the aggressor.*)

CHORUS: O—Aye! (*This is the cry from another darkness. Make it good. Scream.*)

(*At this point Pilgrim drops his stick, holds his hands to heaven in a plea for understanding in the ghost of the man he killed. In a bar of total silence, Ghost holds his stick in a posture of attack, but he is quite still.*)
(*Ghost lowers his weapon, but does not drop it.*)

GHOST: You are not my enemy!

6. Pray for Me

(*Ghost drops his stick on the sforzato, and gently kneels. He does not fall in an anguished manner. The time of anguish is past.*)

GHOST: Pray— for me— O— pray— for me— again!

CHORUS: Pray— for me— O— pray— for me— again. (*Small mouth aperture.*) ü— ü— ü— ü— (*Whistle.*)

(*Stage lights slowly fade.*)
(*Sanctus begins after only a three- or four-second pause.*)

SANCTUS—AN ENTR'ACTE

Act II—On an African Theme

1. The Quiet Hobo Meal

(*Hobo enters right, peers and moves about suspiciously. He carries a small pack and a few small dry branches for a fire.*)
(*Hobo is suddenly suffused with a sense of warm security and rustic tranquility. He stretches, scratches himself, half yawns, and prepares to cook a meal. He drops his pack, his sticks, and dances gaily about looking for others.*)

2. The Lost Kid

(*Hobo has premonition of trouble. Again, he becomes suspicious and nervous, moves cautiously.*)

(*Old Goat Woman trips lightly in, from left. She is constitutionally a gay old woman. She does not see or ignore Hobo. She peers in crooks and crannies for her lost Kid. This is the Old Goat Woman's solo dance.*)

CHORUS: O—uh! O—uh! O—uh! O—uh!

(*Hobo is irritated that his peace is shattered, and tries to ignore the new situation.*)

OLD GOAT WOMAN (*speaking plaintively*): Where—? Where—? Where—?

CHORUS: Buh doo buh doo buh doo buh doo buh doo

OLD GOAT WOMAN: Where—? Where—? Where—?

(*She trips across an open space.*)

CHORUS (*speak*): Buh doo!

(*She reverses.*)

CHORUS: Buh doo!

(*Reverses again.*)

CHORUS: Buh doo!

(*The music is simply a soft rhythmic background for the mocked colloquy between Old Goat Woman and Hobo. It must be so soft that the sounds of imitated speech stand out strikingly. It must be slower than the similar pattern a few lines back.*)

(*Old Goat Woman notices Hobo, scrutinizes him carefully. She speaks to audience.*)

OLD GOAT WOMAN: Hm—! A bum!

CHORUS: Hm—! A bum!

(*Old Goat Woman moves cautiously toward Hobo—all smiles. She moves her jaw vigorously and gesticulates in conjunction with thumb piano, but she makes no sounds.*)

(*Hobo points to his ear to indicate his deafness, but Old Goat Woman takes no notice. Hobo shrugs. He gestures to audience with wide-spread hands, and speaks rhythmically.*)

HOBO: Why (*plaintive glide down*) doesn't she just go away? (*up glide*)

CHORUS: Why (*glide*) doesn't she just go away?

OLD GOAT WOMAN: (*Move jaw.*)

> (*Hobo becomes exasperated, waves frantically for Old Goat Woman to leave him alone. He points vaguely right. Old Goat Woman thinks this means her lost Kid is there, right, and dances happily, making a turn or two before her exit.*)
> (*Old Goat Woman exits. Hobo moves back as Villagers enter.*)

3. Time of Fun Together

> (*Villagers enter from among instruments—seven in Moving Chorus. Wherever possible Moving Chorus should play small hand instruments.*)

CHORUS/HALF: Oo—   Oo—

CHORUS/HALF: Oo— Ho wah tuh Ho wah. Oo— Ho wah too!

Ho wah too!   Ho wah too!

Ho wah   Ho wah too!   Ho wah too!

CHORUS: Oo— oo— oo— oo— oo— woo—ah

CHORUS/HALF: Ho wah! Oo— Woo! oo! ah!

CHORUS/HALF: Ho wah too!   Oo— Woo! oo! ah! Ho wah

Ho wah! Ho wah too!   Ho wah too!

too!   Ho wah too!   Ho wah too!

> [*A low female soloist, a singing Chorus, and a Male No-Voice Chorus perform a long, melismatic, polyphonic passage using unvoiced, breathy sounds or syllables such as* **Muh, Moo, Klu, O,** *and* **La.**]
> (*The Villagers applaud and murmur—no shouting—and begin to disappear among the instruments.*)

4. The Misunderstanding

> (*Hobo returns to the position where he first encountered Old Goat Woman and mimes again the building of a fire.*)
> (*Old Goat Woman enters left. She waltzes in with the new-found Kid cradled in her arms as though it were a baby. The Kid must have a movable jaw that Old Goat Woman can manipulate.*)
> (*Old Goat Woman swings freely—dances joyously.*)

(*Old Goat Woman purrs motheringly over Kid—rocks it back and forth.*)

(*Old Goat Woman and Chorus sing, in celebration of the little found Kid.*)

OLD GOAT WOMAN: Mi O— ma mi—ah!   O mi O ma mi—
CHORUS: Mi   ma   mi O   mi

ah! Mi o mi—ah!   O—   mi!
ma   O ho ho ho ho ho ho ho Mi O— ma mi ah!

O—   mi!
O mi O ma mi ah! Mi o mi—ah!

(*Old Goat Woman approaches Hobo.*)

OLD GOAT WOMAN: (*Mouth movements.*)

HOBO: (*"Talks," gesturing hopelessly.*)

(*Old Goat Woman stares at him, then takes a step downstage.*)

OLD GOAT WOMAN (*speaks to audience, rhythmically*): What a dope!

CHORUS: What a dope!

OLD GOAT WOMAN (*gestures wildly*): I was only trying to thank him!

(*She stares at Hobo, then approaches him again.*)

OLD GOAT WOMAN: (*Mouth movements.*)

(*Hobo stares at her, then takes a step downstage.*)

HOBO (*to audience*): Why doesn't she just go away and leave me alone?

CHORUS: Why doesn't she just go away?

(*Old Goat Woman and Hobo slowly, cautiously, circle each other, like timid boxers.*)

OLD GOAT WOMAN: (*"Talks" to Hobo; mouth movements.*)

HOBO (*to audience*): I'd rather be a bum! (*"Talks" to Old Goat Woman; mouth movements.*)

OLD GOAT WOMAN: (*Mouth movements.*)
HOBO: (*Mouth movements.*)

(*Mouth movements.*)
              (*Mouth movements.*)

(*Old Goat Woman moves downstage.*)

OLD GOAT WOMAN (*to audience*): That— does it!

–Pas de deux—The Quarrel–

OLD GOAT WOMAN: Yoo-oo!

HOBO: Yoo-oo!

OLD GOAT WOMAN: Yoo-oo!

> (*Curious Villagers slowly appear from among instruments to watch the quarrel—only two at first.*)

CHORUS: O— mi O— mi O— mi

> (*In dance terms this is a caricature of a sex quarrel, highly stylized. Principals must not touch.*)

OLD GOAT WOMAN and HOBO (*half-closed mouth*): ü— ü— ü—

CHORUS: O mi O mi O mi O mi O mi O mi

OLD GOAT WOMAN: Ee uh!   ee uh! ee uh!   ee uh!
HOBO: Ee uh!   ee uh! ee uh!

  ee uh! ee uh!   ee uh! ee   ee
          ee uh! ee uh!   Yuh—ee

CHORUS: Yuh—ee yuh—ee

OLD GOAT WOMAN: Ee—   Ee—   Ee—   O—ee—o
HOBO: Ee—   Ee—   Ee—   ee—o
CHORUS: (*Whistle.*) (*Whistle.*) (*Whistle.*)

           O—ee—o ee—   ee— ee—uh
     ee-o   ee—   ee—
  ee-o O—ee—o   ee—uh   ee—uh

CHORUS: Ee—o ee—o ee—o

> (*Old Goat Woman and Hobo are a little weary of their quarrel, but by now the Villagers have become active participants, through dance.*)
> (*Principals are trapped.*)

CHORUS: O—ee o—ee O—ee—o ee—o ee—o ee—o

> (*The preparation for the arrest has a dream quality. This really is not happening—to two innocent people.*)
> (*The Villagers begin to close in. They never touch the two principals—they accomplish the arrest by more subtle means. This is to be an occasion—a trial—therefore time for a celebration, long overdue. "Society" now takes command.*)

CHORUS: Woo— d'woo— d'woo— d'woo—

5. Arrest, Trial, and Judgment
(Joy in the Marketplace!)

(Company begins exuent right, shepherding arrested couple. As they leave, stage lights begin to fade. They circle behind cyclorama and eventually enter left.)

(Lights on. Justice of the Peace is seated on a chair, on small platform, left of center, with two poles supporting it. The poles rest on the shoulders of four tacit musicians. A structure of some sort, on the floor, is actually holding the platform. The four should continue to sing in the Chorus. Justice holds a long arced phone (hearing aid), and huge spectacles with oblong lenses are placed halfway down his nose. He is bare from waist up.)

(Company, with arrested couple, begins to enter right.)

–The Trial Begins–

(Unlike preceding scenes, there is no imitation of speech here. The "dialogue"—the testimony, the Justice's questions, the ejaculations of the Villagers—is accomplished through music, miming, singing.)

OLD GOAT WOMAN: Ee-oh!

HOBO: Ee-oh!

CHORUS: O—wee—o—

JUSTICE: Wee—o—wee—

CHORUS: Ee—yuh—o—

HOBO: Ee—o—

OLD GOAT WOMAN: Ee—yah— oh—

CHORUS: O—wee—o—

JUSTICE: Wee—o—wee—

CHORUS: Ee—yah—o—ah

(As each defendant, or group, "speaks," he or they move toward Justice. He reacts by leaning forward with earphone pointed at speakers.)

Scene from 1969 UCLA production of *Delusion of the Fury*. Act II, Scene 5: Arrest, Trial, and Judgment (Old Goat Woman, Hobo, Justice of the Peace, and Villagers). Photograph by Cecil Charles Spiller.

OLD GOAT WOMAN and HOBO: Ee—o—ee—o—

CHORUS: O—wee—o—

JUSTICE: Wee—o—wee—

CHORUS: Ee—o—ee—o—

OLD GOAT WOMAN: O—ee   yah   Ee—
HOBO: O—ee—oo—ee yuh   Ee—
CHORUS: Ee yah ee yah

  Ee—   O—   ee yah ee—   yah
             O—   ee yah ee—   yah
  ee yah ee yah ee   yah   ee yah ee yah ee yah

OLD GOAT WOMAN: Ee—o—
JUSTICE: Wee—o—wee—
CHORUS: O—wee—o—

– The Judgment –

(Justice stands. Waving drum is handed to him by the bailiff. Justice holds it high with his left hand as a symbol of office—discards the hearing aid. He sings his lines, but he does not hold onto the vowels to the point that they sound like singing. He strikes waving drum viciously and waves it. Consonants must be projected like bullets from a gun. Very slow—deliberate. Arms arch like the letter Ψ with right hand horizontal, somewhat like an Indian dancer.)

(At this point Old Goat Woman is holding Kid so that its face is clearly visible to audience. She manipulates [it] so that its mouth opens wide on the exact beat indicated. The M-A-A-A! sound comes from percussion section.)

JUSTICE: Young man! take your beautiful young wife, and your charming child, and go home—!

KID: M-A-A-A!

JUSTICE: And never let me see you in this court again—

KID: M-A-A-A!

(One of the Musicians, downstage, speaks this line rhythmically to the audience.)

MUSICIAN: Oh, how did we ever get by without justice?

KID: M-A-A-A!

(*Company begins to move, in celebration of this hilariously delightful verdict. Justice, typically, well pleased with himself, leads the procession — carried on his seat — and Villagers escort the little family behind him.*)

CHORUS/HALF: O how— did we ever get by without justice?

CHORUS/HALF: O how—? O how—?
CHORUS/HALF: O how—? O how—?

   O how—?   O how— did we ever get by without
         O how—?

   justice? Justice!   Justice!
         Justice! Justice!   Justice! Justice!

–Dance of Celebration–

CHORUS: Mono mono mono lu-annda mono mono mono Lu-annda mono mono mono Lu-annda mono [etc.]

6. Pray for Me Again

(*The pantheistic deities of precolonial Africa, Asia, America, and Australia come to life — smile divinely, decide that human delusion must be countered by heavenly riot, invoke thunder and lightning, and instill — A STRANGE FEAR!*)

(*Movements become slow, solemn, and end almost totally with the echo of Act I — Pray for Me. Movements, after the Pray-for-Me sequence, should exactly duplicate the dream quality of the Chorus of Shadows — Act I. The music is totally different, but in a dramatic sense this is what is called for.*)

(*The solo voice should have an offstage quality, or an echo chamber quality, as if coming from a distance. The voice must be the same as Act I, and since Ghost and Justice are here stipulated as the same individual, Justice will retire, during the Strange-Fear sequence, to the designated spot.*)

VOICE: Pray— for me—   O— pray— for me— again!

CHORUS: Pray— for me—   O— pray— for me— again!

(*Stage lights begin to fade.*)

Sources and Notes

BITTER MUSIC

Source: microfilm of unpublished typescript in the Lauriston C. Marshall Collection, Harry Partch Archive, University of Illinois Music Library.

Partch described the origins and fate of the typescript to "Bitter Music" in the second edition of his *Genesis of a Music* (New York: Da Capo, 1974):

> I had just returned from the British Museum, Dublin, Italy, and Malta under a grant-in-aid from the Carnegie Corporation of New York. My return was to a jobless America, and I took my blankets out under the stars beside the American River (the river of gold!), carried my notebook, kept a journal, and made sketches. I called the journal *Bitter Music* (it is not included in the list of my work in Appendix III), and I even had a contract for its publication. During the Depression, it might have had a chance, but with war in Europe, the contract was cancelled and I destroyed the effort. I did so without regret, because it had given me a large and already faintly delineated canvas for the collection of ideas that I later called *The Wayward*, of which *U.S. Highball* is a part. (P. 323)

Originally titled "Cause All Our Sins Are Taken Away," the first draft of the journal was completed by 1936, the present version in November 1940 at Anderson Creek, Big Sur. The typescript must still have existed in February 1950 when Partch wrote Lauriston C. Marshall asking for its return in order to destroy it. It had, though, been microfilmed earlier (along with other scores) in Berkeley by Marshall, with whom Partch was sharing a Guggenheim Fellowship.

1. With the exception of the two maps and the graffiti illustration (see pp. 46, 88, and 17, respectively), these pencil or ink drawings could not be reproduced from the microfilm.

2. Everett Ruess has since become legendary in the Southwest. He left

his family in Los Angeles at age sixteen to wander in the deserts of Utah and Arizona, painting, writing, and befriending Indians; he disappeared in the Utah wilderness in 1935 at age twenty. The poem "Wilderness Song"— to which Partch provided music (pp. 117–18)—was first published in an article about Ruess by Hugh Lacy, "Say That I Kept My Dream," *Desert Magazine*, September 1938, 18–20, although Partch notes he quotes from a typescript. The printed version reads:

> Say that I starved; that I was lost and weary;
> That I was burned and blinded by the desert sun;
> Footsore, thirsty, sick with strange diseases;
> Lonely and wet and cold, but that I kept my dream!

3. The Federal Transient Service would give aid to transients who had not resided in a state for twelve consecutive months. The Transient Service (1933–35) was established as part of the Federal Emergency Relief Administration and at one time cared for as many as 300,000 transients.

4. Partch's research trip to England had been funded by the Carnegie Corporation of New York. The grant was administered by the Institute of International Education, New York, whose founder and director at the time was Dr. Stephen P. Duggan (1870–1950).

5. The Civilian Conservation Corps (1933–42) was among the earliest of the New Deal programs and provided work for young single men, primarily on rural projects.

6. *Trails of Music* would later become *Genesis of a Music*.

7. Here Partch quotes from Yeats's letter of January 6, 1934. The parenthetical interpolation is Partch's. (It is not known if Yeats's original letter survives; typed transcript of letter is in the Lauriston C. Marshall Collection, Harry Partch Archive, University of Illinois Music Library.)

8. The president of the Carnegie Corporation of New York, the organization that funded Partch's trip, was Dr. Frederick P. Keppel (1875–1943).

9. Roger Sessions (1896–1985), American composer. Between 1925 and 1933 he had lived and worked mostly in Europe, supported by two Guggenheim fellowships, an American Academy in Rome Fellowship, and a Carnegie Fellowship.

10. Whether Yeats's letter of August 1934 survives is unknown; the parenthetical interpolations are presumably Partch's. Florence Farr (1860–1917), Irish actress and writer, provided music for Yeats's plays and collaborated with him on reciting poetry to musical pitches accompanied by a psaltery. Yeats appended a "Note by Florence Farr upon Her Settings" to his essay "Speaking to the Psaltery," in *Essays* (London: Macmillan, 1924). On Farr's musical ideas, see Josephine Johnson, "The Music of Speech, 1890–1906," chap. 6 in *Florence Farr: Bernard Shaw's "New Woman"* (Totowa, N.J.: Rowman and Littlefield, 1975).

11. Partch had set the 137th Psalm, "By the Rivers of Babylon," at Santa Rosa, Calif., in August 1931 for voice and Adapted Viola.

12. Probably *Plays in Prose and Verse Written for an Irish Theatre* (London: Macmillan, 1922).

13. Yeats describes his meetings with Partch in two letters to Margot Ruddock contained in *Ah, Sweet Dancer: W. B. Yeats, Margot Ruddock*, ed. Roger McHugh (London: Macmillan, 1970), 27–28 and 30–31.

14. Arnold Dolmetsch (1858–1940), scholar, performer, and instrument builder, was among the earliest pioneers in the revival of the performance of Renaissance and baroque music. He had built a psaltery for accompanying the recitations of Yeats and Florence Farr. In a letter to Yeats, Dolmetsch describes his impressions of the meeting with Partch; see *Letters to W. B. Yeats*, ed. Richard J. Finneran et al., 2 vols. (London: Macmillan, 1977), 2:568–69.

15. In the typescript Partch lined out the following sentence: "Maybe Italy does have compensations, after all."

16. Presumably Bertha Knisely Driscoll, Los Angeles music critic, who in 1933 had organized a group of patrons, including the pianist Richard Buhlig and soprano Calista Rogers.

17. Between December 1930 and August 1933, Partch had set seventeen poems by Li Po for voice and Adapted Viola.

18. Harry Partch, "A New Musical Instrument," *Musical Opinion* [London], June 1935, 764–65.

19. Edmund Dulac (1882–1953) provided music for some of Yeats's plays and illustrated many of his books. He is now best known as an illustrator of children's books.

20. Presumably Yeats's letter of February 21, 1935; see McHugh, ed., *Ah, Sweet Dancer*, 133.

21. Kathleen Schlesinger (1862–1953), scholar of the history of musical instruments. In addition to her articles on Greek musical instruments (aulos, cithara, and lyre) in the eleventh edition (1910–11) of the *Encyclopaedia Britannica*, she wrote *The Greek Aulos: A Study of Its Mechanism and of Its Relation to the Modal System of Ancient Greek Music* (London: Methuen, 1939).

22. Partch provided this note: "The Kithara, in the same forty-three-tone-to-the-octave system as the chromatic organ, has been completed—December, 1940." See also the essay "The Kithara," sup., 169–73.

23. George William Russell (1867–1935), visionary poet, painter, economist, and editor, was a close friend of Yeats for over fifteen years.

24. Presumably Osman Edwards (1864–1936), translator of and writer on Japanese drama. No book by him on Yeats is known.

25. From Yeats's essay "Literature and the Living Voice," first published in 1906 and frequently included in collections of his writings. See W. B. Yeats, *Plays and Controversies* (London: Macmillan, 1923), 184.

26. Partch seems to be paraphrasing or quoting from memory. The lines in the Legge translation read: "All things spring up, and there is not one which declines to show itself; they grow, and there is no claim made for their ownership; they go through their processes, and there is no expectation (of a reward for the results). The work is accomplished, and there

is no resting in it (as an achievement)." *The Sacred Books of China*, vol. 1, *The Texts of Tāoism*, trans. James Legge (Oxford: Clarendon Press, 1891), 48.

27. From "Hymn to the Sun and Myself," in *Hard Lines* (New York: Simon and Schuster, 1931), 64.

28. Isadora Duncan (1877–1927), American dancer whose advanced social ideas and innovations in interpretive dance made her a cult figure. Through her free style of movement in which she attempted to recapture the rhythms of Greek dance, she virtually created modern dance.

29. In the setting that follows, Partch again seems to be paraphrasing or quoting from memory. The lines in the Legge translation read: "I seem to be carried about as on the sea, drifting as if I had nowhere to rest" (p. 63).

30. State Emergency Relief Administration. Established in September 1933, SERA provided shelters in cities and work camps away from cities for transients who would accept care and cash in return for work. At its peak in April 1935, over 77,000 individuals received aid.

31. Partch here refers to his song "My Heart Keeps Beating Time" published in 1929 (by Lloyd Campbell Publications, San Francisco). The music was attributed to the pseudonym Paul Pirate, and new words to replace Partch's hobo lyrics were provided by a Larry Yoell. The text in the song that follows presumably is Partch's original lyrics.

32. Later between July 2 and July 4, 1943, in Ithaca, N.Y., Partch set the text of this letter for voice, Adapted Guitar, and Kithara. Titled at first *Letter from Hobo Pablo—Excerpt from "Bitter Music,"* it was later revised in 1955 as *The Letter: A Depression Message from a Friend.*

33. That is, the Mokelumne River.

34. From Arthur Weigall, *Sappho of Lesbos: Her Life and Times* (London: T. Butterworth, 1932), 112.

35. The poet Robinson Jeffers (1887–1962) lived a quiet and reclusive life at Carmel, Calif.; his narrative and lyric poems often are set along the Big Sur coast.

36. Chopin, Nocturne Op. 15, No. 2.

37. A division point is a major freight yard at approximately 500 mile intervals where freight trains stop and change crews.

38. A Salvation Army kitchen.

39. Presumably Mildred Couper (1887–1974), Santa Barbara composer, noted for her quarter-tone piano compositions.

40. Partch provided this note: "The original chromatic organ is dismantled—the keyboard abandoned to a junk pile, the cabinet left in a Santa Barbara garage, while the reeds are being used in building a second chromatic organ—December, 1940."

41. Partch loosely quotes from a letter of October 22, 1935, from Stephen Duggan, director of the Institute of International Education (which had administered the grant), reporting the decision of Frederick P. Keppel, president of the Carnegie Corporation. On December 13, 1940, Partch wrote the Carnegie Corporation advising them he had completed the manuscript

to *Patterns of Music* and offering to send it to them as his final report. (Copies of this correspondence are at the Carnegie Corporation of New York.)

42. Here Partch loosely quotes from a letter he sent to Stephen Duggan on November 28, 1935. (Original is at the Carnegie Corporation of New York.)

END LITTORAL

Source: microfilm of unpublished typescript that Partch later lost or destroyed. Partch had the typescript at least until about 1950 when it was microfilmed along with "Bitter Music" in Berkeley by Lauriston C. Marshall, with whom Partch was sharing a Guggenheim Fellowship. The microfilm is now in the Lauriston C. Marshall Collection, Harry Partch Archive, University of Illinois Music Library. Several ink(?) sketches and a map accompanying the typescript could not be reproduced from the microfilm. A newly drawn and more detailed map is provided in its place.

1. In the typescript, Partch deleted the following paragraph: "It makes me both tired and nervous. For the sake of my equanimity I wish this road would just once go sailing around one of these tops with a bored expression. But this is no sophisticated road."

2. In the typescript, Partch deleted the following sentence: "Nearly everyone is."

3. Noyo: eighty miles south of Cape Mendocino, near Fort Bragg.

4. Warren E. Gilson, Madison, Wis., had privately issued recordings of Partch's *U.S. Highball* (1946) and *Ten Settings of Lyrics of Li Po* (1947).

5. Probably Livia Appel, Partch's editor at the University of Wisconsin Press.

PATTERNS OF MUSIC

Source: typescript of "Author's Preface" (dated December 10, 1940) to *Patterns of Music*, on file at the Carnegie Corporation of New York.

Begun in 1926, *Patterns of Music* was a draft of what later became *Genesis of a Music* (Madison: University of Wisconsin Press, 1949). The preface and table of contents of the more than 260-page typescript were submitted as a partial final report to the Carnegie Corporation of New York, which on June 5, 1934, had provided a $1,500 grant funding Partch's research trip to Europe in 1934–35 (see "Bitter Music," sup., 22).

1. From Hart Crane's poem "Voyages II," in *White Buildings* (New York: Boni and Liveright, 1926).

BACH AND TEMPERAMENT

Source: reprinted from the *Carmel Pine Cone*, July 18, 1941, 10.

In 1940–41 Partch lived at Big Sur, south of Monterey, Calif. On July 21–27, 1941, the nearby city of Carmel held its seventh annual Bach Festival, which prompted this essay.

W. B. YEATS

Source: reprinted from the *Carmel Pine Cone*, October 17, 1941, 7.

In November 1934 Partch visited W. B. Yeats (1865–1939) in Dublin to discuss his projected setting of *King Oedipus* (see also "Bitter Music," sup., 25–26), which was produced at Mills College, Oakland, Calif., on March 14–16, 1952.

1. See "Bitter Music," n. 14.

2. Partch had set the 137th Psalm, "By the Rivers of Babylon," in August 1931, at Santa Rosa, Calif., for voice and Adapted Viola.

3. From Yeats's essay "Literature and the Living Voice," first published in 1906 and reprinted frequently in collections of his writings. Reprinted in W. B. Yeats, *Plays and Controversies* (London: Macmillan, 1923), 184.

4. Yeats, "Literature and the Living Voice," 183–85.

5. From Yeats's translation, *Sophocles' King Oedipus: A Version for the Modern Stage* (New York: Macmillan, 1928), 6.

THE KITHARA

Source: reprinted from the *Carmel Pine Cone*, September 19, 1941, 10.

Partch had visited Kathleen Schlesinger in London in March 1935 (see the account in "Bitter Music," sup., 31–32).

1. Gordon Newell (b. 1950), California-born sculptor, who had worked in Los Angeles and the Carmel–Big Sur area.

SHOW HORSES IN THE CONCERT RING

Source: reprinted from *Circle* [Berkeley], no. 10 (Summer 1948): 43–51.

1. Henry Miller (1891–1980), American writer of sexually frank, naturalistic autobiographical novels, which had a liberating effect on literature and society. Partch may have known Miller through a common group of writers and artists (including Jean Varda, George Leite, Harrydick Ross, and Jaime de Angulo) at Big Sur, Calif., where Miller lived after February 1944.

NO BARRIERS

Source: reprinted from *Impulse* [San Francisco] (Summer 1952): 9–10.

1. Wilford Leach (1929–88), playwright and successful director on Broadway. In November 1950, while living in Gualala, Calif., Partch and Ben Johnston collaborated on composing and taping incidental music for Leach's play *The Wooden Bird*, which was produced at the University of Virginia on January 10–12, 1951.

THE ANCIENT MAGIC

Source: reprinted from *Music Journal*, June–July 1959, 16, 45–47.

A SOMEWHAT SPOOF

Source: written in Champaign, Ill., in September 1960, but not published until 1972 in *Soundings*, no. 2 (April 1972): 59–61, from where it is here reprinted.

1. More precisely, the twelfth root of two: the ratio of the distance between the twelve semitones in an equally tempered chromatic scale can be expressed as the ratio of the twelfth root of two to one ($^{12}\sqrt{2}/1$).

THE UNIVERSITY AND THE CREATIVE ARTS: COMMENT

Source: reprinted from *Arts in Society* 2, no. 3 (1963): 22–23.

In 1963 *Arts in Society* devoted the principal part of an issue to the topic "The Creative Artist Invades the University." The editors reprinted a lecture titled "The University and the Creative Arts," delivered before a meeting of the Association of Graduate Schools, New Orleans, October 24, 1961, by W. McNeil Lowry, director of the Ford Foundation Program in Humanities and the Arts, and invited comments by eight artists and art educators, among them Partch. In his lecture (pp. 8–21), Lowry observed that the university had irrevocably assumed the function of professional training in the arts, but usually with the sacrifice of professional standards. The university must, therefore, develop new modes of cooperation with truly professional art institutions; otherwise, Lowry argued, "Under present conditions, the best service you can perform for the potential artist is to throw him out" (p. 21).

1. "Show Horses in the Concert Ring," *Circle*, no. 10 (Summer 1948): 51. (See sup., 179.)

MONOLITHS IN MUSIC

Source: text of a lecture-demonstration by Partch given before a performance of his *Two Studies on Ancient Greek Scales, Castor and Pollux,* and *And on the Seventh Day Petals Fell in Petaluma;* reprinted from *Source,* no. 1 (January 1967): 103.

The concert featuring Partch's works took place on May 8, 1966, and was presented by the University of California at Los Angeles Committee on Fine Arts Productions as part of its 20th Century Music Series. The published abridged transcription of Partch's lecture omits his description of *And on the Seventh Day Petals Fell in Petaluma,* as well as his demonstration of instruments. The transcription in *Source* is untitled; the present title is editorial.

1. Aristoxenus (fourth century B.C.); his writings are our principal source about Greek music theory.

2. Euclid (third century B.C.), Greek mathematician; two works on music theory survive.

3. Ancient Greek music theory and melodies were based on the concept of the tetrachord (a four-note scale). The principal tetrachords were the diatonic (e.g., E–F–G–A); the chromatic (e.g., E–F–F♯–A); and the enharmonic (e.g., E–E♯–F–A, where the E♯ is only a quarter-tone sharp).

A QUARTER-SAW SECTION OF MOTIVATIONS
AND INTONATIONS

Source: transcribed excerpt from a taped lecture-demonstration presented in absentia to an American Society of University Composers seminar at Tanglewood, Mass., in the summer of 1967. After the excerpt printed here, the taped presentation included excerpts and scales from Partch's compositions. Tape copies of the complete presentation are at the Harry Partch Estate Archive, San Diego, and the Harry Partch Archive, University of Illinois Music Library.

BARSTOW

Source: reprinted from the *Carmel Pine Cone,* September 26, 1941, 10.

Partch encountered the hitchhiker inscriptions described in this essay in February 1940; they formed the basis of *Barstow—Eight Hitchhikers' Inscriptions from a Highway Railing at Barstow, California.* The first version for voice and Adapted Guitar was written in La Mesa, Los Angeles, and Big Sur, Calif., in April and May 1941; it was revised with enlarged instrumentation in 1942, 1943, 1954, and 1968.

1. In the score the line reads, "Why in hell did you come, anyway?"

U.S. HIGHBALL (1943)

Source: typescript in the papers of Otto Luening, Music Division, New York Public Library.

Partch prefixed this "Argument" to a libretto for *U.S. Highball* that he sent Otto Luening on July 7, 1943. After drafting several preliminary librettos, Partch completed the first setting of *U.S. Highball* for voice and Adapted Guitar at Ithaca, N.Y., on March 24, 1943; it was revised and given enlarged instrumentation later that year and again in 1955. (See also Partch's discussion of *U.S. Highball* in *Genesis of a Music,* 320–24.)

U.S. HIGHBALL (1957)

Source: typescript carbon copy in the Lauriston C. Marshall Collection at the Harry Partch Archive, University of Illinois Music Library.

This essay was written in July 1957 at Yellow Springs, Ohio, as a preface to a tentative film script for *U.S. Highball.* The following month in Chicago, Partch met the experimental filmmaker Madeline Tourtelot; they began a film of *U.S. Highball* in 1958, which was completed in 1963. (See also Partch's discussion of *U.S. Highball* in *Genesis of a Music,* 320–24.)

1. The notebook is now at the Harry Partch Estate Archive, San Diego, folder 1.

2. Partch seems in error about the April 4 date, since he had already written to the Guggenheim Foundation on March 26, 1943, from Ithaca acknowledging receipt of the fellowship.

3. Henry Allen Moe (1894–1975) was secretary general of the John Simon Guggenheim Memorial Foundation. As a supporter of Partch and his work since the mid-1930s, Moe had assisted Partch in obtaining Guggenheim fellowships in 1943, 1944, and 1950.

4. The audition was held on November 29; the concert, titled "A Program of Compositions on Americana Texts," was given at Carnegie Chamber

Music Hall on April 22, 1944, and at Brander Matthews Theatre, Columbia University, on May 22, 1944.

5. The version with enlarged instrumentation was recorded in 1958 in Evanston, Ill., with an ensemble conducted by Jack McKenzie and released privately on Gate 5 Records, issue no. 6 and issue B.

KING OEDIPUS

Source: reprinted from program to first performances at Mills College, March 14–16, 1952.

Partch had planned to set Sophocles' *King Oedipus* as early as 1933. His setting of *Oedipus*, which used the W. B. Yeats translation, was written between March and July 1951 and was produced at Mills College, Oakland, Calif., in March 1952. Because permission to issue a recording of the performance was denied by Yeats's literary agent, Partch revised the work with a new translation later that year; a final, revised score was prepared in 1967. (See also Partch's discussion of *Oedipus* in *Genesis of a Music*, 331–34.)

1. From Yeats's essay "Literature and the Living Voice" (1906), in W. B. Yeats, *Plays and Controversies* (London: Macmillan, 1923), 184.

OEDIPUS

Source: transcribed from tape recording of Partch's introduction to a 1954 radio broadcast of *Oedipus;* copy in the Lauriston C. Marshall Collection at the Harry Partch Archive, University of Illinois Music Library. Omitted here are concluding acknowledgments to the performers.

In 1954 Partch's revised 1952 version of *Oedipus* with enlarged instrumentation and a new translation was recorded in Sausalito, Calif., with Allen Louw as Oedipus and ensemble conducted by Jack Hohensee. (Partch had been refused permission by Yeats's literary agent to release a recording of the Mills performance.) On July 16, 1954, the recording was broadcast over KPFA Radio, San Francisco; this essay was an introduction spoken by Partch. (See also Partch's discussion of *Oedipus* in *Genesis of a Music*, 331–34.)

RHYTHMIC MOTIVATIONS

Source: undated typescript enclosed in a letter of September 25, 1952, to Peter Yates; now in the Peter Yates Papers, box 15, folder 6, University of California, San Diego, Central University Library, Mandeville Department of Special Collections.

Partch completed *Castor and Pollux* on July 1, 1952, and *Even Wild Horses* on August 31, 1952, both at Mills College, Oakland, Calif. This essay was written about that time, since it does not mention *Ring around the Moon* (written in 1949–50 and titled *Sonata Dementia*), which was later added to these two works to form the three-part *Plectra and Percussion Dances*. The set of dances premiered at the International House, Berkeley, Calif., on November 19, 1953.

In the paragraphs on *Even Wild Horses*, Partch quotes from *Une saison en enfer* (1873) by Arthur Rimbaud (1854–91) in the translation by Louise Varèse, *A Season in Hell* (Norfolk, Va.: New Directions, 1945).

PLECTRA AND PERCUSSION DANCES

Source: transcribed from tape recording of Partch's introduction at the 1953 premiere; copy in the Lauriston C. Marshall Collection at the Harry Partch Archive, University of Illinois Music Library. Omitted here are concluding comments identifying instruments.

Partch's *Plectra and Percussion Dances* was completed at Mills College, Oakland, Calif., in the summer of 1952; it was premiered on November 19, 1953, at the International House, Berkeley, Calif., and broadcast live over KPFA Radio, San Francisco. (See also Partch's discussion of *Plectra and Percussion Dances* in *Genesis of a Music*, 324–31.)

THOUGHTS AFTER AND BEFORE *THE BEWITCHED*

Source: photocopy of 1955 scenario to *The Bewitched* in the files of Broadcast Music, Inc. The BMI files are now at the Harry Partch Archive, University of Illinois Music Library.

Partch completed the first version of *The Bewitched* in Sausalito, Calif., on January 19, 1955, and an expanded version was written in September of that year. This essay was written in mid-1955 as a preface to an early version of the scenario. The "after and before" of the title presumably refer to after the composing of, and before the production of, *The Bewitched.*

A SOUL TORMENTED

Source: transcribed from tape of the 1957 lecture-demonstration by Partch given before the first performance of *The Bewitched;* a copy of the tape is in the Lauriston C. Marshall Collection at the Harry Partch Archive, University of Illinois Music Library. Omitted from the transcription are the concluding remarks that introduce demonstrations of the various instruments.

The first performance of *The Bewitched*, with choreography by Alwin Nikolais, took place on March 26, 1957, as part of the Eighth Festival of Contemporary Arts, and the piece was presented again the following evening at Washington University, St. Louis. Partch's lecture, titled "A Soul Tormented by Contemporary Music Looks for a Humanizing Alchemy," was delivered on March 24, two nights before the first performance. (See also Partch's discussion of *The Bewitched* in *Genesis of a Music*, 334–40.)

REVELATION IN THE COURTHOUSE PARK

Source: reprinted from *Genesis of a Music*, 340–45.

Revelation in the Courthouse Park was written in Champaign, Ill., and premiered as part of the Festival of Contemporary Arts at the University of Illinois on April 11, 1961. Partch began writing the libretto in August 1959, and the music was completed on June 16, 1960. This essay dates from 1969, when it was written for the second edition of *Genesis of a Music.*

1. Alluding here to the myth of the Aloads, sons of Poseidon, who grew to the size of giants. Attempting to reach heaven to battle the gods, they placed Mt. Pelion on Mt. Ossa, and Mt. Ossa atop Mt. Olympus.

2. [Partch's note:] The climax of the revels in Chorus Three, *Tumble On*, was attained with mat tumblers and with one gymnast on a trampoline. This had been rolled onstage unknown to the audience, at the rear, and with a certain beat of the Marimba Eroica, the trampolinist rose high above those onstage, his feet striking the net with each beat of the Eroica. Knowing of this scene, the gymnasts' coach at the University of Illinois asked me to perform this, with added music, at the NCAA meet, which happened to occur that year (1961) at Illinois. I wrote the script and titled it *Rotate the Body in All Its Planes*. A film was made of the exhibition.

OBSERVATIONS ON *WATER! WATER!*

Source: reprinted from "Observations by Harry Partch," written for the program book accompanying the performances of *Water! Water!* The program book for the University of Illinois performances omits the opening four paragraphs, which are contained in the Studebaker Theater program.

Water! Water! was commissioned by the University of Illinois Illini Union Student Activities Board as its spring 1962 musical. The work was written between May and November 1961 at Champaign, Ill., and was produced at the University of Illinois on March 9 and 10, 1962, and at the Studebaker Theater, Chicago, on March 17, 1962.

Because of his dissatisfaction with the production and its recording, Partch withdrew the Gate 5 recording of *Water! Water!* and did not list or discuss the work in *Genesis of a Music*.

1. Chorus Three of *Revelation in the Courthouse Park* included tumbling routines using Illinois gymnasts. Since the 1961 National Collegiate Gymnastic Championships were being held at the University of Illinois the same month of the premiere of *Revelation*, Partch was asked to prepare a tumbling routine for the occasion. The work, using music from Chorus Three of *Revelation*, was *Rotate the Body in All Its Planes—Ballad for Gymnasts*, which was performed on April 8, 1961.

2. Partch had met the Chicago experimental filmmaker in 1957, and they collaborated on six films: *Windsong* (1958), *Music Studio* (1958), *Rotate the Body in All Its Planes* (1961), *Revelation in the Courthouse Park* (1961), *U.S. Highball* (1963), and *Delusion of the Fury* (1969).

DELUSION OF THE FURY

Source: typescript of prospectus and scenario dated January 17, 1965, in the Barnard Hewitt Collection, Harry Partch Archive, University of Illinois Music Library.

Delusion of the Fury was composed between November 1965 and March 1966 and premiered at UCLA on January 9–12, 1969, with ensemble conducted by Danlee Mitchell and choreography by Storie Crawford. The discussion of *Delusion* in the 1965 prospectus and scenario will be found to differ in small details from that given in *Genesis of a Music*, 350–57.

1. Based principally on *Atsumori* by Seami, in Arthur Waley, *The Noh Plays of Japan* (New York: Grove Press, 1957), 64–73. The son is taken from *Ikuta* by Zembō Motoyasu, in ibid., 74–80.

2. The story "Justice: An Ethiopian Tale," in *African Voices: An Anthology of Native African Writing*, ed. and comp. Peggy Rutherford (New York: Grosset & Dunlap, 1958), 67–68.

U.S. HIGHBALL

Sources: The copy text for the libretto presented above is the 1946 printed libretto that accompanied a privately released recording of *U.S. Highball* issued by Warren Gilson of Madison, Wis. Four additional sources, each representing a different version of the text, were also consulted: two typescript draft librettos, one titled "U.S. Highball: Musical Account of a Transcontinental Hitchhike-Freight Train Hegira" and the other "U.S. Highball: Musical Account of an American Transcontinental Freight Train-Hitchhike Trip" (both in the Harry Partch Estate Archive, San Diego, folder 1); the 1943 score version, titled *U.S. Highball: A Musical Account of Slim's Transcontinental Hobo Trip* (autograph in the Harry Partch Estate Archive, San Diego; for locations of copies of the autograph, see Thomas McGeary, *The Music of Harry Partch: A Descriptive Catalogue*, I.S.A.M. Monographs, no. 31 [Brooklyn, N.Y.: Institute for Studies in American Music, 1990], no. 35b); and the final 1955 score version, titled *U.S. Highball: A Musical Account of a Transcontinental Hobo Trip* (autograph in the Harry Partch Estate Archive, San Diego; for locations of copies of the autograph, see McGeary, *Music of Harry Partch*, no. 35c).

Partch based *U.S. Highball* on a trip he took from California to Chicago in September 1941. To provide the fullest possible account of that trip, passages found (1) only in the final typescript draft and (2) in both the final typescript draft and the 1943 score but *not* in subsequent versions have been collated and interpolated into the text. The former are enclosed in braces (i.e., { }), while the latter insertions appear in angle brackets (i.e., ⟨ ⟩). Editorial clarifications are given in square brackets. Following the 1946 printed libretto, the Subjective (singing) Voice part is set in italics to distinguish it from the Objective (intoning) Voice.

Glossary

Ball the jack: to speed
'bos: hoboes
Bulls: police employed by the railroads
Chuck horrors: indigestion
Coffee and sinkers: coffee and doughnuts
D. and R.G.: Denver and Rio Grande Railroad
Division: a stop on a rail line where train crews are changed

Drag: a slow freight train

Gondola: an open-top freight car

Highball: to get going, speed through

Hole in: to go onto a siding to allow a faster train to pass

Hotshot: a fast freight train

Jungle: a shanty town of shacks built by transients or hoboes

Pot-wallopin': washing dishes

"Short stack, fry 'em on the side, over easy. Coupla babies and a chicken in spuds": short-order cook jargon for two pancakes, a side order of eggs fried over easy, several small bottles or glasses of milk, and (?) an egg scrambled with hash brown potatoes.

OEDIPUS

Sources: The copy text for the libretto presented above is the final 1967 revised score (autograph in the Harry Partch Estate Archive, San Diego; for locations of copies of the autograph, see Thomas McGeary, *The Music of Harry Partch: A Descriptive Catalogue,* I.S.A.M. Monographs, no. 31 [Brooklyn, N.Y.: Institute for Studies in American Music, 1990], no. 18c). Also consulted were the 1951 and 1952 versions of the score (autographs in the Harry Partch Estate Archive, San Diego; for locations of copies of the autographs, see McGeary, *Music of Harry Partch,* nos. 18a–b). When stage directions in the 1951 and 1952 scores are more descriptive of action, lighting, character motivation, delivery, and incidental music than those of the 1967 score, these descriptions have been incorporated into the text in the following manner: directions taken from the 1951 score are enclosed in braces (i.e., { }); those from the 1952 score appear in angle brackets (i.e., ⟨ ⟩). Editorial clarifications are given in square brackets.

Partch's first setting of *Oedipus,* titled *Sophocles' King Oedipus,* utilized the translation by W. B. Yeats. Written between March and July 1951 at Oakland, Calif., it was produced at Mills College, Oakland, on March 14–16, 1952. Although Partch had received Yeats's written permission to set his translation, he was unable to obtain permission from Yeats's literary agent to release a recording of the Mills College production. Consequently, Partch revised the score and provided his own translation in 1952. In 1967 he made a final revision of *Oedipus* and appended the following note to his score:

A rescoring—Summer, 1967—of this work, written first for the W. B. Yeats text, and rewritten and much abbreviated for my own text, from public domain sources, 1952. This score incorporates many changes made during the six months of rehearsals the early part of 1954 in Sausalito, and conforms generally to the two-record set of 1954. . . . (Help with passages not already set to music, from a translation by Jordan Churchill, is gratefully acknowledged.)

THE BEWITCHED

Sources: (1) the "Introduction" is reproduced from the 1955 typescript scenario that followed "Some New and Old Thoughts after and before *The Bewitched*" (see sup., 231); (2) the "Scenario" is reprinted from a mimeograph distributed with the program to the 1957 premiere. Copies of both sources are located at the Harry Partch Archive, University of Illinois Music Library.

Partch's dance satire *The Bewitched* was composed between November 1954 and September 1955 at Sausalito, Calif., and received its first performance at the University of Illinois on March 26, 1957, choreography by Alwin Nikolais, ensemble conducted by John Garvey. The piece was produced again in 1959, with choreography by Joyce Trisler, at Columbia University on April 10 and 11, and at the University of Illinois on April 24. Partch appended the following note to the 1957 mimeograph scenario: "The slow, rather lengthy and contrapuntal melodic passage heard in the Prologue and in Scenes 8 and 10 is based on a chant of the Cahuilla Indians of the southern California desert."

REVELATION IN THE COURTHOUSE PARK

Sources: The copy text for the libretto presented above is the 1960 final full score (autograph in the Harry Partch Estate Archive, San Diego; for locations of copies of the autograph, see Thomas McGeary, *The Music of Harry Partch: A Descriptive Catalogue*, I.S.A.M. Monographs, no. 31 [Brooklyn, N.Y.: Institute for Studies in American Music, 1990], no. 23). Also consulted was the preliminary libretto prepared by Partch shortly before composing the work (carbon copy of typescript in the Barnard Hewitt Collection, Harry Partch Archive, University of Illinois Music Library). When stage directions in the preliminary libretto are more descriptive of action, lighting, character motivation, delivery, and incidental music than those of the 1961 score, these directions have been incorporated into the text and are enclosed in angle brackets (i.e., $\langle \rangle$) to distinguish them from the parentheses used by Partch for stage directions in the full score. Editorial clarifications are given in square brackets.

Revelation in the Courthouse Park was composed between August 1959 and August 1960 in Champaign, Ill., and was first produced at the University of Illinois on April 11, 1961, directed by Barnard Hewitt, conducted by John Garvey, and choreographed by Jean Cutler. Partch based the text for the ancient choruses on *The Bacchae of Euripides*, trans. Gilbert Murray (London: George Allen, 1911).

WATER! WATER!

Sources: The copy text for the libretto presented above is the 1961 full score (autograph in the Harry Partch Estate Archive, San Diego; for locations of copies of the autograph, see Thomas McGeary, *The Music of Harry Partch: A Descriptive Catalogue*, I.S.A.M. Monographs, no. 31 [Brooklyn, N.Y.: Institute for Studies in American Music, 1990], no. 36), whose textual authority supersedes that of the preliminary libretto prepared by Partch shortly before composing the work (mimeographed typescript in the Barnard Hewitt Collection, Harry Partch Archive, University of Illinois Music Library). When the stage directions in the preliminary libretto are more descriptive of action, lighting, character motivation, delivery, and incidental music than those of the full score, these directions have been incorporated into the text and are enclosed in angle brackets (i.e., ⟨ ⟩) to distinguish them from the parentheses used by Partch for stage directions in the full score. Editorial clarifications are given in square brackets.

Water! Water! was composed between May and November 1961 in Champaign, Ill., and was produced on March 9 and 10, 1962, at the University of Illinois and on March 17 at the Studebaker Theater, Chicago. Barnard Hewitt directed the production, with choreography by Jean Cutler, and John Garvey conducted the ensemble.

The refrain "The highest goodness is like water. It seeks the low place that all men dislike" is from Lao-tse (eighth century B.C.). Partch paraphrases the translation by James Legge in *The Sacred Books of China*, pt. 1, *The Texts of Tāoism* (Oxford: Clarendon Press, 1891), 52: "The highest excellence is like (that of) water. The excellence of water appears in its benefiting all things, and in its occupying, without striving (to the contrary), the low place which all men dislike."

DELUSION OF THE FURY

Source: The copy text for the libretto presented above is the 1966 full score (autograph in the Harry Partch Estate Archive, San Diego; for locations of copies of the autograph, see Thomas McGeary, *The Music of Harry Partch: A Descriptive Catalogue*, I.S.A.M. Monographs, no. 31 [Brooklyn, N.Y.: Institute for Studies in American Music, 1990], no. 10).

Delusion of the Fury was begun in Venice, Calif., in November 1965 and was completed in San Diego in March 1966. It was produced at the University of California at Los Angeles on January 9–12, 1969, with ensemble conducted by Danlee Mitchell and choreography by Storie Crawford.

Index

Books in the Series Music in American Life